Someone Else's Music

Someone Else's Music

Opera and the British

ALEXANDRA WILSON

OXFORD
UNIVERSITY PRESS

Oxford University Press is a department of the University of Oxford.
It furthers the University's objective of excellence in research, scholarship,
and education by publishing worldwide. Oxford is a registered trade mark of
Oxford University Press in the UK and in certain other countries.

Published in the United States of America by Oxford University Press
198 Madison Avenue, New York, NY 10016, United States of America.

© Alexandra Wilson 2025

All rights reserved. No part of this publication may be reproduced, stored in a retrieval system, transmitted, used for text and data mining, or used for training artificial intelligence, in any form or by any means, without the prior permission in writing of Oxford University Press, or as expressly permitted by law, by license or under terms agreed with the appropriate reprographics rights organization. Inquiries concerning reproduction outside the scope of the above should be sent to the Rights Department, Oxford University Press, at the address above.

You must not circulate this work in any other form
and you must impose this same condition on any acquirer.

Library of Congress Cataloging-in-Publication Data
Names: Wilson, Alexandra, 1973– author.
Title: Someone else's music : opera and the British / Alexandra Wilson.
Description: [1.] | New York, NY : Oxford University Press, 2025. |
Includes bibliographical references and index. |
Identifiers: LCCN 2025016052 (print) | LCCN 2025016053 (ebook) |
ISBN 9780197803639 (hardback) | ISBN 9780197803660 | ISBN 9780197803646 (epub)
Subjects: LCSH: Opera—Great Britain—20th century. | Opera—Great Britain—21st century. |
Opera—Social aspects—Great Britain—History—20th century. | Opera—Social aspects—
Great Britain—History—21st century. | Classism—Great Britain—History—20th century. |
Classism—Great Britain—History—21st century.
Classification: LCC ML1731.W65 2025 (print) | LCC ML1731 (ebook) |
DDC 792.10941—dc23/eng/20250404
LC record available at https://lccn.loc.gov/2025016052
LC ebook record available at https://lccn.loc.gov/2025016053

DOI: 10.1093/9780197803660.001.0001

Printed by Marquis Book Printing, Canada

The manufacturer's authorized representative in the EU for product safety is
Oxford University Press España S.A., Parque Empresarial San Fernando de Henares,
Avenida de Castilla, 2 – 28830 Madrid (www.oup.es/en or product.safety@oup.com).
OUP España S.A. also acts as importer into Spain of products made by the manufacturer.

Contents

List of Figures	vii
Acknowledgements	ix
List of Abbreviations	xi
1. The Elitism Myth	1
2. Opera for All	23
3. (Dis)-Enchanted Gardens	47
4. Opera Goes to War	72
5. Pageantry and Participation	96
6. Counterculture	121
7. A National Opera?	143
8. The E-Word	165
9. A Perfect Storm	190
10. Twenty-First-Century Blues	214
11. This Sceptic Isle	235
Conclusion	258
Selected Bibliography	269
Index	275

Figures

1.1 Royal Opera House ticket queue, Floral Street, Covent Garden, 31 May 1986. Reproduced with permission from © Clive Barda/ArenaPAL.   18

2.1 Lilian Baylis outside the Old Vic Theatre. Reproduced with permission from © University of Bristol/ArenaPAL.   31

3.1 The Royal Carl Rosa Opera Company, programme for a production of *Carmen*, Streatham Hill Theatre, London, 16 August 1930. Reproduced with permission from © University of Bristol/ArenaPAL.   56

3.2 Audience at Glyndebourne Festival Opera, East Sussex, 1934. Reproduced with permission from © Glyndebourne Productions Ltd/ArenaPAL.   66

4.1 Public queuing at Sadler's Wells to see *Faust*, 1939. Reproduced with permission from © Chronicle/Alamy.   75

5.1 Basil Coleman, Benjamin Britten, Peter Pears, Joan Cross (back view). First run-through of *Gloriana*, Orme Square, London, May 1953. Reproduced with permission from © Royal Opera House/ArenaPAL.   97

5.2 Audience members in the grounds, Glyndebourne Festival Opera, 1958. Reproduced with permission from © Glyndebourne Productions Ltd/ArenaPAL.   104

6.1 Maria Callas among fans at the Royal Opera House for Puccini's *Tosca*, 1965. Reproduced with permission from © Performing Arts Images/ArenaPAL.   137

7.1 Carol Neblett, Sherrill Milnes, Zubin Mehta in a London recording studio for *La fanciulla del West*, June 1977. Reproduced with permission from © Clive Barda/ArenaPAL.   148

8.1 Peter Hall (director) in the control van with Robin Lough. *L'incoronazione di Poppea*, Glyndebourne Festival Opera, 1984. Reproduced with permission from © Glyndebourne Productions Ltd/ArenaPAL.   167

8.2 Jonathan Miller at the London Coliseum, *Rigoletto*, ENO, 8 January 1985. Reproduced with permission from © Conrad Blackmore/ArenaPAL.   176

9.1 Audience entering for a performance of Richard Strauss, *Salome*, Royal Opera House, Covent Garden, April 1997. Reproduced with permission from © Clive Barda/ArenaPAL.   204

11.1 Alfie Boe, Melody Moore, David Stout, Pauls Putnins, *La bohème*, ENO, The London Coliseum, 29 January 2009. Reproduced with permission from © Elliott Franks/ArenaPAL.   236

Acknowledgements

The research in this book was funded by the Leverhulme Trust: I am extremely grateful to the Trust for awarding me a Major Research Fellowship and for subsequently extending it. I would like to thank the staff at the following libraries and archives for their assistance: the Bodleian Library and its Special Collections, University of Oxford; the British Library; the People's Palace archive, Queen Mary, University of London; the Bristol University Theatre Collection; the Royal Opera House archive; the Glyndebourne archive; the Royal Albert Hall archive; the John Lewis Partnership Heritage Centre; and ArenaPAL.

This book has been many years in the planning. I have benefited greatly from conversations with countless friends and colleagues, not least with those who attended the OBERTO opera research conferences I organised with Barbara Eichner. Particular thanks, for long-running conversations about opera and the pernicious elitism stereotype, go to Adriana Festeu, Ian Pace, and Michael Volpe. The dynamic opera community on Twitter/X has been an invaluable resource: thanks to everyone who shared sources and ideas or suggested images. Rupert Christiansen and Richard Morrison generously gave up their time to meet me and share their expertise on how music journalism and the opera world have changed over recent decades. Paul Parker was interested in this project from the outset: he has been a constant source of encouragement, the kindest of friends, and a brilliant proofreader. Any errors that may remain are my own.

Kerry Bunkhall, Hannah Millington, Alessandra Palidda, and Harry Parker acted as much-valued research assistants. To Alessandra I owe additional thanks for covering my teaching at Oxford Brookes University so ably when I was on leave. Being made redundant in the final stages of writing this book was disappointing, to say the least, so I am immensely grateful to the Guildhall School of Music and Drama, and particularly Cormac Newark, for offering me a place of refuge from which to complete it. Once the book was in production, I also benefited from the support of new colleagues at Jesus College, Oxford, where I am honoured to hold a Senior Research Fellowship.

X   ACKNOWLEDGEMENTS

Heartfelt thanks to my fantastic agent Caroline Hardman for her advocacy for this book and determined efforts on my behalf. I am very pleased to be working with OUP again and grateful to Norm Hirschy, Laura Santo, Jodie Keefe, Elakkia Bharathi, and all the music editorial, production and design staff in New York for their assistance in bringing this book to publication. Finally, I must thank my family for their enduring support, sustenance, and patience: Andrew Timms, who works so hard to look after us all, and Sebastian, who has always been, and continues to be, a source of immense delight.

Abbreviations

In footnotes, the following abbreviations are used for commonly referenced periodicals:

DE	Daily Express
DM	Daily Mail
DMir	Daily Mirror
DT	Daily Telegraph
ES	Evening Standard
FT	Financial Times
ILN	Illustrated London News
M&L	Music and Letters
MM	Musical Mirror
MMF	Musical Mirror and Fanfare
MO	Musical Opinion
MT	Musical Times
OVM	Old Vic Magazine
OVSWM	Old Vic and Sadler's Wells Magazine
SE	Sunday Express
ST	Sunday Times
TLS	Times Literary Supplement
VWA	Vic-Wells Association

The following abbreviations are used for archival holdings:

BBC WAC	BBC Written Archives Centre
BUTC	Bristol University Theatre Collection
CPA	Conservative Party Archive, Bodleian Library Special Collections
JLP	John Lewis Partnership Heritage Centre
QMUL	People's Palace Archive, Queen Mary, University of London
RAH	Royal Albert Hall Archive
ROH	Royal Opera House Archive

1

The Elitism Myth

'People who have learned to enjoy opera are lucky', the novelist Noel Streatfeild wrote in 1966. 'They know that to be present at a really great performance of an opera and to appreciate it is a privilege never to be forgotten.'[1] Best remembered nowadays as the author of *Ballet Shoes*, Streatfeild captured countless young imaginations with her books about the arts. Opera, she told her readers, was something special: it contained some of the most wonderful music in the world and nothing was more capable of rousing emotion than the human voice. At the same time, an opera was something ordinary, simply a play told through music, whose tunes—familiar from weddings or listening to a seaside band—were good for whistling in the kitchen or the bath.

Streatfeild realised what anyone who has caught the opera bug realises: that to watch an opera among other people in the darkened auditorium of a theatre or to listen to one with your eyes closed in your own living room is to open a box of delights. The critic Rodney Milnes understood too, though he expressed the point rather differently. For him, listening to an opera was a transformative experience: nobody was, or should be, the same person after watching *The Ring* or *The Makropulos Case*, and even a good performance of *Carmen* should make you look at whoever you were sleeping with through new eyes.[2]

The ultimate multimedia, interdisciplinary art form, opera brings together music, drama, dance, design, and technology in sophisticated and beguiling ways, marshalling vast human and material forces to tell stories about the full range of human predicaments and emotions. Opera deals with subjects that affect and speak to us all: love, desire, illness, death, power, politics, corruption. There is something in it for everyone, though plenty of people believe it is not for them. Some, however, might find their minds changed if they were prepared to explore further. Opera is at once epic in scale and tenderly

---

[1] Noel Streatfeild, *Enjoying Opera* (London: Dennis Dobson, 1966), p. 1.
[2] Rodney Milnes, 'Ever Decreasing Circles', *Opera*, 22/11 (November 1971), 945–953, 952.

2 SOMEONE ELSE'S MUSIC

intimate, addressing global concerns while reflecting our own, very personal, situations and sorrows back at us.

Recently, however, opera has come to be associated with privilege of a different sort from that intended by Streatfeild—not privilege in the sense of having an opportunity to do something special but in the sense of having some sort of unfair social advantage. Despite the many different facets of its appeal, its capacity to make us think about the challenges life throws at us, and the sheer pleasure it gives as a musical, theatrical, and social experience, opera has become an object of profound suspicion and is systematically held up as elitist. Not only that, but it has come to be seen as the *most* elitist of the arts. Opera, we are repeatedly told—at least in the United Kingdom—is expensive and exclusive; ergo, the people who enjoy it must be social and intellectual snobs.

In 2017, a correspondent for *The Daily Express* went so far as to write, 'Ask the man on the Clapham omnibus and it is quite likely he'd rather stick pins in his eyes than attend a performance. The popular image of opera is that it's for posh people, exorbitantly expensive, often incomprehensible and seems to drag on for ever.'[3] The very word 'opera' has become a form of shorthand in the contemporary public imagination for a mishmash of anxieties about money, class, dress, privilege, and social status. These perceptions have become deeply ingrained. Ask the average person on the street why they think opera is elitist and they are likely to respond 'because it is'.

Things were not always like this. Once upon a time, not so very long ago, opera was accepted as a form of entertainment anyone could enjoy if they were so minded to go and see one. Opera has always had a close relationship with popular culture—film, advertising, and even popular music—and in many respects still does. But latterly, for all its joyous and consoling qualities, its ability to make us laugh and cry, opera has found itself on the wrong side in a wider national conversation about the politics of exclusion.

In this book I explore the ways in which debates surrounding opera have changed in Britain from 1920, when it was comfortably accommodated as a form of entertainment for all, to the early 2020s, when it is routinely portrayed as the preserve of the wealthy, the intelligentsia, and some sort of imagined social clique. By examining how debates around opera, accessibility, class, and money have changed over the last century, I explore why attitudes towards the art form hardened and representations of it became so

---

[3] Adrian Lee, 'World of the Opera Elite', *DE* (6 December 2017), 19.

relentlessly negative. At what point did people start calling opera 'elitist' and why? When did opera come to be seen as, for want of a better word, 'toxic'?

In tandem, however, this book also tells a second, more celebratory, story. The supposed chasm between opera and 'ordinary life' has never been as deep as today's lazy stereotypes would have us believe. Countless surprising and heart-warming stories of ordinary people's everyday encounters with opera via performances, recordings, radio broadcasts, film soundtracks, television documentaries, participation in amateur productions, and more will be told here. Many of these defy stereotypes. The book is as much about the shopgirl camping out overnight in the queue for gallery tickets as it is about the jewelled duchess in the stalls. We shall meet working-class people for whom opera performances in South London, the East End, and the industrial cities of the north offered respite from challenging lives. We shall meet people who developed a taste for opera after hearing it at Butlin's, or in an end-of-pier revue, or when on active service overseas. We shall meet opera-singing coalminers and secretaries, and children who devised their own operas for fun. We shall meet people like you, and people like me.

Operatic elitism in six myths

What do people mean when they call opera elitist? When asked in 1998 what the word meant to him, the then Culture Secretary Chris Smith replied, 'If elitism means excluding people from access to things, then we have to fight it very hard.'[4] Few would disagree that elitism, thus defined, is a bad thing. But as we shall see, during the twentieth and twenty-first centuries, access to opera—whether in a theatre, or via recordings (often available from public libraries), broadcasting, or latterly the internet—has very rarely been restricted in the United Kingdom. Even in those instances where access to specific operatic performances has been limited by high ticket prices or low seat availability, opera *in general* has always been available to those keen to seek it out. The idea that opera is elitist because it is inaccessible does not make sense: operatic elitism must mean something else.

Is it about the operas themselves? Contrary to widely held perceptions, most operas, at least those in the standard performing canon, deal with universal themes rather than aloof concerns to which 'the likes of us' cannot

---

[4] Petronella Wyatt, 'Blowing in the Wind', *The Spectator* (28 March 1998), 19–21, 20.

4 SOMEONE ELSE'S MUSIC

relate. They do not demand an advanced level of education to be comprehensible. Some plots can be confusing and reading a summary in advance may enrich the viewing and listening experience, provided you don't mind spoilers. But convoluted storylines are by no means limited to opera: I, for one, have rarely felt anything other than baffled by the plot of a James Bond film.

There are certain dramatic and musical conventions in opera, particularly in early opera, which may seem unusual on first acquaintance. But many activities have rules and practices that can seem alien to the newcomer. As Michael Hurd wrote in 1963,

> No one in England is dismayed by the rules of cricket. We accept the peculiar conventions and proceed to enjoy the game on its own terms. We do not complain that its pace is infinitely slower than that of football—we adjust our scale of time-values and sit out the warm summer afternoons, perfectly content that cricket has its own speed and thus its own sort of thrills. And so it should be with opera.[5]

Meanwhile, there is little that is 'intellectual' about most operas. Indeed, generations of highbrows have argued that some types of opera are not intellectual enough—that Italian opera, for example, is positively lowbrow because it is too tuneful and popular. And to suggest that the music itself is too complex in some way for so-called 'ordinary people' to understand would be spurious, not to say insulting.

Language is often perceived as a particular barrier to the enjoyment of opera. Before the advent of surtitles in the 1980s, opera in a foreign language did, admittedly, demand some effort on the part of the listener in familiarising themselves with the work in advance. As the author of a 1970s opera guide wrote, there was a strong demand for opera in English because 'few in an audience are ready to follow the good example of the heroine of D. H. Lawrence's novel, *The Trespasser*, and undertake to learn German because they want to "understand Wagner in his own language".[6] But this was not a problem, because for most of the twentieth century most opera performed in Britain, except at Covent Garden and Glyndebourne, was indeed sung in English. Since the advent of surtitles, the opera-goer has not needed to know

---

[5] Michael Hurd, *Young Person's Guide to Opera* (London: Routledge and Kegan Paul, 1963), pp. 4–5.

[6] Hamish F. G. Swanston, *In Defence of Opera* (London: Penguin, 1978), p. 278.

any foreign languages. One might even argue that an opera translation in plain modern English is easier to understand than the unfamiliar language of a Shakespeare play. No, it's not just about the operas themselves.

Is it about money? This, surely, is the nub of the issue. So costly are opera tickets presumed to be that regular attendance at the opera is routinely used as an indicator of high socio-economic status. In assessing the rate of inflation on luxury goods in 2018, Coutts Bank compiled a 'luxury basket' of high-end goods and services. The contents? Private school fees, bespoke suits, Aston Martins, oysters, and opera tickets.[7] Meanwhile, the BBC's Great British Class Survey of 2011 found that among those earning over £200,000 per annum, 28.8 per cent claimed to go to see an opera sometimes or often, compared with only 7.4 per cent of those earning below £45,000. But then again, the super-rich also went more regularly to restaurants, gyms, and sporting events: their wealth simply allowed them to do more of *everything*.[8]

It would be futile to deny that there are highly priced opera tickets to be had; some extremely so. There is no getting away from the fact that opera is phenomenally expensive to stage, thanks to the vast number of artistic and administrative personnel who need to be paid and all the material costs of putting on a show. As the critic Francis Toye wrote in *The Listener* in 1933, 'Most of the people who write and talk about opera have usually the haziest idea, to begin with, as to what opera costs.'[9] Time and again across the later twentieth century—as standards of production rose and audiences expected to see ever-more sophisticated sets and costumes—the Royal Opera House's annual reports stressed the need for higher subsidy, since even selling every seat in the house every night could not cover its costs. It is possible for opera to be extremely popular and yet remain uneconomical. The question of how to 'make opera pay', whether through state subsidy, ticket sales, or various forms of patronage or philanthropy, has always been and will always be a vexed one, in the United Kingdom as anywhere else.

Paradoxically, opera's 'extravagance' in certain contexts may be regarded simultaneously as a sign of its supposed 'elitism' and as a selling point. As Nicholas Payne (former Director of the Royal Opera and General Director of English National Opera) observes, opera's 'very lavishness serves as an attraction to the public. From Roman games through opera to modern

---

[7] Kaya Burgess, 'Big Spenders Hit by Inflation', *The Times* (12 December 2018), 19.

[8] Cited in Katharina Hecht, Daniel McArthur, Mike Savage, and Sam Friedman, 'Elites in the UK: Pulling Away?' (The Sutton Trust, 2019), 20.

[9] Francis Toye, 'Covent Garden Opera', *The Listener* (20 December 1933), 944.

6 SOMEONE ELSE'S MUSIC

musicals or blockbuster movies, a big budget is seen as proof of ambition'.[10] But whoever talked about Hollywood films being elitist because they are expensive to make? The problem, for opera, is not so much that it costs a lot to put on a good show as the fact that the public purse is often partially footing the bill.

Country-house opera is often particularly expensive, and its ethos is one of unabashed luxury: this, indeed, is in many ways its appeal to those who attend. Perhaps we might see this as a form of elitism? But the companies involved are usually small, in receipt of no public funding, and could not finance their operations without charging high prices. A positive counterbalance to their perceived exclusivity is the rich employment opportunities they provide for up-and-coming young singers and a broader benefit is that their attractiveness as a social occasion irrespective of the operas being performed gives the companies considerable freedom to revive lesser-known repertory. At Covent Garden, of course, tickets can be eye-wateringly expensive—a practical necessity but a bone of contention for decades at this state-subsidised institution—yet some are available for a price similar to a cinema ticket. Tickets to see a touring opera company at a regional theatre are likely to be little different in price from those on sale at the same venue for a musical.

In fact, studies have shown that going to the opera is, on average, consistently *less* expensive than attending other forms of entertainment such as high-profile rock concerts, the latest West End shows, Premier-League football matches, or Wimbledon.[11] Since nobody would call a concert by the Rolling Stones elitist (top price tickets in 2022 £566, with 'VIP' tickets over £3,000), there must be more to opera's supposed elitism than this.[12] Designer fashion and expensive cars, too, are constructed not as elitist but as aspirational: a whole magazine industry thrives on the premise of people looking at pictures of luxurious things they cannot possibly afford. No, it's not just about the money.

Is it about dress codes? The popular perception of an audience enjoying a night at the opera is one of tuxedos and tiaras. As Robin May wrote in 1977 about an imaginary first-time opera-goer, 'Indoctrination by the invincibly

---

[10] Nicholas Payne, 'Trends and Innovations in Opera', in Anastasia Belina-Johnson and Derek B. Scott (eds), *The Business of Opera* (Farnham: Ashgate, 2015), pp. 17–29, p. 25.

[11] For a comparative list of prices, see Andrew Mitchell, 'It's Time to Scotch the Cliché That Opera Tickets Are Too Expensive', *The Guardian* (3 November 2015), n.p.

[12] https://inews.co.uk/culture/music/rolling-stones-2022-tour-tickets-pre-sale-prices-uk-venues-60th-anniversary-shows-1518240 (accessed 19 March 2024).

THE ELITISM MYTH   7

ignorant will have told him that the theatre will be peopled by the rich in full evening dress (see almost any film or TV play in which there is a "night at the opera" scene).[13] But such formal attire was already falling out of favour at Covent Garden for anything other than gala performances decades ago and is now very much the exception rather than the rule.

Black tie is, of course, still worn at the Glyndebourne Festival and at the various country-house opera festivals that have copied its model. Glyndebourne's founder John Christie encouraged the wearing of formal dress in the 1930s as a mark of respect to the performers—and what was said to be a recommendation effectively 'had the force of law'—though was himself reportedly prone to matching evening dress with a pair of old tennis shoes.[14] The Glyndebourne 'look' has undoubtedly had a strong influence upon the representation of opera in the public imagination. Today black tie is not stipulated, though the steer towards formality remains implicit, with the company encouraging audiences to treat attendance as a special occasion, like going to a wedding.[15]

Formal dress would, however, seem out of place at the London Coliseum, where English National Opera (ENO) has actively encouraged its patrons to 'dress down'. In 2017, the company's then Artistic Director Daniel Kramer stated,

> Although the debate about what to wear to the opera has moved on, with almost all of our audience happily turning up wearing whatever they feel most comfortable in, the way opera is presented in a lot of popular culture can be at odds with this. Opera is the most moving art form on Earth. It has the power to challenge, to entertain, to devastate and to inspire, whether its audience is wearing a tiara and ball gown or a T-shirt and jeans.[16]

Of course, many people enjoy dressing up to go to the opera—opera's popular association with luxury is as alluring to some as it is off-putting to others— but there is certainly no compulsion to do so. Furthermore, nobody cries 'elitism!' when people dress up to go to the races, and there is huge public

---

[13] Robin May, *Opera* (Sevenoaks: Hodder and Stoughton, 1977), p. 6.

[14] Peter Cater, 'Christie, The Grand Old Man of Opera', *DM* (5 July 1962), 3; Wilfrid Blunt, *John Christie of Glyndebourne* (London: Geoffrey Bles, 1968), p. 167.

[15] https://www.glyndebourne.com/your-visit/what-to-wear/ (accessed 21 November 2019).

[16] Kevin Coyd, 'Decoding the Dress Code: What to Wear to the Opera', *The Telegraph* (14 June 2017), n.p.

8 SOMEONE ELSE'S MUSIC

interest in the expensive outfits celebrities wear to film *premières*. No, it's not just about the clothes.

Is it about grand venues? The places where operas are conventionally performed—often historic theatres designed to allow aristocratic opera-goers of ages long-past to display their sartorial elegance—are also habitually depicted as inaccessible spaces. 'High culture's icy palace lets the people in for a drink', announced *The Guardian* in September 2018.[17] The subject of the article was the Royal Opera House's redevelopment of its public spaces, an internal refit that had been given the name 'Open Up'. The author presented the theatre as a 'bastion of exclusivity' with a 'rarefied reputation', closed off to 'hoi polloi'. Cliché piled on cliché as he quoted a project developer as saying, 'You can now look in from the street and see that the operagoers aren't all wearing tuxedos.'

The Royal Opera House is undoubtedly an opulent theatre, but it does not have the prominence within London that opera houses have as civic buildings in major European cities such as Paris or Vienna. Indeed, commentators of the early to mid-twentieth century regularly complained about the 'out-of-the-way-ness' of Covent Garden, situated as it was in a then-shabby part of town next to the fruit and vegetable market and opposite a police station, closer to the fleshpots of Soho than the mansions of Mayfair. There were frequent calls for a more 'centrally located' opera house. Such complaints seem odd—Covent Garden is in the heart of the West End—but evidently some commentators believed that the theatre demanded a setting among London's national artistic or financial institutions rather than popular theatres and shopping emporia.[18] English National Opera, close by, performs in a very large, traditional theatre, the London Coliseum, but it is one that enjoyed a former life as a music hall.

Beyond London, most people who watch live opera do so at theatres that also put on pantomimes, gigs, evenings with stand-up comedians, and so on. Operas are now regularly broadcast to cinemas that also screen blockbuster Hollywood films or performed in imaginative non-theatrical spaces from pubs to railway stations. In 2014, for example, Birmingham Opera Company

---

[17] Oliver Wainwright, 'The Royal Opera House Opens Up: High Culture's Icy Palace Lets the People in for a Drink', *The Guardian* (19 September 2018), n.p.

[18] See proposals for an opera house on the Embankment (Anon., 'Prices for All. Meeting Future Needs', *DT* (9 January 1930), 11) and near the National Gallery or Royal Exchange (Frederick Woodhouse, *Opera for Amateurs* (London: Dennis Dobson, Ltd, 1951), p. 51).

put on a performance in a Tesco supermarket.[19] In none of these places are there esoteric social codes or customs that are opaque to the uninitiated.

Even when it is lavish, need the architecture of opera necessarily be off-putting? It is surely patronising to suggest that 'ordinary people' will feel intimidated or excluded in a building that features classical columns, red carpets, gold paint, or smart facilities. Indeed, a similar monumental or, as the urban historian Rohan McWilliam puts it, 'populist palatial' style was used in the nineteenth century for countless West End theatres, music halls, and department stores precisely in order to attract the aspirational middle classes and even working classes, flattering them into believing that they were honoured, refined guests.[20]

There is plentiful historical evidence of people longing to go to the opera *because* it was staged in glamorous surroundings, and the desire for this relatively affordable taste of luxury still exists. Nicholas Payne writes, 'It would be wrong to conclude that the flexible small-scale models are set to supplant the traditional opera houses. The public continues to seek out the spectacular experience which grand opera can provide.'[21] Likewise, while country-house opera is often at the more expensive end of the operatic market, it surely makes no sense to label it elitist simply for its setting amid elegantly manicured gardens when millions of people visit stately homes annually as a leisure activity. No, it's not just about the venues.

Is it about the audience? Perhaps elitism is merely a synonym for a snooty clientèle, the sort of snobs Helen Fielding pokes fun at in *Bridget Jones's Diary*. ('"They should have refused to let anyone listen to the World Cup tune", hooted Arabella, "until they could prove they'd listened to *Turandot* all the way through".'[22]) Of all the topics discussed thus far, audience demographics and attitudes are the hardest about which to generalise. Speculating about whether people who go to the opera are posh or condescending takes us into the realm of the anecdotal. Every seasoned opera-goer would probably have a story to tell about an encounter with an objectionable fellow audience member, and we shall undoubtedly meet some in this book.

There have certainly always been snobs at the opera. First there are the social snobs. Take, for example, the women who wrote to *The Daily Mail*

---

[19] Belina-Johnson and Scott, *The Business of Opera*, p. 4.
[20] Rohan McWilliam, *London's West End: Creating the Pleasure District, 1800–1914* (Oxford: Oxford University Press, 2020), pp. 4–5.
[21] Payne, 'Trends and Innovations in Opera', p. 27.
[22] Helen Fielding, *Bridget Jones's Diary* (London: Picador, 1996), p. 102.

10 SOMEONE ELSE'S MUSIC

in 1964 to demand that people who bought cheap tickets at Covent Garden be excluded from the bars in the more expensive part of the house.[23] Then there are the intellectual snobs: those who pride themselves on favouring challenging Modernist operas over populist Puccini; those who mock 'traditional' stagings and the audiences who prefer them; those who like to give the impression of being party to privileged information. In a beginner's guide to opera from 1977, Robin May wrote that cliques at the opera could make 'even the sophisticated feel uneasy', huddling in groups sharing insider gossip about singers, conductors, and productions and noisily showing off their knowledge, 'which may make our newcomer feel not only an outsider, but that he is surrounded by that dread tribe, the élitists'.[24]

But does even this make opera, per se, elitist? Cliques can be found in all sorts of walks of life and to presume that everyone who goes to the opera is a snob is as unfair as to presume that everyone who attends a football match is a hooligan. A glance around the foyer at any opera performance, or a brief survey of social media conversations about opera would reveal diverse constituencies simply engaged in lively discussion about an art form they love. In this book, we shall see that opera in Britain has historically attracted many different types of listener, mixed in age and social background, which shows that it is unwise to make generalisations about who opera is 'for'. No, it's not just about the audience.

Is it about the singers? The association between opera singers and glamour is long-standing. The stars of the nineteenth and early twentieth centuries were paid astronomical fees. A stereotype emerged, and developed international currency, about prima donnas and their jewels, as parodied playfully in the character Bianca Castafiore in the *Tintin* comic strips. Maria Callas, with her lavish jewel collection and shipping magnate lover, perpetuated the stereotype in the mid-twentieth century. Even today, a select few star singers are paid large sums to sing and even larger sums to endorse luxury products. And yet nobody ever objects to the colossal wealth of the stars of popular music, who are far richer and greater in number.

Today's few truly wealthy opera singers—the Anna Netrebkos and Jonas Kaufmanns—are very much the exception to the rule. Most jobbing singers earn little more than the national average wage; many earn far less.[25] Singers typically pursue portfolio careers, combining opera with concerts and

---

[23] Mrs P. and Miss M. Wilson, 'Intruders', letter to *DM* (24 April 1964), 12.

[24] May, *Opera*, p. 7.

[25] Antony Feeny, 'The Cost of Singing', *Opera*, 71/10 (October 2020), 1180–1190, 1182, 1189.

THE ELITISM MYTH   11

teaching, just as many in the past sang in musical theatre, operetta, and even pantomime and music hall. When the Covid crisis struck in March 2020, many opera singers found themselves in dire financial straits.

Singers have also not traditionally come from the high social echelons one might expect. As Dave Russell notes, in a study of British singers' backgrounds up to the 1960s, 'very few emerged from elite social backgrounds and a significant minority were born into the manual working class, their path into opera made possible . . . by innumerable acts of individual and collective philanthropy and, eventually, by the benefits of a state-funded higher education system'.[26] None of the singers in his study emerged from the aristocracy, and few from the upper-middle classes, because singing on the stage was still considered vaguely immoral well into the twentieth century; those further down the social scale did not have the luxury of worrying about such considerations. It was, in fact, the lower middle classes who dominated the British singing community in the earlier part of our period—the children of shopkeepers, low-grade office workers, and clerks—many of whose families had only recently achieved social mobility and whose home lives were still essentially working-class.[27]

A surprising number of British opera singers have come from working-class backgrounds proper, and the press—always on the lookout for a rags-to-riches story—has often cheered them on, making a big splash of singers from humble parentage or deprived industrial regions. Poor areas of Wales and the North West, indeed, have produced disproportionately large numbers of British opera singers relative to their population size, thanks to strong traditions in choral singing among Lancashire weavers and in chapel and community singing in the mining villages of South Wales.[28] Although some British singers have been propelled up the social-mobility ladder by their talent, they looked like very ordinary people at the outset.

All that said, it is undoubtedly harder to become an opera singer in Britain today. State funding for training is less generous than it was at mid-century, and the earlier twentieth-century tendency for communities to club together to fund a talented member's musical training (or for employers to pay for it, as the National Coal Board did for the Scottish bass William McCue in

---

[26] Dave Russell, 'Reaching the Operatic Stage: The Geographical and Social Origins of British and Irish Opera Singers, c.1850–c.1960', *Cambridge Opera Journal*, 29/3 (November 2017), 312–352, 335.

[27] Ibid., 329–330.

[28] Ibid., 322–325.

12 SOMEONE ELSE'S MUSIC

the 1950s) has declined.[29] The high cost of course fees is certainly a matter for concern, and something the opera industry must urgently address. More broadly, some of the diverse routes into the profession from other types of singing now appear to have closed, and the recent 'crossover' movement has not offered the path into opera singing we might have expected. Furthermore, the general lack of exposure to opera among the population means young people are less likely to consider singing as a career. All that said, we will continue to encounter singers from unexpected backgrounds in the later chapters of this book.

Is it perhaps *foreign* singers who are presumed to be elitist? For many decades, commentators claimed the British would never take opera to their hearts until it was sung by British singers. But even when Britain had succeeded in producing top-level singers who were respected the world over, the idea that opera was sung by foreigners persisted. Conservative MP Terry Dicks said in a parliamentary debate in 1988, 'I do not believe that an overweight Italian singing in his own language is part of my heritage', leading a reporter for *The Sunday Times* to conclude that, 'for him and for many others, opera is an alien and élitist taste'.[30] And yet a glance at the diverse international make-up of any Premier League football team today surely makes a mockery of the argument that the British cannot embrace forms of culture that are 'performed' by foreigners. No, it's not just about the singers. So what is it about?

No opera please, we're British

All the stereotypes above play into the negative perceptions of opera that circulate in Britain today, but they are only part of the picture. Underpinning them is something else: namely, a form of identity politics. The further one digs into the history of the elitism trope in Britain—including in the decades before the term was used explicitly—the more one realises that it is a multifaceted concept, imbued with specific British anxieties about class and a certain peculiarly British anti-intellectualism: ideas that have long and complex historical roots. Underpinning the opera/elitism debate is a conversation

[29] Feeny, 'The Cost of Singing', 1189; Russell, 'Reaching the Operatic Stage', 333–334; http://www.billmccue.com/about/ (accessed 3 February 2021).
[30] Mark Fisher, 'Opera Needs a Stronger Voice', *ST* (3 July 1988), 31.

THE ELITISM MYTH   13

about national identity, a sense of self—all played out through the prism of culture.

Ever since it arrived in Britain some three centuries ago, opera has prompted apprehension. Britain has an 'opera problem', which never seems to go away, and which has metamorphosed over time. This problem was and is, in large part, bound up with questions of national and class identities. Even at times when opera has been viewed more benevolently there has still been a constant refrain in the background: the idea that opera is an 'imported' art form to which the British are somehow constitutionally immune, which has never become part of civic life here or a permanent institution. Opera has been widely characterised as, to borrow a phrase from Oscar Wilde, 'someone else's music': a form of entertainment for foreigners, aristocrats, intellectuals, and eccentrics. Horticultural analogies have been many and various: opera, in the theatre director Tyrone Guthrie's words, 'has never taken very kindly to British soil. It has never become an indigenous plant, but has remained a delicate, waxy, hothouse exotic'.[31] Yet, as another commentator observed in 1946, to say that the British people didn't like opera was rather like saying they didn't like the ceiling of the Sistine Chapel—many had simply never had the opportunity to experience it.[32]

Opera's perceived connection to the upper classes has coloured its reception in Britain. It originally arrived in early eighteenth-century London as a form of aristocratic entertainment: then and for around a century and a half after, it would be correct to call opera an elite art form, in the sense of playing to a privileged audience, though it would be anachronistic to use the word 'elitist' in its present-day sense. Wealthy Georgians, Victorians, and Edwardians went to the opera to see and be seen. Covent Garden in the nineteenth century was 'fashionable and exclusive' and 'a place for wearing all one's diamonds, and meeting all one's friends', the foreign languages reminding the aristocracy of their prolonged travels around Europe.[33]

The international opera seasons at Covent Garden that were as much a fixture in the aristocratic summer 'Season' as going to Ascot or the Henley Regatta continued in one form or another until World War Two. Even in the late 1950s, Lionel Salter, Head of Music Productions for BBC TV, observed that 'something of this "social" attitude still exists, though to a lesser degree in

---

[31] Tyrone Guthrie, *A Life in the Theatre* (London: Columbus Books, 1987), p. 196.
[32] Desmond Shawe, 'Opera at the Seaside', *ES* (1 October 1946), 9.
[33] J. Daniel Chamier, *Percy Pitt of Covent Garden and the B.B.C.* (London: Edward Arnold and Co., 1938), pp. 19–20.

14 SOMEONE ELSE'S MUSIC

England than in some countries, and certainly less nowadays than fifty years ago, when not to have one's box at the opera was to be out of the swim'.[34] The practice finds its modern equivalent in corporate entertainment at Covent Garden.

The British didn't understand opera, so they ridiculed it. The same objections to opera have been reiterated, decade after decade, century after century: that opera is absurd because characters sing rather than speak; that singers don't always look right for their roles; that the art form can never be taken to the nation's heart when it is sung in another language or even when it is translated from another language. Stephen Williams, who presented programmes about opera on the BBC's Light Programme, summed this up in 1952: 'The average Englishman, rightly or wrongly, finds enough in grand opera to arouse his mockery—ridiculous plots, sawdust heroes, maidens with matronly figures—without the additional stimulus of a silly English libretto.'[35] And although one beginner's guide after another patiently explained that these were merely conventions and that we are perfectly capable of accepting other conventions, the British have shown themselves, when it comes to opera, supremely incapable of suspending disbelief.

The clash between supposedly 'posh' opera and down-to-earth 'real life' has long been fixed in the public imagination as the stuff of comedy. The operatic burlesques of the Victorian era parodied well-known operas, highlighting their perceived absurdities, yet also popularising them among distinctly non-elite audiences. That tradition would continue into the twentieth century in the guise of music-hall and variety skits. And in countless films, television dramas, and adverts, a taste for opera has become shorthand for wealth or pretension. Such clichés are ages-old and, although reductive, often good-natured, affectionate even. Recent charges of 'elitism', by contrast—and it must be stressed that the current notion of opera as elitist *is* recent—are distinctly harder-edged. There is nothing warm or humorous about elitism.

It is one thing to call opera silly, quite another to call it elitist, but over time the two strands of rhetoric have converged. As a correspondent for *The Times* reported in 1959, 'Opera is a difficult candidate for any publicity campaign for it provokes resistance both as a minority culture and as a badge of class; and thanks to cartoonists and the music-hall it takes its place with the desert

---

[34] Lionel Salter, *Going to the Opera* (London: Penguin Books, 1958), p. 91.

[35] Stephen Williams, *In the Opera House* (London: Stratford Place, 1952), pp. 71–72.

THE ELITISM MYTH   15

island and the mother-in-law as a stereotype of absurdity.[36] Meanwhile, in 1968, a correspondent for *The Illustrated London News* wrote: 'Opera is fantastically expensive. It is the most lavish, the most spectacular, the most extravagant form of art. And in a sense it is also ludicrous.'[37] These statements could have been made by the British press at any point over the last century. There is plentiful evidence to disprove these arguments, but once stereotypes take hold, they are almost impossible to shake off. As a correspondent for *The Daily Express* remarked of the British public in 2000, 'Tell 'em "it's elitist" often enough and, sadly, they'll soon begin to believe it.'[38]

The road to elitism, as we might characterise it, did not progress in linear fashion but would take many twists and turns as the decades progressed, spawning countless unlikely ideological alliances along the way. Those who have characterised opera as elitist (either explicitly or in as many words) have included the following eclectic characters. 1930s Conservative MPs who believed sugar beet and allotments more worthy of subsidy than opera and their Labour contemporaries who feared public money might be 'used for the purposes of boosting long-haired foreign artistes.'[39] A populist press that has asked repeatedly why opera needs financial support when football and cinema don't. 1980s left-wing councils who favoured community art and saw opera as for yuppies. Cool-Britannia-obsessed New Labour, which adopted 'anti-elitism' as official government policy. Twenty-first-century Conservatives who bundled up opera with a contempt for metropolitan elites. Contemporary academics who denounce opera for historic associations with power structures.

These are strange bedfellows indeed, and they all bear responsibility for turning a form of entertainment that brings joy to many into a socio-political problem. Trendsetters (or 'influencers' as we might call them today) also play a role in shaping behaviours and opinions: some such people have, historically, helped the cause of opera in Britain, whilst others have hindered it. Even the opera industry itself is not without blame in the way in which it presents itself to potential audience members, and there have been occasions when singers, directors, and opera administrators have shot themselves in the foot by perpetuating the elitism stereotype. But above all, the principal

[36] Anon., 'Popularizing Opera with the Television Audience', *The Times* (1 January 1959), 6.
[37] A. K. Panni, 'The Opera Industry', *ILN* (25 May 1968), 46–47.
[38] Mark Pappenheim, 'Opera', *DE* (24 November 2000), 71.
[39] Adam McKinlay (Labour MP for Glasgow), House of Commons debate, 15 September 1931: 'British Broadcasting Corporation (Grand Opera)', Hansard, Vol. 256.

16 SOMEONE ELSE'S MUSIC

culprit for disseminating and recycling misleading clichés about opera has been the media.

Words, as well as attitudes, have changed over time. 'Elitism' is a modern term, not entering wide circulation until the 1980s, at which point it swiftly became a fashionable buzzword that peppered casual conversations about the arts up and down the land. An early dictionary appearance for the word (1982) defines 'elitism' as 'advocacy or reliance on leadership or dominance by a select group'.[40] There was no overt implication that this was a bad thing, because that 'select group'—the elite—was defined as something good: 'the choice part, the best'. Though 'elitism' was commonly used negatively by the late 1990s, dictionary definitions remained equivocal as to whether the word was necessarily pejorative: it remained 'the belief that society should be governed by a select group of gifted and highly educated individuals', or 'pride in or awareness of being one of an elite group'.[41]

By the turn of the twenty-first century, however, elitism had become something about which every right-thinking person was worried. In 2005, *The Compact Oxford English Dictionary of Current English* suggested as an example, 'The cosy elitism that weakened our education system for a century'.[42] Five years later *The Oxford Dictionary of English*'s example was 'he accused her of racism and white elitism'.[43] Elitism's thoroughly malign, exclusive nature was now made crystal clear, and it was no longer connected to 'elite', a positive term when used adjectivally (though not as a noun) that denotes something of high quality, still often used today as a way of praising those who reach the highest levels in sport.

Latterly, 'elitism' has taken on new nuance. In a period of populist politics, the right refers witheringly to 'metropolitan elites', characterising their political enemies as privileged and aloof from so-called ordinary society and disparaging the arts as a trivial luxury. The left, on the other hand, flings around the word 'elitism' as a way of demonstrating its opposition to everything it sees as bound up with supposed historic privilege. In an age of cultural relativism, a pronounced squeamishness has developed around the so-called 'high arts'. Opera, alas, has become caught in the crossfire of a deepening

---

[40] J. B. Sykes (ed.), *The Concise Oxford Dictionary of Current English* (7th edn) (Oxford: Oxford University Press, 1982), p. 312.

[41] Anon., *Collins English Dictionary* (4th edn) (Glasgow: Harper Collins, 1998), p. 503.

[42] Catherine Soanes and Sara Hawker (eds), *The Compact Oxford English Dictionary of Current English* (3rd edn) (Oxford: Oxford University Press, 2005), p. 322.

[43] Angus Stevenson (ed.), *Oxford Dictionary of English* (3rd edn) (Oxford: Oxford University Press, 2010), p. 569.

culture war and is disparaged and held to account from both ends. This, as I shall argue in the conclusion, has actively harmed the cause of artistic accessibility: told that opera is 'not for the likes of them', potential new audience members are likely to be put off giving it a try.

Opera's hidden history

To find a positive model for the future of opera in Britain, we need to look to the past. To characterise the British as resolutely antagonistic towards and dismissive of opera would be to misrepresent matters entirely. Since the later nineteenth century, another type of opera-going developed in Britain alongside the glittering scene at Covent Garden. By the late Victorian era, opera had become very popular among both the middle and even the working classes, who encountered it through rough-and-ready productions of opera in English that were put on by touring companies in the London suburbs or provincial towns and cities. An early pioneer of this model was the troupe set up by Carl Rosa, who began his operations in Liverpool in 1869. He established what a later commentator called 'a sort of operatic Woolworth's, a vast company which could give opera to the nation cheap before the nation was aware that it wanted it'.[44] More people still got to know operatic tunes by listening to brass bands in their local park (Italian operatic numbers a speciality), or hearing barrel-organists on the corner of the street as they walked to work, or watching an operatic skit in the music hall. Opera could even be heard in pubs and working men's clubs.[45]

By the 1920s, it would be no exaggeration to say that opera had become a genuinely popular form of entertainment, its democratisation hastened by the wireless, gramophone records and the initiatives of enterprising opera evangelists such as Lilian Baylis, who built up a loyal audience of working-class opera lovers at the Old Vic in south London. Opera functioned as an integral part of an emerging middlebrow culture—audiences treated a night at the opera little differently from a night at the cinema and were happy to incorporate opera-going into a broader mixed diet of entertainment.[46]

[44] Chamier, *Percy Pitt of Covent Garden*, p. 129.
[45] Russell, 'Reaching the Operatic Stage', 318.
[46] See Alexandra Wilson, *Opera in the Jazz Age: Cultural Politics in 1920s Britain* (New York: Oxford University Press, 2019).

18 SOMEONE ELSE'S MUSIC

Figure 1.1 Royal Opera House ticket queue, Floral Street, Covent Garden, 31 May 1986. Reproduced with permission from © Clive Barda/ArenaPAL.

Throughout the 1930s and 1940s, opera continued to function as a form of popular entertainment in Britain, performed in theatres grand and humble, and heard by people of all social classes in concert and variety halls, restaurants, and cinemas, and on the radio. A new generation discovered opera during World War Two, and in the brave new post-war era, Britons were converted to public subsidy for opera—a concept that had previously attracted immense criticism. At the turn of the 1950s, *Homes and Gardens* declared that 'Grand Opera has certainly become, since the war, as much a British as a Continental institution. It is no longer the hobby of the millionaires, but the newly discovered delight of the millions'.[47] In the 1970s, opera was regularly broadcast on prime-time television; in the 1980s, performances of it packed out rock stadiums. Fans continued to queue for cheap tickets at Covent Garden as they had for decades (see Figure 1.1).

Across the course of the twentieth century, then, the British enthusiastically took opera to their hearts. Although opera remained, throughout this

---

[47] Charlotte Haldane, 'Grand Opera ... Delight of the Millions', *Homes and Gardens* (December 1949), 20–21, 21.

period, something that prompted controversy and debate, it was only at the end of the century that Britain's relationship with opera became fundamentally more negative, as a concerted campaign was waged to depict it as elitist. Unfortunately, this stereotype became so ingrained that the nation collectively forgot its own rich history of popular opera-going.

Opera is arguably the most international of the arts, and the present-day conversation about opera and elitism is certainly not limited to the United Kingdom. However, this is a topic on which it is not possible to make global generalisations, bound up as it is with local contexts and questions of national identity. Opera's reception, cultural meanings, and social position have varied greatly between different countries at different moments in time: the nuances of the elitism conversation, for example, are not the same here as they are in the United States, even if the two debates are now converging.

The politics of opera and its funding are very different in Britain from that in countries which have historically had more vibrant indigenous operatic traditions. Take the contrast with Germany (where opera houses are often seen as providing a municipal service), with its numerous provincial repertory companies, subscription system, and altogether friendlier attitude towards opera in general. Opera has tended to be perceived as less elitist in countries where full or near-full state subsidy was generous (the former Soviet Union and Eastern Europe) and more elitist in those where the staging of opera was funded via the philanthropy of private donors (the United States). In Britain we have a mixed model, with a larger burden of covering opera's costs falling on the box office than elsewhere. As we shall see, the introduction of the first, short-lived subsidy for opera here in the early 1930s led to public outrage and was a factor in turning public opinion against the art form. Yet ironically opera was viewed more positively at the point when it began to be subsidised generously after World War Two.

Authors of countless books about opera have regaled British readers with wondrous tales from Italy, where errand-boys and fishermen could (supposedly) be heard whistling opera, which enjoyed the status of popular song. As one such writer observed in 1977 (though this has begun to change), 'In these countries, and others, like France, with a long operatic tradition, there is no need continually to defend opera, its traditions, its audiences, its opera houses, and its subsidies.'[48] By contrast, in Britain, opera has always needed

---

[48] May, *Opera*, p. 4.

20 · SOMEONE ELSE'S MUSIC

defending by its advocates. Increasingly, they do more than defend it: they apologise for it.

Examining the British relationship with opera over the last century can tell us much about broader attitudes towards culture in this country and questions of national identity. What is it that makes a nation? The factors that make us feel British have been slippery and elusive and have changed over time. Historically, the British have been bound together by institutions—the Church of England, allegiance to royalty, support for empire, and pride in our parliamentary system—and by the physical buildings and visual emblems (flags, statues, and so on) that go with them. In our more sceptical age, most if not all of these institutions have become the subject of controversy or even outright condemnation, characterised as more divisive than unifying.

Of course, there was always far more to the intangible sense of Britishness than this. It was also to do with certain shared attitudes, values, sense of humour, and an understanding of social 'manners', but the consensus of what those were started to fray with the dramatic attitudinal shifts of the 1960s. Certain features of our landscape have also been constructed as quintessentially British, from the gently undulating hills of the Cotswolds to the beaches of Cornwall, while characteristic sights of our urban environment—red pillar boxes and phone boxes—remain emblematic even as they become almost redundant in practical purpose. Individual people, from comfortingly familiar newsreaders to beloved actors, seem to sum up something of our collective character as they are embraced as 'national treasures'.

Sport forges a sense of belonging, of identification, of course, but so too do the arts. The British have historically found a sense of shared identity in both 'high art'—their pride in Shakespeare, Austen, or the Romantic poets (though again, in our more pluralistic, canon-sceptical age, old certainties seem to be shifting)—and, perhaps even more strongly, in popular entertainment. From the Beatles to Britpop, popular music has bound the nation together, as have the television programmes that the whole nation watched together in the days before unlimited digital channels, whether a royal wedding or the *Only Fools and Horses* Christmas special. The nation has rejoiced in films that seem to sum up quintessential, often quirky aspects of the British character: the buttoned-up would-be lovers in *Brief Encounter*; Hugh Grant's bumbling upper-middle-class men in *Four Weddings and a Funeral* and *Notting Hill*. The clash of 'high' and 'low' cultures in films from *My Fair*

Lady to *Billy Elliott* has been exploited to rich effect and become a national speciality.

The national relationship with classical music, let alone opera, has, however, been far more ambivalent. In the mid-eighteenth century, Dr Samuel Johnson called opera 'an exotic and irrational entertainment', and the stereotype has been wheeled out ever since as justification for British antipathy towards the art form. And when the German music critic Oscar Schmitz famously called Britain 'the land without music' in 1904, the stereotype did not seem to trouble most Britons greatly, concerning though it was for members of the musical establishment who were keen to put British composition on the international map. Some commentators on the national character went so far as to characterise Britain's relative lack of productivity in the field of opera as an asset. In 1911, for example, Cecil Forsyth argued that while the Italians might be better than the British at writing operas, they were infinitely worse at winning wars.[49] The implications about national strength and virility hardly need spelling out.

Thus, classical music has been used as a tool of nation-building to a relatively small extent in Britain, save for the association of composers such as Elgar and Vaughan Williams with the Empire and a certain type of reified English pastoralism. (These composers are, of course, indelibly associated with The Last Night of the Proms, the one annual classical music event that does attract mainstream attention, but that has been strongly criticised in recent years precisely for its overt patriotism, even—some would contend— its jingoistic flavour.) Opera has rarely been used in the pursuit of British nation-building, with a very few exceptions, because of our relatively weak tradition of operatic composition—but also perhaps because of a certain embarrassment about opera's heightened emotions. (As one commentator put it in the 1940s, opera demands 'a love of exhibitionism foreign to the English temperament'.[50]) Yet the art form has certainly prompted strong feelings and endless controversies, which have been deeply bound up with debates about national identity.

This book uses opera—an art form both loved and loathed by the British—as a lens through which to trace the broader history of changing cultural attitudes and values in the United Kingdom, from 1920s Reithian

---

[49] Cecil Forsyth, *Music and Nationalism: A Study of English Opera* (London: n.p., 1911), p. 2.
[50] M. M. L., 'What Is Wrong With English Opera To-day?', *Coventry Evening Telegraph* (undated press clipping from 1947, ROH archive).

ideals about art's civilising qualities to contemporary culture wars. This in turn helps us understand how ideas of Britishness have changed over the last century, and how they are connected to deep-seated anxieties about class, education, and money. Telling the story of modern Britain through the unexpected prism of opera sheds new light on well-known, defining historical moments, including the Depression, the British wartime experience, the Festival of Britain and subsequent Coronation, the 1960s decline of deference to 'the Establishment', Thatcherism and yuppie culture, New Labour and 'Cool Britannia', and even Brexit. It is only by tracing shifting British attitudes towards the arts over a long period that we can really understand the arguments that are taking place around so-called 'high culture' today. The controversies and scandals opera has prompted over the last century, and the debates about who it is 'for' reveal a great deal about the national sense of self—who Britons think they are and who they want to be.

2

Opera for All

In 1923 two young sisters, Louise and Ida Cook, bought a gramophone. It was a matter of compulsion. Quite by accident, Louise had wandered into a public lecture at the Board of Education by the composer and music educator Sir Walford Davies. Davies was a musical evangelist, an early adaptor of the gramophone and wireless as educational tools, and later presenter of the long-running radio series *Music and the Ordinary Listener*. Although Louise knew nothing about music, she was entranced and resolved that she too must have a gramophone. The sisters were working girls, still living with their parents: Louise had a job in the civil service; Ida was a typist. Louise paid for the gramophone using a work bonus. They had been raised to believe that if you wanted something, you had to work hard to get it. It was an ethos they would take to extremes.[1]

Louise and Ida decided that they could afford a maximum of ten records. Their first inclination was to choose orchestral pieces, until the shop assistant suggested they try vocal recordings. She played them one by the soprano Amelita Galli-Curci, the biggest female recording star of the day, and they were hooked. Galli-Curci was scheduled to tour Britain the following year, so the sisters saved up to go and hear her at the Albert Hall, where 'celebrity concerts' were a regular feature. The musical cognoscenti of the day looked down on them, arguing that they attracted a crowd more interested in stardom than in music, but such events were important in creating an audience for opera. After the concert, the Cook sisters were desperate to see Galli-Curci on stage. The problem was that she sang opera only in New York.

And so New York it would have to be. Despite having very little money, Louise and Ida made the most ambitious of plans. They calculated that if they skipped lunches and walked rather than taking the bus for two years, they would raise enough money for the trip. They wrote to tell Galli-Curci; astonishingly, she promised that if they made it to New York, she would give them free tickets and invite them to dinner. And, true to her word, she did,

---

[1] The sisters' story is told in Ida Cook, *We Followed Our Stars* (London: Hamish Hamilton, 1950).

24 SOMEONE ELSE'S MUSIC

because by the end of 1926, the two determined sisters had saved the necessary funds. They would go on to become close friends with Galli-Curci, making further visits to her apartment on Fifth Avenue and her home in the Catskill Mountains.

The sisters were clearly exceptionally determined and enterprising women who would go on to lead extraordinary lives. During the 1930s, they would use the money Ida made from writing Mills & Boon romances to help Jewish refugees flee to Britain, and travel to Germany themselves to smuggle out friends' valuables. But their initial encounter with opera reflects a common 1920s trend. Time and again, contemporary newspapers and magazines tell stories about ordinary people—office workers, schoolteachers, miners—stumbling across opera and developing a passion for it. This opera 'contagion' spread by two means: word of mouth (Ida converted fellow typists into opera enthusiasts) and an interest in new technology. Gramophones were in vogue: everybody coveted one. And, strange as it might seem to us now, opera recordings were bestsellers.

Arias were short enough to fit neatly on to records, and gramophone companies were keen to confer respectability on their brand by associating with the glamorous world of opera. Global recording artists like Enrico Caruso were the rock stars of their day, adored by audiences and an inspiration to aspiring singers, such as Edgar Evans, who, as an eight-year-old growing up on a farm in Wales, decided to become an opera singer after hearing Caruso on the wireless.[2] Galli-Curci's records were bought by people of every social background, from a Merseyside cleaning lady to Uncle Matthew in Nancy Mitford's *The Pursuit of Love*, a thinly veiled caricature of the author's father, Baron Redesdale.[3]

It was inevitable that before too long the new opera converts would want to see 'the real thing'. Ida Cook and her friends went to Covent Garden religiously during the two-month international season that ran from May to July. Nobody dressed up to sit in the gallery, and it was not possible to book tickets in advance: you had to hire a camp stool, set it up first thing to mark your spot, go to work, and return later. The 'galleryites', often seen as the 'real' opera lovers, were passionately devoted to their cause. They adored the music and became fanatical about particular singers, but there was more to it than this: communities, friendships, and romances were formed in the

---

[2] Robert Little, *Edgar Evans—Extempore* (St Albans: Bob Little Press and PR, 2005), p. 16.
[3] Rita Nellie Hunter, *Wait Till the Sun Shines, Nellie* (London: Hamish Hamilton, 1986), p. 2; Nancy Mitford, *The Pursuit of Love* (London: Penguin, 1949), p. 21.

queue. So much in demand were gallery tickets, which by 1929 cost between 3s. 6d. and 7s. 6d., that people were turned away nightly.[4]

The popular press sometimes poked fun at opera as a hobby of the rich—and there certainly were rich people in the Covent Garden stalls and boxes, wearing white tie, furs, velvet opera coats, and jewels. Yet as the case of the Cook sisters illustrates, the 1920s was a vital decade in the democratisation of opera, and the idea of opera as elitist in the sense we mean it today would have seemed incomprehensible. Longstanding prejudices against opera as a strange foreign import were still present in the 1920s. But at the same time there was a genuine sense of opera as something for all—more entertainment than 'art'—and as something that might fit into the tastes of the average man in the street as easily as a film or popular novel.

During the late Victorian and Edwardian eras, opera had reached large numbers via brass-band arrangements, music-hall skits, and performances by touring opera companies. All continued into the 1920s, though the bands and music halls had nothing on the wireless and the gramophone as methods of popularisation. The number of touring companies declined after the war, making a visit even more of 'an event' in the calendar of any provincial town. Audiences from across the class spectrum turned out to watch companies like the British National Opera Company (BNOC) and Carl Rosa Opera Company. The musicians received a particularly warm welcome in the north. Manchester was an important musical centre: the local Labour MP J. R. Clynes went so far as to advocate (unsuccessfully) for a government subsidy for opera, knowing it would be favoured by his constituents.[5] Leeds, too, was opera-mad. Everywhere outside of the Covent Garden International Season, opera was sung in English. This was regarded as non-negotiable: as Paget Bowman of the BNOC announced in 1926, 'Opera for the people must be in the language the people understand.'[6]

Opera popped up in numerous contexts beyond the conventional theatre or concert hall. Many people encountered it in restaurants and cafés, and initiatives such as the Carl Rosa's presentation of operatic scenes at a central London Lyons Corner House were seen as particularly effective in attracting women to opera.[7] You could hear opera in the cinema, too: operatic arias

---

[4] Fidelio, 'Mystery of Covent Garden', *The Sphere* (29 June 1929), 696.

[5] Jonathan Rose, *The Intellectual Life of the British Working Classes* (New Haven, CT: Yale University Press, second edition 2010), pp. 201–202.

[6] Anon., 'Opera in English', *DM* (15 November 1926), 7.

[7] Anon., 'Grand Opera at Lyons', *FT* (25 October 1923), 8; Anon., 'Women and Opera Going', *DM* (10 January 1924), 15.

26 SOMEONE ELSE'S MUSIC

were sometimes performed live before or during the screening of silent films. There were even films *of* operas, with famous singers appearing in them, although obviously their voices went unheard. Operatic numbers regularly featured in variety shows at the London Palladium and in concerts by orchestras at resorts like Llandudno.[8]

Gathering around the piano to sing remained a popular form of domestic entertainment, and operatic numbers were sung alongside parlour songs. The future Prime Minister Edward Heath wrote that he 'did not come from a particularly musical family', yet his father frequently sang an aria from *Il trovatore*, 'Ah! I have sigh'd to rest me' ('Ah, che la morte'), which the family simply regarded as 'a good tune'.[9] Amateur opera companies thrived, often concentrating on Gilbert and Sullivan, but sometimes tackling *Carmen* or *Faust* in English. Progressive employers also encouraged their employees to participate in opera: 800 workers from the London area Co-operative societies sang in a concert performance of *Carmen* at the Albert Hall in 1927.[10]

The left-leaning Rutland Boughton, whose hit opera *The Immortal Hour* enjoyed a 500-perfomance West End run between 1922 and 1926, wanted to foster a native school of opera, part of a wider socialist project to raise the artistic consciousness of workers.[11] His Glastonbury Festival, established in 1914, was still running in the early 1920s, bringing together amateur chorus members with professional principals to present operatic versions of British myths; some cast members went on to be hired by touring companies. Alongside the main Festival, the organisers ran a Festival School, introducing children to the business of putting on opera. George Bernard Shaw wrote in 1916: 'The Glastonbury young man will become a cultured human being with highly cultivated senses and a highly trained character. He will be carried right over the dangerous period of life, past the temptations of drink and worse things. The success or failure of this Glastonbury scheme is a matter concerning the welfare of the English population.'[12]

---

[8] Programme, 'All Star Matinée', The Palladium, 1 April 1926. BUTC, MM/REF/TH/LO/PAL/2; Eleanor Allen, *Heddle Nash: Singing against the Tide* (London: Jubilee House Press, 2010), pp. 59–64, p. 78.

[9] Edward Heath, *Music: A Joy for Life* (London: Sidgwick and Jackson, 1976), p. 7.

[10] Rose, *The Intellectual Life*, p. 79.

[11] John Lowerson, *Amateur Operatics: A Social and Cultural History* (Manchester: Manchester University Press, 2005), pp. 137–138.

[12] Cited in Rutland Boughton, *The Glastonbury Festival Movement* (Bloomsbury: Somerset Folk Press, 1921), p. 20.

OPERA FOR ALL 27

Ambitious, socially minded teachers in mainstream schools also put on productions of opera with their pupils. A Mr Charles T. Smith adapted Mozart's *The Magic Flute* for performance by his twelve-year-old schoolboys in a deprived area of the Isle of Dogs in 1920, demanding high standards of performance and inviting major music critics to attend the show. Smith reported that the experience was a transformative experience for children and parents alike, all of whom were encountering opera for the first time.[13]

Opera was regularly front-page news, and everybody had a good laugh when they read about the latest antics of whichever international opera star had just arrived in London. None of this could be described as elitist. Opera was something that drew people in, rather than holding them at arm's length. Opera was fun, and one might even go so far as to say it was fashionable. Once given a taste of it, people wanted more—people of all classes.

Benevolent culture

If the Cook sisters showed an exceptional degree of determination in their devotion to opera, their spirit of enquiry was not unusual for the era. While 'self-improvement' is often characterised today as a rather self-indulgent mindset of the leisured middle classes, it was not seen as such in the 1920s. Many people, at that time, had a strong determination to 'better themselves', whether for purposes of social mobility or simple intellectual satisfaction, by reading widely, joining libraries, going to lectures, attending concerts, singing in choirs, or playing instruments.

In some cases, this desire for knowledge was self-driven: gramophone clubs, where people talked animatedly about the latest recordings, sprang up around the country. In other cases, people were encouraged to improve their understanding of a particular subject by others who were already 'in the know'. The music appreciation movement was thriving, and there was a huge appetite for public lectures and beginners' guides. Some of the beneficiaries— like Louise Cook at the public lecture—were middle class. Others were not. The bass-baritone Geraint Evans's father, a Welsh miner, for example, spent his spare time taking a correspondence course in music theory.[14]

---

[13] Charles T. Smith, *The School of Life: A Theatre of Education* (London: Grant Richards, Ltd, 1921).

[14] Geraint Evans with Noël Goodwin, *Sir Geraint Evans: A Knight at the Opera* (London: Michael Joseph, 1984), p. 3.

28 SOMEONE ELSE'S MUSIC

The Victorian ethos of self-improvement for the working classes lingered on into the interwar era. This was a movement pioneered by the political left—radicals, trade unionists, and the cooperative movement. It promoted literacy and access to the literary classics, as well as participation in drama and music. Nowadays the idea of the middle classes attempting to 'improve' the working classes by foisting 'their' culture upon them is widely regarded as ideologically suspect. But in the 1920s, broadening access to culture was viewed far less problematically, with the recipients themselves often reporting feeling inspired and empowered rather than patronised. As Jonathan Rose writes, 'It is sometimes argued that the working-class pursuit of education was an accommodation to middle-class values, a capitulation to bourgeois cultural hegemony. Actually, it represented the return of the repressed.'[15]

The fact that opera was something for everyone in the 1920s is illustrated most clearly by the pioneering work of Lilian Baylis at the Old Vic. Inspired by the late Victorian ethos of Christian Socialism, Baylis's aunt Emma Cons had established a respectable, alcohol-free music hall at the Victoria Theatre in the late nineteenth century, with the aim of diverting socially deprived locals from a life of drink, violence, and vice.[16] Eventually Baylis took over the institution and began to put on opera performances, initially as a series of arias strung together as tableaux to form a concert. She soon abandoned variety acts, began to focus on full-length operas, and watched their popularity grow.

By the time our story starts in 1920, the theatre, affectionately renamed 'the Old Vic', had established itself as the people's opera house, putting on opera in English, interspersed with Shakespeare plays (then less popular than and subsidised by the opera), for an audience of largely working-class south Londoners, plus others who travelled from further afield. It was the only British operatic enterprise with a permanent base that performed year-round. Touring companies were always, self-evidently, on the move, and opera was presented at Covent Garden only irregularly, primarily during what director Tyrone Guthrie called 'a brief, star-spangled, outrageously expensive International Season'.[17]

---

[15] Rose, *The Intellectual Life*, p. 23.

[16] On the Old Vic, see Susie Gilbert, *Opera for Everybody: The Story of English National Opera* (London: Faber and Faber, 2009).

[17] Guthrie, *A Life in the Theatre*, p. 100.

The Old Vic might put on so-called 'grand opera', but it was hardly grand in any other sense of the word. Everything was run on a shoestring. Soloists were paid a pittance and, not being on long contracts like the resident drama company, fitted their commitments to the theatre around other engagements.[18] Sometimes they were plucked off the street. Heddle Nash, a young man who sang with end-of-pier concert parties, wandered in for an audition, was told by Baylis to sing some top notes, and was cast on the spot as the Duke of Mantua in *Rigoletto*. Baylis depended to a large extent on soloists who already knew the music, could take on roles at short notice, and were prepared to take low fees, her motto being 'Dear God, send me good tenors … but please send them cheap'.[19]

The chorus was made up of enthusiastic amateurs—clerks, shop assistants, and telephone operators willing to sing for nothing, or almost. The fact that most had other jobs meant that such rehearsals as they had took place after working hours in a disused pub; the orchestra, for other reasons, could only rehearse in the mornings on alternate Tuesdays when the theatre was closed, and the two rarely met.[20] Unsurprisingly, performances were static and slapdash. Chorus members wore one of three standard costumes (a stock peasant outfit, a Germanic tabard, or lace and a shawl) and sets were recycled.[21] Facilities at the theatre were poor: leading ladies had to get changed in Baylis's office, leading men in a cupboard.

For all these practical limitations, the Old Vic was ambitious and succeeded in garnering respect from prestigious figures within the musical establishment. It pioneered the performance of Mozart operas—then comparatively little known in Britain—in new translations by Edward J. Dent, a Cambridge don who was advisor to the company. These made the audience laugh, something that was unknown at Covent Garden, where many audience members could not understand the finer details of the original-language text.[22] The company had begun by performing Verdi and Donizetti crowd-pleasers but in time began to tackle more unusual and challenging works, even *Tristan and Isolde* with an inadequate band of eighteen players.[23]

---

[18] Anon., 'Across the Footlights', *OVM*, 3/10 (December 1928), 1–2, 1.

[19] Allen, *Heddle Nash*, p. 77, p. 81.

[20] Editorial Notes, *OVM*, 8/1 (May 1920), 1.

[21] Ibid.; Michael Stapleton, *The Sadler's Wells Opera* (London: Adam and Charles Black, 1954), p. 7.

[22] Richard Findlater, *Lilian Baylis: The Lady of the Old Vic* (London: Allen Lane, 1975), pp. 155–156.

[23] Anon., *A History of Sadler's Wells and English National Opera* (London: ENO, 1980); Rev. Thomas Gough, 'The 1920–21 Opera Season', *OVM*, 7/2 (April 1921), 3; Findlater, *Lilian Baylis*, p. 158.

30 SOMEONE ELSE'S MUSIC

Accessibility was the watchword of the Old Vic. The cheapest tickets cost no more than a packet of cigarettes or a glass of beer. The company announced in 1920 that 'we feel that the People's Theatre and Opera must always be within the reach of the poorest, and as long as the most expensive seat is 3/- and the cheapest 3d. we know the Vic. is fulfilling its proper function.'[24] The 2,000-seat theatre was packed out on a nightly basis, and audience members stood four or five deep in the standing areas, with many being turned away on Saturdays.[25] The atmosphere was relaxed and welcoming: people came along in their ordinary work clothes; the audience clapped after arias, and nobody looked askance.

Baylis believed fervently in the idea of art for all. She argued that theatre was not 'an excuse for wonderful evening gowns and jewels', or the preserve of 'varsity men and women'. Rather, it was 'a crying need of working men and women who need to see beyond the four walls of their offices, workshops and homes into a world of awe and wonder'.[26] She believed that theatre was the most accessible form of art for the man and woman in the street, being comprehensible even to the illiterate, and stated that 'all art is a bond between rich and poor; it allows of no class distinctions'.[27] But she also believed in giving people what was good for them, at least what she believed was good for them, saying, 'My people . . . must have The Best. God tells me The Best in music is grand opera. Therefore my people must have grand opera.'[28]

Baylis had, then, achieved something that would strike us nowadays as astonishing: she had created an audience for opera where there had not previously been one, in the unlikeliest of circumstances. Some audience members came to the theatre seeking refuge from their abysmal dwellings and went on to take opera very seriously indeed. By the 1920s, critics regularly commented on the fact that the Old Vic had the best audience in town—committed, intelligent, and well-informed—and Heddle Nash (himself raised in industrial south London) told the audience after a performance in 1926 that it was the most appreciative he had ever sung to.[29] The audience's enthusiasm also demonstrated the absurdity of the clichés about the British being incapable of appreciating opera. As a commentator observed in 1920, 'Given opera, in

---

[24] Anon., 'Editorial Notes', OVM, 8/1 (May 1920), 1.

[25] Guthrie, A Life in the Theatre, p. 101; H. A., 'Opera for the People', OVSWM, 1/1 (January 1931), 3–4, 3.

[26] Cicely Hamilton and Lilian Baylis, The Old Vic (London: Jonathan Cape, 1926), p. 189.

[27] Ibid., p. 189.

[28] Guthrie, A Life in the Theatre, pp. 96–97.

[29] Heddle Nash, 'A Contrast in Audiences', OVM, 6/7 (March 1926), 3.

their own language and at prices suited to a modest purse, the rank and file of English men and women are as keen on opera as any foreign audience.'[30]

Crucial to the development of the audience at the Old Vic was the sense of community that Baylis created, which encouraged people to come back again and again. The idea that opera audiences seek to exclude others from their special club is one of the persistent clichés that has attached itself to the art form in recent times. However, nothing could have been further from the truth at the Old Vic. The fostering of operatic communities can be both exclusive and inclusive; creating the sense that audience members could become part of the Old Vic 'family' was a welcoming strategy, a vital part of ensuring that the endeavour felt accessible to all (see Figure 2.1).

This was achieved via a variety of means. First, the company petitioned the audience on which works it wanted to hear; thus, the audience helped shape the programme and felt it owned a stake in the company.[31] Second, audience

Figure 2.1 Lilian Baylis outside the Old Vic Theatre. Reproduced with permission from © University of Bristol/ArenaPAL.

---

[30] Lucas Malet, 'An Appreciation', *OVM*, 5/1 (February 1920), 3.
[31] Findlater, *Lilian Baylis*, p. 189.

32 SOMEONE ELSE'S MUSIC

members were invited to pay a small subscription to join the 'Old Vic Circle' and take part in social events with singers, managers and other enthusiasts. Most notable was the 'Cutting of the Twelfth Night Cake', an annual celebration that took place on stage, featuring music-making, storytelling, and a grand triumphal march around the theatre.[32] This custom would survive for decades, and as time went on the Circle would also organise numerous fancy-dress dances, parties for children, and social events for the elderly.[33]

All of this was down-to-earth and welcoming: opera as something ordinary, rather than something extraordinary. *The Old Vic Magazine*—circulation 3,000 copies a month by 1926—helped to foster the feeling of a 'family' organisation by publishing birth, marriage, and death notices for company personnel.[34] It also published regular chatty articles in which singers talked about their passion for playing football or the humble trades they would have entered had they not been discovered.[35] The fact that the Old Vic was organised on repertory lines—using a regular troupe of singers, whom listeners saw as friends—was a crucial factor in its fostering a loyal local audience. This was a model that would be used at English National Opera decades later in the 1970s and 1980s and is found extensively in present-day Germany. It is something conspicuously absent, for the most part, in Britain today.

The example of the Old Vic, then, resolutely counters any notion that opera was the preserve of an elite during this period. As the company's conductor Charles Corri observed in 1928:

> The musical side of our work here is supported mainly by people who have not too many pennies to spend on amusement, and apparently choose opera because it gives them the greatest diversion. In fact, it might almost be said that British music in general is mainly supported by the workers. It is for such people that we cater; and it is a great honour to do so; for the future of British music lies in their hands. There is plenty in the daily papers about the lost cause of opera; but I wish some of the gentlemen who write about it would look in some Saturday night at the Old Vic.[36]

---

[32] Anon., Editorial notes, *OVM*, 5/1 (February 1920), 1.

[33] Findlater, *Lilian Baylis*, p. 208, pp. 218–219.

[34] Anon., 'The "Old Vic." Circle', *OVM*, 5/1 (February 1920), 4.

[35] For example, Herbert Simmonds, 'Singing and Sports', *OVM*, 4/7 (January 1926), 3–4; Robert Naylor, 'How I Became a Singer', *OVM*, 5/10 (February 1929), 2–3, 2.

[36] 'Charles Corri's Foreword', *OVM*, 5/9 (February 1928), 2.

OPERA FOR ALL   33

Corri's words make a mockery of the notion that opera is not 'working-class' culture. A decent proportion of the singers who emerged during this period were manual workers: take, for example, the cotton-mill worker Norman Walker who began training at the Royal Manchester College of Music in 1929 and became a professional bass.[37] And there were many working-class people in the 1920s opera audience. We shall see time and again that a taste for opera cut across all class boundaries in the first part of the twentieth century; indeed, that the *most* enthusiastic opera patrons were often at the lower end of the social scale. As *The Tatler* reported in 1921, after 60,000 people bought tickets for a four-week opera season in Hammersmith, 'it's pretty evident that if the "classes" aren't very musical, and only go to the opera to talk and be seen, the "masses" are musical at any rate'.[38]

Eastenders

The Old Vic was not an isolated example of working-class opera-going: there was also an enthusiastic following for opera in the East End. How far removed this area was from London's cultural mainstream is revealed by the critic Ernest Newman's description of it in 1922 as 'some part of London of which I have no personal knowledge but that is vaguely known to me as the East End' and by his pondering of the consequences for the West End when 'hungry, dirty mobs from the docks' realised the cultural riches on which they had hitherto been missing out.[39] But Newman was badly out of touch, for the East End had a thriving musical scene.

Many renowned instrumentalists had put on concerts in East London throughout the Edwardian era.[40] Visiting opera troupes were welcomed at theatres such as the Alexandra on the Stoke Newington Road, where the O'Mara company put on a season in 1926, staging two performances a night—adopting the 'twice nightly' system commonly used in music halls in order to pack in double the listeners, a practice that must have placed a heavy vocal toll on singers.[41] Opera also had a presence via street music: Rossini and Bellini melodies would have been particularly well-known by the

[37] Russell, 'Reaching the Operatic Stage', 326.
[38] Anon., 'The Letters of Evelyn—Continued', *The Tatler* (12 October 1921), 36–38, 37–38.
[39] Ernest Newman, 'The Week in Music', *Manchester Guardian* (16 March 1922), n.p.
[40] Alan Bartley, *Far from the Fashionable Crowd: The People's Concert Society and Music in London's Suburbs* (n.p.: Whimbrel Publishing, 2009), p. 229.
[41] Figaro, 'The Operatic World', *Musical Opinion*, 49/580 (January 1926), 359–361, 360.

34   SOMEONE ELSE'S MUSIC

residents of Clerkenwell, where the local Italian community had long made a living (albeit meagre) from the barrel organ.

A particularly important East-End venue was the Queen's Building, or 'People's Palace', on the Mile End Road. This complex opened in 1887 in the Victorian spirit of 'rational recreation'—an attempt by social reformers to bring about the intellectual improvement of working people. From the 1870s, cultural institutions were set up in the heart of the 'slum-dwelling neighbourhoods'; the East End was perceived to be an area of particular concern.[42] Musical initiatives in the area included the foundation of the People's Concert Society, which organised chamber-music concerts in halls, Settlement Houses, schoolrooms, and public baths, and the Popular Musical Union, which trained locals in four-part singing.[43] The latter mirrored the thriving amateur music scene in industrial towns and cities up and down the country, often closely associated with the labour movement.[44]

The People's Palace featured a concert hall, library, gymnasium, swimming pool, dance hall, and other leisure facilities, and by the 1920s, the activities on offer included dances and an array of sports and concerts.[45] Operatic music was presented to audiences in different formats: variety programmes presented by visiting 'concert parties'; classical chamber recitals; and orchestral concerts.[46] In 1925, the People's Palace Choral and Orchestral Societies put on a complete concert performance of *Faust* using 300 performers; *Cavalleria rusticana* followed later the same year. Society members were drawn from the local community, giving the East-End poor the chance to perform alongside well-known singers who were hired to play principal roles. Touring opera companies also visited.

In 1923, the world-famous soprano Dame Nellie Melba performed at the People's Palace in a charity concert, singing operatic arias alongside popular songs such as 'Coming Through the Rye' and 'Swing Low, Sweet Chariot'. Two thousand tickets sold out a fortnight in advance, as Mile End and Mayfair came together, with distinguished West-Enders in conventional opera dress sitting by rows of men in cloth caps. Melba herself had priced

---

[42] Brad Beaven, *Leisure, Citizenship and Working-Class Men in Britain, 1850–1945* (Manchester: Manchester University Press, 2005), p. 28.

[43] Bartley, *Far from the Fashionable Crowd*, pp. 54–55, p. 57, p. 279.

[44] See Duncan Hall, '*A Pleasant Change from Politics': Music and the British Labour Movement between the Wars* (Cheltenham: New Clarion Press, 2001).

[45] Programme of forthcoming attractions at the People's Palace, October 1924, No. 1. QM/1/10/5.

[46] All concerts drawn from programmes at the QMUL archive.

OPERA FOR ALL   35

the cheapest tickets at only 1s. 3d., to allow people of all backgrounds to attend, and tailors from Whitechapel, chemical workers from Bethnal Green, bricklayers from South Hackney, and labourers from Poplar all turned out in force.[47] It was, as *The Manchester Chronicle* put it, 'the first time in musical history that a prima donna who can pack Covent Garden offered her vocal wares at bargain sales rates', and local reporters wondered at the fact that 'the love of good music is innate even with the poor of East London.'[48]

The flourishing of working-class opera-going in Britain was underpinned by a philanthropic zeal of a sort that might have been characterised as patronising had it been proposed in later times. But whatever the underlying motives, its benefits were tangible, as it ignited a spark of genuine curiosity on the part of audiences and encouraged them to explore other forms of culture that might well, otherwise, have been the preserve of an elite. Opera was fun and it offered a form of escapism. As *The Old Vic Magazine* reported in 1928: 'If only some millionaire had the imagination to realise what an evening spent in hearing great drama or fine music means to those whose lives are cramped and stunted by poverty and lack of beauty.'[49] Elitist opera most certainly was not.

Top hats and tiaras

Opera-going had another face in 1920s Britain, of course. The aforementioned millionaire was probably sitting four and a half miles to the west, in a box at Covent Garden. Post-war summer seasons resumed at Covent Garden in 1919 and 1920, becoming, once more, a fixture of 'the Season', like going to Ascot or the Henley Regatta. This was thanks to the efforts and enthusiasm of Sir Thomas Beecham and bankrolled in part by his wealthy mistress, the opera-loving society hostess Lady Cunard, estranged wife of Sir Bache Cunard, scion of the shipping line. Financial setbacks, partly the result of the heavy entertainments tax that had been introduced in 1916, partly the result of Beecham being declared bankrupt and his opera company going into liquidation, later put things on hold, but the international seasons on pre-war

---

[47] Anon., 'Melba for 1s', *The People* (28 January 1923), n.p.; Anon., 'Way Down East', *The Yorkshire Telegraph* (25 January 1923), n.p.

[48] Londoner, 'Melba in the Mile End Road', *The Manchester Chronicle* (25 January 1923), n.p.; Anon., 'Way Down East'.

[49] G. C. Ashton Jonson, 'Opera at the Old Vic', *OVM*, 8/9 (May 1928), 2–3, 3.

36 SOMEONE ELSE'S MUSIC

lines resumed in 1924. The theatre was used for very different purposes for the rest of the year, including dances, film screenings, variety shows, and boxing matches, as well as being rented out on a short-term basis to other touring opera companies. The incongruity of this mixed usage was sometimes noted by the press, as, for example, when a newspaper reported that, during a dance, 'echoes of *Tristan and Isolde*, of *La bohème* were drowned in the whine and cough of the saxophone'.[50]

Covent Garden's two-month summer programme of international opera was undoubtedly glamorous, attracting as it did the crème de la crème of foreign singers. British singers were rarely heard during 'the Season', though they might perform with visiting troupes at other times of year. The casting of Oldham-born Eva Turner as Turandot at Covent Garden in 1928 was a highly notable event. Newspaper headlines reporting her triumph the morning after the performance repeatedly stressed her Englishness, Britishness, or Lancashire roots, *The Glasgow Daily Record* even opting for 'British and Unashamed'.[51] And not only was Turner British, but she was of working-class stock, the daughter of a cotton-mill engine driver.

Members of royalty continued to attend the opera, and although the British aristocracy was well into decline by the 1920s, members of the upper class still turned out in force at Covent Garden. It was a venue where they would encounter other grand people: the annual subscription list was considered a matter of such public interest that the names on it were printed in the press. Some Covent Garden habitués were undoubtedly there purely for reasons of social prestige, and it seems unlikely that everyone who went was engaged by the music. Perhaps this was for the best. The international season offered glittering star names, but the performances had their quirks. Operas were officially presented in the original language, but in practice audiences were often presented with 'polyglot' performances, in which singers performed in whichever languages they had learned the work: a 1920 *Madama Butterfly* featured singers performing in Swedish, English, and Italian.[52]

Nevertheless, accounts of superficial audience goers and a poor artistic experience were sometimes overstated. W. J. Turner, a critic for *The Illustrated London News*, wrote in 1926 that the so-called 'popular public'—by which he

---

[50] Anon., '2,000 People Jazz among Ghosts', unattributed press clipping (26 February 1925). BUTC, MM/2/TH/LO/COV/53 (1925–1928).

[51] Linda Esther Gray, *Dame Eva Turner: 'A Life on the High Cs'* (New Malden: Green Oak Publishing, 2011), pp. 124–125.

[52] Anon., 'The Letters of Evelyn—Continued', *The Tatler* (2 June 1920), 280–282, 282.

meant people attending purely for the social experience—made up a comparatively small part of an otherwise well-informed audience of real music enthusiasts, who were prepared to sit through Wagner's *Ring*, in German, without cuts. All tickets for such performances would sell out well in advance, the cheapest selling particularly fast, and although all cost four times what a similar seat would cost in an ordinary West End theatre, the audience knew that it would be getting something—in terms of the operas themselves, if not necessarily their execution—'absolutely first-rate'. Turner acknowledged that a potential audience needed to be given a taste of foreign operas in order to discover it liked them, but would ultimately find them to be 'no more remote from its "natural" palate than are tea, coffee, wine, beer, and all the delicacies of the modern store, from West Indian grape-fruit to Russian caviare or Greek honey'.[53]

Dressing up during the Season was still de rigueur in the stalls and boxes—men in white tie and silk hats; women in evening dress and jewels—although there was a growing recognition of the fact that the dress code was impractical for modern life. One journalist noted in 1927 that the practice was deterring office workers who had no time to go home and change before a performance at seven.[54] As time went on, the dress code began to relax somewhat. Nevertheless, the act of going to Covent Garden remained 'an occasion', and it spawned an array of ancillary fashionable activities. The resumption of the international seasons meant not only the return of upper-class opera-going but also the return of luxury dining in the area, both before and after performances. *The Daily Mail* reported that fashionable restaurants were, once more, 'reminders of pre-war brilliance' and noted that 'only a visit of international opera is able to provide the exclusive and cosmopolitan atmosphere of the *diner de l'opéra*', whose dishes bore the names of opera stars or the characters they played.[55]

Going to the opera at Covent Garden remained a way of showing off one's wealth. Hiring a pit-tier or grand-tier box to seat four people for all fifty performances of the Season was expensive: £472 10s. in 1929, 19 per cent up on the previous year.[56] On the other hand, there were, as we have seen,

---

[53] W. J. Turner, 'The World of Music: The Musical Season', *Supplement to the ILN* (17 April 1926), iv.

[54] Anon., 'The Talk of London', unattributed press cutting (4 May 1927). BUTC, MM/2/TH/LO/COV/53 (1925–1928).

[55] Anon., 'Revival after 14 Years', *DM* (6 May 1924), 7.

[56] Anon., 'Dearer Opera Seats', *DM* (17 November 1928), 18.

38 SOMEONE ELSE'S MUSIC

cheap tickets available in the gallery if one were prepared to queue, sit in discomfort, and tolerate a distant view of the stage. These seats attracted a lively crowd of Soho Italians and East-End clerks, as well as many from the Old Vic crowd. From time to time, the theatre experimented with seasons at 'popular prices', but on the whole, Covent Garden was simply not large enough to put on 'budget' opera and cover its running costs. As T. C. Fairbairn, manager of the Fairbairn touring opera company, wrote, it was better to put on operas at the Albert Hall, Alexandra Palace, People's Palace, or Crystal Palace, where tickets could be priced on a par with those for cinema.[57]

There would be countless moments in later decades when Covent Garden would be painted as 'the problem' for opera in Britain: a bastion of elitism. Occasionally, snide comments in the 1920s press about it being aloof, 'un-British', and so on can also be found. For the most part, however, the glamorous activities at Covent Garden were portrayed by the press at this time as a marvel at which one might wonder—a source of pride, even, in an era when having a thriving opera house that could compete with those in other major international cities was seen as an indicator of being a civilised nation.

Thus, the press was largely respectful of the well-heeled people who made up the bulk of the audience during the international season. In part this reflected a deference for society's leaders that many would now regard as old-fashioned. But more importantly, the press appreciated that this demographic was essential. Even if in some cases relatively uninterested in the music itself, the wealthy people going to Covent Garden simply because it was the place to be seen were a vital part of the economy that allowed opera to flourish, since in the days before public subsidy Covent Garden could not function without their support. It was, in effect, their financial investment in the enterprise that made the art form available to the serious enthusiasts in the gallery.

The novelist Aldous Huxley went so far as to propose that although social climbers who patronised the arts might seem laughable, there were reasons to be grateful to them. He wrote in 1927:

> If there were no intellectual snobbery—if the philistines, the stupid, and the ignorant refused to pay their tribute to taste, learning, and talent—research and all serious artistic effort would simply be starved out of existence. Snobbery immensely increases the public which support these activities; it

---

[57] T. C. Fairbairn, 'British Opera', letter to the editor of *The Daily Mail* (4 November 1925), n.p.

gives them a financial backing which they would not otherwise have. Let us be duly thankful, then, for snobbery.[58]

This is a question that has always hung over the whole operatic enterprise and that makes people feel uncomfortable today: is indulging a wealthy audience a price that simply has to be paid for opera, costly as it is, to flourish?

Covent Garden might be a place of endless fascination, its activities widely reported in the press, from profiles of glamorous young singers in *The Tatler* to salacious stories about divas behaving badly. But in terms of the broader culture of 1920s opera-going, it was the exception to the rule: an exotic curiosity, unrepresentative of and detached from how most people experienced opera, which was in a provincial theatre and in English. Covent Garden might best be viewed as a sort of supranational entity, in competition not with other London theatres but opera houses in distant lands. It competed at a global level for the best international singers—though it was increasingly unable to match the exorbitant fees on offer in the Americas, where some singers preferred to stay year-round, segueing from a winter season in New York to a second winter season at the Teatro Colón in Buenos Aires, which paid the highest fees in the world.[59]

It would not be going too far to say that Covent Garden was so cosmopolitan as not to be regarded as really 'British' at all. People sometimes talked about the theatre as if it were a kind of national opera house, but, as a critic wrote in 1938, 'it is not, never has been, anything of the kind'.[60] In the 1920s and for decades after, then, British operatic culture had two quite different faces: there was 'international' opera (Covent Garden, later followed by Glyndebourne) and there was 'national' opera (everything else). The two were entirely separate entities, and the tension between them would grow and grow, in ways that over time began to fuel the idea that opera was—or could be—in some way elitist.

[58] Aldous Huxley, 'Snobs', *DM* (7 April 1927), 10.
[59] Anon., 'Opera Problems', *DM* (2 November 1925), 8; Anon., 'Great Opera Singers', *DM* (20 March 1928), 21.
[60] Francis Toye, 'The Charm of Music', *ILN* (22 October 1938), 745.

40 SOMEONE ELSE'S MUSIC

Technology and democratisation

Worlds away from the oddity that was Covent Garden, the audience for opera was ever-expanding in the 1920s, thanks to the democratising power of new technologies. Gramophone records of arias had been best-sellers throughout the 1910s and remained so: recordings of Caruso or Chaliapin were as likely to be heard belting out of the windows of Durham miners' cottages as they were from the salons of Kensington.[61] Broadcasting, on the other hand, was entirely new. The first opera was transmitted on the BBC in 1923—a performance of *The Magic Flute* by the BNOC at Covent Garden.

Many listeners encountered opera for the first time via radio, were encouraged to learn more by programmes such as 'The Foundations of Music', and were suitably motivated to seek out staged performances or even to take up singing. The tenor Geraint Evans, who was brought up in the 1920s and early 1930s in an impoverished Welsh pit village, heard his first Wagner as a child on a wireless his grandmother had been given by the Blind Institution. He later wrote: 'I wasn't conscious at the time that I was listening to Wagner—all I knew was that it was wonderful and I wallowed in every phrase'.[62] As the broadcaster Percy Scholes said, music had previously been the preserve of a small group of people who happened to live in the places where it was being performed, but 'henceforth, it belongs to everybody'.[63]

At this stage, 'highbrow' material was mixed in with general programming, including variety shows and dance-band music: everyone was given the same broad mix of programming. Thus, most listeners would have encountered some opera. A proportion of the studio performances broadcast on the BBC were designated 'libretto operas'. A cheap printed booklet containing a synopsis, libretto, and composer biography was made easily available to listeners in advance. The BBC reported that this initiative had 'proved itself to be one of the outstanding features of the Corporation's musical activities' and initial sales of 60,000 per booklet swiftly rose to 100,000.[64]

The BBC sought to reach different sorts of people with its opera broadcasts. First, they would, undoubtedly, have appealed to those who were

---

[61] Rose, *The Intellectual Life*, p. 203.

[62] Evans, *Sir Geraint Evans*, p. 5.

[63] Percy Scholes, *Everybody's Guide to Broadcast Music* (London: Oxford University Press, 1925), p. 10.

[64] Anon., *BBC Handbook 1928*, p. 93; 'Minutes of the Inaugural Meeting of the Advisory Committee on Opera, to the BBC', 13 December 1926 (BBC WAC R6/75 Advisory Committees. Opera Advisory Committee: Minutes. Files 1-2, 1926–1927; 1936–1937).

already aficionados, who found the wireless a useful complement to their opera-going habits. Some even argued that listening to opera in this manner was preferable, because it removed the more tedious aspects of a night in the theatre. Writing in the 1929 *BBC Handbook*, Hamilton Fyfe characterised broadcast opera as a liberation from dressing up in white tie, latecomers who trod on your foot, 'obese' singers posing as fervent young lovers, and productions that did not reflect the composer's intentions.[65]

But the BBC also sought to 'enlighten' listeners new to opera. As Cecil Lewis, a founding executive, stated, 'The poor, the ordinary people in the street never heard an opera in their lives ... And then suddenly there it was, in their ears ... everybody's excitement and interest in life was lifted: they hadn't known; now they began to know.'[66] In its 1928 handbook, the organisation expressed its ambition to take the best musical performances to all, including the shepherd on the downs, the crofter on the farthest Hebrides, the labourer in a squalid slum tenement, or the lonely housebound invalid.[67] All of these people could sit 'together' with the patrons in the stalls and hear the best music in the world.

The language used to express this point is different from what we might expect to see nowadays, and some may baulk at the Reithian BBC's paternalistic attitude, but the underlying spirit of the message is not so far removed from today's access agenda. Good quality music was to be made available to all. Of course, not everyone wanted it: there were complaints that the BBC was inflicting highbrow music on listeners, and one correspondent wrote to express his disgust at the 'vile' programming of 'foreign garbage'.[68] But it was there for anyone willing to give it a try.

The BBC strove to aid listeners' understanding with supplementary materials, such as features in *The Radio Times*, but there was also an assumption that audience members should put in some work themselves. A contributor to the 1929 *BBC Handbook* explained that listening to and understanding music took some effort but no more so than watching a football match—watching a Cup Final with no understanding of the rules would not give the spectator much enjoyment.[69] The analogy was carefully chosen to appeal to a wide audience and is consistent with other attempts during this

---

[65] Hamilton Fyfe, 'Now That the Opera Comes to Us!', *BBC Handbook 1929*, pp. 135–140, pp. 135–136.

[66] Cited in David Hendy, *The BBC: A People's History* (London: Profile Books, 2022), p. 38.

[67] Anon., *BBC Handbook 1928*, p. 84.

[68] Scholes, *Everybody's Guide to Broadcast Music*, p. 39.

[69] Anon., 'On Listening to Music', *BBC Handbook 1929*, pp. 171–172, p. 171.

42 SOMEONE ELSE'S MUSIC

period to liken opera to sport to broaden its appeal. And there is plentiful evidence that listeners *were* prepared to work hard on understanding music, fuelled by the music-appreciation movement and autodidacticism across all social strata.

The battle of the brows

Though never called elitist in the 1920s, opera become embroiled in a heated interwar debate known as the 'battle of the brows'.[70] Troubled by the growth of the lower middle class and the expansion of the commercial mass media after World War One, intellectual elites strove to defend their position of authority by attempting to categorise various forms of art and police who had the right to consume and enjoy what. Intense debates took place about what was highbrow, what was lowbrow, and what was middlebrow, a new buzzword. The debate was also bound up with Modernism and how it set itself apart from more traditional forms of artistic representation and redefined the relationship between artist and audience.

Commentators who seized upon the glamour of bejewelled opera-goers in the stalls at Covent Garden and concluded opera should be placed in the box marked 'highbrow' made two fundamental errors. First, they overlooked the fact that highbrowism was an intellectual rather than a social phenomenon. Second, they were evidently ignorant of the thriving culture of middle- and indeed working-class opera-going, a context in which going to an opera was considered little different from going to see a film.

The concept of the 'brows' was more to do with tastes and attitudes than wealth or class. In this respect, discussions about what was highbrow differed from today's debates about what is 'elitist', which are largely concerned with perceptions (however mistaken) of social exclusion, rather than with the cultural objects themselves. According to Dmitri Mirsky, in a study of the British intelligentsia of the interwar period, the word 'highbrow', in the British context, signified '*the esthetic intellectuals*, those who are "advanced" in their literary and artistic tastes, read books which the common philistine herd cannot understand, and enjoy paintings which most people would find monstrosities'. The highbrow, often taken to mean someone with

---

[70] See Wilson, *Opera in the Jazz Age.*

a lofty forehead, actually signified, Mirsky argued, 'a person who arches his eyebrows in a superior manner to scorn the common philistine herd'.[71]

Highbrowism was to do with intellectual snobbery, then. This had little to do with opera because the highbrows were often to be found arching their eyebrows *at* opera, which, in the main, they considered trite and ridiculous. Opera failed the highbrow test at almost every turn. The highbrows of the 1920s revered cultural 'purity', and opera was considered 'impure', both as a composite art form (music, text, drama, and dance combined) and as a collaborative one (created by a team of artists rather than a lone genius). It was also too closely allied for comfort to the worlds of commerce and celebrity to be taken seriously. In its emotionalism, opera fell foul of the prevailing modernist tendency to prioritise form over feelings. Put simply, opera was too popular with the masses to count as highbrow.

The works of Wagner—long, musically complex—might qualify on aesthetic grounds for highbrow status, though again that status was brought into question by their popularity. Avant-garde modernist operas would have qualified but were almost never heard in Britain at this time. For all these reasons, opera seemed to sit closer to the middlebrow than the highbrow. Occasionally it even seemed to approach the realms of the lowbrow, with critics dismissing the works of the Italian *verismo* school as sensationalist crowd-pleasers full of cheap tunes.

Opera was said in the 1920s to be a form of music that had a particular appeal to the 'man in the street', an almost fabled contemporary archetype, synonymous with middlebrow tastes and middle-class attitudes. He was the sort of person who lived in the suburbs and commuted into London to work as a clerk, who took his family for an annual holiday at the seaside, who enjoyed sport, popular novels, variety shows, and films, and had—in the eyes of the highbrows who looked down on him—conservative, petit-bourgeois tastes. He was intelligent but not intellectual, took his opinions from his daily paper, and knew what he liked. Just an average man, in other words.

The 'man in the street' would typically have encountered opera via touring-company performances. When an opera company came to town, it was eagerly anticipated by people of all classes. The business model could not possibly have functioned had the companies targeted only the well-to-do; one commentator in 1923 called the man in the street 'the main prop of the

---

[71] Dmitri Mirsky, *The Intelligentsia of Great Britain*, trans. Alec Brown (London: Victor Gollancz, 1935), p. 90, p. 89; original emphasis.

44 SOMEONE ELSE'S MUSIC

box office'.[72] Like the Old Vic troupe, these companies saw themselves as providing opera for all. They had to: with around two hundred personnel and twenty-five truckloads of scenery on the road simultaneously, attracting full houses was imperative.[73] Members of local amateur opera companies sometimes joined the chorus, offering an additional way for local communities to get involved.[74]

Performances were rough-and-ready. John Barbirolli recalled that on his appointment as conductor of the BNOC he was required to conduct *Romeo and Juliet*, *Aida*, and *Madame Butterfly* in the first week on only three hours' rehearsal.[75] Costumes and sets were often shabby and recycled between shows. Casts were usually comprised of adequate jobbing singers, although very occasionally a star emerged from within the ranks, such as when Eva Turner (as Madam Butterfly) was heard by the Argentine conductor Ettore Panizza, who arranged for her to audition in front of Toscanini.[76] The swift leap Turner made from the Scala Theatre near Tottenham Court Road (home of touring and amateur troupes) to La Scala, Milan, was unusual indeed.

The BNOC's programme for its 1927 residency in Aberdeen shows the range of operas, mixed in nationality and style, that an audience could typically expect to hear in a week:

Monday: *The Barber of Seville*
Tuesday: *Dusk of the Gods*
Wednesday: *The Magic Flute* (matinée); *Manon* (evening)
Thursday: *Mastersingers*
Friday: *The Marriage of Figaro*
Saturday: *Madame Butterfly* (matinée); *Aida* (evening)[77]

It is worth noting that all opera during this period was billed as 'grand opera' unless it was light or comic opera. This gave companies an air of prestige—just as hotels might call themselves 'The Grand'—rather than striking

---

[72] J. A. Forsyth, 'Opera and Operatives', *Middlesex County Times* (28 March 1923), 2.

[73] Shapland Dodds, 'National Opera Bookings', letter to *The Western Mail* (26 March 1925), 9.

[74] Lowerson, *Amateur Operatics*, p. 115, p. 117.

[75] Raymond Holden (ed.), *Glorious John: A Collection of Sir John Barbirolli's Lectures, Articles, Speeches and Interviews* (London: The Barbirolli Society, 2007), p. 131.

[76] Gray, *Dame Eva Turner*, p. 5.

[77] Anon., 'Week of Opera at His Majesty's Theatre: BNOC's First Visit to Aberdeen', *Aberdeen Press and Journal* (21 October 1927), 3.

audiences as aloof. Performances were typically complemented by a range of talks and lectures.

Though listeners did not make much distinction on the basis of nationality between the works they saw during a touring company's visit, as all were performed in English, Italian repertory was an obvious operatic 'entry point' for audiences, and staples such as *Il trovatore* and *Madama Butterfly* were wildly popular. An opera such as *Aida* offered spectacle, *La bohème* sentimentality, and the double bill of *Cavalleria rusticana* and *Pagliacci* a frisson of thrillingly un-English passion.

More surprising, perhaps, was the popularity of Wagner's works, excerpts from which were among the best-selling gramophone records of the day. It was hearing a recording of the prelude to *Die Walküre* in 1929 that led the six-year-old George Lascelles, son of Princess Mary, and later (as Earl of Harewood) a hugely important opera advocate in twentieth-century Britain, to develop an early passion for the composer.[78] Though we might expect Wagner's works to have been regarded as too complex for audiences relatively new to or unfamiliar with opera, one commentator proposed that their use of motifs made them particularly easy for the musical 'layman' to grasp.[79] Wagnerian music dramas were seen as a particular draw when a touring company came to town, even if they had to be performed with drastically reduced orchestration.

For highbrow commentators of the 1920s, the fact that opera attracted the man in the street put it beyond the pale. Opera's integrity was supposedly compromised by its easy appeal to the so-called unsophisticated listener and the 'illegitimate' ways in which such a listener typically listened to it. The man in the street was often said to be drawn to opera either by listening to 'bleeding chunks' on gramophone records or at concerts, or after being attracted by aspects other than the music itself: the story, visual spectacle, or a star singer.

The man in the street enjoyed opera alongside a range of other forms of entertainment. This was a defining characteristic of the middlebrow: people enjoying a bit of this and that, as so-called 'high' and 'low' cultures sat comfortably side by side. As Karen Arrandale pithily puts it, Britain in the 1920s was 'a cultural world where the Ballets Russes were on the same bill at the

---

[78] The Earl of Harewood, *The Tongs and the Bones: The Memoirs of Lord Harewood* (London: Weidenfeld and Nicolson, 1981), p. 4.

[79] Anon., 'A Tilt at Grand Opera', *The Liverpool Echo* (24 February 1923), 4.

46 SOMEONE ELSE'S MUSIC

Coliseum as "Winston's Wonderful Water Lions".[80] Opera fitted comfortably into a cultural diet that might also include variety shows, cinema, football, and *Messiah* at Christmas. Of course, opera, like serious drama or literary fiction, was never going to attract people in the same numbers as films or sporting matches, but it occupied the same mainstream entertainment world.

The eclectic middlebrow mindset could be either a good thing or a bad thing, depending on your own position within the battle of the brows. Treating opera as if it were just another enjoyable pastime was key to the expansion in its popularity during this decade. Yet for highbrows, this undiscriminating way of consuming culture was to be deplored, while opera's accessibility further undermined its intellectual status. Anyone could hum its tunes, enjoy its costumes and scenery, swoon with its hero and heroine. Thus, the highbrows of the 1920s had little use for it: it offered them no opportunity to demonstrate their intellectual credentials.

Opera, notwithstanding such snobbery, remained a part of the mainstream British cultural conversation during the 1920s. Throughout the decade there was a genuine sense of opera for all—or at least for anyone who chose to take an interest. Opera was fun, enjoyable, a good night out—there was something vibrant about it that made people keen to find out more. Of course, making live opera available to everyone was often a challenge, not for a lack of audience enthusiasm or bad box office but because of the high costs of putting it on. Money was always popular opera's Achilles heel (as was demonstrated when the BNOC folded in 1929). But nobody could have predicted how controversial opera would become in the next decade, when the prospect of funding it from ordinary people's taxes changed the stakes entirely.

---

[80] Karen Arrandale, 'The Scholar as Critic: Edward J. Dent', in Jeremy Dibble and Julian Horton (eds), *British Musical Criticism and Intellectual Thought, 1850–1950* (Woodbridge: Boydell, 2018), pp. 154–173, p. 164.

3

(Dis)-Enchanted Gardens

Philip Snowden, Chancellor of the Exchequer in Ramsay MacDonald's Labour government, had a keenly musical wife. Ethel Snowden (née Annakin), a socialist and former women's-suffrage campaigner, was one of a group of influential interwar patronesses who used their proximity to powerful politicians to campaign for causes that were close to their hearts. While Lucy Baldwin, wife of Stanley Baldwin, agitated for better maternity care, Ethel Snowden turned her focus towards the arts, and in 1930 she was instrumental in persuading her husband to attempt something previously unthinkable: to pay for opera out of public funds.

The subsidy scheme of 1930 was the culmination of years of discussion about how opera should be funded. During the 1920s various subscription schemes had been mooted, such as Sir Thomas Beecham's grandly named 'Imperial League of Opera', which invited opera enthusiasts to donate to the costs of creating a new national opera company and house. All such projects ultimately failed, and subsidy was always dismissed as a pipe dream. Snowden's scheme—the first serious proposal to subsidise any of the performing arts—was a laudable one, but it could scarcely have come at a worse moment, at the height of the Depression. An almighty row ensued about the suitable use of taxpayers' money and whether one should pay for activities one did not personally pursue—arguments that are still alive and well today. The subsidy question also kick-started a debate about national cultural identity: how much did the British value the arts in general, and to what extent were they willing to take an interest in—and pay for—art forms that were not 'home-grown'?

Money for opera

The Chancellor's proposal was that the government would award a grant of £5,000 for the last quarter of 1930, followed by £17,500 a year for five years from 1931, to the BBC, which would use the money to support opera at

48 SOMEONE ELSE'S MUSIC

popular prices at Covent Garden and in the provinces.[1] The BBC—already working closely with the theatre in the broadcasting of opera—would supplement the sum to an annual total of £25,000, and any remaining funds needed would come from private subscriptions.[2] The Postmaster-General would administer the subsidy scheme as part of his remit of managing wireless licences and fees.

Objections to the subsidy scheme came from both sides of the House. Eight Conservative MPs put forward a motion opposing the subsidy in light of the present economic situation.[3] Others asked why opera was being prioritised over cinema or Shakespeare, or 'worthier' causes ranging from sugar-beet production to foundling children.[4] Even Sir Alfred Butt, who combined being a Conservative MP with managing the Theatre Royal Drury Lane, felt that the government should not be 'promising to give the nation's money for the most expensive, most luxurious and least widely appreciated form of stage production'.[5] Though an opera enthusiast himself, he argued that it was neither 'a national pastime' nor 'a national passion', like football, crossword puzzles, horseracing, or musical comedy.[6]

Protectionist or even chauvinistic attitudes, meanwhile, coloured responses from the Labour backbenches, as is exemplified by an exchange between the Glaswegian Labour MP Adam McKinlay and the Postmaster-General, the Rt. Hon. William Ormsby-Gore:

> Mr McKinlay: 'Is there any guarantee that the money so granted will not be used for the purposes of boosting long-haired foreign artistes? I want a guarantee that the foreign voice production expert will not exploit British nationals who are able to take their part in opera.'

> Mr Ormsby-Gore: 'It is not within my competence to discriminate between long-haired and short-haired performers. It is not within the control of my Department.'[7]

---

[1] HoC debate, 20 November 1930: 'Grand Opera (Government Grant)', Hansard, Vol. 245.
[2] HoC debate, 1 December 1930: 'Grand Opera Government Grant', Hansard, Vol. 245.
[3] Anon., 'Opera Subsidy Opposed', DT (27 November 1930), 11.
[4] HoC debate, 2 December 1930: 'Grand Opera (Government Grant)', Hansard, Vol. 245; HoC debate, 18 June 1931: 'Grand Opera (Government Grant)', Hansard, Vol. 253; Anon., 'Opera Subsidy Criticism', DT (22 November 1930), 13.
[5] Sir Alfred Butt, 'Sir Alfred Butt's Attack on Opera Subsidy', DM (26 November 1930), 7.
[6] Sir Alfred Butt, letter to The Times (17 December 1930), n.p.
[7] HoC debate, 15 September 1931: 'British Broadcasting Corporation (Grand Opera)', Hansard, Vol. 256.

(DIS)-ENCHANTED GARDENS 49

Press condemnation of the subsidy was extensive. An article in *The Jedburgh Gazette* in March 1931—by which time the nation was entering full-blown economic crisis—encapsulates the full panoply of objections to it.[8] Its author, George A. Short, asserted that opera was only for a 'little coterie' of (apparently) no more than ten thousand people, and there was a clear conflict of interest in the Chancellor funding his wife's hobby. Opera was also undeserving because it was un-British and 'ridiculous to our matter-of-fact minds' with its stout performers and absurd plots. You and I, Short argued emotively, were having to find money to pay taxes 'by the sweat of our face', only for the money to be spent supporting 'what, after all, is essentially a Continental form of art'. The tone of this article is strikingly more bilious than debates about opera in the 1920s.

A set of national prejudices against opera, many still familiar today, asserted, or reasserted, themselves around the subsidy debate, and foreign observers looked on askance. Paul Cohen-Portheim (a German-born Jewish artist and travel writer based in London) reflected on the fact that the use of public funds in Germany to support opera—£200,000 a year for the Berlin State Opera alone—encouraged the population to 'naturally regard it as their own'.[9] But this did not seem to be the British mentality. The fact that other European nations were able to subsidise and support their arts sectors without public opprobrium tells us much about a peculiarly British philistinism that would influence attitudes towards the arts throughout the century.

Some people wrote to the papers arguing that the subsidy would do much to support theatrical workers, attract tourists, raise funds via the Entertainments Tax, and make tickets more affordable.[10] Elsewhere, more predictable utilitarian attitudes prevailed. A reader wrote to *The Daily Telegraph* to protest that Mr Snowden expected struggling industry to save itself, whereas he was willing to a grant a subsidy to opera, 'about which the worker does not care a row of beans'.[11] A used-car dealer called Robert Moffat Ford even attempted to bring a High Court injunction against the granting of the subsidy. The judge refused the interim *ex parte* injunction but offered

---

[8] George A. Short, 'Talks on Music. (7.) The Opera Subsidy', *The Jedburgh Gazette* (6 March 1931), n.p.

[9] Paul Cohen-Portheim, *The Spirit of London* (London: Batsford, 1935), p. 74.

[10] Anon., 'Subsidising Opera', letter to *DT* (17 December 1930), 11; J. F. Hall, 'Cheap Seats Full', letter to *DT* (28 November 1930).

[11] 'Non-political Parson', 'Choice of Benefits', letter of 27 November 1930 to *DT* (29 November 1930), 9.

50   SOMEONE ELSE'S MUSIC

Moffat Ford a hearing the following week if he could produce the necessary paperwork. Though the stunt was widely reported in the press, Moffat Ford appears to have ultimately dropped the motion, but not without trying (unsuccessfully) to persuade the judge to waive the costs.[12]

Resistance to the subsidy also came from less foreseeable quarters. The conductor Sir Thomas Beecham, taking offence after the breakdown in negotiations between the Imperial League of Opera, the government, and Covent Garden, was opposed.[13] The entrepreneur Charles Manners, founder of the now-defunct Moody Manners touring opera company, was opposed.[14] The *Sunday Times* critic Ernest Newman, who could not see why a majority should pay for the pleasures of a minority, was opposed.[15] Ralph Vaughan Williams, however, saw it as a symbolic moment—music had been acknowledged by government to be a vital part of life rather than a luxury— and the critic Harvey Grace called for opera to be funded on the same basis as galleries, libraries, and museums.[16]

After so much gnashing of teeth, the subsidised season finally went ahead in September 1931, starting with *The Bartered Bride*, followed by works by Wagner, Verdi, Puccini, Strauss, Rossini, Bizet, and Smyth, all performed in English by British singers. A proud Mrs Snowden declared that she would not rest until Britain had a Ministry of Fine Arts.[17] Within a few months, however, the subsidy's future was in jeopardy, thanks to further financial crises, the abandonment of the Gold Standard, a general election, and the formation of a National Government.[18] In October 1932 the Postmaster-General announced that the subsidy would be suspended and although the BBC would continue to fund Covent Garden, there was to be no resumption of the formal government subsidy.[19]

---

[12] Anon., 'Objection to Grand Opera Subsidy', *The Nottingham Evening Post* (5 December 1930), 11; Anon., 'Opera Subsidy', *DT* (10 December 1930), 14; Anon., 'Citizen and Opera Subsidy', *DT* (13 December 1930), 6.

[13] Anon., 'Imperial League of Opera: Statement by Sir Thomas Beecham', *DT* (17 December 1930), 8.

[14] Charles Manners, 'The Financial Problem of National Opera: By the People For the People', *M&L*, 7/2 (April 1926), 93–105, 94–95.

[15] Cited in Anon., 'The Opera Subsidy', *MMF*, 11/1 (January 1931), 1.

[16] Steven Edward Martin, 'The British "Operatic Machine": Investigations into Institutional History of English Opera, c. 1875–1939', unpublished PhD dissertation, University of Bristol (2010), p. 209; 'Feste', 'Ad Libitum', *MT*, 76/1109 (July 1935), 620–622, 621.

[17] Anon., 'English Season at Covent Garden: Mrs Snowden's Party', *DT* (14 September 1931), 8.

[18] Martin, 'The British "Operatic Machine"', pp. 213–214.

[19] HoC debate, 31 October 1932: 'Grand Opera (Government Subsidy)', Hansard, Vol. 269; Martin, 'The British "Operatic Machine"', pp. 214–218.

The Snowdens had demonstrated laudable ambitions, but ultimately, as *The Daily Telegraph* had predicted back in 1930, it had been a case of 'doing the right thing in the wrong way and at the wrong time'.[20] The negative way in which the scheme was reported meant that opera came to be viewed afresh as the pursuit of the rich. It also fuelled a debate among members of the musical establishment about the 'right' and 'wrong' sorts of opera to subsidise. And one type, in particular, found itself at the centre of the spotlight.

The Covent Garden problem

The fact that the subsidy gave favoured treatment to Covent Garden was a key factor in the controversy, notwithstanding aspirations to attract a new audience. Clichés about Covent Garden that had been expressed with good humour during the 1920s were now harder-edged. The critic A. H. Fox-Strangways argued that Covent Garden was 'a show, given by a rich man, paid for as a luxury by those who can afford it, employing instrumentalists who take no personal pride in it and foreign singers to whom it is a convenient milch-cow'.[21] Much of this was unfair, though there was certainly truth in the point about singer fees: the American Rosa Ponselle was paid £210 per performance in 1930, and £300 the next year, whereas fellow cast members received sums of £45–£70.[22]

The Musical Mirror argued that the government had made a fundamental error in granting the subsidy not to a touring company such as the Carl Rosa, but to Covent Garden, or 'society's pet pekinese', which the editor described as attracting 'the very people who care no more for opera as an art than they do for the equity of hunting the fox'.[23] Covent Garden's clientèle is here characterised as members of Society who divided their time between their country estates and their grand London houses. So what was Covent Garden actually like in the 1930s? What was stereotype and what was reality?

Although the aristocratic audience was steadily being tempted away by jazz and nightclubs, opera at Covent Garden remained a fixture of the 'Season', alongside Royal Ascot, Lords, and the Chelsea Flower Show. Society

[20] H. C. B., 'The Muddled Subsidy, *DT* (4 December 1930), 12.
[21] The Editor, 'Opera and the Musician', *M&L*, 13/2 (April 1932), 119–125, 124.
[22] Memo, Estimated Expenditure from 11/6/30 to 5/7/30. ROH archives file: Business Papers Pre-War 1919, 1920, 1926, 1928, 1929, 1930 (2) BOX ONE, 18/2/1; List of singer payments, 1931. ROH archives file: C.G. Opera Syndicate 1929–1931.
[23] Anon., 'Carl Rosa Society's Claim', *MMF*, 11/5 (May 1931), 145.

52 SOMEONE ELSE'S MUSIC

and the opera world were still intimately connected: it was not unusual for society hostesses to throw parties at glamorous hotels for opera stars.[24] Performances were interrupted by a lengthy dinner interval, in which audience members would pick their way delicately through the straw and discarded cabbage leaves of Covent Garden market to get to the Savoy or Romano's on the Strand.[25]

Covent Garden's old-fashioned model of glamour was increasingly criticised. E. H. Tattersall of *The Daily Mail* characterised the patrons of Covent Garden in 1937 as not only preoccupied with fashion and social advancement, but also 'a set of shocking musical snobs'.[26] It is surprising to find this type of talk in *The Daily Mail*, a paper that paid zealous attention to Society and its doings, yet there was, perhaps, something about the opera that made it more suspect than other, heartier, aristocratic pursuits. Privilege and 'foreignness' were intertwined at the opera in ways that made some people feel suspicious. Going to the opera during the Season meant sitting through five weeks of performances sung in German, then a further five weeks in Italian: this was something for an audience of cosmopolitan outlook. *The Daily Record and Mail* even made the striking claim in 1939 that the entire Covent Garden enterprise was only possible because it was being bankrolled by wealthy Jews.[27]

Despite being entirely untypical of the opera-going experience as most people knew it, Covent Garden remained the institution that epitomised the art form. The theatre retained an allure in the public imagination, and yet it was a paradox. The venerable old building was now in a fragile state: it was coming to the end of its lease as an opera house and faced the threat of demolition, as Westminster City Council planned to regenerate the market. The slow line of magnificent motorcars that drove down Bow Street each evening created an incongruous spectacle when set against fruit-and-veg crates and the police station opposite.[28] And its very architecture was coming to seem dated and fusty compared with the ultra-modern theatres such as the Savoy and Adelphi, remodelled in art-deco style, which were springing up in the West End. Covent Garden represented, for some, an ossified type

---

[24] Anon., 'Miss Winnie Melville's Wonderful Party', *The Tatler* (13 May 1931), 296.
[25] Karl Silex, *John Bull at Home*, trans. Huntley Paterson (London: George G. Harrap & Co., 1931), p. 93.
[26] E. H. Tattersall, 'Opera Snobbery', *DM* (8 December 1937), 12.
[27] Anon., 'Opera or Not?', *The Daily Record and Mail* (13 February 1939), 13.
[28] A Special Correspondent, 'Driving to the Opera', *DM* (5 May 1930), 11.

(DIS)-ENCHANTED GARDENS   53

of opera-going. *Time* magazine reported from America that 'a traditional side show of London's Season . . . is opera at elderly, fuddy-duddy Covent Garden'.[29]

And yet, the in-crowd still enjoyed the glamour. *The Tatler* regularly printed photographs of aristocratic women in satin, ermine, and diamonds, their male companions in white tie or ceremonial military dress. Some of the fashions at Covent Garden were becoming more modern, more dynamic, even scandalous. Women in daytime two-piece suits, women with their hair dyed pink, violet, or green, women not wearing stockings: all made headlines.[30] And in 1936 there was the 'sensation' of a woman wearing trousers to Covent Garden for the first time—emerald, accordion-pleat trousers with a black satin jacket and violet sash, no less.[31] To highbrow commentators, all of this epitomised the frivolity of the place. Harvey Grace of *The Musical Times* poured misogynistic scorn on women who were prepared to sit for four hours having their hair waved, their eyebrows plucked, and nails enamelled, but who struggled to sit through 'the operatic stretches that separate the dress-and-diamond parades'.[32]

Interestingly, however, even on occasions where opera was a very dressy event, this was not regarded as a sign of 'elitism'. In 1936 *The Daily Mail* reported the story of an eleven-year-old boy, Leonard Gunton, who had written to Thomas Beecham asking if he could hear *Aida*, an opera he had been told about by his schoolmaster. His father, an assistant mechanic from Leytonstone, had queued outside Covent Garden from 5 a.m. but failed to obtain tickets. Beecham obliged and an interviewer reported that 'it was the grandest night of his life and what impressed him most was the number of lovely women in the audience with their magnificent jewels and beautiful gowns'.[33] The glamour of opera was not necessarily off-putting: for some it merely intensified the art form's allure.

Indeed, the music critic Francis Toye argued in 1933 that 'the man in the street' took a vicarious pleasure in the reputation and fashionable associations of Covent Garden. He wrote: 'They become to him a kind of symbol of national well-being; they are a tribute to London's prestige. He may only be able to afford to go to Sadler's Wells, but he likes to know that

---

[29] 'Music', *Time* (26 June 1939), 64.

[30] Anon., 'Pink Hair Is on the Way: Fashions That Have Startled Opera Audiences', *The Evening Telegraph* (6 June 1936), 4.

[31] Special 'Daily Mail' News, 'Woman in Trousers at the Opera', *DM* (9 May 1936), 11.

[32] 'Feste', 'Ad Libitum', *MT*, 76/1109 (July 1935), 620–622, 620.

[33] Our Social Editress, 'Boys' Night at Covent Garden', *DM* (16 May 1936), 14.

54 · SOMEONE ELSE'S MUSIC

Covent Garden is there—a possibility, a hope, an ideal.'[34] Opera in its most glamorous manifestations was something to take pride in—more aspirational than aloof.

Opera still remained highly popular among the 'galleryites' and a three-day queue for the opening of the 1934 Season broke records.[35] Covent Garden also put on a regular season of cheaper operas in September, once the aristocracy had decamped to the country, followed by a tour to northern cities with the London Philharmonic Orchestra. British singers had an opportunity to star in these performances. The popular press had a field day whenever a singer of humble origins was serendipitously 'discovered', such as when Beecham engaged a young woman he had seen in a pantomime, or when a dairy farmer's son from Swindon was hired to sing Manrico in *Il trovatore*.[36]

Though some of these singers already had stage and concert experience, others were genuinely discovered out of nowhere. Enid Marilynn James, an Oxford Street salesgirl, was literally plucked off the street. A chance encounter with Admiral Sir Henry Campbell, aide-de-camp to King George V, after both stopped to assist people injured in a motoring accident, led to introductions to arts patrons and teachers and ultimately a Covent Garden début.[37] Edgar Evans, meanwhile, was discovered by a talent scout when singing in a London pub while on a rugby trip from Wales in 1935. He was introduced to a singing teacher at the Royal College of Music, and after paying for lessons by taking on a milk round, he was offered a contract to sing at Sadler's Wells.[38]

The Depression encouraged Welsh miners with good voices to look for training and work in singing that they might otherwise never have pursued, the need to earn a living trumping longstanding moral concerns about theatrical life. After Trevor Anthony won the bass category at the 1934 National Eisteddfod, a local appeal raised enough money for him to train at the Royal Academy of Music. He would go on to perform at Covent Garden, the Proms, and to create the role of the Voice of God in Britten's *Noye's Fludde*.[39] The stereotypes about Covent Garden were therefore not quite

[34] Francis Toye, 'Covent Garden Opera Reviewed', *The Listener* (20 June 1934), 1045.

[35] Anon., '3-Days Queue for Opera', *DM* (30 April 1934), 10.

[36] Harold Conway, 'Principal Girl as Opera Star', *DM* (21 September 1935), n.p; Anon., 'Former Milk Boy Is Covent Garden Star', *DM* (16 May 1939), 9.

[37] 'Shopgirl Opera Star Last Night', unidentified press cutting, 27 May 1936. BUTC, MM/2/TH/LO/COV/58 (1936).

[38] Little, *Edgar Evans—Extempore*, pp. 2–3.

[39] Russell, 'Reaching the Operatic Stage', 324.

all they might seem: ordinary British people from across the class spectrum were embracing opera, even at this most august and seemingly un-British of institutions. As for opera beyond the West End—well, that was something else entirely.

Popular opera

Opera House, a 1935 novel by Marjorie Richards, opens with a party of English tourists disembarking from a cruise-ship and being shown an opera house in the fictional Mediterranean resort of Cortesa. The tourists include a Kilburn butcher, a hardware buyer for a store in Clapham, a jerry-builder, and three spinster sisters from Balham. They are awed by the building but mistake the Italian language on the posters for French, laugh at the singers' names, and say they prefer jazz to 'Italian oojahs singing opera'. But a few linger as the party moves on, tempted to know more. 'Wouldn't it be lovely if we could be there tonight? I've never seen *La Traviata*.' 'Wasn't it *Carmen* we saw at the Old Vic?'[40] The protagonists of this novel think they don't know opera, but they do.

Popular opera continued to thrive in the 1930s. Touring companies came and went but were still a vital force for taking opera to the regions, even if many theatres had turned into picture palaces. Some of these companies were still run on cooperative lines, helping audiences to feel involved by allowing them to vote on new works to be added to the repertoire.[41] Company employees lived resolutely 'ordinary' lives. Accounts submitted to the Mass Observation social research organisation of the daily routine of a Miss Una Cheverton, who worked for an unnamed opera company, suggest that she was a 'fiddle player' in the orchestra but also that she was expected to undertake mundane duties like buying costume fabrics from Selfridge's.[42] Lodging in a different room every week, she attempted to make each homely by placing familiar objects on the mantlepiece: a cherished photograph; a tin of cold cream; a postcard of Greta Garbo bought at Woolworth's.

In the East End, opera was back at the People's Palace in 1936, following a five-year hiatus after a fire. There were debates about whether it should be

[40] Marjorie Richards, *Opera House* (London: Hutchinson and Co., 1935), p. 13.
[41] Herman Klein, 'The Carl Rosa Society: Choice of Opera by Plebiscite', *MMF*, 11/3 (March 1931), 107.
[42] Mass Observation. Cheverton, U., D. S. 247 (1937).

56 SOMEONE ELSE'S MUSIC

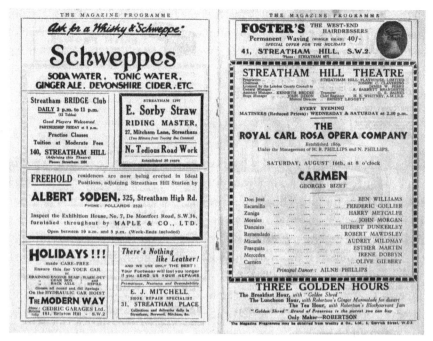

Figure 3.1 The Royal Carl Rosa Opera Company, programme for a production of *Carmen*, Streatham Hill Theatre, London, 16 August 1930. Reproduced with permission from © University of Bristol/ArenaPAL.

rebuilt or relocated, but many locals appealed for its reconstruction, particularly the Jewish community.[43] The new art-deco theatre was opened by the King in 1936 and was described by one commentator as being 'slightly in the manner of super-cinemas'.[44] The Carl Rosa Company visited regularly, selling tickets for 2s.–5s. for a reserved place and 1s. for unreserved.[45] The company expressed its particular pleasure at performing at the venue, because the audience was so familiar with the operas, coming back as many did night after night.[46] Even the magazine *Poultry World* reported on the ambitious programme of opera on offer at the theatre and remarked that 'culture is lively in the East End!'[47]

---

[43] Anon., 'Ghetto Gossip', *East London Observer* (5 December 1931). QM/1/17/8.
[44] Anon., 'People's Palace', *Liverpool Daily Post* (17 August 1938), n.p.
[45] Advertisement in *The Hackney Gazette* (21 January 1938), n.p.
[46] Anon., 'Friends of the People's Palace', *East London Advertiser* (20 August 1938), n.p.
[47] Mabel Hadley, 'East End Opera', *Poultry World* (30 September 1938), n.p.

As in the 1920s, there were grassroots attempts to make the case of opera for all. In 1930, Edward Baritz, a well-known radio lecturer, gave a talk at the Jowett Hall in Bradford (a temperance hall-turned-cinema leased by the Independent Labour Party). He made the case that the great majority of composers had written their works while poverty-stricken, asserting that music was 'largely the product of proletarian minds'. Baritz railed against the fact that England was 'the only country where opera was not supported by the state' and was thus seen as a form of entertainment for the aristocracy and the bourgeoisie.[48]

A manifesto for working-class opera would have gone down well in Bradford, an industrial centre with many arts enthusiasts, even if the town had recently suffered some decline. The novelist J. B. Priestley revisited his hometown in 1933 when undertaking a coach tour of England. He noted that the communities who had fostered the arts in Bradford in the Edwardian years—foreigners and wealthy industrialists—had departed, the latter now, thanks to motoring, 'turning themselves into country gentlemen'. The town's main concert hall and theatre had turned into cinemas, prestigious European musicians no longer visited, and the population had become poorer. Yet repertory theatre was still flourishing, and teachers, typists, cashiers, and artisans devoted their free time to putting on performances. 'Operas, musical comedies, farces, dramas, the place hums with them', Priestley mused.[49]

Of course, broadcasting was an ever-more important mechanism for disseminating music, with the early 1930s seeing a rapid expansion in radio ownership. The BBC continued to receive hostile correspondence, including from a man who stated that 'when the word opus is mentioned I switch off', and more popular music began to be broadcast over the course of the decade.[50] Nevertheless, the BBC remained committed to broadcasting opera and listeners remained appreciative. In 1938, 27 per cent of middle-class listeners expressed an interest in 'grand opera' broadcasts and 47 per cent in broadcasts of light opera. The figures for working-class listeners for these genres were 15 per cent and 30 per cent, respectively, but with working-class listeners outnumbering middle-class listeners two to one, absolute numbers in each of the groups were similar.[51] *The Listener* emphasised the ways in

[48] Anon., 'Opera for the Rich Only: Lectures on British Attitude Towards the Arts', *The Yorkshire Post* (6 January 1930), 14.

[49] J. B. Priestley, *English Journey* (London: William Heinemann, 1934), p. 199.

[50] Anon., *BBC Handbook 1940*, p. 20; Simon J. Potter, *This Is the BBC: Entertaining the Nation, Speaking for Britain? 1922–2022* (Oxford: Oxford University Press, 2022), p. 55.

[51] Rose, *The Intellectual Life*, pp. 204–205.

58 SOMEONE ELSE'S MUSIC

which broadcasting was helping to create an 'immense mental revolution' by disseminating culture. The fact that the magazine, allied with the BBC, advocated for broadcasting should come as no surprise, but the fact that it placed 'opera taking new life' as the first benefit on the list is worthy of note.[52]

Cinema, meanwhile, was posing a greater threat to opera than it had during the 1920s, with the arrival of 'talkies' and 'super cinemas' offering a lavish array of entertainments. *The Musical Times* reported in 1930 that not long ago 'the man in the street received music preferably through the prism of opera: in general, he eagerly followed the events occurring in this sphere and was always well acquainted with them', whereas now 'the hegemony of opera, so far as the general public is concerned, appears to have been transferred to the cinematograph.'[53] The manager of the Carl Rosa Company reported in 1938 that the influence of films was 'definitely beneficial to popular opera', remarking that people were increasingly coming to an opera having heard its tunes in the talkies, such as when Grace Moore sang 'One Fine Day' in the 1934 film *One Night of Love*.[54]

Finally, snippets of opera could be heard unexpectedly as people went about their daily lives. In the gargantuan marble-floored lobbies of West End hotels such as the Regent Palace and the Strand Palace, both run by the restaurant chain J. Lyons and Co., bands played Wagner and Puccini. Together with the hotels' billiard rooms, smoking rooms, and writing rooms, these performances played a role in creating an aura of affordable glamour at a moderate price for a clientèle made up of businessmen and tourists of modest means.[55]

All of the above points to an eclectic and lively operatic scene for those inclined to take an interest, and many opera propagandists boasted of the massive explosion of interest in opera as a popular art form. *The Old Vic and Sadler's Wells Magazine* declared in 1936, 'One of the most striking social phenomena of modern times is the revival of the love of grand opera . . . not merely among a select coterie of "highbrows" but among the general entertainment-seeking public.'[56] Numerous major London-based

---

[52] The Editor, 'Our Cultural Revolution', *The Listener* (10 June 1931), 966.

[53] Leonid Sabaneev, trans. S. W. Pring, 'Opera at the Present Day', *MT*, 71/1049 (1 July 1930), 593–596, 593.

[54] Anon., 'Friends of the People's Palace', *East London Advertiser* (20 August 1938), n.p. QM/1/17/17.

[55] Cohen-Portheim, *The Spirit of London*, p. 87; Thomas Harding, *Legacy: One Family, A Cup of Tea, And the Company That Took on the World* (London: Windmill Books, 2019), pp. 180–182.

[56] Alan Bland, 'The New Season at the Wells', *OVSWM*, 33/3 (September–October 1936), 7–8, 7.

companies even saw it as part of their remit to foster a love of the arts among their employees and customers. Barclay's Bank, Pearl Assurance, and the Stock Exchange all had operatic societies that performed at the Scala Theatre near Tottenham Court Road.[57]

Numerous 1930s sources suggest that opera was being patronised to a *greater* extent by poorer people than by the very wealthy. The conductor John Barbirolli wrote of playing operatic seasons all over the country that attracted packed audiences in the pit and gallery, but noted that 'the wealthier people, the so-called leaders of Society, are too often conspicuous by their absence'.[58] Barbirolli argued that it was important to face the unpalatable truth that 'the British upper classes today have little use for culture of any kind'. This was unfortunate, as the operatic economy depended upon support from across the class spectrum, but such anecdotes offered a sharp riposte to those who assumed opera to be the pursuit of an elite. The new reality was that, as Robert Stuart, manager of the Oxford University Opera Club, put it, 'those who appreciate opera well represented cannot afford to make it pay; while those who can and ought to afford to make it pay will not'.[59]

New companies

Attitudes towards opera were becoming more polarised during the 1930s, as even enthusiasts were increasingly conflicted about which operatic model should be prioritised. Some members of the musical establishment believed opera should be cheap, modestly staged, and in English; others thought opera an 'exotic' product, which should be performed to connoisseurs in luxurious surroundings.[60] The idea still held sway, as it had in the 1920s, that there was 'national opera' and there was 'international opera', and never the twain shall meet.

Two new operatic companies that were established in the 1930s epitomise this fundamental divide. In 1931 Lilian Baylis opened the Sadler's Wells Opera in Clerkenwell with the aim of putting on near-nightly shows in English at 'prices . . . low enough to suit all purses'.[61] Three years later John

---

[57] J. Stanley-Verde, 'Opera as a Recreation', *MMF*, 11/2 (February 1931), 70.

[58] John Barbirolli, 'Is British Opera Doomed?' *The Music Lover*, 3/24 (10 February 1934), 7.

[59] Robert Stuart, 'Opera and the Talking Film', *MO*, 54/637 (October 1930), 41–42, 41.

[60] R. H. M., 'The Enchantment of Glyndebourne, *The Listener* (24 June 1936), 1224.

[61] Anon., 'Sadler's Wells', *The Listener* (8 July 1936), 95.

60 SOMEONE ELSE'S MUSIC

Christie established Glyndebourne Festival Opera for his singer wife Audrey Mildmay, staging performances in a specially built theatre on their family estate in East Sussex. Both institutions would shape perceptions of opera in the 1930s, and prompt discussion about who it was 'for'.

Discussions of the early Sadler's Wells were characterised by a genuine sense of excitement that the country might finally have the national opera company so many had long desired. Baylis's Old Vic had already proved that cheap, high-quality opera was not only possible, but capable of creating demand on the part of the working classes, demonstrating that, as *The Listener* put it, 'Shakespeare and opera are not mere luxuries for the man of learning and the musician, but healthy sustenance for which the better part of the big British public are eager'.[62]

Baylis had first spotted the empty shell of the derelict Sadler's Wells from the upper deck of a bus during World War One.[63] The theatre had previously served as a music hall, cinema, and roller-skating rink, and was situated in a formerly genteel but now squalid district.[64] Eventually the purchase, rebuilding, and fitting out of the theatre were achieved via a large-scale public appeal and support from the Carnegie United Kingdom Trust.[65] The completed theatre offered spacious, pleasantly decorated public areas, excellent acoustics, and the easiest parking of any theatre in London—an important consideration in a city now clogged with traffic.[66] But the setting was scarcely 'grand', taxi drivers didn't know where Rosebery Avenue was, and the conductor Geoffrey Toye remarked, 'You can't have an opera house here. There are no boxes. People won't come.'[67]

Baylis, however, wasn't concerned with boxes or their inhabitants. She recognised how key the working classes were to the economics of popular opera: for the venture to succeed, all parts of the house needed to be full nightly. The claim made by *The Old Vic and Sadler's Wells Magazine* that the extension of opera to Sadler's Wells would ensure that 'tunes from *Butterfly* and *Pagliacci* will be hummed from Islington to Streatham Hill, whistled by

---

[62] Anon., 'Sadler's Wells', *The Listener* (12 March 1930), 440.

[63] Anon., 'The Story of Sadler's Wells', *MT*, 78/1135 (September 1937), 781–786, 781.

[64] Guthrie, *A Life in the Theatre*, p. 102.

[65] R. P. P. Rowe, 'The Old Vic and Sadler's Wells', *Music & Letters*, 13/2 (April 1932), 141–146, 141.

[66] Anon., 'The Story of Sadler's Wells', 781; Silex, *John Bull at Home*, p. 159.

[67] Guthrie, *A Life in the Theatre*, p. 103; Anon., 'Sadler's Wells Theatre', *The Times* (8 January 1952), 4.

every errand boy from Peckham to Camden Town' may sound far-fetched, but was grounded in the success of the Old Vic.[68]

The Vic-Wells enterprise was part of a broader interwar 'People's Theatre' movement. As Priestley continued his coach journey up to Tyneside, through areas of ever-greater deprivation, he found numerous theatrical collectives, an offshoot of the vast network of clubs that were set up for the unemployed during the 1930s.[69] Local communities put on plays like *Peer Gynt* and *The Trojan Women* at the People's Theatre in Newcastle and organised concert parties for the unemployed of Gateshead.[70] The warmth with which such endeavours were greeted illustrated a growing desire among the poorest to look, as Priestley put it, towards the arts for 'little windows into a world of ideas' in the darkest of times.[71]

People's theatres favoured melodramas, thrillers, and crime dramas, as audiences welcomed any kind of 'strong emotion'.[72] One can see a natural affinity between this type of audience and the 'high drama' of opera. The British, or at least the English, middle classes were known for emotional self-control, and a certain degree of primness and prudishness. This, combined with lingering Victorian perceptions of theatre's immorality, meant eyebrows were still raised at passionate opera, particularly of the Italian type. But Baylis spotted that there was great potential for building an audience for opera among the more open-minded working classes, and it was here, in grassroots theatre rather than amid the bright lights of the West End, that Britain's strongest future as an operatic nation seemed to lie.

Sadler's Wells, which seated 1,640, was packed in January 1931 for the company's first production, *Carmen*.[73] Baylis had found an audience ready and waiting at Rosebery Avenue, just as she had at the Waterloo Road, including young men of about 19 or 20 who were new to opera.[74] The fact that the launch of the company coincided with the subsidy furore merely stimulated publicity. Unfortunately, however, Sadler's Wells was hampered by the same economic forces, and by the autumn, ticket sales had begun to

---

[68] H. A., 'Opera for the People', *The Old Vic and Sadler's Wells Magazine*, 1/1 (January 1931), 3–4, 3.

[69] Juliet Gardiner, *The Thirties: An Intimate History* (London: HarperPress, 2011), pp. 141–146.

[70] Priestley, *English Journey*, pp. 296–304.

[71] Ibid., p. 198.

[72] Paul Cohen-Portheim, *England the Unknown Isle*, trans. Alan Harris (London: Duckworth, 1930), pp. 190–191.

[73] H. H., 'Sadler's Wells Opera: *Carmen* as Opening Production', *DT* (21 January 1931), 8.

[74] Herbert Hughes, 'World of Music', *DT* (17 January 1931), 15.

62   SOMEONE ELSE'S MUSIC

fall.[75] Regular supporters were exhorted to drum up audiences by giving tickets to overworked friends or to buy them as birthday gifts; some patrons were already distributing flyers on trains or sneaking them into library books.[76] Sadler's Wells was £3,000 in deficit after its first year, and by 1934 it was apparent that the policy of running two theatres as a joint enterprise was not working.[77] To cut down the costs of transporting sets and costumes, Baylis decided that each theatre should concentrate on the area in which it was drawing larger audiences, so in 1936 opera moved wholesale to Sadler's Wells, with the Old Vic focusing on Shakespeare.[78]

Sadler's Wells's aim was to put on opera for all, and not only that, but to do it to a high standard (there was now a professional chorus). But as the director Tyrone Guthrie noted, the company also had an air that was 'worthy rather than exciting; a little dowdy, a little stodgy; they were something which no theatrical performance can afford to be—snob repellent'.[79] There was little to attract the smart set but much to attract ordinary people. *The Listener* reported that 'operas are produced there in such a way that the public feels that they are real living works of art, and not museum pieces, occasionally brought out from under their glass show-cases for the delectation of a handful of fashionable and snobbish individuals whose object in going to the opera is less to listen to the music than to exhibit themselves'.[80] Historian Daniel Snowman recalls his father talking about going to Sadler's Wells after a day's work in an insurance office, growing to love opera and building up a treasured collection of gramophone records to get to know them better.[81] This willingness to study the operas at home and come to performances well-prepared was typical of audiences at Baylis's theatres.

Sadler's Wells enjoyed immense public goodwill, and this was reflected in many different sectors of the press. It might come as a surprise to find support for urban, working-class Sadler's Wells in the pages of *Country Life*, a magazine that sandwiched features about opera between others about the hunting

---

[75] Rowe, 'The Old Vic and Sadler's Wells', 142–143.

[76] Lilian Baylis, 'Wanted: 2,000 People! Not Pounds!', *OVSWM/1* (September–October 1931), 2–3, 3.

[77] Rowe, 'The Old Vic and Sadler's Wells', 142–143; Michael Stapleton, *The Sadler's Wells Opera* (London: Adam and Charles Black, 1954), 9; Anon., 'Sadler's Well and The Old Vic: The Policy of Joint Enterprise', *The Times* (24 April 1934), n.p.

[78] George Warrington, 'At the Theatre: Old Vic. and Sadler's Wells', *Country Life*, 81/2100 (17 April 1937), 435–436, 436.

[79] Guthrie, *A Life in the Theatre*, p. 197.

[80] Anon., 'Sadler's Wells', *The Listener* (8 July 1936), 95.

[81] Daniel Snowman, *Just Passing Through: Interactions with the World* (Bristol: Brown Dog Books, 2021), p. 25.

(DIS)-ENCHANTED GARDENS 63

scene or polo, but the magazine enthusiastically endorsed the company's high standards and prices that 'make good opera available to the most impecunious'.[82] *Country Life* was also—less surprisingly—an avid supporter of idyllic, bucolic Glyndebourne, which ushered in the 'country-house' model of opera that has had a significant impact upon popular conceptions of the art form in this country ever since. The magazine's property pages advertised numerous lavish country homes that were within striking distance of the theatre and could be rented for the opera season.[83] The international model at Glyndebourne also intersected well with *Country Life*'s regular articles about foreign opera festivals aimed at well-heeled, well-travelled readers.[84]

Glyndebourne was, undoubtedly, a small, perfectly formed operatic enterprise, a thing of beauty on luxurious lines. John Christie insisted on high artistic standards, hiring top singers and players and visiting European opera houses to observe their modus operandi. As *Country Life* reported, 'Every detail had to be right—and is'.[85] Because Christie took opera seriously, he expected the audience to as well. Evening dress was expected, and early programmes emphasised the formality of the proceedings, with silence to be strictly observed and audience members to arrive in their seats five minutes ahead of curtain-up.[86] Critics found themselves in their element. It was also the perfect setting for the musicians, who could work together intensively in a country-house atmosphere that afforded them better conditions than regular theatres, as well as an escape from the cares of day-to-day life.[87]

But was Glyndebourne elitist? Admittance was primarily restricted to the well-to-do. Tickets were expensive at £2 (or 20 guineas for a box)—with a limited number available at 30s.—and there were no 'galleryites' here.[88] *The Listener* admitted that 'this is not opera for the masses; it is admittedly opera de luxe, run for the benefit of a public which has money to spend but enough sense to realise that in spending it at Glyndebourne it is not only encouraging a very valuable artistic enterprise, but gaining for itself pleasure

---

[82] Anon., 'London Entertainment: The Opera', *Country Life* (14 May 1938), 516.

[83] For example, 'Stanmer Park, Sussex', advertisement for Curtis & Henson, London, *Country Life*, 83/2157 (21 May 1938), ix.

[84] See, for example, Anon., 'Bayreuth and the Wagner Festival', *Country Life* (17 May 1930), lxxxviii–xc; and 'Winter and Spring in Italy', Italian State Tourist Department advertisement, *Country Life* (26 January 1935), xxvii.

[85] Anon., 'Woman to Woman: Genius at Glyndebourne', *Country Life*, 85/2212 (4 June 1938), lxvi.

[86] Glyndebourne Festival Opera House, Mozart Festival programme, 1935.

[87] R. H. M., 'The Enchantment of Glyndebourne', *The Listener* (24 June 1936), 1224.

[88] John Jolliffe, *Glyndebourne: An Operatic Miracle* (London: John Murray, 1999), p. 265; Anon., 'Mozart in a Sussex Garden', *Nottingham Guardian* (16 May 1934), n.p.

64 SOMEONE ELSE'S MUSIC

and satisfaction of a kind that can be found nowhere else in the country'.[89] Perceptions of the enterprise playing to a leisured elite were intensified by the unusual shape of the evening. Performances started early—making it impossible to attend after work—and there was a long interval during which a full dinner (or 'banquet') was served.[90] Rumours that the festival might try to attract holidaymakers from Brighton and Eastbourne were swiftly quashed.[91]

A sense of community developed among the attendees that gave it something of the atmosphere of a special club.[92] There is a discernible air here of a select group of people cherishing something beautiful and wanting to keep it to themselves: arguably, elitist participants in an elite enterprise. And yet there was another side to Glyndebourne, for a subsection of the audience was made up of music-loving shopworkers of all ranks from the John Lewis Partnership, who were given tickets in gratitude for their hard work by the opera-loving CEO John Spedan Lewis, a great friend of Christie's.[93]

Christie was at pains to emphasise the fact that the music must always remain central to the Glyndebourne enterprise. He was keen to differentiate it from Covent Garden: Glyndebourne performances were not something to be 'sandwich[ed] between interviews and a society party'.[94] And although he was always keen to attract influential or grand people, Christie's model of opera was not, as he saw it, just about seeing and being seen. It was a celebration of good art, and if the tickets were expensive, it was purely a necessity, since 'opera cannot be cheap and good'.[95] As it was, the venture would lose money, even if every seat were sold, but Christie was prepared to bear the brunt of it, since 'it may mean the revival of opera in England. That's all that matters'.[96]

Like Covent Garden, Glyndebourne was regarded as something international that operated in an elevated world of its own. There was a vogue in British artistic circles in the 1930s for all things German, and it was to Germany and Austria that Christie looked for inspiration, making trips to

---

[89] R. H. M., 'The Enchantment of Glyndebourne', *The Listener* (24 June 1936), 1224.

[90] Glyndebourne Opera programme, *Macbeth* (23 June 1938); Glyndebourne Opera programme, *Don Pasquale* (dress rehearsal, 27 June 1938). British Library shelfmark X.435/859.

[91] Eric Blom, 'Glyndebourne Opera Festival', *MT*, 75/1097 (July 1934), 651–652, 651.

[92] Edwin Evans, 'Music: The Opera Season', *Time and Tide* (29 May 1937), 717–718, 718.

[93] Anon., 'Glyndebourne and Wimbledon', *The Gazette of the John Lewis Partnership*, 20/21 (25 June 1938), 675.

[94] Anon., 'Opera in Country', *Glasgow Evening Times* (29 May 1934), n.p.; Blunt, *John Christie of Glyndebourne*, p. 161.

[95] Our Special Correspondent, 'Grand Opera in a Tudor Mansion', *The Daily Sketch* (16 May 1934), n.p.

[96] Our Special Correspondent, 'Opera-Making in a Garden', *Morning Post* (16 May 1934), n.p.

Bayreuth, Munich, Salzburg, Vienna, and Dresden.[97] Christie searched the world for the best soloists, and his singers were coached by the Italian Mariano Stabile; the artistic direction was by Dr Fritz Busch and Professor Carl Ebert. The repertoire was, of course, resolutely foreign—exclusively Mozart in the first few seasons—and sung in the original. Christie told a dinner of Sussex women musicians in 1936 that he would be prepared to stage a British opera if any composer could produce one 'which the staff at Glyndebourne regard as really good'.[98] One offended composer, Julius Harrison, retorted that Christie would be disappointed if he expected British composers to come rushing to offer their works to an organisation that was 'essentially German'.[99]

In 1936, *The Musical Times* reported that 'there has been some discussion, largely casuistical, as to how far Glyndebourne is a foreign institution planted in Sussex and how far a British institution that gives a cachet to the foreigners whom it employs'.[100] Yet surprisingly positive comments could be found in the mainstream press. *The Daily Mail*, for example, did not carp about Glyndebourne being foreign but called it 'one of the most charming experiences of the season' and praised 'Mr Christie's wonderful little opera house . . . in the Sussex Downs'.[101]

Nevertheless, Christie often found himself in a double bind, particularly when it came to criticisms about expense. He wanted to put on something of artistic worth for the benefit of all discerning listeners but had to charge high prices to make the model work. As Glyndebourne became more fashionable, its exclusivity became more of a selling point. In 1938 Christie defended himself in *The Listener* against what he termed 'unfriendly criticism' that his theatre was 'a rich man's hobby' and 'an exotic product run by an amateur and intended only for the benefit of a small minority of wealthy and leisured musical snobs'.[102]

Christie insisted that,

We do not aim at any particular class of public, and we have helped many poor people to hear the performances, just as many others have saved up

[97] Blunt, *John Christie of Glyndebourne*, p. 115; Anon., 'Mozart at Glyndebourne', *Country Life*, 81/2106 (29 May 1937), 586.
[98] Our Own Correspondent, 'Chance for British Opera', *DT* (9 March 1936), n.p.
[99] Anon., 'Glyndebourne and English Opera', *DT* (14 March 1936), n.p.
[100] W. McN., '*Don Giovanni* at Glyndebourne', *MT*, 77/1120 (June 1936), 553.
[101] Anon., 'Looking at Life', *DM* (9 May 1935), 10; Edwin Evans, 'Opera on the Downs', *DM* (28 May 1935), 15.
[102] John Christie, 'Glyndebourne as I See It', *The Listener* (16 June 1938), 1308–1309.

Figure 3.2 Audience at Glyndebourne Festival Opera, East Sussex, 1934. Reproduced with permission from © Glyndebourne Productions Ltd/ ArenaPAL.

to come here because they thought it was worth it. They cannot, perhaps, come as often as they like, but then neither can they have Van Dycks nor Botticellis in their sitting-rooms.[103]

Glyndebourne was a special treat, a taste of affordable luxury—something that perhaps sat at odds with puritanical, thrifty British instincts.

Christie also prided himself upon his altruism: he saw Glyndebourne as serving the local community, creating an estate wherein locals found employment for life, and thinking not only of the audience but of their staff by providing a chauffeurs' bar, where patrons' drivers could relax.[104] Nor did these arguments about public good come solely from Christie himself. In 1938, *The Listener* stated that opera in 1930s Britain was being fuelled in

---

[103] Ibid., 1309.
[104] Marcus Binney and Rosy Runciman, *Glyndebourne: Building a Vision* (London: Thames and Hudson, 1994), p. 23, p. 47.

(DIS)-ENCHANTED GARDENS   67

large part by 'a small group of altruists'—including Christie and the now-late Lilian Baylis, who had died the previous year.[105] It is noteworthy that Christie and Baylis—ostensibly such different impresarios—should be categorised together in this way, as disinterested, benevolent parties.

In raising the standards of operatic performance, Glyndebourne did much to get opera taken seriously in Britain and encouraged other British opera companies to raise their game. It had, as the authors of a 1939 book about opera put it, been 'responsible for the conversion of many objectors to a better frame of mind about opera as a legitimate and delightful form of art'.[106] Once again, perhaps, we might reflect on Aldous Huxley's words from the 1920s about there being reasons to be grateful to the snobs.

From fun to stuffiness

If opera at Glyndebourne was very definitely 'art', the opera most Britons saw was better characterised as what critic Francis Toye called 'part of an entertainment routine'.[107] The man in the street, it was often said, knew what he liked and liked what he knew. He approached opera on the same level as other forms of entertainment, coming to realise soon enough that opera's conventions were little different from those of cinema—the close-up, the flashback, and so on.[108]

Interwar opera was often low-budget and amateurish. But in 1930 the novelist Hugh Walpole wrote that he revelled in its absurdities, which, combined with glorious music, were precisely what made opera, for him, so enjoyable. Walpole took delight in anticipating where things might go wrong, whether out-of-tune singing, over-acting, or a dozy conductor.[109] Opera's excesses, too, were something in which to take delight. People frequently complained about fat Wagner singers, but for Walpole, 'they should be fat; they should be enormous; they should be mountains high and mountains broad and all the scenery should be mountains high and mountains broad as well; and then in that world of gods and goddesses you do move

---

[105] Ralph Hill, 'Symphony Concerts for the Plain Man', *The Listener* (27 October 1938), 916.

[106] Frank Howes and Philip Hope-Wallace, *A Key to Opera* (London: Blackie and Son Ltd, 1939), p. 12.

[107] Francis Toye, 'The Economics of Opera', *The Listener* (5 March 1930), 403.

[108] Francis Toye, 'Studies in Musical Heresy—VII', *The Listener* (27 July 1932), 142.

[109] Hugh Walpole, 'The Adventure of the Opera', *The Listener* (21 May 1930), 896.

68 SOMEONE ELSE'S MUSIC

to an extraordinary sense of splendour and ecstasy that is beyond your own human and daily knowledge'.

The joy of more realist operas, on the other hand, derived not so much from escaping into a fantasy world as from seeing one's own inner emotions writ large. (It may not be insignificant that Walpole was a closet homosexual.) You might not know any cigarette girls or have lived with desperadoes in the mountains, but you could still imagine yourself as one of the characters from *Carmen*. Everyone could relate to opera in some way, and the key to enjoying it, Walpole proposed, was to go to it with an open mind, and to be 'ready to take whatever may be going to come and then to receive it joyfully'.

It was not unusual to see newspapers promoting operas on their anti-cerebral qualities, such as when *The Daily Telegraph* promoted *Hansel and Gretel* as a work that could particularly appeal to young people because 'it has a story demanding no deep intellectual concentration and containing no abstruse philosophical or allegorical meaning'.[110] But while those in the habit of going to see opera didn't regard it as intellectual, the opera industry had to fight against a growing perception that the broader classical music scene was forbiddingly so.

Antagonism towards all things intellectual was growing during the 1930s; indeed, anti-intellectualism was being constructed as a defining element of the national character.[111] George Orwell attacked the English intelligentsia for their 'severance from the common culture' and their cosmopolitanism, taking their cooking from Paris and their opinions from Moscow; they were 'detached from the common people' and therefore 'un-English'.[112] Opera was not really intellectual—indeed, highbrows still saw it as lowbrow—but the 1930s press began to bundle it in with other forms of music that most definitely were.

Modernist music of this era was perceived to be inaccessible—indeed, many of its proponents believed that it should not *be* accessible, that it would be compromised and degraded if brought into contact with market forces. It attracted much derision in the press, one commentator arguing that to put too much modernist music on a concert programme was like filling a menu with dishes for vegetarians—eccentric at a time when the British diet was

---

[110] Anon., 'Municipal Opera Success: Four Day Season at Hastings', *DT* (27 December 1930), 6.

[111] Sarah Collins, 'Anti-intellectualism and the Rhetoric of "National Character"', in Jeremy Dibble and Julian Horton (eds), *British Musical Criticism and Intellectual Thought, 1850–1950* (Woodbridge: The Boydell Press, 2018), pp. 199–234, p. 204.

[112] George Orwell, *The Lion and the Unicorn* and *The Road to Wigan Pier*, cited in ibid., p. 211.

dominated by meat and two veg.[113] In time, classical music in general began to be tarred with the same brush and even opera began to be seen as part of the same obscure, intellectual world as modern music. This was a perception shaped by the fact that there was no longer a ready supply of new popular operas, as the art form moved inexorably towards becoming a museum culture. Audiences yearned in vain for a successor to Verdi and Puccini who would write accessible, tuneful works characterised by sincere emotion. But emotion was becoming, instead, the preserve of the cinema.

Time and again, commentators reported the fact that the self-styled musical cognoscenti hated opera.[114] Yet these severe intellectuals, not interested in opera themselves, seemed determined to put everyone else off enjoying it as well. Music critic Richard Capell summed things up pithily in *The Daily Mail*: the cause of opera in Britain had two enemies, 'both the open ones, the Philistines, and the insidious ones, the capricious snobs'.[115] In some ways, this still holds good today.

John Barbirolli expressed concern that highbrows were becoming a veritable menace: whereas the true music-lover was broadminded in tastes and outlook, the highbrow was 'a self-opinionated, disgruntled individual who adopts a patronisingly possessive attitude towards music, musicians, and the public, that might be considered amusing were it not so often definitely harmful'.[116] Barbirolli wrote that highbrows were driving people to avoid performances and switch off their wirelesses in droves. Told that he was listening in 'the wrong way', the average opera-goer would 'probably shrug his shoulders and decide that, after all, this opera stuff must be too deep for him and that musical comedy is more in his line'.

All this was rather ironic, given that it was widely agreed by the 1930s that most people's cultural tastes sat somewhere in the middlebrow. The idea of separate spheres for different forms of entertainment was seen as outdated: commentators observed that the younger generation might be found in the concert hall one night and at the racing-track the next.[117] People tended to be 'highbrows' or 'lowbrows' from time to time, not consistently.[118] Thus, the development of an aura of forbidding intellectualism around classical

---

[113] Denys W. Harding, 'The Social Background of Taste in Music', *MT*, 79/1143 (May 1938), 333–335, 333.

[114] 'Deva' (John Foulds), 'Challenges', *MM*, 10/11 (November 1930), 322.

[115] Richard Capell, 'Don't Croak about British Music', *DM* (22 February 1932), 10.

[116] John Barbirolli, 'The Musical Highbrow Menace', *The Music Lover*, 3/26 (24 February 1934), 5.

[117] Leslie Baily, 'Points from Letters: Gilding the Pill?', *The Listener* (6 June 1934), 972.

[118] Anon., 'Creating a Demand', *The Listener* (30 January 1929), 98.

70   SOMEONE ELSE'S MUSIC

music was as reactionary as it was unfortunate. It also revived the notion that opera was somehow contrary to the British character. As a commentator wrote in *The Illustrated London News* in 1933: 'Popular entertainments reflect accurately the culture, morals, ideals, temper, as well as the standards of literacy and taste, of the great mass of the people ... The Opera, the Chamber Concert, the Art Exhibition, the "highbrow" play, are not broadly and truly expressive of the national character'.[119] Someone else's music, indeed.

By the 1930s the people who set the trends, whose opinions mattered, were no longer the same as they had been—and the new trendsetters had a different attitude towards the arts. The idea that a knowledge of music might be a valuable social asset was declining—opera mattered less to the 'in-crowd'. Denys W. Harding argued in *The Musical Times* in 1938 that 'the social prestige of good taste in music is now much lower than it was' and that 'the profession of good taste in music is now less important as a social qualification than it once was—less expected, less invited, and less sanctioned socially'.[120] People no longer automatically took their cue in matters of good taste from the leisured elite who had historically been vital in patronising the arts. As the balance of wealth transferred from land-owning to commerce and manufacturing, a nouveau riche was becoming the new elite, and it was one less interested in the pursuits the old aristocracy had favoured.[121]

The new arbiters of taste were men of industry and commerce. In a decade obsessed with modernity, when owning a car was a sign you had made it, it was men such as Lord Nuffield, of Morris Motors, who were the heroes of the hour. Nuffield was a philanthropist, but his interests lay in science and technology rather than the arts. In the past, a social climber would have been embarrassed to be a philistine, Harding argued, but now the situation had entirely reversed, to the point where 'in the ordinary world of industry and commerce a developed taste for music is regarded as at best a harmless idiosyncrasy, and to admit it openly to any great importance in one's scheme of values would be a handicap rather than an advantage'.[122]

None of this was good news for British opera, which continued to function on a sporadic basis and whose audience was enthusiastic but scattered and factionalised. Opera still sat comfortably in the broader middlebrow

---

[119] G. F. H., 'The World of the Theatre', *ILN* (2 September 1933), 354.

[120] Denys W. Harding, 'The Social Background of Taste in Music', *MT*, 79/1143 (May 1938), 333-5, 333.

[121] Ross McKibbin, *Classes and Cultures: England 1918–1951* (Oxford: Oxford University Press, 1998, repr. 2013), p. 40.

[122] Harding, 'The Social Background of Taste in Music', 334.

entertainment world, but the subsidy row, the prominence in the media of glamorous models of opera-going, and the posturing of snooty intellectuals began to harden attitudes against it among people who had not encountered it for themselves.[123] And finally, the 1930s saw the rise of a new breed of taste-setters from the world of industry that had little time for things like opera. In response to all these factors, the glimmers of the opera-elitism rhetoric—albeit using different terminology from that in common currency today—started to emerge.

---

[123] Figaro, 'The Operatic World', *MO*, 54/637 (October 1930), 23–24, 23.

4

Opera Goes to War

In 1948 the soprano Joan Hammond received two fan letters. The first came from a squadron leader with Bomber Command who had been held as a prisoner of war in an underground room in Poland with twenty other RAF officers in 1941. Somehow, the men had managed to acquire a portable gramophone and a handful of records, of which one, featuring Hammond singing arias from *Gianni Schicchi* and *Tosca*, had become a particular favourite. The prisoners played it in the darkness each night and many times during the day and noticed that Germans guards would also come to listen. The man thanked Hammond for the fact that her recording gave the officers 'a real sense of freedom, not, alas, of the body but of the spirit' and wrote, 'Should a parallel situation arise and I find myself again having to battle with the seeming "powers of darkness" I know I shall again find inspiration from your song.'[1]

The second letter Hammond received came from a woman who described herself as 'the wife of a Yorkshire working man' who had been forced by ill health to take a low-paid job. She explained that 'many adversaries have kept my hubby and I poor in material things, but our mutual love of music has made us, oh so very rich, in our little home.'[2] Recently she had heard Hammond on 'Woman's Hour' and been inspired to write. The woman explained that her son had served as a fighter pilot in Malaya. His collection of records, including Hammond's 'One Fine Day', had formed the basis for a music appreciation club he had set up with his fellow pilots: whoever flew to Calcutta would pick up a new record. One day in 1945, the engine of her son's Thunderbolt fighter plane failed. He was buried at Kuala Lumpur.

The woman explained to Hammond that her records had become a source of enormous solace, writing:

---

[1] Joan Hammond, *A Voice, a Life* (London: Victor Gollancz Ltd, 1970), p. 242.
[2] Ibid., p. 242.

OPERA GOES TO WAR 73

Our boy's collection was returned to us in the steel carrying cases he had bought, and although they are a little worn and scratched with usage, they are our dearest possessions. We can unite with him, as we sat by our fireside, listening, as so many of those pilots listened before, in so many cases, they went out on the last flight. They are a very great comfort to us, and I am sure you will be glad to know that your lovely voice gave courage, enjoyment, and a belief that there was still so much that was beautiful in the world, to live and fight for . . . May you be able to give joy and pleasure to ordinary folks like us for many a long day.[3]

Opera was, for both of Hammond's correspondents, associated with hope. These are powerful and moving stories, of people listening to opera without prejudice and taking comfort from it. There was evidently no sense, at this time, of opera being the preserve of an elite. People from all backgrounds continued to encounter opera during the war, whether on the home front or posted overseas, even as the world had changed—and in some cases fallen apart—around them.

Interwar debates about who was or wasn't a musical highbrow largely fell by the wayside during the war. Discussions about who went to Covent Garden were irrelevant, since Covent Garden was closed; so too was Glyndebourne, now being used as an evacuation centre.[4] With the cliché of the aristocratic opera-goer in furs and jewels receding from view, some of the negativity surrounding the art form that had set in during the 1930s abated. By the end of the war, opera had become extremely popular in Britain, and once it was over people began to talk tentatively of ambitions for a whole new cultural landscape, with opera for all at its heart. Might opera even finally be accepted as a form of truly 'British' culture?

Opera in London and the regions

One can almost hear the sigh with which *The Daily Mail*'s Corrie Knox remarked in April 1940, 'I wish dreary people would not waste stamps, and my patience, writing to tell me that all entertainment must stop because "we are living in the shadow of death".[5] But if a few disapproving, puritanical

[3] Ibid., p. 244.
[4] Jolliffe, *Glyndebourne*, p. 39.
[5] Corrie Knox, 'Show Time', *DM* (4 April 1940), 10.

74   SOMEONE ELSE'S MUSIC

types felt that the arts should be put on hold during the war, for the most part the nation craved the distraction of wartime entertainments both 'high' and 'low'.

At the onset of war, the government, expecting widespread bombardment of London, declared that places of entertainment where large groups of people gathered must close. It was a decision that caused anger in the theatrical community. In letters to *The Times*, theatre manager Oswald Stoll argued that 'entertainment is necessary to the morale of the people . . . it is not logical to close theatres and cinemas and to open churches to crowds', while George Bernard Shaw called the closure of theatres and cinemas 'a masterstroke of unimaginative stupidity. During the last war we had 80,000 soldiers on leave to amuse every night'.[6] As months passed without air-raids, theatres began to reopen, at least for matinées, and most had resumed operations by Christmas 1939. Theatrical performances came to be an important form of escapism in the spring and early summer of 1940, both for those on the home front and for soldiers on leave. But with the coming of the Blitz, all theatrical performances in London were halted once more.

Covent Garden became a commercial dance hall with a rotating bandstand—'doing its bit', as Desmond Shawe-Taylor put it, 'like an elderly *prima donna* who obliges at a NAAFI concert with a spirited performance of "Tipperary"'.[7] It would not reopen for opera until 1946. Sadler's Wells, meanwhile, was turned into a refuge for the newly homeless—250 people, who slept on mattresses in the stalls and bars, or on the stage.[8] The Vic-Wells company relocated its headquarters to the Victoria Theatre in Burnley and from there embarked on a series of extensive national tours, run by the soprano Joan Cross. From 1943, these were organised in collaboration with CEMA (Council for the Encouragement of the Arts), the forerunner to the Arts Council of Great Britain, which had been established in 1940. Towns and cities clamoured for the company to visit: the manager of the Hull New Theatre reported receiving letters daily from patrons who were keen to see the troupe.[9]

[6] Andy Merriman, *Greasepaint and Cordite: The Story of ENSA and Concert Party Entertainment During the Second World War* (London: Aurum, 2013), p. 11.

[7] Desmond Shawe-Taylor, *Covent Garden* (London: Max Parrish, 1948), p. 69; Anon., 'Back to Opera at Covent Garden', Unattributed press clipping, 22 April 1944, BUTC, Covent Garden box 1939–1946 MM/2/TH/LO/COV/64-69.

[8] Joan Cross, 'An Experiment in Opera', in Tyrone Guthrie, Edwin Evans, Joan Cross, Edward J. Dent, and Ninette de Valois, *Opera in English* (London: John Lane the Bodley Head, 1945), pp. 18–24, p. 18.

[9] Anon., 'Opera Scheme for Hull', *Hull Daily Mail* (2 March 1940), 1.

Figure 4.1 Public queuing at Sadler's Wells to see *Faust*, 1939. Reproduced with permission from © Chronicle/Alamy.

The company had to work with limited resources, giving heavily cut-down performances with piano accompaniment, reduced casts, and a skeleton staging. Tours were made arduous by heavy snowfall, gruelling rail travel,

76 SOMEONE ELSE'S MUSIC

struggles to find digs, and bombing raids.[10] But despite these difficulties, the company of fifty adapted, performing the nine operas in its repertoire to the best of its ability.[11] Some theatres baulked at booking an opera company, considering it 'box-office poison', but the company defied expectations and audiences were enthusiastic from the off.[12]

From time to time Sadler's Wells ventured back to London, usually performing at the New Theatre in St Martin's Lane. In 1944, the company was playing at the Haymarket Theatre when performances were disrupted—although not terminated—by bombing. The soprano Elisabeth Parry, who was in the audience for *Madam Butterfly* and *La bohème*, recalled: 'Bells would ring loudly in the auditorium every time a doodlebug came in our direction. Anyone was at liberty to get up and go, but no one moved and the singers and orchestra carried on as if nothing was happening, even when a doodle engine cut out overhead to be followed by a bang that shook the theatre.'[13]

The fact that 'ordinary people' were treating opera as a form of entertainment just like any other is captured in testimonials gathered as part of Mass Observation. Respondents reported going to see Sadler's Wells one night and *Gone with the Wind* or *The Life and Death of Colonel Blimp* the next, or wrote of knowing opera-going bus conductresses or customers who were 'definitely not . . . highbrow'.[14] Joan Hammond, on tour with the Carl Rosa, recalled an occasion when a woman had come to the box office, asked what was on, and gone away with two tickets despite not even knowing what an opera was.[15] Of course, many of those who had encountered opera via these scaled-down tours had no understanding of what opera could be like when realised in full, but the enterprise had certainly stimulated an appetite to learn more.

New audiences

There was much talk in the war of a large potential audience for opera, though nobody knew how large it really was. The serious newspapers were in broad

---

[10] Cross, 'An Experiment in Opera', p. 20.
[11] Stapleton, *The Sadler's Wells Opera*, p. 10.
[12] Guthrie, *A Life in the Theatre*, p. 200, p. 233.
[13] Elisabeth Parry, *Thirty Men and a Girl: A Singer's Memories of War, Mountains, Travel, and Always Music* (Guildford: Allegra, 2010), p. 216.
[14] Diarist-5221_125/126; Diarist-5331_261.
[15] Hammond, *A Voice, a Life*, p. 127.

agreement that Britain had pursued a fundamentally wrong course when it came to opera. Establishing permanent companies in major cities around the country, along the lines of Sadler's Wells, could have created the thriving operatic culture for which there was genuine demand. Instead, the baronets and bankers who might have been able to provide the necessary funds had, as *The Times* put it, 'thrown their money down the *cloaca maxima* of Covent Garden'—a striking image, for the cloaca maxima was the biggest sewer in Ancient Rome.[16]

The unusual circumstances of the war had revealed a taste for opera in unexpected quarters, and there was a widespread sense that the nation was becoming more cultured. *The Observer* reported that 'opera, ballet, and the great orchestras were never busier or more popular', while *The Daily Mail* told stories of tram drivers delighting in Tchaikovsky and waitresses revelling in Wagner.[17] Perhaps only serious art had the power to be cathartic. As *The Daily Mail* continued: 'People really engrossed with tragedies find flippant entertainment, bright lights, and cart-wheeling legs out-of-key with their mood so that they grate, merely enhancing their own discomfort or unhappiness.'[18] Countless people now realised that things they had previously assumed to be too highbrow for them were actually within their intellectual grasp.

CEMA was an exercise in state patronage—designed to support the arts whose more traditional forms of patronage were on the decline—and opera was at the heart of the project. It had emerged out of conversations between Dr Thomas Jones, secretary of the Pilgrim Trust—a charity set up in 1930 by the American philanthropist Edward Harkness that had funded a prewar programme of travelling exhibitions called 'Art for the People'—and two peers, Lord Macmillan (Minister of Information) and Lord De La Warr (President of the Board of Education). All were keen to avoid a 'black-out of culture' during the war.[19] The Pilgrim Trust put up initial funding, with the government taking over from 1940. John Maynard Keynes, chairman from 1942 to 1946, lobbied contacts in the Treasury and managed to raise nearly a quarter of a million pounds of state aid for the arts by the end of the war.[20]

---

[16] Anon., 'Real Opera-Goers: Bus Men and Bank Clerks', *The Times* (22 June 1940), 4.

[17] Anon., 'Comment', *The Observer* (31 December 1944), 4; Guy Ramsey, 'Big Money in Good Music', *DM* (20 April 1943), 2.

[18] Ramsey, 'Big Money', 2.

[19] Andrew Sinclair, *The Need to Give: The Patrons and the Arts* (London: Sinclair-Stevenson, 1990), p. 121.

[20] Beaven, *Leisure, Citizenship and Working-Class Men in Britain*, pp. 224–225; Sinclair, *The Need to Give*, p. 122.

78 SOMEONE ELSE'S MUSIC

CEMA was conceived as a more upmarket alternative to its competitor ENSA (Entertainments National Service Association), which put on entertainment for troops and factory workers but toured to similar venues and played to similar audiences. (Some operatic music eventually crept into ENSA programmes too, when the association fell under the direction of record producer Walter Legge.[21]) CEMA organised concerts in air-raid shelters, hostels, hospitals, and military bases—some 1,476 in 1942–1943, to audiences of between 20 and 1,000 people. Furthermore, it put on 4,543 concerts in factories, repeating them for workers on night shifts.[22]

Joan Hammond was engaged to perform at a series of troop concerts: smoky, noisy affairs in front of restless audiences at Chelsea Barracks and Croydon Air Force Base. Though she was advised by her agent to learn popular songs because 'no one will want to listen to operatic arias or serious songs until the war is over', she persisted and received a warm response.[23] Victoria Sladen, an aspiring opera singer who had performed in seaside concert parties, revues, and pantomime, also used to sneak arias into her CEMA concerts.[24] And *The Daily Mail* reported that concerts by opera singers were 'proving "big hits" at armament works'.[25]

In taking art to new audiences and encouraging them to seek out more, CEMA was the polar opposite of elitist, though some might regard it as patronising nowadays in its 'civilising' slogan 'The Best for the Most'. Historians have tried to claim that initiatives such as CEMA failed to 'impart high culture to the masses'.[26] But there is plentiful evidence to counter, for example, Jörg Weingärtner's claim that 'two of the three art forms which CEMA propagated, straight drama and classical music including opera, were forms of entertainment of the higher strata of society, from which the working and lower middle classes were excluded'.[27] Such audiences had not been excluded from opera in the interwar period, and they embraced it with even greater enthusiasm during the war.

[21] Merriman, *Greasepaint and Cordite*, pp. 140–145.
[22] Anon., *The Arts in War Time: A Report on the Work of C.E.M.A 1942 and 1943* (London: Council for the Encouragement of Music and the Arts, 1944), p. 11.
[23] Hammond, *A Voice, A Life*, p. 98.
[24] Victoria Sladen, *Singing My Way* (London: Rockliff, 1951), p. 52.
[25] Daily Mail Reporter, 'Workers go Classical', *DM* (18 March 1940), 5.
[26] For instance, Beaven, *Leisure, Citizenship and Working-Class Men in Britain*, p. 226.
[27] Jörg Weingärtner, *The Arts as a Weapon of War: Britain and the Shaping of National Morale in the Second World War* (London: Tauris, 2006), p. 8.

Operatic encounters abroad

Many servicemen experienced live opera for the first time when stationed abroad. Such performances were sometimes scrappy, but they piqued soldiers' curiosity. The record reviewer Martyn Goff reminisced in the 1950s about a performance of *Rigoletto* he had heard in Algiers, in which the quartet was reduced to 'a "Goon Show" level'; George Lascelles, the future Earl of Harewood, attended a chaotically staged performance of *Werther* in the same city.[28] Just after VE Day, Ted Heath was leading a battery charged with rebuilding an opera house at Herrenhausen, near Hanover, and he and his troops soon had the opportunity to hear performances on the reconstructed stage.[29]

The soprano Elisabeth Parry was recruited as a soloist with an ENSA musical group under the auspices of the Royal Army Medical Corps, put together to entertain the troops in Paiforce (the Persia and Iraq force). The troupe undertook a circuit from Baghdad to Cairo in 1943–1944, giving troop shows and recording concerts for broadcast around the region, with Parry a lone woman in a crowd of men. Though some of the concerts were of light music, there were also regular classical concerts, at which Parry sang arias from *Rigoletto*, *Tosca*, and *Faust*.[30] Walter Widdop, Dennis Noble, and Miriam Licette, some of the major British opera stars of the day, were on tour elsewhere in the region. Opera recordings also offered comfort to the troops. The writer Jimmy Robertson, a contributor to *Gramophone* magazine, would be killed in active service in 1941, but wrote before his death of finding a small band of gramophone enthusiasts on all four ships on which he had served, and of the way in which a shared interest in classical music served as a way of binding people together.[31]

It was in Italy, however, that the largest number of service personnel first encountered opera, with *The Daily Express* reporting in 1944 that 'one of the biggest surprises of our "invasion" of Italy has been the way the men have become opera fans'.[32] It all started with a group of enterprising army officers who came up with the idea of reforming the company at the bomb-damaged

---

[28] Martyn Goff, *A Short Guide to Long Play* (London: Museum Press, Ltd, 1957), pp. 119–120; Harewood, *The Tongs and the Bones*, p. 39.

[29] Heath, *Music: A Joy for Life*, pp. 74–75.

[30] Parry, *Thirty Men and a Girl*, pp. 37–98.

[31] Naomi Jacob and James C. Robertson, *Opera in Italy* (London: Hutchinson, 1948), p. 101.

[32] Sunday Express Correspondent, Rome, 'Men from the "Eighth" Are Opera Fans Now', *The Sunday Express* (3 December 1944), 5.

80   SOMEONE ELSE'S MUSIC

Teatro Bellini in Catania, Sicily, for the benefit of Allied troops in the Central Mediterranean Forces. The building was patched up; stage machinery and lighting were put back into service. There was a shortage of scenery, costumes, props, scores, and indeed sopranos, so a collaborative arrangement was made with the Teatro Massimo in American-controlled Palermo, and resources and performers shuttled by US troop-carrier planes between the two. Ticket sales for the Bellini's inaugural production of *La bohème* rose from 140 to 1,280 per night across a single week, with full houses thereafter.[33] The British and American troops subsequently took over the Teatro San Carlo in Naples and ran it on similar lines, with ten performances a week at 'cinema prices'.[34] In due course, as the Allies moved north, similar companies were established in other Italian cities, including Bari, Rome, Florence, Padua, Venice, and Trieste, and performances were broadcast on the radio.[35] By the end of the war, over four million British service personnel were estimated to have seen opera performances and Spike Hughes reported that 'in every town the same thing happened: the British soldier took to grand opera as if it were in his blood'.[36]

Naomi Jacob, a Ripon-born author, actress, and broadcaster, distinctive for her masculine attire, cropped hair, and monocle, had moved to Italy before the war.[37] She was a keen opera enthusiast who had first encountered it via touring company performances. Recalling performances at the San Carlo, she wrote that soldiers began to flock in ever-growing numbers once they had realised that operas were not 'some strange kind of "highbrow" entertainment' but 'fine, full-blooded dramas' with music that was suitable for whistling in the bath.[38] The men were punctual, read their programmes assiduously, and gave performances their rapt attention.

In 1948 Jacob wrote a book about opera aimed explicitly at the men and women who had encountered it in Italy. She dismissed the idea that opera was for an elite, writing:

---

[33] Spike Hughes, 'Operation Opera on Tonight', *DE* (4 September 1946), n.p.

[34] H. G. Sear, 'Operation Opera', *Daily Worker* (6 September 1946), n.p.; Anon., 'Neapolitan Nights', *Manchester Guardian* (23 August 1946), n.p.

[35] Jacob and Robertson, *Opera in Italy*, p. 233, p. 132.

[36] Anon., 'The C.M.F. San Carlo Opera Company's Début at Covent Garden', *ILN* (14 September 1946), n.p.; Hughes, 'Operation Opera On Tonight', 2.

[37] Merriman, *Greasepaint and Cordite*, p. 130.

[38] Jacob and Robertson, *Opera in Italy*, p. 39.

OPERA GOES TO WAR 81

For years many people insisted that opera was a kind of entertainment for "highbrows" and exclusive intellectuals. The war proved that it was the kind of entertainment which was appreciated universally by all types and all classes. There had always been a kind of implication that opera was "difficult to understand", that to listen to it necessitated a special kind of musical training. What rubbish![39]

In the introduction to Jacob's book, W. J. Smith, later Director of Music at Alleyn's School in Dulwich, argued that the war had been pivotal in changing British attitudes towards opera and building a genuine audience for it. Although the touring companies and the Vic-Wells companies had done valiant work during the interwar period, even they had not been able to create an opera-loving public on any scale—opera, Smith wrote, 'remained a foreign and exotic taste rather like the food one used to eat in Soho'.[40] By 1948, however, he was able to report that 'today this is changed, and is changing still further' thanks to two factors: the Sadler's Wells tours and the troop performances in Italy.[41]

Post-war opera

The rupture of the war created a desire for radical reform. A whole new operatic landscape needed to be created and an audience for it fostered, building on the gains made during the war. The need for subsidy now seemed inevitable: a 1946 Gallup Poll found that 52 per cent of the population supported it, versus 27 per cent against.[42] CEMA was relaunched as the Arts Council of Great Britain, with a remit of 'developing a greater knowledge, understanding and practice of the fine arts exclusively, and in particular to increase the accessibility of the fine arts to the public'.[43] John Maynard Keynes stated in 1945: 'At last the public exchequer has recognised the support and encouragement of the civilising arts of life as a part of their duty'.[44]

The Arts Council supported professionals, favoured the large national companies, and, although not exclusively metropolitan, had a certain bias

[39] Ibid., p. 16.
[40] W. J. Smith, introduction to ibid., p. 11.
[41] Ibid., pp. 11–12.
[42] Rose, *The Intellectual Life*, p. 204.
[43] Tom Sutcliffe, 'Subsidising the Arts', *The Spectator*, 247/7992 (12 September 1981), 12–14, 12.
[44] Arts Council of Great Britain, *First Annual Report*, 20–21.

82 SOMEONE ELSE'S MUSIC

towards London—factors that would later lead some to describe it as elitist.[45] Keynes declared a certain missionary zeal to carry the arts throughout the land but never neglected the importance of London itself, stating that 'it is . . . our business to make London a great artistic metropolis, a place to visit and to wonder at'.[46] Covent Garden would be the jewel in the crown: now was the time for Britain to have a permanent opera. It was only Arts Council funding that could make this possible.

Retrospectively, this was characterised as paternalistic and unpalatable. John Pick wrote in 1980 that in favouring the activities of CEMA over those of ENSA, the government chose to support 'a high-minded, highly selective notion of the arts', while Raymond Carr wrote in 2000, 'A product of Bloomsbury, [Keynes] was an elitist'.[47] Keynes spoke explicitly about civilisation and cultivation: terms that make people nervous now. Yet is there anything actually elitist about these ideals? Certainly, there is plentiful evidence that CEMA and the early Arts Council genuinely reached people of varied backgrounds, and that such people felt enthused rather than patronised. By the end of 1948 it was reported that there had been a marked increase in those attending the opera.[48]

Although the Arts Council was not the invention of any one political party, the left was particularly idealistic about introducing people from all backgrounds to 'high culture'.[49] This was an attitude that would be important in fostering a wider engagement with opera during the early and mid-twentieth centuries, though it was a position from which the left would later substantially retreat. J. B. Priestley observed in 1947 that for more than half a century, the various Socialist and Labour parties had been claiming to represent artists and to promote the arts in the community; now, with the first majority Labour government, their moment had come to make good on these pledges.[50] The arrival of the Arts Council was broadly accepted across the political spectrum, though there were pockets of resistance, one Conservative MP arguing that the money should be spent on cooking fats instead.[51]

---

[45] Patricia Hollis, *Jennie Lee: A Life* (Oxford: Oxford University Press, 1997), p. 249.

[46] John Tooley, *In House: Covent Garden. 50 Years of Opera and Ballet* (London: Faber and Faber, 1999), p. 206; Arts Council of Great Britain, *First Annual Report*, 23.

[47] John Pick (ed.), *The State and the Arts* (London: City University, Centre for the Arts, 1980), p. 10; Raymond Carr, 'An Ardent Bloomsbury Patriot', *The Spectator* (16 December 2000), 76–78, 77.

[48] Anon., 'Interest in the Arts Growing', *The Morning Advertiser* (24 November 1948), n.p.

[49] Sir Hugh Willatt, *The Arts Council of Great Britain: The First Twenty-Five Years* (London: Arts Council of Great Britain, 1973), p. 3.

[50] J. B. Priestley, *The Arts under Socialism* (London: Turnstile Press, 1947), p. 25.

[51] Anon., 'Fats Before Music', *Nottingham Guardian* (19 February 1947), n.p.

OPERA GOES TO WAR   83

Eccentric objectors notwithstanding, there was a sense of considerable optimism surrounding opera after the war, both in terms of new ventures and in terms of an expanding audience. In a lecture at the University of Liverpool in 1945, Edward J. Dent, a long-time advocate for popular opera, went so far as to state that 'fifteen years ago I should have felt obliged to defend opera as a form of art but that is no longer necessary'.[52] *The Daily Express* reported that 'the most ridiculous art-form ever invented' was 'proving more popular than anybody ever imagined'; there had been copious operas on the BBC recently and 'the public loves it all'.[53] The servicemen who had acquired a taste for opera in Italy continued to patronise it back at home and people were replacing or at least complementing the 'cinema habit' with 'the opera habit', treating it as a routine pastime.[54] Victor Hely-Hutchinson, the BBC's Director of Music, wrote of 'a corporate appreciation and desire for music of a kind, and on a scale, that has never been seen in Britain before'.[55]

Within a couple of years of the war, London's operatic life was vibrant once more. A report published by a group called PEP (Political and Economic Planning) noted that there was now 'more opera in London than at any other time in this century', and argued that the first foundations of a genuine national opera had been laid.[56] In autumn 1947, audiences in the capital had the opportunity to watch an astonishing twenty-three different operas performed by five companies and at one point could choose between four concurrent productions in London of a single opera, *Rigoletto*.[57] Beyond Sadler's Wells and the resident Covent Garden Company, there were also performances at Covent Garden from the Vienna State Opera and the English Opera Group (which also performed at Sadler's Wells).[58] Italian opera was back at the Stoll Theatre, and the New London Opera Company was giving high-quality performances of an all-Italian repertoire at the Cambridge Theatre.

Opera met pop culture at the Royal Albert Hall, as an audience of 5,000 came to hear American baritone Lawrence Tibbett—star of the Met and

[52] Anon., 'New Attitude to Opera: Professor Dent's Lecture', *The Liverpool Daily Post* (23 October 1945), 3.
[53] Nicholas Hallam, 'Gone! The Plomley Touch', *DE* (31 October 1946), 2.
[54] Anon., 'Towards English Opera', *Beckenham Journal* (22 February 1947), n.p.
[55] Victor Hely-Hutchinson, 'The Rising Tide of Music', *BBC Year Book 1945* (London: British Broadcasting Corporation, 1945), pp. 44–47, p. 44.
[56] Anon., 'The Opera in Britain', *Planning*, 15/290 (8 November 1948), 147–162, 148, 149, 147.
[57] The Earl of Harewood, 'Opera in London', *Tempo*, 6 (Winter 1947–1948), 4–9, 4; J. C. B., 'A Londoner's Retrospect', *Manchester Guardian* (31 December 1947), n.p.
[58] Anon., 'The English Opera Group', *VWA*, 22 (July 1948), 3–4, 3.

84 SOMEONE ELSE'S MUSIC

musical films such as MGM's *Cuban Love Song*.[59] The Hall also hosted a series of weekly 'Opera Promenade' concerts by the London Symphony Orchestra, in conjunction with the National Music for Youth Movement. Each concert showcased arias and ensembles from three operas, whose plots and music were discussed at length in the programme. The concerts were extremely popular, to the extent that the programmes began to include a postage-paid postcard inviting people to book ahead to avoid disappointment, since previous concerts had sold out well in advance.[60]

There was also an appetite for more opera beyond London and a particularly notable development was the establishment of Welsh National Opera. Initially an amateur group, it was the brainchild of John Morgan, a former Carl Rosa baritone, who with his fiancée Helena Hughes Brown proposed to the Cardiff-based choral conductor Idloes Owen the idea of setting up an opera troupe in 1943. By the spring of 1946, the company was putting on its first performances at the Prince of Wales Theatre, Cardiff. These attracted coachloads of audience members from the Valleys and led to enquiries from prospective singers, among them miners, secretaries, housewives, shop assistants, and nurses. Many only knew sol-fa and could not read music but were recruited to the troupe on the strength of having good voices. All parts were cast from within the company with the exception of the tenor Tudor Davies, who was brought in as a star attraction.[61]

Most of the post-war companies were deeply concerned with the idea of opera for all. Sadler's Wells, of course, had an established reputation in this respect and continued to assert its status as the leading provider of opera for the people on returning to its Islington base. In 1947 its company magazine boasted: 'Sadler's Wells is not a commercial theatre. It exists for the benefit of the people, for whom it was designed, and depends upon their support for its development. The question of price is one of the greatest importance to Opera and Ballet lovers. SADLER'S WELLS PROVIDES THE ANSWER. Prices of the seats range from 1/- to 9/-.'[62] The company continued to posit itself as a cooperative enterprise, petitioning audiences on the works they wanted to see.[63]

---

[59] Roy Johnson, 'Tibbett Delights 5,000 Fans', *DE* (10 June 1947), 3.
[60] Programmes, March 1948–December 1949, RAH archive.
[61] Richard Fawkes, *Welsh National Opera* (London: Julia MacRae, 1986), pp. 1, 4, 8, 11.
[62] Anon., 'Sadler's Wells is the People's Theatre', *VWA*, 10 (April 1947), 4.
[63] Anon., 'Last Night of Opera Season', *VWA*, 32 (June 1949), n.p.

OPERA GOES TO WAR 85

The company relaunched itself for the post-war age by staging the *première* of Britten's *Peter Grimes*. This certainly galvanised interest, with tickets selling out in three days. The choice of opera was a deeply symbolic gesture, both on account of its newness and its nationality. Sadler's Wells had always performed in English, of course, but allying itself with the composer who epitomised the much-desired flowering of British opera was part of a strategy to change the image of opera in the United Kingdom. Tyrone Guthrie welcomed the fact that the opera would give British singers an opportunity to express themselves 'in a natural and authentic way' at long last, after so many years spent performing in 'tepid translations of torrid Mediterranean art'. Later, in 1948, opera writer Stephen Williams would reflect that *Peter Grimes* had been born not merely with a silver spoon in its mouth but with 'a whole canteen of cutlery', as an opera on an English subject by an English composer, which appeared at the most opportune of moments, when there was post-war euphoria and an emerging new audience for opera.[64] Its success in drawing the crowds—as a piece of modern music, at a time when modern art generated controversy—was a truly astonishing phenomenon, and it showed what a 'democratic' sort of opera could look like.

The English Opera Group was founded by Britten, John Piper, and Eric Crozier after the war in order to perform the former's operas. Its launch pamphlet stated that the Group believed the best way to create an English repertory was through the encouragement of young composers, poets, and playwrights and by commissioning works requiring small performing resources.[65] The company made its debut at Glyndebourne in June 1947, reviving *The Rape of Lucretia* and giving the *première* of *Albert Herring*. Unfortunately, the relationship between Britten and Christie soon became a strained one, culminating in what Christie's son called a 'total estrangement on each side—sad but inevitable' given their contrasting personalities.[66]

The Britten performances, together with a few short summer seasons—of which Kathleen Ferrier in Gluck's *Orfeo* in 1947 was a highlight—and one-off concerts, represented the sum total of activity at Glyndebourne during the late 1940s.[67] An angry disagreement with Thomas Beecham about casting and other aesthetic matters scuppered a collaboration that was planned for

---

[64] Stephen Williams, *Come to the Opera!* (London: Hutchinson and Co., 1948), p. 34.
[65] Cited in Stephen Williams, 'Future of British Opera', *The Stage* (17 April 1947), n.p.
[66] George Christie, *A Slim Volume. Glyndebourne: An Anecdotal Account* (Lewes: Glyndebourne Productions, 2016), p. 17.
[67] Blunt, *John Christie of Glyndebourne*, p. 258.

86   SOMEONE ELSE'S MUSIC

a grand reopening in 1946.[68] The post-war economic situation meant that Christie could not afford to finance the festival, and it would not resume on pre-war lines until the early 1950s, when alternative funding models were found. He busied himself instead with founding the Children's Theatre at Toynbee Hall and subsequently establishing the Edinburgh Festival—an initiative that had opera at its heart and aimed to promote understanding between nations.

The New London Opera Company, the brainchild of the Russian impresario Jay Pomeroy, was an interesting phenomenon, setting itself up in 1946 in competition with both Sadler's Wells in terms of target audience and Covent Garden in terms of artistic ambition. Italian repertory was a speciality, with performances in the original language, as the company sought to cater to the generation that had discovered opera in wartime Italy, and even to cast them. (The brothers William and Murray Dickie, an ex-lieutenant colonel and ex-naval rating, took on the roles of Figaro and Almaviva in *The Barber of Seville.*) The company advertised itself as a non-profit-making organisation that aimed to raise the standard of British opera production and train British singers, giving them the chance to sing alongside international performers. Most important was its aim to bring 'the *real thing* within reach of young working people'.[69]

The Daily Express lauded the company for achieving what would previously have been thought impossible: performing opera in Italian to full houses without a tiara in sight, and attracting an audience that included 'scores of saleswomen from the West End shops, who come in reduced-rate parties'.[70] This was part of a larger trend for opera trips, including to Covent Garden, for factory, civil-service and local-government staff. In most cases, the employee organising them was an ex-serviceman.[71]

Unfortunately, the company foundered in 1948 as a result of Pomeroy's personal financial difficulties, which predated the founding of the opera company. He had made his money in black-market whisky, exploiting a tax loophole that had been legal at the time. But after the government closed it in 1943, retrospective punitive measures were applied and Pomeroy was left with financial liabilities of £400,000, eventually being declared bankrupt.[72]

---

[68] Ibid., pp. 244–253.

[69] Anon., 'Opera for All' (unattributed press cutting, 1947, ROH archive); original emphasis.

[70] Roy Johnson, 'The Menuhins Pull in £5,000', *DE* (1 April 1947), 3.

[71] Anon., 'London Operas' £10,000 A Week', *DT* (19 January 1948).

[72] Ian Wallace, 'Two Years of Glory', *Opera*, 47/12 (December 1996), 1420–1426, 1420.

OPERA GOES TO WAR   87

The collapse of the company was nothing to do with a lack of interest in opera; indeed, it had, for two years, posed a direct threat to Sadler's Wells in attracting the same sort of committed, non-pretentious audience. What is more surprising is that Covent Garden was also beginning to lure away listeners who would naturally have patronised Sadler's Wells.

Covent Garden for all

Covent Garden reopened in September 1946 with a season by the San Carlo Opera Company from Naples: a symbolic occasion indeed, since this was the company that had entertained so many British troops during the war.[73] Proceeds from the first performance went to the Soldiers', Sailors' and Air Force Families Association, and in the audience were many service personnel, such as ex-Desert Rats Alf Bates and John Western, of Canning Town, a lorry driver, and a builders' labourer.[74] Demob suits and khaki uniforms mingled among the tail coats; medals sparkled among the jewels.

Thereafter, it was time to launch the theatre's new, permanent company, with a production of Purcell's *The Fairy Queen* in December 1946, which Dent called 'an appropriate symbol of the new enterprise: a proclamation of our faith in the greatest of English musicians'.[75] For the first time, Covent Garden was to become a year-round home for opera and ballet: the ballet transferred from Sadler's Wells, but for opera, an entirely new company would be formed. It was announced that singers and music staff would be, with extremely few exceptions, British, though the appointment of an Austrian, Karl Rankl, as music director, prompted some discontent.[76] Operas were henceforth to be performed in the vernacular, a policy document stating: 'The Trust believes that the development of opera in England, and indeed the formation of a style of performance, depends to a large extent on the use of English.'[77]

---

[73] Anon., 'The C.M.F. San Carlo Opera Company's Début at Covent Garden', *ILN* (14 September 1946), n.p.

[74] Anon., 'The Army's Opera', *The Tatler* (25 September 1946), 399; Anon., 'Desert Rats Go Again to the Opera', *The Daily Herald* (6 September 1946), n.p.

[75] Royal Opera House, *A Review 1946–1956*, p. 5, p. 8.

[76] Anon., 'Royal Opera House, Covent Garden. Statement of Policy', BUTC, MM/REF/TH/LO/COV/66, Covent Garden, the Royal Opera, April 1940–c.1945, p. 10.

[77] Ibid., p. 13.

88 SOMEONE ELSE'S MUSIC

At the helm of the new company was David Webster, formerly the manager of the Liverpool Bon Marché department store and General Manager of the Liverpool Philharmonic. Webster had demonstrated an imaginative flair for the artistic in his retail work, laying on in-store fashion shows, arranging art exhibitions, and inviting Edith Sitwell to perform *Façade* wearing leopard skin and gold tissue.[78] Webster was a mass of contradictions: a socialist who argued that the theatre should be 'popular, not just aristocratic', yet drank champagne throughout the interval and had his own table at the Savoy Grill.[79]

The company now ran on repertory lines, with singers hired for forty-two weeks of the year on an exclusive basis.[80] The idea was to foster a genuine team effort and to raise standards of musical ensemble in the process. Vocal standards among the newly formed British troupe were, however, generally agreed to be insufficiently high, since many early recruits had little experience beyond singing oratorio.[81] Audiences responded frostily, and this led to back-tracking on the policy of all-British casting with almost immediate effect.[82]

The assumption was that guest artists would usually sing in English, but soon enough the dreaded polyglot performances began to return. Often it was a case of a cover artist stepping in for an ailing colleague with no time to relearn the words, but sometimes star singers simply refused to sing in English, such as when Boris Christoff sang *Boris Godunov* in 1949.[83] Singers would even, inexplicably, shift languages mid-performance.[84] Polyglot performances were reviled, but opera in English was also not uniformly popular: some audience members refused to book English-language performances and ticket sales rose whenever a foreign star was on the bill.[85] *The Observer*'s correspondent characterised this as arrant pretentiousness, writing, 'This snobbish finding of virtue in incomprehensible words is peculiar to our country; most foreign opera companies sing in their own tongues. Is there in London a body of middle-aged opera-goers who once made the

---

[78] Montague Haltrecht, *The Quiet Showman: Sir David Webster and the Royal Opera House* (London: Collins, 1975), p. 34, p. 48.

[79] Ibid., pp. 17–18, p. 21.

[80] Royal Opera House, *A Review 1946–1956*, p. 7.

[81] Tooley, *In House*, p. 9.

[82] Barnes, 'Everything in the Garden', 349.

[83] Arthur Jacobs, 'So Please Sing It in English', *DE* (21 November 1949), 3.

[84] 'Figaro', 'Opera in English', letter to *The Observer* (9 October 1949), 5.

[85] Anon., 'Opera Policy Defended', *The Times* (7 January 1949), 2.

OPERA GOES TO WAR 89

grand tour of Europe and want to dream that they are in Vienna or Dresden again?'[86]

For all these teething troubles, the initial steps were felt to have been achieved in the Covent Garden Opera Trust's ambitious programme of plans for 'the establishment of opera in England on a secure and lasting basis; not as an exotic luxury, imported from time to time for the benefit of a fortunate minority; but as a normal amenity of civilized life, a school in which all who wish to do so may learn discrimination'.[87] All seats were now available to book rather than reserved for subscribers, and ticket prices were reduced to just above the average West End price for the best seats and as little as 2s. for the cheapest.[88] People came in huge numbers, queuing for several days with deckchairs, rugs, and thick coats. The detachment of opera at Covent Garden from the aristocratic 'Season' was in some respects a vital turning point in transforming British attitudes towards opera—at least temporarily.

It was announced in 1948 that Covent Garden would become state-owned, as the government served notice on the current lessees, the music publishers Boosey and Hawkes, at the end of their five-year lease the following year. The Ministry of Works' purchase of the theatre would not mean any governmental involvement in the running of the House; it was, however, a guarantee against its being turned into a cinema or dance hall.[89] Prices would be kept low to attract a wide public, and according to Sir Ernest Pooley, the Arts Council's chairman, the new state opera and ballet house would be 'no snob show'.[90]

In contemporary press reports, both general and specialised, one senses a genuine enthusiasm for the nation to get behind opera as an enterprise that could finally become truly British. There was employment to be gained from such an enterprise: for British composers, who usually presumed there was little point writing operas; for large numbers of chorus and orchestra members; for backstage and technical staff; and of course for aspiring principals. Given that it had long been the case that British singers stood almost no chance of being hired for leading roles at Covent Garden, it was a

---

[86] Anon., 'Comment', *The Observer* (19 October 1947), 4.

[87] Anon., 'Opera at Covent Garden', *Tempo*, 4 (Summer 1947), 19–21, 19.

[88] A Special Correspondent, 'Building a New British Opera at Covent Garden', *The Observer* (13 January 1946), 7; David L. Webster, 'The Reopening of Covent Garden', *VWA*, 1 (March 1946), 1–3, 3.

[89] Anon., 'State to Buy Covent Garden Opera House', *The Western Mail* (26 July 1948), n.p.

[90] Anon., 'State Opera House "Will Be No Snob Show"', *DMir* (26 July 1948), n.p.

90 SOMEONE ELSE'S MUSIC

truly ground-breaking moment when the post-war company started actively talent scouting.

Some commentators were sceptical, remarking on the comparatively poor training available in Britain, and pondering whether a singer named Agnes Bottle would have to call herself Lucrezia Remigiani or Magda Stoffelheim.[91] But in the summer of 1946, Rankl and his staff really did tour Britain holding auditions, and singers were indeed allowed to perform under their own names. Four thousand auditioned and those signed up, whether as principals or chorus members, came from all walks of life. Some were former members of the Carl Rosa and Sadler's Wells or employed in music in some other capacity; others came from entirely unrelated backgrounds. Servicemen turned up in considerable numbers, as did Welsh miners.[92]

The re-envisioning of Covent Garden as an 'English' institution and with it its sudden transformation as no longer 'elite' reveals something telling about British perceptions of opera that is relevant for our entire century. In times and in contexts when opera is presented as and perceived to be 'international', it has been perceived as grand, snobbish, elite, and latterly 'elitist'. In contexts where it has been presented in English, with all-British casts, it has often been viewed more kindly. We shall see repeatedly that the opera/ elitism stereotype is bound up with a nationalistically driven suspicion of the foreign and the cosmopolitan.

Shaping tastes

After the war, opera no longer seemed stuffy and remote, but there was an awareness that active steps would have to be taken to maintain the momentum of the war years in terms of participation in cultural activities. The Musicians' Union published a report appealing for the provision of music to be seen as a vital 'social service' alongside education, health, and public libraries.[93] In the welfare-state era, art came to be considered as something essential to day-to-day life. As J. B. Priestley argued in an address to the

---

[91] Ernest Newman, 'Towards English Opera', ST (9 February 1947); Beachcomber, 'By the Way', DE (5 September 1944), 2.

[92] Anon., 'Miner Will Sing at Covent Garden', DMir (20 August 1946), n.p.

[93] Music Development Committee of the Musicians' Union, 'Music and the Borough Councillor', London, April 1947, 4; 13.

Fabian Society, 'art is not really like the icing on the cake, it is far more like the yeast in the dough'.[94]

The audience for the arts started to grow as a result of changes in Britain's educational system; notably, the 1944 Education Act provided free education for all, raised the school leaving age to 15 and expanded higher and adult education. Its vision drew upon the interwar theories of William Henry Hadow, Vice-Chancellor of Sheffield University and a musicologist, who recommended that schools lay the foundation for a lifelong love of and interest in the arts, while the McNair Report of 1944 placed a strong emphasis upon the teaching of music appreciation as a way of creating 'healthy tastes'.[95] These ideals were promoted particularly strongly in grammar schools, which opened the cultural horizons of many whose families were neither privileged nor highly cultured.

Furthermore, the ethos of autodidacticism was still flourishing at this time. Priestley observed that when people were introduced to the arts, many would 'discover a new source of interest and enjoyment, in a rather mild fashion', but a few would find a particular art form to be a 'revelation'. They might be 'quite rough chaps' or 'mousy little women'—people one ran into at exhibitions, concerts, theatres, or in bookshops who 'talk with enthusiasm and discrimination of work that you would have thought much too difficult for them'.[96] The very capriciousness of it—the fact that the real aficionados were often the least likely seeming people—was the reason why 'people in general should have an opportunity to experience good art, however original and difficult it may seem to be. The more people have this chance, the more of these new understanders and appreciators we shall discover'.

There was still demand for introductory guides to opera. In a 1947 survey about reading habits, a female clerk aged 22 wrote enthusiastically about buying Pelican books, singling out as an example Edward J. Dent's book *Opera*.[97] A male respondent wrote that volumes on art, opera, town-planning, and history were books 'I feel should be in my library', though he admitted he just dipped in.[98] Whether or not respondents were new to opera

---

[94] Priestley, *The Arts under Socialism*, pp. 7–8.

[95] Kate Guthrie, *The Art of Appreciation: Music and Middlebrow Culture in Modern Britain* (Oakland: University of California Press, 2021), pp. 114–115, 119

[96] Priestley, *The Arts under Socialism*, p. 18.

[97] 'Book Buying Habits', report by the Mass Observation Study TopicCollection-20_10191-10203, 31 April 1947, 11.

[98] Mass Observation Study TopicCollection-20_10445.

92   SOMEONE ELSE'S MUSIC

is not made clear, but it is likely, given that the Pelican imprint was published with the autodidact in mind.

Stephen Williams, the author of one such beginners' guide, prefaced his book thus:

> Dear Reader: I imagine you are as one
> Who, loving opera, has of late begun
> To puzzle out the reasons of his love;
> Why some works fall below, some rise above
> The common level; why some pilgrims flee
> From Verdi, who to Wagner bend the knee.
> Perchance in opera houses you have sat,
> And wondered what the devil they were at;
> Perchance your records are in foreign tongues—
> So baffling when exhaled from foreign lungs.
> You listen to my broadcast talks and doubt 'em—
> I know, because you write to me about 'em,
> Demanding, in a general opera 'quiz',
> A guide book on the subject. Here it is.[99]

This poem tells us much about British attitudes towards opera in the 1940s. Opera was regarded as comical, but the humour was affectionate. It continued to be regarded as 'foreign', but people had an appetite not only to find out more about it but to know the things that insiders knew. And as the audience for opera grew, companies were able to become more adventurous, introducing listeners to new, unusual repertory.

The launch of the Third Programme in 1946 was a major development in efforts to improve musical taste. The station consciously set about fostering an audience and promoting excellence for all, as well as harbouring rather grandiose ambitions to be a civilising force across Europe. Whereas broadcasting had hitherto been generalist, with listeners receiving a mixture of light and serious material, the division into three programmes led to greater specialisation. William Haley, Director General of the BBC from 1944, conceived of society, intellectually, as a sort of 'pyramid', with 'a lamentably broad base and a lamentably narrow tip': the three networks would map on

---

[99] Williams, *Come to the Opera!*, p. 12.

to the three levels of the pyramid, through which a listener might, in time, ascend.[100]

Those involved in setting up the Third Programme were determined not to 'dilute' the sometimes challenging material on offer, but this prompted a long-running debate, which has persisted into the Radio 3 era, about how to 'hook' and hold on to new listeners.[101] The Third Programme's founders anticipated that its audience would include both 'habitués' and 'aspirants' but they could be from any background: the Director General of the BBC stated that 'it can be assumed the audience will include the most intelligent receptive people in all classes'.[102] Listeners from humble backgrounds who would attribute their later artistic success, at least in part, to listening to the Third Programme included Peter Hall, Peter Maxwell Davies, and Harold Pinter.[103]

The Third Programme was, unsurprisingly, a 'minority' station, accounting for only 7 per cent of evening listening in 1946, though its class demographic was not entirely predictable. A 1947 study found that 23 per cent of listeners were upper-middle class, 44 per cent lower-middle class, and 33 per cent working class.[104] Potential listeners may have been put off by negative reports that caricatured it as highbrow, as the station that 'plans to give us five hours of opera one evening and four hours of Shaw another', which required a 'new, more earnest listening technique'. *The Daily Mail* even advised readers to display a warning light at the front door to deter visitors, saying 'Silence; Third Programme in Progress'.[105] Suspicious members of the public wrote letters of complaint to newspapers, stating that nobody they knew listened to it and that its only listeners were 'the genuine and the pseudo intellectual'.[106]

The BBC's opera planning committee met in January 1947 and agreed there should be at least one opera per week on the Third Programme.[107] But opera could also be heard on other stations. The Home Programme

[100] Cited in Humphrey Carpenter, *The Envy of the World: Fifty Years of the BBC Third Programme and Radio 3, 1946–1996* (London: Phoenix, 1996), p. 9.

[101] Kate Whitehead, *The Third Programme: A Literary History* (Oxford: Clarendon Press, 1989), p. 1, p. 11.

[102] Ibid., p. 50; Cited in P. H. Newby, 'The Third Programme', Lunch-time lecture, Broadcasting House, 20 October 1965, 3 (available at the British Library).

[103] Carpenter, *The Envy of the World*, pp. 49–50.

[104] Whitehead, *The Third Programme*, p. 54, p. 57.

[105] Cecil Wilson, 'Sh-Sh! The Third Is on the Air', *DM* (30 September 1946), 3.

[106] Carpenter, *The Envy of the World*, p. 72.

[107] 'Findings of the Informal Meeting Held on Thursday January 16th 1947 to Discuss the Future Planning Policy of Opera Broadcasts', BBC WAC R/27/375/4 Music Gen Opera: Policy File 4, 1947.

94 SOMEONE ELSE'S MUSIC

broadcast special operas that could be considered an 'event' (such as performances by foreign companies visiting Covent Garden), short operas, and Sunday operas; there was also a popular 'variety' programme, 'Ring Up the Curtain', which included excerpts of opera.[108] Even the Light Programme featured opera from time to time: in 1946 the management discussed the availability of good continental performances of 'popular operas' that could be recorded for broadcast on the station.[109]

In 1946, opera reached an audience that may strike a present-day reader as very unexpected indeed, at an event that confounds all simplistic notions of opera being elitist. Opera went to Butlin's. After performing at Covent Garden, the San Carlo troupe was engaged to give a concert at the Odeon Cinema in Southend, and then to perform at the popular holiday camps. Unlikely as it may seem, the entire enterprise set up shop at the Filey Butlin's for two weeks, performing *La bohème*, *The Barber of Seville*, and *Cav and Pag* (all in Italian) in the ballroom. Tickets for camp residents and members of local musical societies were free, with a small charge of 5s. for those coming from outside, and buses were laid on from Leeds, Bradford, York, and Huddersfield.[110] Interest was intense, particularly among servicemen who had been stationed in Italy: all tickets for the first night were sold out within an hour of booking opening.[111] The troupe performed to 5,000 listeners in all, before moving on to Skegness.[112]

Billy Butlin, founder of the holiday camp company, embarked upon a deliberate strategy of attracting people back to the camps by putting on entertainment by the comedy stars who had entertained the nation during the war. At the same time, he took conscious steps to change the camps' image by inviting companies such as the San Carlo, Bristol Old Vic, and LSO to perform.[113] Campers reported that they preferred traditional variety shows; nevertheless, Butlin's experiments in introducing audiences to 'highbrow' entertainment were not entirely unsuccessful. The war years, he argued, had proved that 'the appreciation of classical music, ballet and opera is not

---

[108] Ibid.

[109] Memo from Mr T. W. Chalmers to Opera Director, 13.12.46, 'Popular Opera for Light Programme'. BBC WAC R27/375/3 Music Gen Opera: Policy File 3 1944–1946.

[110] Our London Staff, 'Covent Garden Opera for Filey' (unattributed press clipping, ROH archives); Anon., 'Italian Grand Opera for Butlin Theatre', *Lincolnshire Star* (5 October 1946), n.p.

[111] Anon., 'C.M.F. Opera at Filey: Big Draw', *Yorkshire Evening Post* (9 October 1946), n.p.

[112] Sandra Trudgen Dawson, *Holiday Camps in Twentieth-Century Britain* (Manchester: Manchester University Press, 2011), p. 164.

[113] Ibid., p. 162, p. 164.

limited to any one section of the community', and he had first-hand evidence to back up his claim.[114]

Butlin had been involved in organising the Ministry of Labour's wartime 'holidays at home' initiative, which encouraged people to participate in leisure activities in their home town during their annual holiday at a time of severe fuel shortages.[115] Large urban spaces were turned into 'seaside' resorts, with circuses, funfairs, donkeys, and Punch-and-Judy Shows, as well as participatory sports, all making for a bank-holiday atmosphere that extended across the entire summer.[116] However, performances of plays, symphony concerts, ballets, and operas were also part of the scheme, as CEMA and the Pilgrim Trust also got involved. Victoria Park in Hackney, East London, was commandeered in 1943 for a range of entertainments, with *The Times* reporting in August that 'a big crowd listened with obvious pleasure to a first-class rendering of *Il trovatore* by the Royal Carl Rosa Company'.[117]

Insofar as the music critic Desmond Shawe was concerned, the Butlin's venture was the ultimate litmus test for opera in Britain. If a casual holiday crowd at Butlin's on a wet November evening in Skegness could embrace opera, any of the British could, and the only challenge left was to provide plenty of it, not only in London but in places like Blackpool, Huddersfield, or Perth.[118] Figures like Butlin had to be guided by commercial motivations, but there was also an idealistic spirit to the enterprise. It was all based on the premise that Britain had fought to preserve what was 'best' in European civilisation and the ideal of creating 'good citizens' via 'good culture'.[119] Paternalistic? Certainly. But also enjoyable. By the late 1940s, opera really was for everyone.

---

[114] Ibid., p. 164.

[115] Ibid., pp. 138–139.

[116] Chris Sladen, 'Holidays at Home in the Second World War', *Journal of Contemporary History*, 37/1 (January 2002), 67–89.

[117] Jerry White, *The Battle of London, 1939–45: Endurance, Heroism and Frailty Under Fire* (London: The Bodley Head, 2021), p. 208; Sladen, 'Holidays at Home', 83.

[118] Desmond Shawe, 'Opera at the Seaside', *ES* (1 October 1946), 9.

[119] Trudgen Dawson, *Holiday Camps*, pp. 164–166.

5

Pageantry and Participation

It was the night of the century. Glamour had returned to Covent Garden after the long period of post-war austerity. 'Glorious', said the crowd of 5,000 outside the theatre. 'That was the word that summed it all up: Glorious.'[1] They watched agog as a succession of fabulously attired stars and politicians made their way into the theatre. Nehru was there. Norman Hartwell was there. Even Douglas Fairbanks Jr. was there. And then, finally, there *she* was, accompanied by her husband, mother, and sister: Britain's new, young, beautiful Queen, who had been crowned at Westminster Abbey only six days before.

Benjamin Britten, the composer of the moment, in whom so many hopes for Britain's musical future had been invested, had been commissioned to compose a new opera to mark the Coronation (see Figure 5.1). The occasion was a symbolic celebration not only of British artistic achievement but of post-war renewal and prosperity, projecting to the watching eyes of the world a display of opera *de-luxe*, with free-flowing champagne, copious flowers, and lavish decorations.[2] An elaborate system of special entrances and rope cordons were set up at the theatre, with Yeomen lining the barriers to keep the royal guests away from the rest of the audience.[3] Social hierarchies were made visible, even though the jewels sparkled just as brightly on either side of the barrier.

This was not the first glitzy royal gala performance of a new British opera to attract the great and good; nor would it be the last. Covent Garden boasted that Her Majesty's government was increasingly using its performances to offer hospitality to foreign royalty, heads of state, and other important visitors.[4] This was a matter of national pride, a form of cultural propaganda, and such occasions became a form of spectacle in themselves. Describing the

---

[1] Anon., 'Glory ... Glory ... Gloriana', *DE* (9 June 1953), 3.
[2] Lorna Gibson, *Beyond* Jerusalem: *Music in the Women's Institute, 1919–1969* (Aldershot: Ashgate, 2008), p. 68.
[3] Anon., 'Express Diary', *DE* (9 June 1953), n.p.
[4] Royal Opera House, *A Review 1946–1956*, p. 23.

Figure 5.1 Basil Coleman, Benjamin Britten, Peter Pears, Joan Cross (back view). First run-through of *Gloriana*, Orme Square, London, May 1953. Reproduced with permission from © Royal Opera House/ArenaPAL.

diplomatic cars arriving at a performance of Rimsky Korsakov's *The Golden Cockerel*, *The Daily Express* reported that people-watching was 'the main pleasure at these occasions'.[5]

The Queen and Prince Philip gave the impression of being interested in and appreciative of *Gloriana*, and came well-prepared, having been given a private preview by Britten and the singers Joan Cross and Peter Pears at a dinner party hosted by the Earl and Countess of Harewood. The Queen clapped for eight minutes and was reputedly delighted by the *première*. However, the well-to-do audience, expecting a flattering tribute to the new Queen, took umbrage—particularly at a scene in which Elizabeth I removed her wig and was depicted as almost bald—and responded to the work frostily, giving it only muted applause or even leaving in the interval.

The Covent Garden audience was quite different on an ordinary night: there were no tiaras or tailcoats at *Gloriana*'s second performance, when it received eleven curtain calls.[6] Nevertheless, the theatre was starting

---

[5] William Hickey, 'Express Diary', *DE* (1 July 1954), n.p.
[6] Anon., 'A Bow for Britten', unidentified press clipping (12 June 1953). BUTC, MM/2/TH/LO/COV/88.

98 SOMEONE ELSE'S MUSIC

to become associated once again with 'fashion'—indeed fashion shows were sometimes presented in the building.[7] *The Daily Express*, despite doing much to fuel Covent Garden's glamour, also satirised it in a cartoon that showed a couple in evening dress on the stairs of an opera house, posing for a press photographer. The caption read, 'But darling, if I'd stayed in Paris and heard it on the Third Programme, no one would ever KNOW how much music means to me!'[8]

A sense of 'internationalism' was also returning. The director Tyrone Guthrie argued that Londoners now liked their opera as New Yorkers did: large-scale, opulent, sung by stars in foreign languages, and 'sold at a price which prohibits wide popularity and gives the performance great snob appeal.'[9] Though training home-grown singers remained a priority, the company was increasingly striving for international standards of performance. Using foreign principals was necessary to cast certain roles, but also to meet the demands of an increasingly well-informed, discerning audience that had been exposed via recordings to the world's best singers. Although the theatre officially maintained its post-war English-language policy, it was becoming more difficult to persuade foreign singers to perform in English; Callas, for one, simply refused, and others made it a condition of their appearance in the Coronation season that they be allowed to sing in the original.[10] In 1956, the Company's Opera Sub-Committee convened to discuss the language policy. Performances in the original language, from time to time, would, the committee felt, both improve box-office takings and entice foreign singers.[11] Covent Garden suddenly seemed worlds away from the pared-down, national company of the late 1940s.

The subsidy row redux

The renewed association between opera and glamour was a backward step for the art form's public image. The expectations of the 1940s had not come to fruition and the tone of reportage about Covent Garden started to become hostile and suspicious. The theatre's manager David Webster had promised

[7] Anon., 'The World of Fashion', *Queen* (18 January 1950), n.p.
[8] Osbert Lancaster, 'Pocket Cartoon', undated *DE* clipping, BUTC, MM/2/TH/LO/COV/84.
[9] Guthrie, *A Life in the Theatre*, p. 195, p. 196.
[10] Haltrecht, *The Quiet Showman*, p. 216.
[11] Minutes of a Meeting of the Opera Sub-Committee held on Wednesday 15th November 1956. ROH archives file: ROH/2/2/50.

PAGEANTRY AND PARTICIPATION   99

to make the theatre 'popular, not aristocratic', yet in the eyes of the press it was becoming, once again, 'Continental' and 'precious'.[12] Covent Garden appeared to be reneging on its post-war idealism to become a truly national company, yet continued to receive the public funds that had been justified by that ideal. The annual subsidy granted to the theatre rose exponentially over the 1950s: from £150,000 in 1952 to £270,000 in 1956, and in 1959 Conservatives advocated for £500,000.[13] Other companies, however, were facing such severe financial difficulties that *The Daily Mail* remarked in 1957, 'The threat is plain. Unless art gets more money it will cease to be part of the national life. Theatres, concert halls, opera houses, and art galleries will be the privilege of those who live in or near London and three or four other cities.'[14]

Nevertheless, the Arts Council staunchly defended the Covent Garden subsidy, pointing out in 1952 that 'grand opera' (as opposed to post-war 'utility opera') demanded a scale of presentation that could not be funded through ticket sales.[15] Even if all 2,000 seats were occupied, a performance still cost £540 more than could be taken at the box office, and raising ticket prices would undermine the company's efforts to attract as many people of different incomes as possible.[16] In response to the perennial argument that if a minority wanted an amenity, it should pay for it, the Arts Council hit back at such 'rugged individualism', at a time when society was increasingly willing to take on a collective financial responsibility for such things as libraries, swimming pools, and playing fields. Interestingly, however, the authors of this report identified an interesting paradox: that many people happy to see municipal funds spent on a gallery or museum would resist it for a concert hall or theatre, on the grounds that they saw the former as educational and the latter as mere entertainment.[17] Perhaps this is a mindset the musical world still has to try to change.

There remained a paternalistic impulse to arts subsidy at this time, of a sort that would later become unfashionable but that did much for the

[12] Daily Mail Reporter, 'Covent Garden "Too Precious"', *DM* (13 June 1956), 3.
[13] Daily Mail Reporter, 'Closed Doors at Opera', *DM* (13 November 1952), 5; Express Political Correspondent, 'Opera Chief to Ask M.P.s for Cash', *DE* (20 June 1956), n.p.; Express Staff Reporter, 'Tory Chiefs Plan Aid for the Arts', *DE* (1 July 1959), 11.
[14] Peter Black, 'Money, Money, Money', *DM* (10 October 1957), 8.
[15] Arts Council, 'The State and the Arts', *Seventh Annual Report, 1951–52* (London: The Arts Council of Great Britain, 1952), 3–9, 3.
[16] Daily Mail Reporter, 'Closed Doors at Opera', *DM* (13 November 1952), 5; Royal Opera House, *A Review 1946–1956*, p. 21.
[17] Arts Council, 'The State and the Arts', 5.

100   SOMEONE ELSE'S MUSIC

democratisation of the arts at the time. Lord Bridges, former head of the Home Civil Service, argued in an Oxford lecture that it did not matter if the poor did not consciously want museums and the arts, because 'they ought to want them, and will be better people when they have got into the habit of having them'.[18] Bridges also defended the Arts Council's London-centric focus, arguing that if the best of the arts were presented in the capital, wider dissemination would follow, as the regions were inspired by London's shining beacon.[19] The prevailing view of the time, in any case, was that it was better to have a few world-class institutions than to spread the funding too thinly and risk diluting quality.

Covent Garden argued that subsidy allowed it to provide the training and employment that would foster a national school of opera in Britain. But maintaining opera on the scale at which it was put on at the Royal Opera House was about more than this: it was a mark of civilisation, something fundamental to the image, reputation, and identity of the country. The company declared that 'it may seem a curious form of national pride, but any European country deems it essential to its dignity to have a national opera house in its capital, and sometimes municipal opera houses in its largest cities'.[20] London needed a permanent opera company working at the highest international level, and this could not be provided by the company in its post-war guise. Nor, it was obliquely suggested, could such a role be taken by any other British company. As Covent Garden argued,

If in the metropolis, if in the largest city in Europe we want opera of a scale and standard worthy of being called national, in the sense that the British Museum and the National Gallery are so regarded, then there is only one house in which it can find a home and that is Covent Garden ... All over the world it stands for quality and a high tradition, and it is only here that we can show that we are in the company of the great, in scale and standard.[21]

Thus, this most foreign of art forms had become an essential national institution. But many journalists, MPs, and members of the public were exasperated by the constant calls for more money. All the clichés of the 1930s

---

[18] Anon., 'The State and the Arts', *TLS* (22 August 1958), 471.
[19] Lord Bridges, *The State and the Arts: The Romanes Lecture* (Oxford: The Clarendon Press, 1958), p. 11.
[20] Royal Opera House, *A Review 1946–1956*, p. 17.
[21] Ibid., p. 24.

PAGEANTRY AND PARTICIPATION   101

returned. Opera was, once again, the hobby of the aristocracy. ('Is this not a vast sum of public money for a nation which is said to be living on a financial trapdoor to spend on an institution which does little else than entertain London's tiaras and tailcoats?'[22]) Opera was, once again, a frivolous luxury. ('If a few Londoners want this bottle of champagne, they should pay more for it themselves instead of humping the cost on to the nation's back.'[23]) Opera was, once again, reserved for a metropolitan elite. ('There is a firm feeling that far too large a proportion of the Arts Council's money is being gobbled up in London.'[24]) Opera was, once again, taking money away from more worthy local musical enterprise. (MPs argued that grants should be given instead to provincial performances of *Messiah*.[25]) And opera was, once again, something for foreigners, as this parliamentary exchange between Harold Macmillan and a Socialist Party MP illustrates:

JULIAN SNOW (SOC, LICHFIELD AND TAMWORTH): 'Is it not a fact that English art has a right to be encouraged?'
MACMILLAN: 'It is encouraged to the extent of £885,000 this year.'
MR SNOW: 'Mostly on German artists at Covent Garden.'[26]

Talk of champagne, pampered audiences, and a 'feather bed' opera house, as the manager of the New Theatre Hull called Covent Garden, sounds suspiciously close to today's elitism rhetoric.[27] But the representation of Covent Garden in the press was far removed from the picture that emerges from the theatre's internal reports, of a company that was deeply committed to opera itself and determined to attract a wide audience, decades before the external imposition of the 'access agenda'. It was an organisation that was under increasing pressure to perform to the highest levels and genuinely wanted to engage people but was in a financial double bind.

The renewed debate about subsidy and so-called luxury opera showed how opera had become embroiled in broader controversy about national identity. For Covent Garden, 'Britishness' meant being able to hold one's

[22] Anon., 'Cash and Culture', unidentified press cutting, 1 August 1952, BUTC, MM/2/TH/LO/COV/85.
[23] Ivor Brown, 'Where the Money Goes', *The Observer* (15 January 1950), 6.
[24] Unidentified press clipping (13 June 1956) quoting Conservative MP Kenneth Thompson, BUTC, MM/2/TH/LO/COV/97.
[25] Anon., 'Opera House Grant "Leaps to £150,000"', *DE* (3 July 1953), 5. Noel Goodwin, 'Covent Garden Comes Clean!', *DE* (9 January 1959), 6.
[26] Unidentified press clipping (13 June 1956), BUTC, MM/2/TH/LO/COV/97.
[27] Express Staff Reporter, 'Feather Bed Opera House He Calls It', *DE* (21 June 1956), n.p.

102   SOMEONE ELSE'S MUSIC

head up high on the international stage, showing the nation could present the arts at the highest level. The nation desired opera and ballet of high quality, 'for they are part of the European tradition that we are all anxious to sustain. They are needed for a full musical life, and their distinctive contributions to our national culture are as important to us as they are to the rest of the world.[28] The press's definition of Britishness, however, fell back on far less positive stereotypes about utilitarianism and protecting the public purse.

Glyndebourne and the fashionable set

Glyndebourne began the decade in financial difficulty. Unsubsidised except for one-off funds for the Festival of Britain, it was entirely dependent on private funding. The 1950 season was only made possible thanks to a generous guarantee against loss from (John) Spedan Lewis, son of the founder of the John Lewis Partnership.[29] Lewis had been a keen supporter of Glyndebourne from the off. Each summer he would take up residence at the Grand Hotel in Eastbourne and take eight or ten guests to each performance, inviting them to listen to recordings with him in advance and providing them with a score to follow during the performance. Furthermore, he would block-book in the region of sixty tickets to distribute among senior company partners, sending them a list on which to state their preferences for performances and dates, whether they were interested in opera or not.[30]

The John Lewis Partnership Music Society, which put on performances of opera from 1947, was founded as part of the company's broader aim of community-building and giving workers educational, cultural, and recreational opportunities. It was coordinated by Lewis's wife Beatrice and gave performances throughout the 1950s in the restaurant of Peter Jones on Sloane Square. Interestingly, there was a broader operatic theme to the mid-century John Lewis enterprise. During the war, Lewis had hired Rudolf Bing, the co-founder of Glyndebourne and later General Manager of the New York Met, to work at Peter Jones. Bing initially helped customers work out what they could buy with their clothing coupons, subsequently becoming assistant to the Director of Selling, and eventually running Ladies' Hairdressing.[31]

---

[28] Royal Opera House, *A Review 1946–1956*, p. 23.
[29] Jolliffe, *Glyndebourne*, p. 59.
[30] Victoria Glendinning, *Family Business: An Intimate History of John Lewis and the Partnership* (London: William Collins, 2021), p. 210.
[31] Ibid., pp. 238–239.

PAGEANTRY AND PARTICIPATION   103

Underwriting the Glyndebourne Festival after the war to the tune of £12,500 was Lewis's largest act of operatic benevolence.[32] Another substantial lifeline came when Nicolas 'Miki' Sekers, director of the West Cumberland Silk Mills at Whitehaven, not only donated all the fabrics required for a 1951 production of *Don Giovanni* but proposed the idea of a lavishly illustrated season programme book. The idea was that it would attract advertisers willing to pay a high fee and be a useful long-term fundraising strategy for the company, as turned out to be the case.[33]

As Glyndebourne got back on its feet, its renewed glamour began to compound the public perception that opera was exclusive and foreign. Though the theatre's décor was more like a school hall than an opera house, ticket prices (4 guineas by the end of the decade) spoke of luxury, and the general atmosphere was said to be 'much more "exclusive" than Covent Garden at its most formal'.[34] Tickets were hard to obtain: a correspondent to *The Spectator* complained that for two years he had tried without success and that once he had been informed that all seats had gone to members of the 'Glyndebourne Circle' before public booking opened.[35] *The Tatler* took every opportunity to feature the fashionable set in black tie, evening dress, and fur jackets enjoying the gardens.[36] Evening dress was still required as a mark of respect, with John Christie stating: 'Glyndebourne is an ideal. The ideal is not the servant of the public. On the contrary the public must be the servant of the ideal. Take it or leave it.'[37]

Some people who attended Glyndebourne exhibited an aura of insufferable social snobbery, even in a context where most audience goers were relatively well-to-do. A reader wrote in to the *Spectator* in 1957 to complain about picnickers. There had been picnics at Glyndebourne since 1935, though they were initially confined to the carpark.[38] Now the practice was spreading to the grounds, prompting this correspondent to write: 'To spread out your beastly, bank-holiday mess in the garden or by the lake is the very bottom

---

[32] Blunt, *John Christie of Glyndebourne*, p. 266.

[33] https://www.glyndebourne.com/membership/the-origins-of-the-festival-society/ (accessed 3 March 2022); Blunt, *John Christie of Glyndebourne*, p. 270.

[34] Philip Hope-Wallace, 'Opera at Glyndebourne', in Anna Instone and Julian Herbiage (eds), *Selections from the BBC Programme Music Magazine* (London: Rockliff, 1953), pp. 110–113, p. 111; Jolliffe, *Glyndebourne*, p. 267; Salter, *Going to the Opera*, p. 36.

[35] J. D. K. Lloyd, 'Catering at Glyndebourne', letter to *The Spectator* (27 June 1958), 840.

[36] Jennifer, 'A Vintage Season for the Debutantes', *The Tatler* (13 February 1957), 271–274, 274.

[37] Cecil Smith, 'Summer Cinderella Sparkles', *DE* (11 June 1953), 3; John Christie, 'Is It Snobbery to Dress Up?', letter to *DE* (6 July 1953), 4.

[38] Blunt, *John Christie of Glyndebourne*, p. 177.

Figure 5.2 Audience members in the grounds, Glyndebourne Festival Opera, 1958. Reproduced with permission from © Glyndebourne Productions Ltd/ ArenaPAL.

of bad manners. Grease-proof paper, orange peel and empty bottles do not sully the beauty of Mr Christie's grounds.'[39] Disgusted to find benches 'reserved' by picnic baskets and mackintoshes, he continued: 'The perpetrators of this outrage, needless to say of such people, having erected their unsightly monument to ill-breeding, and having ensured, to their own sole and selfish advantage, that no one else could sit there throughout the evening, were elsewhere—presumably swilling tea'.

How ironic this seems today, given that lavish picnics have become fundamentally associated with the Glyndebourne experience; indeed, in the 1980s, *The Spectator* was publishing articles advising the smart set on what to pack in a fashionable Glyndebourne hamper.[40] But perhaps, in a sense, this correspondent was not only irritated by selfish bench-hogging, but cack-handedly trying to make an argument that the music, rather than the social experience, ought to be the point of going to the opera. This too was Christie's argument,

[39] Richard Greet, 'Glyndebourne Food', letter to *The Spectator* (21 June 1957), 811.
[40] Nigella Lawson, 'Salad Days Al Fresco', *The Spectator* (20 June 1987), 37.

PAGEANTRY AND PARTICIPATION 105

every time he was forced to defend himself against charges of snobbery: that musical excellence was everything.

Glyndebourne was never going to offer opera on democratic lines. One contemporary commentator employed culinary metaphors, writing, 'Not for Mr Christie the *spaghetti con burro* of the popular Italian Opera, nor the heaven-sent manna of the Wagner cult, but caviare.'[41] Yet Christie's intentions remained as good-hearted as they had been in the 1930s. He was, in the words of *The Observer*, 'an example of that kind of wealthy Englishman who devotes himself to the development of some art, craft or science which he believes has value both in itself and to his fellow men.'[42] Carl Ebert, interviewed upon his departure from Glyndebourne, where he had been artistic director for twenty-five years, called the enterprise 'a patriotic ambition, not the hobby of a rich man.'[43] This patriotism, it had to be said, was sometimes rather lost on the wider world. Although, for a certain social set, Glyndebourne was becoming as quintessential a part of an English summer as going to Wimbledon or Lord's, the perception among the public at large was rather different, *The Observer* writing of the enterprise in 1952 that 'almost everything about it is foreign.'[44]

The expanding audience

For all the growing discontent with Covent Garden, for all the sense that Glyndebourne was a rarefied world apart, there remained a widespread belief in the 1950s that opera was for anyone who cared to take an interest. It was still often presented as an accessible form of popular culture, and it was not unusual to find the author of a book on opera likening singers to 'favoured film stars of today' and explaining that Puccini's works combined 'the naturalism of real life with the popular sentimentality of magazine stories.'[45]

Opera was only inaccessible in this period to the extent that not enough performances were being put on to meet demand. Covent Garden and Sadler's Wells were regularly full and demand was particularly high for the cheapest seats, particularly from young listeners.[46] Sadler's Wells

---

[41] Woodhouse, *Opera for Amateurs*, p. 49.
[42] Anon., 'Profile: John Christie', *The Observer* (15 June 1952), 2.
[43] Our Special Correspondent, 'Unique Opera House', *The Times* (27 May 1959), 7.
[44] Anon., 'Profile: John Christie', *The Observer* (15 June 1952), 2.
[45] Salter, *Going to the Opera*, p. 112, p. 130.
[46] Ibid., p. 11, p. 12; P.H.-W., 'The London Opera Season', *The Manchester Guardian* (13 November 1950).

106   SOMEONE ELSE'S MUSIC

continued to bill itself as the 'people's theatre, where opera and ballet are given with teamwork but without stars, at prices everyone can afford', and launched a new cheap ticket scheme for 15- to 25-year-olds.[47] At Covent Garden, students and schoolchildren queued for the gallery, huddled up in duffle-coats, polo-necked sweaters, and boots.[48] Around the time of his 14th birthday, the young Daniel Snowman and a schoolfriend turned up during their half-term break cheekily hoping to have a look around, and the doorman simply let them in to watch a rehearsal. (The young woman going through her paces on stage, and about to make her Covent Garden debut, was one Maria Meneghini Callas.[49])

Even the more expensive seats were still something a family could afford for a special occasion. Irene Gass's 1957 book for young readers, *Through an Opera Glass*, opens with a description of a fictional family going to Covent Garden for a birthday treat.[50] The children are engrossed by the music and dancing, and talk animatedly in the interval about devising their own operetta. Their mother, meanwhile, daydreams about what Covent Garden must have been like in the nineteenth century, when women wore diamond tiaras and travelled to the opera in carriages, rather than by Tube. This account encapsulates the state of operatic culture during the 1950s: opera was a site of dreams and fantasies for children and adults alike, but it was also accessible to ordinary people—even perhaps at its most glamorous if they saved up.

Audience expectations were rising. When an Italian company put on a slapdash performance at the Stoll Theatre, *The Observer* retorted that 'if Italy is to show England her superiority in opera, such a company as this should choose a less sophisticated and more readily grateful place than London'.[51] Standing in the queue for tickets at Covent Garden would give any observer the impression that 'we are all connoisseurs now'.[52] Even a rise in booing was taken to be an indicator that audiences were becoming more discriminating, though *The Times* lamented the fact that audiences had borrowed their operatic manners from 'the third-rate Italian opera house', rather than emulating 'German seriousness'.[53] Finally, the foundation of *Opera*—a specialist

---

[47] Cecil Smith, 'Come On Now . . . Strike Out a Bit!', unattributed press clipping, 1 May 1951, BUTC, MM/2/TH/LO/COV/82; Anon., 'New Public for Opera', *The Times* (24 November 1959), 3.
[48] Eve Perrick, 'On Everybody's Toes', *DE* (18 November 1950), 3.
[49] Snowman, *Just Passing Through*, p. 29.
[50] Irene Gass, *Through an Opera Glass* (London: George Harrap and Co., 1957), pp. 145–149.
[51] Eric Blom, 'An Abundance of Opera', *The Observer* (10 May 1953), 13.
[52] *Royal Opera House Annual Report 1958–1959*, p. 9.
[53] Our Music Critic, 'Behaviour at the Opera', *The Times* (11 July 1958), 12.

PAGEANTRY AND PARTICIPATION   107

magazine that examined opera in depth and without apology—also seemed evidence of the fact that a serious musical connoisseurship was developing in Britain. Audiences were becoming more open-minded about even the most challenging works. When *Wozzeck* was put on at Covent Garden, *The Evening Standard* wrote: 'Do not be dissuaded from hearing Wozzeck because it is supposed to be highbrow. Even if your brow is so low that a flat cloth cap won't stay on your head without falling over your eyes, this music will rinse and ring in your ear.'[54]

Meanwhile, opera in the regions was expanding. By 1950 Welsh National Opera had seventy-five singers and a resident orchestra, and was maintaining troupes in Cardiff and Swansea, their members including miners, schoolteachers, clerks, and housewives, who received training from professionals at Covent Garden and Sadler's Wells.[55] An ambitious schedule of tours was being planned, throughout Wales and into England. Meanwhile, Sadler's Wells and the Carl Rosa also continued to tour, first independently, then combining resources following a merger, and people made considerable efforts to see them. The music writer Patrick Carnegy remembered cycling twelve miles from Rugby School to the Coventry Hippodrome in 1959, writing, 'So Sadler's Wells became for myself and thousands of others a gateway into opera, at affordable prices whether on tour or back in Rosebery Avenue.'[56]

Meanwhile, the Arts Council's new troupe 'Opera for All' drove around in a six-seater van with a few props, presenting potted operas or lecture recitals with piano accompaniment in towns from Fort William to Bishop's Stortford. Similar, but focusing on schools, was 'The Opera Players', a company co-founded by Elisabeth Parry, back from her wartime tour of the Middle East. She later recalled, 'I shall never forget the first "Bohème" to a school of physically handicapped children in a very poor area of Islington, using the coke stove in the narrow hall as the attic stove, with a lad in a wheel chair in the front row crying all through the last act and saying after that it was smashing.'[57]

And then, of course, there continued to be ways of encountering opera by chance, as singers both young and old sang in pubs and clubs. The veteran tenor Tudor Davies, who had sung opposite Melba at Covent Garden, could

---

[54] Ronald Duncan, '25 Years On The Way—*But Worth Waiting For!*', *ES* (25 January 1952), n.p.
[55] Anon., 'Wales Needs a National Opera House', *Herald of Wales* (21 October 1950), n.p.
[56] Patrick Carnegy, 'Blood on the Carpet', *TLS* (1 January 2010), 3–4, 3.
[57] Parry, *Thirty Men and a Girl*, p. 266.

108 SOMEONE ELSE'S MUSIC

be found in 1950 performing in a working men's club in Burnley.[58] Around the same time, the young Rita Hunter (daughter of a gas stoker) was singing in clubs around Liverpool, at the beginning of a career that would ultimately see her singing at the Met.[59]

Technically, then, opera was reaching regional audiences—but there was still potential for improvement. The Calouste Gulbenkian Foundation produced a report which concluded that there was a 'tendency for opera to become unduly limited to the metropolis and about half-a-dozen large cities', and called for more to be done.[60] The Foundation expressed concern that universities, in particular, were not doing enough to encourage the arts, and urged them to set up gramophone-lending libraries.[61] For the role of technology in popularising opera was beginning to be recognised as never before.

Broadcasting and the long-play revolution

By the turn of the 1950s, 80 per cent of the population were listening to BBC broadcasts, and it was acknowledged that broadcasting was a particular boon for opera, which was harder to access live in some areas than other types of music.[62] Opera was plentiful on the Third Programme: seventy-five broadcasts in 1951, rising to eighty in 1954, including obscure older works, new commissions, and relays from foreign festivals.[63] For keen listeners, a particular operatic broadcast was an event worth noting in the diary. Daniel Snowman, then a teenager, recalls listening to a Gigli concert in bed with the radio half an inch from his ear at low volume to avoid detection by his parents for breaking Sabbath rules.[64]

Of course, the Third Programme did not reach a mass audience—only those who sought it out—but the BBC itself was at ease with the fact that the station was designed for a minority audience with specialist, cosmopolitan tastes. Over time, however, the Third Programme began to attract

---

[58] Russell, 'Reaching the Operatic Stage', p. 318.

[59] Hunter, *Wait Till the Sun Shines, Nellie*, p. 31.

[60] Lord Bridges, Diana Albemarle, Noel Annan, and George Barnes, *Help for the Arts* (London: The Calouste Gulbenkian Foundation, 1959), p. 60.

[61] Ibid., p. 133.

[62] Anon., 'The Arts and Entertainment', *The Times* (2 January 1950), 18; Anon., 'English Musical Growth', *TLS* (24 August 1951), xxix.

[63] Andrew Porter, 'Opera and the Radio', *Opera*, 3/4 (April 1952), 203–248, 203; Anon., 'Music', *BBC Handbook 1955* (London: British Broadcasting Corporation), 60–63.

[64] Snowman, *Just Passing Through*, p. 45.

PAGEANTRY AND PARTICIPATION   109

criticism for its 'highbrow' content, *The Leicester Evening Mail*, for example, complaining that it was 'almost entirely monopolised by the long-haired and long-winded'.[65] In 1953, *The Sunday Express* launched a campaign to 'scrap the Third', asking, 'For whom does the programme cater? Nobody can pretend that the conversation and interests of ordinary educated listeners embrace such subjects ... few will be found outside university common-rooms, Arts Council tea parties and societies for specialists.'[66] But this was not true. A Glaswegian iron-foundry worker wrote to the *Radio Times* to say that he and his co-workers had learnt much about music, literature, and philosophy from the Third.[67] Similarly, the singer Victoria Sladen, a former secretary, wrote, 'The radio helped me to become familiar with music I would never have heard otherwise, and now, with the coming of the more high-brow Third Programme, even more wonderful riches are at the disposal of the listener.'[68]

Complaints before the war about the mixture of 'high' and 'low' items on radio—the fact that everyone had to listen to the same thing—had led to the division into the Home, Light, and Third.[69] However, there was now a perception that the Third was 'ghettoising' classical music, creating, as *The Times* put it, 'a little highbrow rock pool, so that the ultimate effect, they say, of this considerable broadcasting venture has been to impoverish rather than to enrich the fare of the ordinary listener.'[70] Nevertheless, listeners could still hear around ten to fourteen operas or operettas a year on the Home Service, as well as highlights on the Light Programme's 'Come to the Opera'.[71]

By 1957, it was feared that the Third Programme might be merged once again with the Home Service. Peter Laslett, a Third Programme producer and Cambridge don, produced a leaflet encouraging listeners to express their concerns to the BBC management.[72] He argued that the Third was emblematic of the nation's recent intellectual progress, providing a symbolic meeting place for the nation's growing number of arts graduates, and the professional classes who demonstrated an ever-increasing appetite for culture. But it

---

[65] Whitehead, *The Third Programme*, p. 59, p. 60.
[66] Ibid., pp. 209–210.
[67] Ibid., p. 210.
[68] Sladen, *Singing My Way*, p. 42.
[69] Whitehead, *The Third Programme*, p. 45.
[70] Sykes, 'Achievement of the Third Programme', viii.
[71] Memo from Controller, Home Service, 3 June 1954. BBC WAC: R27/375/7 Music Gen Opera: Policy File 7 1952–1954; Sladen, *Singing My Way*, p. 92.
[72] Peter Laslett, *The Future of Sound Broadcasting: A Plea for the Third Programme* (Oxford: Basil Blackwell, 1957), p. 3.

110   SOMEONE ELSE'S MUSIC

was not only to these people that the station sought to speak. The key point, Laslett emphasised, was that 'the essence of the Third Programme is that it is always there, for anyone who cares to listen'. It might make intellectual demands upon the listener, but in terms of ease of access it could not credibly be said to be elitist.

The number of people with a television was small at the turn of the decade: famously it was the Coronation that stimulated the mass purchase of sets. But opera was there from the start: in 1950 Britten's *Let's Make an Opera* was televised directly from the Theatre Royal, Stratford, and the BBC billed a modern-dress production of *Pagliacci* as 'an outstanding event in the history of television opera'.[73] When *Don Giovanni* was televised from Glyndebourne in 1954, *The Daily Express* wondered whether it was a mistake to take up nearly two hours of millions of viewers' time with opera, but concluded that it was 'spellbinding' and stated, 'What a relief to get away from the inanities of recent programmes like "Dear Dotty" and those experimental parlour games'.[74]

Televised opera had the potential to reach large new audiences, and so it would in due course, but initial audience responses were somewhat muted. In a 1952 poll, opera emerged as the least popular item on television, liked by only 29 per cent of viewers (though even this seems respectable), the most popular items being news reels (98 per cent) and plays (95 per cent).[75] Two years later, however, the Head of Music Programmes at BBC TV, Kenneth Wright, claimed a broadcast of *Tosca* would typically attract an audience around two-thirds the size of that for a popular vaudeville. Wright argued that BBC television had '*proved beyond doubt* there is vast public who, though unaccustomed to opera, are nevertheless ready to accept it as entertainment'.[76]

Opera on television also prompted negative feelings. It was hard to promote to those inclined to consider opera ridiculous, television being a medium that inclined to a greater extent than theatre towards realism. (The answer, *The Times* proposed, was to present specially written new works 'carefully drained of everything implied by the word "operatic"'.[77]) It was equally hard to make the case for television opera to those who considered

---

[73] Anon., 'Report of the Year's Broadcasting', *BBC Year Book 1951* (London: British Broadcasting Corporation), 97–129, 112.

[74] Cyril Aynsley, 'Mozart Beats the Panel', *DE* (30 July 1954), 3.

[75] Anon., 'You Say This About TV', *DE* (8 May 1952), 6.

[76] Robert Cannell, 'It's Time TV Was Taught to Add', *DE* (19 January 1954), 4; original emphasis.

[77] Anon., 'Popularizing Opera with the Television Audience', *The Times* (1 January 1959), 6.

PAGEANTRY AND PARTICIPATION   111

opera too rarefied for such a populist medium. In 1958, Lionel Salter, head of the BBC's music department, laid into professional musicians who sneered at television's musical offerings, calling them guilty of 'the most damnable form of artistic and intellectual snobbery'.[78] Television, Salter stressed, had to appeal not only to music lovers but also to people with 'no strong views on the subject' who 'might yet be won over with encouragement and persistence'.

Opera also featured in programmes with a wider entertainment appeal. Vic Oliver, a star of variety and radio, featured it in his variety show 'Vic Oliver presents'.[79] *The Times* presented this as 'smuggling in opera in disguise': what we might call a sort of 'Trojan horse' approach that is still sometimes used by TV commissioners today. Opera could also still be heard in the cinema, and one way of attracting a mass audience was to use star actors and actresses in the main roles, voiced by unseen professional singers. The year 1957, for example, saw the release of an *Aida* with the title role sung by Renata Tebaldi but mimed on screen by Sophia Loren.[80]

This was also the era of the 'long-play revolution', with LPs being introduced into the United Kingdom by Decca in 1950.[81] Many of the big-budget studio recordings of opera made at this time remain classics today. Listeners were now able to listen to high-quality performances of the world's greatest singers and choose between competing recordings of the same work. Although young people were often said to be being lured away from classical music by jazz and dance music, some certainly became fans of opera via LPs. Colin Wilson, author of the bestseller *The Outsider* (1956), rushed out at the age of twenty-four to spend his first royalties on a gramophone and a large pile of second-hand opera LPs.[82] Recordings also remained an important means of introducing children to opera in the home. Tony Hall (b. 1951), later Chief Executive of the Royal Opera House, recalled being introduced to opera by hearing Wagner's *Tannhäuser* in short segments on old 78s at his grandparents' house in Birkenhead.[83]

The Times noted in 1959 that LPs had created a new generation of opera connoisseurs who listened to them and followed along with a score.[84] Though

[78] Our Own Correspondent, 'Television Music Defended', *The Times* (3 January 1958), 10.
[79] Anon., 'Report of the Year's Broadcasting', *BBC Year Book 1951* (London: British Broadcasting Corporation), 97–129, 112.
[80] Snowman, *Just Passing Through*, p. 51.
[81] Goff, *A Short Guide to Long Play*, p. 14; Edward Sackville-West and Desmond Shawe-Taylor, *The Record Guide* (London: Collins, 1951), p. 31.
[82] Colin Wilson, introduction to John L. Brecknock and John Kennedy Melling, *Scaling the High Cs: The Musical Life of Tenor John L. Brecknock* (Lanham, MD: The Scarecrow Press, 1996), p. 2.
[83] Bryan Appleyard, 'On an Even Keel', *The Sunday Times* (18 June 2006), 6–7, 6.
[84] Our Music Critic, 'Abiding Problems of English Opera', *The Times* (30 October 1959), 4.

112 SOMEONE ELSE'S MUSIC

this might seem quaintly earnest, there was still at this time a certain ethos of autodidacticism, an understanding that complex art forms demanded some effort on the audience's part. Stephen Williams advised readers that the best way to understand an opera was to play it through at the piano when they got home from the theatre. He wrote that, in understanding the music, 'you will not only have enjoyed yourself, but you will know *why* you enjoyed yourself. And that, surely, is the right and privilege of every civilised man'.[85] Here we come back to Noel Streatfeild's argument with which this book began. To know opera was a privilege—but in the positive sense of a gift one could give to oneself.

Have-a-go opera

Opera, then, was presented to new audiences as something that was both fun and funny, so long as you were prepared to put in a bit of work. Enjoyment and amusement could also be derived from performing it. Author Irene Gass encouraged her young readers to try to recreate the performances of the Florentine Camerata. While this might sound preposterously ambitious, even pretentious, what Gass had in mind was something very simple. Children should choose a Greek myth, find dressing-up outfits, play the mouth organ or recorder, or even bang a pan, and communicate in a mixture of speech and song. Gass wrote: 'At the end of the performance you will probably find that everybody has had a good laugh . . . And I wonder how near you will have got to the real thing.'[86] Children could then devise operatic scenes of their own, based on events in their own lives.

Gass presented opera as something down-to-earth. The Florentine Camerata, she explained, loved to talk about Greek drama 'just as to-day men love to talk about cars or planes or golf', and their names were as ordinary to Italians as John Smith or David Brown would be here.[87] Though it might seem idiotic that someone would *sing* a request, when he could simply *say* 'Fish and chips, please', or that someone would sing a song about his house being on fire rather than ringing the fire station, these were simply

---

[85] Stephen Williams, *You and the Opera: A Pocket Guide* (London: MacDonald and Evans, Ltd, 1952), p. 17; original emphasis.
[86] Gass, *Through an Opera Glass*, p. 14.
[87] Ibid., p. 12.

PAGEANTRY AND PARTICIPATION 113

conventions that must be accepted, just as people accepted the unusual language in a Shakespeare play or a church sermon.[88]

In stark contrast, W. H. Auden argued in 1951 that opera was fundamentally not participatory, and that this was why the British had never fully embraced it. He imagined a scenario where a village attempted to put on a performance of *Hamlet*. The result might be crude but 'would convey enough of the work's greatness to be worth attending'.[89] Attempting to do the same thing with *Don Giovanni* wouldn't work: the cast simply wouldn't be able to sing the notes. In have-a-go Britain, then, with its long history of 'am dram', opera was a problem.

Nevertheless, some ambitious amateur groups *were* putting on adventurous repertory, even works rarely staged professionally. Glasgow's Grand Opera Society put on Berlioz's *Benvenuto Cellini*, *Idomeneo*, and *The Trojans*; there was a production of Borodin's *Prince Igor* in Swindon; and the Workers' Music Association was commissioning new operas by English composers.[90] The John Lewis Music Society was noteworthy for giving the first performance in England of *Rusalka*, in 1950, and staged other obscure works such as Wolf-Ferrari's *The Inquisitive Women*, Weber's *Abu Hassan*, and Boieldieu's *La Dame blanche*.[91]

Particularly impressive were the efforts of the Birmingham-based Midland Music Makers. Set up as the Gooch Street Choir in the early 1930s to sing worship music and G&S, the group rebranded itself as an opera troupe after the war.[92] It began tackling works such as *Boris Godunov*, followed in the 1950s by *The Huguenots*, *Masaniello*, *The Sicilian Vespers*, and *Rienzi*, encouraged by member Leslie Deathridge.[93] His son, the Wagner scholar Professor John Deathridge, whose mother also sang principal roles with the company, wrote later that the Midland Music Makers 'helped to introduce some significant works of international stature to opera enthusiasts in Britain at a time when they were little known'.[94]

Such groups were vehicles for the democratisation of opera among industrial workers, some of whom went professional, like the tenor John

[88] Ibid., p. 9.

[89] W. H. Auden, 'Reflections on Opera', *The Observer* (16 September 1951), 6.

[90] Salter, *Going to the Opera*, p. 170.

[91] Programme for *La Perichole*, JLP Opera Society, 1961. JLP archive file 696/iv.

[92] Michael Walpole (ed.), *Midland Music Makers Opera: The First Fifty Years, 1946–1996* (Birmingham: Midland Music Makers, n. d.), p. 6.

[93] Ibid., p. 16.

[94] John Deathridge, *Wagner Beyond Good and Evil* (Berkeley: University of California Press, 2008), xii.

114   SOMEONE ELSE'S MUSIC

Brecknock, originally an apprentice engineer at a Midlands ironworks.[95] Intriguingly, however, the authors of a Calouste Gulbenkian report of 1959 suggested the regulars who were interested in the adult education movement, with its ethos of self-help and self-improvement, who loyally attended lectures on art, literature, and music, were themselves 'a self-enclosed *élite*', failing to 'leaven the whole lump'.[96] The report called for greater efforts to 'bring the arts home to the provinces at large, not to the staunch small groups of the already converted'.

This seems to sit uneasily with the example of someone like the baritone Thomas Allen, who heard no opera as a child in a County Durham pit village, but for whom music would become a passport to a different life after his voice was noticed by a teacher at grammar school. Decades later, Allen said he would struggle to describe his upbringing without it sounding like a Catherine Cookson novel, and told an interviewer, 'I was Billy Elliot... Where I came from everyone who could pull themselves up by their bootstraps did just that. We knew there was a choice if we could find out how to make it. It was up to us.'[97] It seems troubling that ordinary people, discovering opera for themselves, enjoying it and even devoting their lives to it, as Allen did, should be constructed as 'an elite'.

Opera performances in schools and youth clubs were widespread, with the National Council of Social Service's Advisory Committee on Amateur Opera publishing a list of recommended works, such as *Hansel and Gretel* or Gluck's *Orpheus*.[98] *Dido and Aeneas* was so commonly done that the author of a book about amateur opera, Frederick Woodhouse, wrote, 'No musically inclined boy or girl should leave school without an experience as performer or listener of Purcell's masterpiece.'[99] Woodhouse advocated that children also be taken to watch operas, and the more advanced the better, though preferably *Tristan and Isolde* or *Peter Grimes* rather than 'the highly spiced' Italian repertoire.[100]

Woodhouse was delighted by the enthusiasm with which youngsters were embracing opera. But he noted that there was sometimes a problem. It was

[95]   Russell, 'Reaching the Operatic Stage', p. 319.
[96]   Anon., 'Help for the Arts', *TLS* (19 June 1959), 369.
[97]   Nicholas Wroe, 'Cutting It at the Opera', *The Guardian* (5 December 2013), n.p.; Fiona Maddocks, 'Fanfare for the Common Man', *The Observer* (3 December 2000), n.p.
[98]   Anon., 'List of Operas and Operettas for Schools and Youth Clubs' (London: National Operatic & Dramatic Association, 1957).
[99]   Woodhouse, *Opera for Amateurs*, p. 85.
[100]   Ibid., pp. 83–84, p. 87.

PAGEANTRY AND PARTICIPATION   115

not so much the lack of suitable works to perform as 'the diffidence of staff arising from a quite exaggerated respect and awe of "opera"'. He argued that 'it would remove a stumbling-block, not only for schools but for a section of the public, if the word "opera" could be superseded or anyhow shorn of its exotic and pompous significance'.[101] This most striking of statements sums up an essential paradox at the heart of opera reception in twentieth-century Britain. For all the ordinary people queuing in the rain outside Covent Garden, for all the children devising their own operas, there was still an obstinate cliché that opera was alien, foreign, and pretentious—to the extent that some recoiled from the very word. And so persistent has this idea been—despite all evidence to the contrary—that it seems unshakeable in Britain. We are not too many steps away, here, from the contemporary elitism stereotype.

Britishness (again)

Opera was clearly still too alien for some to accept in the 1950s. There would always be literal-minded Brits who were so perplexed by opera's perceived absurdities—'ridiculous tubby men pretending to be mighty heroes and huge, hefty, horsy women trying to persuade us that they are fragile little girls dying of consumption', as Stephen Williams put it—that they would never be able to see opera-singing as anything other than foreign.[102] The rationale that one simply had to use one's imagination with opera, just as one would when watching a Shakespeare play, where nobody would expect to see live deer walking about the stage in the Forest of Arden or witches flying on real broomsticks in a performance of *Macbeth*, was lost on such people.[103]

It was not only lowbrows who struggled with opera. The anonymous author of an extraordinarily hostile review in *The Times Literary Supplement* of Eric Walter White's book, *The Rise of English Opera*, not only insisted that opera was 'unquestionably' a minority taste but also argued that 'it has never seemed necessary, as it has to some other nations, to have, defiantly, *our* theatre, *our* opera; to show that we too could do it; to possess a national opera'.[104] The British might sometimes reflect on how art forms such as opera

---

[101] Ibid., p. 84.
[102] Williams, *You and the Opera*, pp. 4–6.
[103] Ibid., pp. 11–12.
[104] Anon., 'Star in the Ascendant', *TLS* (27 July 1951), 468; original emphasis.

116 SOMEONE ELSE'S MUSIC

could be tailored to the national taste, but always cheerfully reminded themselves that Britain had 'Wimbledon, Lord's, and more important things'. Opera, here, was held up—as it would be so many times across the course of our century—against sport and found wanting. Britain, it seemed, would always prioritise the body over the mind. Yet, interestingly, the sporting world itself was keen to do something about the perceived divide between the two spheres. In 1952, the Football Association organised a competition to mark its ninetieth anniversary, in which prizes worth £3,000 were awarded for art works with a footballing theme, to bridge 'the gulf between the Hearty and the Highbrow'.[105] Yet the *TLS* reviewer persisted in stressing the culturally alien nature of opera, writing, 'Opera is not cricket, after all; mostly it is foreign; sometimes even worse than that'.[106]

The author's tone was coloured by a striking puritanical prejudice. He or she spoke of the British having 'an allergy, perhaps, to the whole idea, a resistance to the idea of voice, the singing voice, as a means of dramatic expression, the voice as queen of instruments, voluptuous and unavoidably sexual in its overtones'. Opera was too sensual, too licentious. Although this trope was not ostensibly related to the elitism idea per se, it was one strand in a general British squeamishness about opera that rendered it, to quote this author verbatim, a 'sort of slightly suspect art'. Even by the 1950s it had not been possible to shake off the old Puritan idea that the theatrical world was immoral.

For the British, a Calouste Gulbenkian report noted, it was not enough for the arts to be beautiful: they also had to be 'morally or socially justified', had to be proved categorically to have 'a use'. Its authors noted that 'Great Britain is almost unique among European countries in that the mass of her people have never associated the practice of the arts either with their own pleasure or the greatness of their country'.[107] This utilitarian mindset was vital in shaping the elitism stereotype and in explaining why it set in so deeply in this country. If the arts served no obvious purpose and could not even be held up as a source of enjoyment or national pride, then it was only logical that these expensive pursuits should be characterised as a frivolous luxury.

And yet, there is also evidence from the 1950s of opera being reclaimed as a British art form. Opera featured prominently in the celebrations surrounding the Coronation, harking back repeatedly to the first Elizabethan era. In

---

[105] Stanley Rous (Secretary, Football Association), 'Art for Sport's Sake', letter to *The Times* (23 October 1952), 7.
[106] Anon., 'Star in the Ascendant'.
[107] Anon., 'Help for the Arts', *TLS* (19 June 1959), 369.

addition to *Gloriana*, there were other significant operatic performances in the weeks either side of the Coronation and a radio broadcast of Rossini's *Elizabetta Regina di Inghilterra*.[108] A thousand amateur performers in Elizabethan costume took part in a pageant based on Edward German's comic opera *Merrie England* in the grounds of Luton Hoo in Bedfordshire, and many other societies staged the work around the country.[109]

Opera also featured prominently in the Festival of Britain, which ran from May to September 1951 to mark the centenary of the Great Exhibition. The Festival was an exercise in national pride, its advance programme announcing it would be a 'landmark in Britain's history', in which 'the whole of Britain will be on show' by displaying its achievements past and present and its ambitions for the future in the arts, sciences, technology, architecture, and design.[110] Exhibitions on the South Bank and at the Science Museum celebrated the nation's history and its technological prowess, respectively.[111] The Festival was an exercise in propaganda, displaying British wares to the world, but also British culture—making a statement about who the Britons were.

It is striking that opera played a role in this 'act of national autobiography', as the then Home Secretary Herbert Morrison put it, in a way it would not in later eras (no opera featured in the opening ceremony of the 2012 London Olympics, for instance).[112] The Chancellor of the Exchequer granted the Arts Council £400,000 of additional funding for Festival of Britain events.[113] Covent Garden, Sadler's Wells, and Glyndebourne featured prominently in the celebrations, the first performance of Vaughan Williams's *The Pilgrim's Progress* was an important *première*, and the Arts Council organised an opera-writing competition, attracting over 100 submissions.

With state funding for musical training now generous—over 70 per cent of students at the Royal Manchester College of Music were in receipt of bursaries by 1958—audiences were getting used to seeing more British singers on stage.[114] There was still interest in glamorous foreign stars at

---

[108] 'BBC Third Programme: Plans for Coronation Week' (London: BBC, 1953).

[109] Our Special Correspondents, 'Coronation Celebration Plans', *The Times* (14 January 1953), 3.

[110] Anon., *Advance Programme for the Festival of Britain 1951* (London: Festival of Britain, 1950), 1.

[111] Ibid., 2–6.

[112] Cited in Peter Mandler, *The English National Character: The History of an Idea from Edmund Burke to Tony Blair* (New Haven: Yale University Press, 2006), p. 208.

[113] Anon., 'The State and the Arts', *Sixth Annual Report, 1950–51* (London: The Arts Council of Great Britain, 1951), 4.

[114] Russell, 'Reaching the Operatic Stage', 333.

118 SOMEONE ELSE'S MUSIC

Covent Garden—even if Equity expressed objections throughout 1956 to the hiring of foreign performers—but commentators were starting to pay attention to down-to-earth, unpretentious Brits.[115] There was, of course, one who reigned supreme in the nation's affections, and that was the former telephone operator Kathleen Ferrier. Loved for her endearing personality and rags-to-riches backstory, Ferrier's death from cancer in 1953, aged only 41, prompted an outpouring of national grief. She was both a serious contralto and a 'fun-loving Lancashire lass, unspoilt by fame'.[116] Though Ferrier was not exclusively an opera singer, Britten wrote *The Rape of Lucretia* for her, and her devastating final performance—during which part of her left femur disintegrated—was in Gluck's *Orfeo* at Covent Garden.

In December 1954, *The Daily Mail* announced on its front page that it was launching a competition, whereby a £1,000 prize in memory of Ferrier would be awarded to a young female singer.[117] Over the years to come, the *Mail* would regularly profile the ordinary women who had impressed judges in the regional heats of the Ferrier Award. The finalists in the first year included teachers, shorthand-typists, and a hospital receptionist, and the winner, a Miss Jean Reddy of Burnley, was a telephone operator, like Ferrier herself.[118]

Singing competitions more broadly were a popular phenomenon of this era. In 1952 MGM sponsored 'The Great Caruso Competition' to coincide with the British release of the Mario Lanza film.[119] And in the same year, a Royal Albert Hall concert in aid of the National Playing Fields Association included on the programme a 'Search for Opera and Concert Star' contest, the winners to be awarded a camera, a session at a photographic studio, or an Ascot Gas Water Heater.[120] These events were not so far removed from the popular talent shows found on radio and television (*Opportunity Knocks* was a staple of the Light Programme and would move to ITV in 1956) or indeed at holiday camps.

In quite different vein, serious operas by British composers were now starting to enter the public consciousness, in an operatic renaissance kickstarted by *Peter Grimes* that one commentator likened to 'some

---

[115] ROH/2/2/32-59 Minutes and Papers from the Opera Sub-Committee (1955–57).

[116] Percy Cater, 'She Gave up Love for Art', *DM* (30 September 1955), n.p.

[117] Cater, '£1,000 prize for a girl singer in memory of Kathleen Ferrier', *DM* (15 December 1954), 1.

[118] Cater, 'A Wonderful Night for a Singer', *DM* (24 November 1955), n.p.; Cater, 'A Night of Triumph For Miss Reddy', *DM* (26 November 1955), n.p.

[119] Russell, 'Reaching the Operatic Stage', 333.

[120] Royal Albert Hall archive file RAHE/1/1952/172.

PAGEANTRY AND PARTICIPATION 119

long-dormant volcano thrust suddenly above the surface of the ocean'.[121] Walton, Tippett, and Berkeley were even finding their works in demand from European opera houses, a development that was 'startling and unprecedented'.[122] Covent Garden took *Peter Grimes* to the Théâtre de la Monnaie in Brussels and the Paris Opéra and *Billy Budd* to the Théâtre des Champs Elysées for the 'Masterpieces of the Twentieth-Century' Festival in May 1952.[123] All of these were clear attempts to vaunt the good health of British artistic achievement on the international stage.

Opera composition was being encouraged and stimulated in all sorts of unexpected contexts. In December 1957 the John Lewis Partnership placed adverts in daily newspapers and the specialist music press announced a competition for a full-length opera in English, suitable for amateur performance. The winning work, which would be performed in the fourth-floor auditorium at the company's new flagship store on Oxford Street, was announced in May 1959 as Hugo Cole's *The Tunnel*, about a disaster on the Victorian railways.[124] A reception to announce the result was attended by the musical great and good and critics from the major London newspapers.[125]

All this led to considerable optimism about opera in Britain, and there were even suggestions that older prejudices were starting to disappear. In the introduction to a pocket guide to the opera, Sir Steuart Wilson, Deputy General Administrator at the Royal Opera House, wrote: 'In the next generation . . . apologies for Opera will not be necessary, I think, for Opera will be a convention which is accepted because it is established'.[126] *The Times* also seemed giddily optimistic about the future of opera in Britain, arguing that 'many factors have combined during the past half-century to convert an anti-operatic majority among musicians and a wide-spread ignorance among the general public to a realization that [opera] is an essential part of the art of music, that it is a fine flowering of a national culture, that it is an interest and a delight to an ever-widening circle of people

---

[121] Anon., 'Advances in British Music', *TLS* (29 August 1952), viii.
[122] Anon., 'English Musical Growth', *TLS* (24 August 1951), xxix.
[123] *A Review 1946–1956*, p. 10.
[124] Anon., 'Winner of Opera Competition', *The Times* (27 May 1959), 7.
[125] Anon., 'The Opera Competition', *The Gazette of the John Lewis Partnership* (30 May 1959), n.p.; Memorandum 12368, 'Reception—26 May', Social Secretary to the Chairman (22 May 1959), JLP archive file 268/37.
[126] Sir Steuart Wilson, Foreword to Williams, *You and the Opera*, p. xii.

120   SOMEONE ELSE'S MUSIC

in our egalitarian society'.[127] And finally, an author for the *TLS* wondered whether Britain's opera problem might disappear altogether in future, speculating that 'the observer in the year 2001, knowing the outcome, may well smile as he looks back at our anxieties for opera'.[128] How wrong he would ultimately turn out to be.

[127] Our Music Critic, 'The Covent Garden Controversy', *The Times* (6 July 1956), 11.
[128] Anon., 'English Musical Growth'.

6

Counterculture

A man in black tie leans back in his stylish blue convertible Jaguar E-Type to reach for the picnic basket on the backseat. He is well-turned out, sophisticated, his hair neatly slicked back. His young female companion has bobbed hair and a loose, off-the-shoulder floral dress. This was how the Glyndebourne festival chose to promote itself in a publicity photograph on the cover of *The Tatler* in 1963.[1] It was a far cry from the images of the festival that had appeared in the magazine in the 1950s, featuring dowager duchesses with precision-set waves and fur jackets. There is something rather James Bond-esque about the man depicted in this image, and Bond was a character who had captured the nation's imagination when the first film in the franchise, *Dr No*, was released the previous year. Styled like this, opera almost seemed cool—and being cool mattered a great deal in the 1960s.

It was a hard sell making opera seem fashionably youthful, at a time when it was increasingly coming to be perceived as stuffy, out-of-date, and perhaps even that new word, 'square'. Opera-goers' sartorial choices were coming under renewed scrutiny. In 1962 Katharine Whitehorn, a former model and fashion editor at *The Observer*, wrote an observational piece about the types of people who frequented Covent Garden. There were, of course, still plenty of glamorously dressed women, but scattered among the smart set was an assortment of badly dressed eccentrics. Whitehorn poked fun at a man in a brown corduroy jacket, another with a square signet ring, and a 'concave character drinking tonic through a straw', whose description brings to mind a rather effete-sounding man who couldn't fill his dress shirt, didn't know basic social etiquette, and wasn't man enough to take hard liquor. There were frumpish women as well, including one so badly dressed 'in a high-necked white blouse and a piece of anklelength blackout' that Whitehorn concluded that she '*must* have been seriously interested in music'.[2]

---

[1] *The Tatler* (12 June 1963), cover.
[2] Katharine Whitehorn, 'Why Such Excellence in the Evenings?', *The Observer* (8 July 1962), 26; original emphasis.

122   SOMEONE ELSE'S MUSIC

The Observer was equally contemptuous of the audience over in unpretentious Islington. Its chief music critic, Peter Heyworth, often given to trenchant views, wrote disparagingly of 'our own great regiment of puritans, sipping their pale-grey coffee at Sadler's Wells', who looked witheringly at the celebrity circus that surrounded Callas at Covent Garden and asked themselves what it had to do with opera.[3] Thus he caricatured an audience often regarded as Britain's 'real opera lovers' as drab, humourless people so austere in their pursuit of art for art's sake that they were determined to deprive themselves even of a decent drink. What people drank at the opera seems to have preoccupied commentators to an unusual extent during the 1960s and become a sort of shorthand for broader matters of taste. At Covent Garden, a bartender reported that the drinks consumed at the theatre varied according to repertoire, with Wagner attracting heavy beer drinkers, *Carmen* drawing in those who liked spirits, and the crowd for *La bohème* being 'all sherries and gins'.[4]

This was a decade when opera criticism and opera reportage were so extensive that one commentator wrote, '*The Times*, *The Financial Times* and *The Guardian* have so much about opera in them that the operamaniac should move near a public library if his pocket will not stand the strain.'[5] But much of the commentary was negative, as if the media had suddenly turned against opera. Again and again, the left-wing broadsheets in particular took issue with unfashionable people who enjoyed opera, caricaturing them not only for their tastes in clothes (and drinks) but for their tastes in repertory and singers.

Inverted snobbery was rife. Covent Garden was, at this time, still attracting huge numbers of 'galleryites'. In 1964, 200 people queued in the cold for three days, determined to secure a cheap standing position for Callas's *Tosca*.[6] A star singer remained a huge box office draw. A few years earlier Philip Hope-Wallace had noted sarcastically in *The Guardian* that rarities at Covent Garden attracted little attention, 'yet, mysteriously, if Tebaldi is in the offing or the name Zeffirelli is billed, the box office is besieged and office girls are lying out under sacks all night in Floral Street'.[7] Whereas reports of the Covent Garden queue from earlier in the century had admired the

---

[3] Peter Heyworth, 'Callas Returns to Milan', *The Observer* (11 December 1960), 27.
[4] Anon., 'Yes, It's Wagner That Drives Them to Drink', *DM* (26 October 1962), 4.
[5] Robin May, *Operamania* (Wimbledon: Vernon and Yates, 1966), p. 49.
[6] Untitled photograph, *The Observer* (2 February 1964), 3.
[7] Philip Hope-Wallace, 'Opera and Ballet in 1961', *The Guardian* (21 December 1961), 5.

COUNTERCULTURE 123

fans' hardy stoicism or rejoiced in the diverse audience for opera, Hope-Wallace's remark emits barely veiled contempt. There were, presumably, people of varied occupations queuing, yet he seized upon lowly 'office girls' and mocked them for their interest in female stars. These shallow women watching other shallow women could not, he implied, possibly be interested in art itself.

This was a variation on a perennial theme—self-styled highbrows had been sneering at 'canary fanciers' for centuries, and star singers continued to be seen as trivial, on account of the publicity given to their extra-musical activities. Callas's activities were front-page news, whether she was being ordered to rest by her doctor, cancelling an appearance, or giving evidence at the High Court. However, it seems ironic and more than a little unfair that people should have been mocked for clamouring to see star singers in a decade when hero-worship of singers, albeit of a different type, would go off the scale.

The mention of Zeffirelli exuded snobbery too. Critics were widely sceptical about film directors venturing into opera directing, using it as evidence that opera was overly emotional and catered for 'a cinema audience'. A writer for *The Illustrated London News* suggested that opera was for stupid people because audiences were told 'in pictures' what the music meant—'this is the angry bit, this is love, this rejection, and so on'.[8] Thus, the ages-old caricature of the dim-witted opera fan returned with a vengeance.

From reading reports such as these, one could be forgiven for thinking opera was patronised only by peculiar people: the nerdy and 'square'; the stupid and rich; plus a few sad and desperate starstruck girls willing to sleep overnight on pavements. In this we can see a precursor of today's notion that opera is for the over-educated, the wealthy, and the eccentric—an idea that is constantly wheeled out with the apparent intention of making it off-putting to everyone else. There were often politically driven agendas to such caricatures. Robin May, author of several introductory guides to opera, argued in 1966 that the number of people going to the opera simply because it was 'the thing to do' was being grossly exaggerated, 'especially by philistines eager to cut operatic subsidies', a comment that anticipates today's opera-funding debate eerily.[9]

[8] A. K. Panni, 'The Opera Industry', *ILN* (25 May 1968), 46–47, 46.
[9] May, *Operamania*, p. 1.

124   SOMEONE ELSE'S MUSIC

The left-wing press was particularly keen to stress opera's irrelevance to modern life, calling it a 'fringe activity' and a frivolous luxury, and arguing that nobody gave a fig what was going on at Covent Garden.[10] This much is unsurprising, given that this was a decade in which the left was increasingly preoccupied with the rejection of traditional bourgeois society and dispensing with its language, values, culture and ideology, even in some quarters calling for Marxist-inspired revolution. As Jonathan Rose notes, the 1960s was also a decade when a new generation of middle-class, university-educated 'Bohemians' started to display contempt for the 'culturally conservative working class', including the humble autodidacts of earlier decades.[11] Nevertheless, criticisms of opera were not limited to the left-wing press. *The Illustrated London News* dismissed Glyndebourne as 'a socially anachronistic institution'.[12] Even *The Spectator* argued that Covent Garden no longer commanded the awe as a cultural institution it once had, being, for most people, 'a nothingness, a thing perhaps at most glanced at in the papers', or worse, a tourist-trap and 'mausoleum'.[13]

Some people directly involved in the opera business were, by the 1960s, inclined to regard it with scorn, as if it were something passé with which they barely wished to be associated. In 1965 Richard Rodney Bennett's *The Mines of Sulphur* was premiered at Sadler's Wells, yet he admitted that he didn't go to the opera himself, telling an interviewer, 'I hate the palaver of the theatre. It's like the Covent Garden mystique and the sort of "camp" surrounding opera in the recent past. The large majority of so-called opera fans are not really interested in music—those potty Glyndebourne audiences, all hampers and long dresses.'[14]

The journalist Bernard Levin wrote in 1970 that opera was 'under increasingly fierce attack at the end of the decade as an irrelevant and expensive bauble, kept up, at huge cost to the vast majority who were entirely uninterested in it, for the pleasure of the tiny handful who doted on it'.[15] And yet, he proposed, 'the more opera, as an art-form, appeared absurd, moribund and socially indefensible, the more clear it became that it, alone among art-forms,

---

[10]   Peter Heyworth, 'Callas Returns to Milan', *The Observer* (11 December 1960), 27; Hope-Wallace, 'Opera and Ballet in 1961', 5.

[11]   Rose, *The Intellectual Life*, p. 462.

[12]   Anon., 'New Policies Take Shape at Glyndebourne', *ILN* (27 May 1967), 19.

[13]   Clive Barnes, 'Everything in the Garden', *The Spectator* (20 September 1964), 348–351, 348.

[14]   Anon., 'Anti-Camp Composer', *The Observer* (21 February 1965), 23.

[15]   Bernard Levin, *The Pendulum Years: Britain and the Sixties* (London: Jonathan Cape, 1970), p. 366.

provided in the Sixties that which the other arts had foresworn: certainty'. Thus, perhaps people who enjoyed opera clung to it ever more keenly. But how casually opera appeared to have been dismissed, even by its own practitioners, becoming—at least according to a sceptical press—a 'nothingness', of no interest to an indifferent nation.

Civilisation?

The broader attitudinal shifts of the 1960s did the image of opera few favours. Many of the old mores, social norms, and ideas about culture and civilisation were starting to change, with a questioning of the rigid social hierarchies and unhesitating respect for authority that had lived on into the 1950s. Class barriers were breaking down, and paternalism and 'the Establishment' were being rejected by everyone from radical activists to Oxbridge graduates-turned-comedians.[16] Roy Strong argues that the 1960s marked the end of what he calls 'consensus culture': 'the preservation and transmission of the old aristocratic and bourgeois culture', the defence of excellence against populism, the idea that the arts bore with them a moral as well as an aesthetic dimension.[17]

All this had consequences for the arts, as the supposed hegemony of high culture was comprehensively rejected by the end of the decade. It is unsurprising that opera in particular should have been hit hard by the changing mores of the era, bound up as it was in many people's minds—however unfairly—with the upper classes, the Establishment, and the perceived stuffiness of decades past. Opera seemed particularly conventional in its buildings, its modes of presentation (updated productions were still some years off), and its audiences, when compared with the new vogue for experimental theatre and artistic 'happenings'.

Opera was also, of course, worlds apart from the popular music that was becoming a genuine lingua franca and increasingly driving classical music into the shade. As Peter Aspden put it, many decades later,

[16] Arthur Marwick, *The Sixties: Cultural Revolution in Britain, France, Italy, and the United States, c. 1958–1974* (Oxford: Oxford University Press, 1998), p. 3, p. 143.
[17] Roy Strong, *The Spirit of Britain: A Narrative History of the Arts* (London: Hutchinson, 1999), p. 664, p. 642.

126   SOMEONE ELSE'S MUSIC

when the 1960s arrived, the mission to bring high art to everyone was ambushed by a popular culture that was catchy, technologically accessible to all ... And so intensified the two-cultures dichotomy of the post-war world. Popular, or "low", culture—television, film, pop music, fashion—became clever in promoting itself to a mass audience; "high" culture, battered and bruised, turned inwards into specialised, almost academic niches.[18]

Of course, some of the headline claims about the 1960s being a decade of revolutionary change have been overstated. Though the modernising impulses of the era certainly had a long legacy, affecting how British society would develop over the coming decades, most people did not frequent the King's Road or embrace flower power. The 1960s was a decade of contradictions, of old and new attitudes sitting side by side in often uncomfortable juxtaposition, as old certainties started to come under scrutiny and were in some cases rejected. This is a point well illustrated by conversations about the idea of 'civilisation'. The year 1969 saw the broadcast of the landmark television series of that name. But elsewhere there was a growing discomfort around the word, as the whole idea of what culture was—and whether 'civilisation' mattered—was coming under scrutiny.

Landmark arts organisations had often, up until this point, been seen as emblems of a 'civilised' nation. Such language was still used in the 1960s, and not only by learned professors, critics who were out of step with the times, or reactionary habitués of the Covent Garden stalls. For example, on relaunching Sadler's Wells at the Coliseum in 1968—with a desire to draw in new listeners—the opera administrator Stephen Arlen uttered the words 'Opera is an investment in civilization'.[19] The civilisation argument was invoked regularly in discussions about arts subsidy: it was a marker of a civilised nation that it would support the finer things in life. In a book for young opera-goers, for instance, Michael Hurd argued that 'a nation that can boast of no artistic ability can hardly claim to play a part in civilization ... it is in Art that we see the soul of a people reflected and intensified'.[20] That same year, Covent Garden argued in favour of operatic subsidy on the grounds

[18] Peter Aspden, 'New Dawn', *FT* (17–18 April 2010), Life & Arts section, 1–2, 1.
[19] Panni, 'The Opera Industry', 46–47, 47.
[20] Hurd, *Young Person's Guide to Opera*, p. 39.

COUNTERCULTURE 127

that 'first, and this is in the end the ultimate reason, it fosters an art of high excellence which is intrinsically good in itself'.[21]

The idea of art being a marker of civilisation and a thing of value on its own merits that did not need to be justified in terms of extra-musical benefits was starting to be questioned in this period. There was vague talk of the postmodern ideas that were taking root in American universities, rejecting boundaries between 'high' and 'low' and celebrating pluralism. Within this framework, certainties about what constituted 'civilisation' were no longer quite as clear-cut as they had been, and the very definition of what constituted 'culture' was becoming a point of disagreement. In a 1962 memorandum, the Granada TV production company advocated against using the words 'highbrow' or 'lowbrow', which it characterised as 'snob words', because 'culture today does not reside only, even mainly, in the Royal Opera House, the Arts Council, Sadler's Wells and the Old Vic. They tend to be the custodians of yesterday's things, some of them good, some of them not so good. Culture is also to be found around people like Louis Armstrong, Gene Kelly and Tony Hancock'.[22]

Confidence was faltering at the BBC, meanwhile, surrounding the status of the Third Programme. The Corporation decided to reform its networks in 1967, rebranding them as Radio 1, 2, 3, and 4, a format that has survived to the present. Some felt that in doing away with the 'highbrow' Third Programme, the BBC had lost its idealism, in an era when popular culture reigned supreme. Many BBC producers were privately appalled by the move away from Reith's mission to 'educate by stealth', whereby someone listening to one type of programming might leave the radio on and stumble across something entirely different.[23] The move towards specialised channels ran the risk of placing classical music in a ghetto: it was now far less likely that a casual browsing listener would encounter an opera, in full or in excerpts, by chance.

The decade also had new ideas about equality and 'fairness': it was, after all, the decade that saw the beginnings of the move towards comprehensive education, offering the same opportunities for all. (Or which, depending on your view of things, signalled the beginning of the end for the grammar-school system that had created the sort of social mobility that allowed men

[21] Royal Opera House Annual Report 1962–63, 4. BUTC, MM/2/TH/LO/COV/121 (January–March 1963).
[22] Anon., 'Snobbery About Kinds of Brow', *DT* (14 September 1962), 23.
[23] Snowman, *Just Passing Through*, p. 195.

128 SOMEONE ELSE'S MUSIC

of humble backgrounds, such as Wilson, Heath, and Major, to become prime ministers.) In 1963 a *Daily Mail* columnist provocatively asked readers what they thought about unfairness, arguing that it was an unavoidable price one had to pay to have good things in life. Without the 'unfair' wealth of a few individuals, for example, the world would not be able to enjoy some of the world's great art collections. Without unfairness there could be no luxury, and this journalist argued that we all need something luxurious to aspire to, whether it be opera at Covent Garden, a fast car, or garden ornaments. But he acknowledged that the view was becoming an unfashionable one, writing that socialists 'would burn down St Paul's Cathedral, the National Gallery and Sir Malcolm Sargent, all of them the product of unfairness, if the flames were needed to warm a single child that was cold with hunger'.[24] If opera was coming to be seen as the product of 'unfairness', then that was a problem, and so the seeds of the elitism stereotype began to be sown.

New participants, new audiences

Despite the repeated messaging in the press that opera was stuffy and old-fashioned, and with its tacit claim to be 'the best' now in question, many people continued to enjoy opera in the 1960s and a surprising number tried it for the first time. Historian Arthur Marwick has argued that, for all the adventurous, eclectic, experimental art of the decade, most people's tastes remained fairly conservative, particularly when it came to audiences for classical music. He writes: 'Educational advance, growing affluence, social change, meant that the audience for traditional classical music was steadily growing.'[25]

Opera is hardly the music we would associate with 1960s youth culture, and it was doubtless a minority taste; nevertheless, there is evidence that opera's appeal among the young was growing during the 1960s, as a specially commissioned Arts Council report of 1969 confirmed.[26] The Royal Opera House's new Friends scheme, founded in 1962, soon attracted 1,200 student members, while Sadler's Wells announced in 1968 that half its audience was

---

[24] Peter Black, 'Does Luxury Deserve Such a Bad Name?', *DM* (27 September 1963), 10.
[25] Marwick, *The Sixties*, p. 334.
[26] Arts Council of Great Britain, *A Report on Opera and Ballet in the United Kingdom, 1966–69* (Colchester: Benham and Company, 1969).

COUNTERCULTURE   129

under 35.[27] *The Daily Mail* ran a profile in 1965 of three Clapham schoolboys given special dispensation by their headmaster to take time off to join the Covent Garden queue.[28]

Children also continued to discover opera via participation. Opera was still being performed in schools, but whereas the emphasis had previously been on children performing operas such as *The Magic Flute* or *Dido and Aeneas*, youngsters were now encouraged to create their own works, in keeping with a broader shift towards community art. Sylvia Boarder's book *They Made an Opera* documented two operas created by primary-school pupils, prompted by one of the children having seen Britten's *Let's Make an Opera*. Starting with the idea of a crowd of sailors, the children devised their own chorus, storyline (based on research in the public library and visiting Hampton Court), and in due course an entire opera about Sir Walter Raleigh. This involved writing words, making up tunes, constructing scenery, finding costumes, deciding on casting, direction, and finally giving a performance, and one child said, 'Acting in our own opera was the most exciting thing we ever did. I shall always remember it.'[29] The teacher spoke of the many and varied skills this model of 'active learning' had given them and nowhere in her account of the experiment did she refer to opera as something strange or elitist.

Another book about staging opera in schools (Terence Dwyer's *Opera in Your School*) did begin, however, from the starting point that negative perceptions might have to be overcome. The author of the book had, himself, previously disliked opera, associating it with 'screeching fat sopranos and incomprehensible plots, together with personal boredom and even misery.'[30] Yet here he was, stating that any school could put on an opera. The author advised schools to be ambitious in the repertory they chose, listing sixty-three recommended works, including *Bastien and Bastienne*, *Savitri*, *Amahl and the Night Visitors*, *Acis and Galatea*, and the ubiquitous *Dido and Aeneas*. There was an assumption, at which many would now baulk, that different 'types' of children would be capable of performing different types of work. A more advanced list was therefore provided for grammar and public

---

[27] *ROH Annual Report 1964–65*, p. 6. ROH archive file: Royal Opera House Annual Reports—1946/56–71/72; Peter Lewis, 'Opera Comes in from the Desert', *DM* (21 August 1968), 8.

[28] Brian O'Shea, 'Ticket Time for Covent Garden Campers', *DM* (5 May 1965), 7.

[29] Sylvia Boarder, *They Made an Opera* (London: University of London Press, Ltd, 1966), p. 23, p. 31.

[30] Terence Dwyer, *Opera in Your School* (London: Oxford University Press, 1964), p. 1.

130 SOMEONE ELSE'S MUSIC

schools, including *The Marriage of Figaro, The Magic Flute, The Bartered Bride,* and *Hugh the Drover*.[31]

Dwyer's book took a more formal approach than Boarder's, providing job specifications for staff (producer, MD, stage manager, dance director), detailed diagrams of how to group the chorus, instructions on how to plan a rehearsal schedule, and advice on all aspects of performance. In other words, this book, having started out with a cliché about opera, swiftly moved on to treating a school performance as if it were a full-scale professional show, treating the children's endeavours with the utmost seriousness, giving them as full an 'operatic education' as possible. Both of these books, then, took opera for children seriously and presented it without prejudice, but in very different ways.

Direct participation also introduced opera to adults who might never have given it a prior thought. June Gordon, Countess of Haddo, set up an opera company for the workers on her family estate, Haddo House, about twenty miles north of Aberdeen. Gordon had established a choral society at the House when her husband inherited it in 1945, recruiting estate workers and persuading these initially reticent singers to tackle progressively more difficult choral repertoire.[32] Soon the Haddos began to expand the operation, adding drama and an orchestra into the society's activities, enlisting the Queen Mother as a patron, and recruiting distinguished soloists, such as Heather Harper and Janet Baker for a Mozart Requiem in 1964.[33] Following a foray into Gilbert and Sullivan, the group was, by the 1960s, prioritising opera and putting on performances of works such as *Carmen* and *Macbeth*. The operation was an egalitarian one, involving shepherds and shopkeepers ('No social boundary was recognised, or, if distantly observed, was promptly ignored'): all that mattered was enthusiasm, camaraderie, and a decent ear.[34]

Opportunities were also expanding for talented people from ordinary backgrounds to train as opera singers. The Bridges Report of 1960 had recommended that a new advanced opera school should be established, giving postgraduate students the opportunity of practical training in a workshop environment, with the idea that they would progress to working with the major opera companies.[35] To this end, the London Opera Centre was

---

[31] Ibid., pp. 124–135.

[32] Eric Linklater, *The Music of the North* (Aberdeen: The Haddo House Choral Society, 1970), p. 4.

[33] Ibid., p. 15, p. 12.

[34] Ibid., p. 7.

[35] Anon., 'London Opera Centre: Report of the Committee Appointed by the Governing Body to Investigate Recent Criticisms of the Centre' (London: St Clement's Press, 1964), p. 26.

established in 1963 at the former Troxy Cinema on the Commercial Road in Stepney, an art-deco building which had been the largest and one of the most luxurious cinemas in England when it was built in the 1930s. It closed in 1960, its original audience having been relocated in post-war slum clearances, and sat unused for three years, becoming progressively shabbier until it was reopened as the opera training centre and a rehearsal space for Covent Garden.[36]

The Troxy used to resound to a rather different type of song—Vera Lynn, Gracie Fields, Petula Clarke, and Cliff Richard—but the opening of the London Opera Centre seemed fitting, given the earlier tradition of East End opera. The Centre, which would remain active until 1978, offered a training to students who did not come from particularly privileged backgrounds; one of the first cohort, for example, was a bricklayer.[37] Generous funding was provided by the Peter Stuyvesant Foundation (based on funds from tobacco sales) and the Count Cinzano Opera Scholarship (which offered students an opportunity to sing abroad).[38] Some students would go on to establish international careers: one particularly successful early course participant was Kiri Te Kanawa.

A new audience for the arts emerged in the 1960s that was socially diverse, intelligent but not pretentious, and keen to be informed about new developments. In his book *The Plain Man's Guide to the Opera*, Ernest Reynolds argued that opera—for all its purported 'uncoolness'—now had widespread appeal, whereas twenty years ago it had attracted only a minority.[39] He delighted in the possibilities audiences now had to supplement their operatic knowledge through broadcasts, recordings, and even holidays to major European operatic centres, continental travel no longer being the preserve of a leisured elite.[40] It was not incongruous in the 1960s to find a serious opera critic waxing lyrical about listening to five-and-a-half hours of Wagner at the Coliseum (Reginald Goodall's production of *Mastersingers*) in a publication such as *The Daily Express*.[41] *The Times Literary Supplement* noted that 'the old gap between highbrows and middlebrows seems to be closing.'[42]

---

[36] https://troxy.co.uk/about-us/history/ (accessed 3 September 2023).

[37] Anon., 'London Opera Centre: Report', p. 34.

[38] Anon., 'London Opera Centre', *FT* (1 May 1965), 7; Anon., 'More Money for Singers', *The Times* (16 April 1966), 12.

[39] Ernest Reynolds, *The Plain Man's Guide to the Opera* (London: Michael Joseph, 1964), p. 127.

[40] Ibid., p. 10.

[41] Alan Blyth, 'Musical Marathon at Just the Right Pace', *DE* (26 August 1968), 4.

[42] Anon., 'Whose Criterion?', *TLS* (8 January 1960), 20.

132 SOMEONE ELSE'S MUSIC

Opera did not, of course, address the fashionable 'kitchen sink realism' of the era, and seemed worlds apart in many ways from the new wave of British drama and film, which focused upon the lives of working-class communities. It also seemed far removed from the forms of working-class expression that were finding a voice in popular music. That said, the operatic world made some concessions to the changing ethos of the era. New operas were beginning to be written on more 'democratic' subjects, such as Thea Musgrave's *The Decision*, about a mining accident, which premiered at Sadler's Wells in 1967.[43]

Opera on television was now well-established and viewing figures were rising. In 1965/6, the highest audience for an opera on television was a broadcast of *La bohème*, which attracted 125,000 viewers, a respectable figure for BBC2, where the norm was usually closer to 25,000. Shifting opera onto BBC1, however, brought it to a vastly larger audience, with audiences of between 1 and 3 million not uncommon in the second half of the decade, whilst a series of six opera programmes presented by Tito Gobbi attracted 2.75 million viewers.[44] On ITV, meanwhile, opera often appeared in the context of arts magazine programmes and chat shows attracting high audiences. The fact that Geraint Evans made an appearance on 'Secombe and His Friends' in 1966 (a programme that attracted almost 7.25 million viewers) is noteworthy.[45] Other guests on the show included Tony Hancock, Danny La Rue, Spike Milligan, and Peter Sellers.[46] Evans and Secombe sang the *Pearl Fishers* duet together, harking back to the days of opera in the variety hall.

Singers continued to move flexibly between different genres of music, as they always had. A pop singer called David Hughes, briefly known as 'Mr Heart Throb', signed with Glyndebourne to sing in *Idomeneo*.[47] The bass-baritone Ian Wallace, though singing regularly with Scottish Opera and at opera houses around Europe by the 1960s, also performed a popular one-man show, featuring arias alongside ballads and comic songs (particularly the works of Flanders and Swann, becoming indelibly associated with their song 'The Hippopotamus'). Wallace also presented television programmes that introduced a wider audience to opera, such as 'Singing for your Supper'

---

[43] Michael Reynolds, 'Drama in a Disaster Pit', *DM* (1 December 1967), 16.
[44] Arts Council of Great Britain, *A Report on Opera and Ballet in the United Kingdom*, pp. 63–65.
[45] Ibid.
[46] https://www.imdb.com/title/tt0261280/fullcredits (accessed 19 November 2021).
[47] Barry Norman, 'From Pop to Opera', *DM* (30 November 1963), 8.

(a series of half-hour introductions to operas) and was well-known as one of the stars of the Radio 4 quiz show 'My Music'.

Meanwhile, new opportunities continued to arise for people to go and see live opera, and to access the arts in general. The Labour MP Jennie Lee, the UK's first Minister for the Arts, trebled the Arts Council's grant in six years, from £3.2 million in 1964–1965 to £9.4 million in 1970–1971, with 1966–1967 seeing the largest ever single rise in arts funding.[48] Lee was an important figure from the left who saw no incompatibility between excellence and access, and who understood the long and noble tradition of working-class participation in the arts, recalling that touring opera companies had been given an extremely warm welcome whenever they visited the Scottish mining community where she had grown up.[49] Lee was keen to foster different types of artistic creativity in places beyond the major London institutions, though she remained supportive of the latter. This ongoing commitment to 'high art' and traditional institutions meant that Lee enjoyed support from both sides of the House of Commons, the Conservatives seeing her as their 'pin-up girl' (as she herself put it) for supporting Covent Garden.[50]

Lee was particularly active in diverting money towards artistic activity in Scotland, Wales, and the regions more generally.[51] One of her personal regrets on leaving office was her failure to oversee the opening of a long-planned permanent opera house in Edinburgh, thanks to wranglings between the Treasury and Edinburgh City Council.[52] Discussions surrounding the project were coloured by the suggestion of elitism. *The Daily Telegraph* wondered whether there was demand for an opera house beyond the festival season, asking, 'Would a subsidised opera house be just an occasional "socialite" rendezvous for the wealthy or cater for a genuine appetite for music?'[53] Upon learning that a visiting opera troupe from Florence drew 80 per cent of its audiences back home from Tuscan locals and only 20 per cent from tourists, the same author expressed scepticism about whether Edinburgh—a city keener on bingo than the high arts—would be able to achieve anything similar. (Commercial bingo, made legal after the Betting

---

[48] Sean Day-Lewis, 'Miss Lee Promises £2½ Million More for Arts', *DT* (25 February 1966), n.p.
[49] Rose, *The Intellectual Life*, p. 198.
[50] Hollis, *Jennie Lee*, p. 363.
[51] Ibid., pp. 250–251.
[52] Ibid., p. 269.
[53] Normal Riley, 'Wrangle Over Opera House Rekindled', *DT* (26 August 1969), n.p.

134 SOMEONE ELSE'S MUSIC

and Gaming Act of 1960, was all the rage and characterised by some parts of the press as a sign of the nation's moral decline.[54])

However, other positive developments were afoot north of the border during the 1960s. 1961 saw the first performances by Scottish Opera, set up by Alex (later 'Sir Alexander') Gibson, a pianist and conductor who, after training in London, returned to Glasgow to direct the Scottish National Orchestra. During the 1950s he had conducted the Glasgow Grand Opera Society, an ambitious amateur operatic society, and by the early 1960s he had set about establishing Scottish Opera with like-minded friends who were keen amateur musicians, music teachers, and music enthusiasts. The company took a democratic approach to its casting, holding auditions in London, Manchester, and Glasgow in order to attract graduates from the conservatoires, and made it easy for singers to move between chorus and principal roles.[55]

Opera for All, meanwhile, the Arts Council's venture to introduce new audiences to opera, fell under the auspices of Scottish Opera in 1966. The group put on 255 stage performances in 1967–1968 and 252 the following year, staging small operas like Cimarosa's *The Secret Marriage* and scaled-down versions of *La bohème* and *Rigoletto*. They set up shop in towns across the United Kingdom that could never in other circumstances have hoped to have seen any opera, among them Bacup, Settle, and South Shields. Despite this, the perception of operatic culture being London-centred remained: sizeable towns and cities that received no visit from an opera company between 1966 and 1969 included Brighton, Reading, Southampton, and York.[56]

Many now believed that opera was becoming impossible to access at the country's most 'elite' companies. Glyndebourne had a seven-year waiting list and allocated 70 per cent of tickets on a priority booking system.[57] When *The Ring* was staged at Covent Garden in 1964, for the first time in four years, all tickets sold out in two days to subscribers to a subscription list that gave them priority booking, some twelve days before tickets were meant to go on sale to the general public.[58] By 1965 the theatre was offering a subscription voucher system, which offered ten tickets for the price of nine on the understanding

---

[54] David Kynaston, *Modernity Britain: 1957–62* (New York: Bloomsbury, 2014), p. 562.

[55] Cordelia Oliver, *It's a Curious Story: The Tale of Scottish Opera 1962–1987* (Edinburgh: Mainstream Publishing, 1987), pp. 14–15, p. 93.

[56] Arts Council of Great Britain, *A Report on Opera and Ballet in the United Kingdom*, p. 18, pp. 68–69.

[57] Anon., 'Opening Night at Glyndebourne', *The Tatler* (15 June 1960), 608.

[58] Anon., 'Ring a Ring o'Ring', *The Observer* (6 September 1964), 23.

that the purchaser would attend less popular as well as best-selling shows. The system was shrouded in mystery, with Covent Garden refusing to say how many people held the vouchers.[59] The company denied there was a problem, however, David Webster writing to *The Observer* to complain at its 'misleading' reporting of the situation and stating that the only limitation on ticket sales was the physical size of the house.[60] The newspaper responded to Webster's letter with an acidly worded note, stating: 'All theatres may face the same box-office problems, but not all provoke the same ill-feeling that Covent Garden does.' Yes, Covent Garden was in the press for all the wrong reasons yet again.

Opera wars in the West and East End

By now it was obvious that the post-war formula at Covent Garden was not working: the rough-and-ready opera-in-English approach was alienating the theatre's core audience and had reduced Covent Garden's distinctiveness. It had tried to be 'a large-scale Sadler's Wells', as *The Guardian* put it, but the audience that was in search of cheap, relatively modest performances in English had largely remained loyal to Sadler's Wells itself. Touring to cities such as Oxford, Leeds, and Manchester was resulting in typical losses of £9,000–£10,000 a week and big international stars would not tour.[61] Nor would they relearn roles in English, and as time went on the company found itself merely paying lip-service to the English-language policy; the guiding principle of using predominantly British singers had also been quietly sidelined.[62] Even the Arts Council admitted in 1969 that 'it felt impossible to reach the highest international level by using only British artists and singing only in English'.[63]

The conductor George Solti arrived at Covent Garden in 1961, with an aspiration to make Covent Garden the best opera house in the world. In terms of language policy, he struck a compromise, proposing all comic and Slav operas be given in English and everything else in the original, though an exception was made for *Wozzeck* in 1964, in whose case a combination

[59] Julian Holland, 'I'm Sorry to Introduce a Sour Note at the Opera, But . . ', *DM* (5 July 1965), 6.

[60] David Webster, letter to *The Observer* (13 September 1964), 28.

[61] Our Own Reporter, 'North Gets a Lesson in Self-Help—On Opera', *The Guardian* (23 March 1961), 26.

[62] Heyworth, 'The State of Covent Garden'; Tooley, *In House*, p. 5.

[63] Arts Council of Great Britain, *A Report on Opera and Ballet in the United Kingdom*, p. 10.

136 SOMEONE ELSE'S MUSIC

of German language and atonal music was considered a step too far.[64] A return to international opera gave a boost to the much-derided star system, and stars were expensive: some were being paid as much as £1,000 a week by the mid-1960s.[65] In some ways this might be seen as reinforcing the idea of opera as something elite, if not elitist, bolstering long-standing clichés about opera's exoticism and snobbish people who would only tolerate opera so long as it was 'foreign'. Yet, on another view, one might note that the return to this model was driven by public demand: audiences were making it very clear once again that what they liked best was watching Callas (Figure 6.1) or Sutherland. Compelled, once again, to defend its use of foreign singers in the face of press criticism, the company stated that it still needed to buy singers in to sing particular roles, and declared emphatically that 'it is our duty to present artists of special eminence whom the public has a wish and a right to hear'.[66]

Thus, Covent Garden, having long wrestled with the conundrum of whether to be international or national, therefore finally decided that only a hybrid model could work. This was both a good thing for opera in Britain, ushering in a period of improving artistic standards, to the satisfaction of audiences and critics, and a bad thing, heralding the end of many of the laudable ambitions of the post-war era, which had done good work in confronting the negative perceptions surrounding Covent Garden and opera in general. Of course, the new international model was not the same as it had been during the pre-war period: this would be all-year-round international opera, the term a signifier for quality rather than exclusivity.

Solti's innovations, in casting and in programming, were expensive. Even with annual subsidy of £1.25 million and audiences averaging over 90 per cent of capacity, the Royal Opera House claimed to be existing from hand to mouth, with annual expenditure exceeding £2.25 million and large debts by the end of the decade.[67] But the company argued that high-quality art was 'intrinsically good in itself', and emphasised aspects of its operation that were for the national good. In providing opera at the highest standard, Covent Garden was providing an educational function, acting as a seedbed for the nation's most talented performers, and acting as 'an essential feature of the

---

[64] Clive Barnes, 'Everything in the Garden', *The Spectator* (20 September 1964), 348–345, 349; Edward Greenfield, 'Wozzeck at Covent Garden', *The Guardian* (30 October 1964), 11.
[65] Holland, 'I'm Sorry to Introduce a Sour Note', 6.
[66] *Royal Opera House Annual Report 1962–63*, p. 11. ROH archive file: Royal Opera House Annual Reports—1946/56–71/72.
[67] Anon., 'Royal Opera Appeal', *DM* (19 December 1969). 9; Panni, 'The Opera Industry', 46.

Figure 6.1 Maria Callas among fans at the Royal Opera House for Puccini's *Tosca*, 1965. Reproduced with permission from © Performing Arts Images/ArenaPAL.

attractions of a metropolitan centre', for 'the business and life of contemporary London would be substantially reduced if it were not for the fame of its music, its theatre and its galleries'.[68] Such unabashed confidence in London as a great metropolitan centre, in the importance of cultivating a civilised life there, and of the benefits of art for art's sake, with no reference to any utilitarian function, are striking. A defence of opera on these grounds would be unimaginable in later decades. Striking, too, is the fact that opera—of all art forms—was being held up as central to the cultural activities that made Britain great.

Nevertheless, Covent Garden was under attack, even from voices within the wider theatrical world. In 1965 Peter Cadbury, chairman of the theatre ticket agency Keith Prowse, complained at such large sums of public money being spent on minority productions for a fringe audience, such as 'the Covent Garden "orgy" opera, *Moses and Aaron*', rather than on conventional

[68] *Royal Opera House Annual Report 1962–63*, p. 4.

138 SOMEONE ELSE'S MUSIC

theatre.[69] And Len Harper, Chairman of the Sunderland Empire Theatre Committee, aggrieved at the fact that his own theatre got no Arts Council funding because it put on variety shows, complained that taxpayers' money was used to fund productions from which 'only the intellectual minority benefit', with almost half of all available funds going annually to Covent Garden and Sadler's Wells. The unfortunate headline given by *The Guardian* to his letter was 'The Arts Council and Top-Hat Culture'.[70] Top hats had barely been seen at Covent Garden for decades, except at special gala performances, and the thought of them being worn at Sadler's Wells was absurd. Yet Covent Garden was being increasingly characterised, once again, in terms of the old clichés about luxury and inaccessibility. State performances for visiting royalty and the introduction from 1961 of a flashy annual opera gala patronised by the Queen Mother (albeit as a fundraising venture) also presented an image of luxury and expense.[71] The resident company changed its name from the Covent Garden Opera Company to the Royal Opera in 1968.

In 1964, in a gesture to the long-suffering galleryites, the gallery was made more welcoming, the old wooden benches on stone steps being replaced by tip-up seats.[72] The necessary period of closure for renovation and rewiring—combined with a rising salary bill—led to a 'grave deterioration' in the House's finances, which would preoccupy it for some years.[73] A tiny fraction of the costs were passed on to audiences via ticket prices, but the increases came in a way some found unfair. Price rises were proportionally steeper in the gallery seats than in the more exclusive parts of the house: gallery tickets had more than trebled since 1946 (increasing from 2s. 6d. to 8s. 6d.), while seats in the stalls had only doubled (from 17s. 6d. to 35s.).[74]

There was more bad press for the theatre in 1964 when it became embroiled in what *The Daily Mail* called 'the biggest row that opera in this country has had for many a year'.[75] Covent Garden was responsible for the administration of the London Opera Centre at the Troxy. The institution had replaced an earlier opera training centre, the National School of Opera,

---

[69] Anon., 'Mr Cadbury's Plea for "Conventional Theatre"', *The Guardian* (28 August 1965), 12.

[70] Len Harper, 'The Arts Council and Top-Hat Culture', letter to *The Guardian* (13 January 1965), 10.

[71] Anon., 'When Royalty Steps Out', *DM* (20 October 1960), 9; Lord Drogheda, *Double Harness: Memoirs by Lord Drogheda* (London: Weidenfeld and Nicolson, 1978), p. 273.

[72] Haltrecht, *The Quiet Showman*, p. 20.

[73] *Royal Opera House Annual Report 1964–65*, p. 5. ROH archive file: Royal Opera House Annual Reports—1946/56–71/72.

[74] Anon., 'Callas, Costs and Queues', *DM* (30 July 1965), 4.

[75] Julian Holland, 'It's Murder at the Opera!', *DM* (6 June 1964), 8.

COUNTERCULTURE 139

which had been established in 1948 at Morley College by Sadler's Wells soprano/manager Joan Cross and Anne Wood. In 1964, Cross and Wood became embroiled in a row with the Centre's director (Professor Procter-Gregg), ultimately leading to the resignation of all concerned.[76] In a damning report, Cross and Wood expressed their regret that the new Centre had not simply been established on the existing premises, and that their views were not taken into account when it came to setting company policy.[77]

Many of Cross and Wood's concerns were about practicalities and niggling details of the running of the enterprise: the costliness of the building; the lack of a proper stage; bold claims in the prospectus that could only disappoint students; approaches to teaching that they perceived to be too 'academic' and so forth.[78] But one cannot help but detect a more fundamental clash between Cross, a product of the Vic-Wells companies, and an enterprise associated with Covent Garden. Indeed, her press statement said, 'We have always held the view, and stated it, that there is no *natural* relationship between an opera school and an international opera house.'[79]

The deal that had been struck with Covent Garden ostensibly stated that the Centre would be able to uses the premises, administrative support, and artistic resources of the Royal Opera and the Royal Opera would be able to use the Troxy from time to time as a rehearsal space. But this was not how things turned out in practice. The relationship became an uneasy one, and Cross and Wood objected in particular to the fact that students from the Centre, who were usually admitted to dress rehearsals at Covent Garden, had been denied entry to watch a dress rehearsal of *Tosca* starring Callas.[80]

Expense, luxury, snobbery, exclusivity. These were stereotypes Covent Garden wanted to counter—and it was trying hard to do so. In 1967, it collaborated with the BBC on the first live transmission of a complete opera on television, with a broadcast of *La traviata*—a significant step in taking its performances to much larger audiences.[81] By the end of the decade there was much talk of the opportunities that might be provided in the early 1970s by the relocation of the fruit-and-vegetable market. A redevelopment of

[76] Anon., 'London Opera Centre Criticisms Answered', *FT* (10 September 1964), 24.
[77] Anon., 'London Opera Centre: Report of the Committee Appointed by the Governing Body to Investigate Recent Criticisms of the Centre' (London: St Clement's Press, 1964), pp. 8–9.
[78] Ibid., p. 27, p. 37.
[79] 'Press Statement by Miss Joan Cross CBE and Miss Anne Wood', 23 April 1964. Reprinted in Anon., 'London Opera Centre', p. 24; original emphasis.
[80] Ibid., p. 32; p. 12.
[81] *Royal Opera House Annual Report, 1972/1973*, p. 6. ROH archives file: Royal Opera House Annual Reports—1972/73–1991/92.

140 SOMEONE ELSE'S MUSIC

the theatre would allow not only for better rehearsal spaces and facilities for musicians but for audience spaces that removed some of the old social hierarchies that were built into the architecture of the building. The management noted that it was no longer the case that the habitués of the stalls and the gallery were of a different economic and social bracket and that it was 'preposterous' that patrons could not mix, even during the intervals, because of having to use different entrances.[82]

Interviewed in 1965 by *The Daily Mail* about who the theatre was for, David Webster covered every base. He stated:

> At Covent Garden we aim to present opera and ballet for everybody interested or likely so to be in these arts, and not for one class or strata socially, one wage or salary group, rich or poor, a high-brow or a low-brow, the musically educated or the chap who simply states he knows what he likes. We present it, too, for the growing population exposed to music in schools and for those who want music as relaxation, entertainment, something for their leisure, for intellectual fulfilment or anything else.[83]

This sounded very much like the ethos of another company that had long stressed its welcoming, populist credentials—and it was one that was about to move much closer to Covent Garden.

There was confident talk in the early to mid-1960s of Sadler's Wells moving to a new 'national opera house' beside the National Theatre. However, to the disappointment of the company, escalating costs of the South Bank project in general meant that the plan never came to fruition, with the government withdrawing financial support in 1966 and the GLC refusing to contribute without the government.[84] In 1968 it was confirmed that the company would, instead, move up west, to the Coliseum on St Martin's Lane, a move it hoped would allow the company to gain greater prominence in London and attract a larger audience.[85] The company gave its last performance at Sadler's Wells on 15 June 1968. It was, fittingly, *Peter Grimes*—the opera with which the theatre had reopened after the war. The move to the Coliseum commenced in August with a *Don Giovanni* directed by Sir John Gielgud, designed by Derek Jarman, and conducted by Charles Mackerras: the first performance

---

[82] *Royal Opera House Annual Report 1966–67*, p. 4. ROH archive files: Royal Opera House Annual Reports—1946/56–71/72.

[83] Anon., 'Callas, Costs and Queues', *DM* (30 July 1965), 4.

[84] Anon., 'Opera Maniacs', *The Guardian* (16 August 1962), 6; Anon., 'Ring a Ring o'Ring', 23; Hollis, *Jennie Lee*, p. 264; Anon., *A History of Sadler's Wells* (London: English National Opera, 1974), n.p. BUTC, MM/REF/TH/LO/COL/48 (January–March 1974).

[85] Anon., 'Sadler's Wells for Coliseum', *The Times* (6 February 1968), 6.

COUNTERCULTURE 141

was a sell-out, the house 'crammed to the last seat and the last half-inch of standing room'.[86]

The Coliseum was a theatre with an appropriately populist past, designed by Frank Matcham in 1904 for the music-hall impresario Oswald Stoll and intended to be the largest and grandest variety hall of its era, which had latterly (from 1963 to 1968) been used as a Cinerama wide-screen cinema. On the day of the move, *The Daily Mirror* flagged up the theatre's roots in popular culture, reporting that 'the arias of Mozart will tonight soar happily above the stage trodden by Vesta Tilley and Lily Langtry—and a theatre will be reborn', and reminding readers that this was the venue that had staged many a popular triumph, from Sarah Bernhardt to *Annie Get Your Gun*.[87] We might have expected a tabloid newspaper to remark on this with a degree of humour or cynicism, but the move was reported without 'side': this article concluded simply by stating that the new premises would 'give more people an opportunity to see good opera'. Similarly *The Daily Mail* applauded the arrival of opera in the West End, writing, 'For the first time in our era, opera is pitching alongside the hardened old hands of show business, confident that it can pull the customers in as well as they can.'[88] Sadler's Wells was 'raring to prove that the British public will go to the opera for a night out, without any of the mystique of Covent Garden attached'.

Two permanent companies presenting opera in very different ways now rubbed shoulders just a handful of streets apart. With international opera back on the agenda at Covent Garden, the language issue became a way for the companies to differentiate themselves. However, the similarity of interior design aesthetics between the two companies' homes—both overflowing with red velvet and gilt—may have begun to blur the line between the two in the public's mind. The aesthetic of the old Sadler's Wells Theatre was described, variously, as 'utility, almost austerity', 'plain, unadorned, rather dull, rather small', and even 'positively hideous within', whereas the Coliseum was 'opulent, almost aggressively decorated ... stagey in the grand manner'.[89]

It was harder now to go on seeing Sadler's Wells as the British equivalent of continental theatres for the people such as Paris's Opéra Comique and Berlin's Komische Oper.[90] The intimacy of a smaller theatre had been

[86] William Mann, 'Big Welcome at New Wells', *The Times* (22 August 1968).
[87] David Clemens, 'Scene', *DMir* (21 August 1968), 14.
[88] Lewis, 'Opera Comes in from the Desert', 8.
[89] Stephen Arlen interviewed by Ursula Robertshaw, 'A New Home for London Opera', *ILN* (31 August 1968), 18–19; Bernard Levin, 'Bernard Levin', *DM* (7 February 1968), 6.
[90] Patrick Carnegy, 'Blood on the Carpet', *TLS* (1 January 2010), 3–4, 4.

142   SOMEONE ELSE'S MUSIC

lost, pushing the company towards larger-scale repertoire. There were also, suddenly, far more seats to fill: 2,400 as opposed to 1,450. The company promised to keep 2,000 tickets at 'present Finsbury prices'; the remaining 400 would be more expensive but still cheaper than the equivalent tickets at Covent Garden.[91] There was certainly great public interest in the move to the Coliseum: £45,000 was taken in advance bookings, and by April 1969, the company was reporting an increase in attendances of almost 50 per cent compared with the last season at Sadler's Wells (though of course there were far more seats to be filled).[92]

Sadler's Wells also hoped to attract new *types* of people to the opera. Relocating had the disadvantage of moving further away from its loyal local audience. In a more prominent situation, however, close to Trafalgar and Leicester Squares, the theatre would be able to attract curious passers-by and tourists, including people who might ordinarily go to see musical theatre. Stephen Arlen, the company's Managing Director, wanted to make the Coliseum 'the theatre in which newcomers to opera learn about the medium'.[93] These could be important people: even Jennie Lee, who rarely went to Covent Garden, enjoyed sitting in the chairman's box for first nights at the Coliseum.[94] But more importantly, Arlen's aim was to 'bring home to a carpenter, or a motor mechanic, that opera is not some strange minority rite, but a play with music, and good, tuneful music too' and to 'attract a public that has never seen opera before, people who have thought of opera as snob art'.[95] In its new setting, then, Sadler's Wells was aspiring to return to first principles, reviving the aspirations of Baylis. Opera might be facing fresh challenges in the 1960s, but the arrival of a new, year-round 'people's opera', in the very heart of the West End, was surely a beacon of hope in the cause of opera for all.

---

[91] Anon., 'Sadler's Wells Policy to Be Maintained', *The Times* (29 April 1968), 13.

[92] Stephen Arlen interviewed by Ursula Robertshaw, 'A New Home for London Opera', *ILN* (31 August 1968), 18–19, 19; Henry Raynor, 'Sadler's Wells Reviews its First Year at Coliseum', *The Times* (5 December 1969), 7.

[93] Alan Blyth, 'Sadler's Wells Takes Over the Coliseum', *The Times* (23 May 1968), 13; Henry Raynor, 'Sadler's Wells Reviews Its First Year at Coliseum', *The Times* (5 December 1969), 7.

[94] Hollis, *Jennie Lee*, p. 294.

[95] Ursula Robertshaw, 'A New Home for London Opera', *ILN* (31 August 1968), 18–19, 18; Eric Mason, 'Sadler's Wells Moves to West End', *DM* (26 April 1968), 11.

7

A National Opera?

Christmas, on early 1970s television, was synonymous with light entertainment. As families up and down the land gathered around the set on Christmas night, they could usually look forward to a Disney film, a pantomime, a sitcom like *On the Buses*, or a variety show with Ken Dodd. But in November 1972, ITV announced a radical, unthinkable plan. On Christmas night, it would show an opera. Moreover, it would not even show a really popular opera with tunes everybody knew, like *Aida* or *La bohème*, but Verdi's *Macbeth*.

In truth, ITV itself had reservations about this unorthodox plan. The idea had been imposed upon it by the recently formed Independent Broadcasting Authority, which had rejected the original Christmas schedule proposed by the station and dictated that there should be more serious programming.[1] ITV executives were up in arms, arguing that it would be 'suicidal' to broadcast the opera in the most coveted ratings spot of the year, driving viewers straight into the arms of the BBC, which would be broadcasting light entertainment as usual.[2]

The proposed broadcast, recorded by Southern Television at Glyndebourne the previous August, became front-page news. For the tabloids, the IBA was being a 'killjoy', inflicting gloomy opera on people who were already miserable enough. *The Daily Mail* argued, 'When you remember that the nation hates opera even more, if that were possible, than it hates Shakespeare, to offer a combination of the dreaded pair to the ITV audience was a splendid act of defiance.'[3] It was *The Daily Telegraph*—a newspaper that published a good deal of high-quality arts journalism—which came closest to the charge of elitism, baulking at what it saw as high art being forcibly imposed upon the nation from above by a 'new model Establishment', acting like Victorian Salvationists purporting to enlighten

---

[1] Shaun Usher, 'Cut the Comics at Christmas ITV is Told', *DM* (10 November 1972), 1.
[2] Leslie Watkins, 'Exit Macbeth to Cheers', *DM* (11 November 1972), 11.
[3] Peter Black, 'Entertainment/2', *DM* (28 December 1972), 19.

144 SOMEONE ELSE'S MUSIC

the masses. A peculiarly British combination of anti-intellectualism and patriotism was much in evidence in the newspaper's depiction of a nation under assault from cosmopolitan elites, culminating in the comment 'Better England free than England cultivated against its will'.[4]

Following the rebellion at ITV, the IBA eventually relented and postponed the broadcast until 27 December, scheduling it immediately, after *The Benny Hill Show*, in the naïve hope that viewers who enjoyed slapstick and double entendres might remain tuned in.[5] In fact, the viewing figures for *Macbeth* were better than might have been hoped. About 4.5 million viewers watched the start and although numbers dropped away, 2.5 million were still watching at the end.[6] Although this was far lower than ITV's regular viewing figures in the same 9.30 p.m. slot (around 10 million), the figures were high for opera and better than those BBC2 might expect for any kind of programme. Plans went ahead for Southern Television to return to Glyndebourne for filming the next summer.

Even sceptical journalists were converted. Peter Black of *The Daily Mail*, the journalist who had argued that the nation hated opera, found elements in *Macbeth* that were akin to popular culture. The Macbeths resembled movie gangster chiefs, Lady Macbeth recalled the wicked queen in Disney's *Snow White*, and the opera was packed full of 'cheerful Italian folk tunes', the witches' incantation resembling 'a Neapolitan patter song in six-eight time for entertainer and café chorus'.[7] Opera might not be panto, but looked at in a certain way, it wasn't too far removed from it.

Such connections between opera and popular culture were not so far-fetched in the 1970s. A few years later Queen released 'Bohemian Rhapsody' (1975), an operatic parody complete with 'bombastic choruses, sarcastic recitative and distorted Italian operatic phraseology', which spent nine weeks at number one.[8] It is interesting to note that opera was not something Queen's members perceived to be 'foreign'. Freddie Mercury was well-known for his eclectic musical tastes, and Brian May later said that all members of the band had absorbed a lot of classical music subliminally through their parents, writing, 'It's part of our English upbringing.'[9]

---

[4] Anon., 'The Cultural Salvationists', *DT* (11 November 1972), 14.
[5] Maurice Weaver, 'Enter Verdi—on ITV', *DT* (28 December 1972), 9.
[6] Sean Day-Lewis, 'Opera Worry for ITV', *DT* (24 January 1973), 15.
[7] Black, 'Entertainment/2'.
[8] Ken McLeod, 'Bohemian Rhapsodies: Operatic Influences on Rock Music', *Popular Music*, 20/2 (May 2001), 189–203, 192.
[9] Cited in ibid., 192.

A NATIONAL OPERA? 145

Astonishing as it may seem now, the 1970s tabloid press began to embrace opera as the decade progressed. In 1975 *The Daily Mirror* took the unlikely step of choosing Monteverdi's *The Return of Ulysses to His Homeland* as its pick of the week for the August bank holiday and at Christmas it billed a broadcast of *La bohème* as 'not to be missed'.[10] In 1978 it encouraged readers to watch *The Magic Flute*, reporting, 'This is television at its best. See what you think.'[11] The paper's reporting about opera was enthusiastic and respectful, only occasionally veering into the sort of language we might expect from the 'gutter press', such as when it billed *Carmen* as 'sex heavily wrapped in culture . . . full of heaving bosoms and lascivious goings-on'.[12] Certainly, none of this discussion of opera was given an 'elitist' frame.

Audience numbers that had previously been in the thousands were now in the millions. For the most part, however, the BBC itself was not at this stage using viewer figures as a metric of worth. In 1972 David Attenborough, then Director of Programmes at BBC Television, said about audience size: 'Nearly always it is quoted as though it were a measure of quality. Oddly, some regard a high figure as an indication of excellence, whereas others see it as proof of precisely the reverse.'[13] It was still accepted that a programme could be of high value even if its viewing figures were comparatively low—though even an audience of four million meant that one person in fifteen was watching, a far from negligible figure.[14]

A key figure in getting more opera on television was Humphrey Burton, Head of BBC TV's Music and Arts programmes, whom *The Daily Mail* approvingly called 'the most important single patron of the arts since the medieval Venetians'.[15] Across the course of the decade, under Burton's tenure, the number of operas on BBC television had risen from three a year in 1970 to around eighteen in 1979.[16] In the autumn of 1979, audiences could watch, amongst other things, a documentary about Pavarotti; broadcasts of *La Gioconda* and *Tosca* at peak time on successive Saturday nights; Solti

---

[10] Anon., 'Pick of the Week', *DMir* (24 August 1975), 22; Anon., 'Sounds Super!', *DMir* (27 December 1975), n.p.

[11] Anon., Untitled article, *DMir* (30 December 1978), 11.

[12] Ann Pacey, 'Henry, You're a Little Devil', *DMir* (30 April 1978), 21.

[13] David Attenborough, 'Audience Figures', *BBC Handbook 1972* (BBC: London, 1972), pp. 12–15, p. 12.

[14] Joan Bakewell and Nicholas Garnham, *The New Priesthood: British Television Today* (London: Allen Lane, 1970), p. 127.

[15] Martin Jackson, 'Mainstream . . .? It's Become Even More Like a Backwater', *DM* (8 December 1979), 22–23, 22.

[16] Ibid., 23.

146　SOMEONE ELSE'S MUSIC

conducting *Arabella*; and a new commission, *The Rajah's Diamonds*.[17] Burton believed that an opera or ballet was capable of generating as much interest as a film or a play, and stated, 'I believe I am in business to provide pleasure and that pleasure should not be confined to some coterie or elite but should be made accessible to everyone.'[18]

Some in broadcasting now saw the Reithian notion of giving people what was good for them as rather aloof, and in 1978 the BBC launched a survey to find out whether 'people who don't often watch our programmes think they are too elitist or aimed over their heads'.[19] Nevertheless, there remained a bullishness in the 1970s about what TV could achieve in terms of fostering an audience for the arts, the BBC even declaring in 1976 its ambition to 'change the whole nature of the British attitude to the weekend' and discourage people from going to the pub by putting more opera on television.[20] The Corporation was perhaps naïve in its belief that people were *only* going out drinking because there was nothing to watch of a high enough quality on television. Nevertheless, it expressed its intention to 'fight the pub' by putting on more broadcasts of opera, concerts, and ballets on Saturdays and special arts features and documentaries on Sundays.

By the 1970s, then, there was a confidence and a sense of ambition on the part of both the BBC and ITV that the arts could genuinely enrich people's lives. But perhaps what really mattered was whether people were willing to make the leap from catching a snapshot of opera on television to seeking out a live performance. As opera evangelist Robin May wrote, despite valiant efforts on television to persuade ordinary people that opera *could* be for them, 'only in the opera house is an opera-lover made'.[21] Television had to work hand-in-hand with local opera provision if the British were really to be encouraged to take opera to their hearts.

Opera for everyone

Televised opera was certainly encouraging some people to seek out live performances. Himadri Chatterjee, today a retired operational research

[17] David Gillard, 'How the Arts Broke the Snob Barrier', *DM* (13 October 1979), 22.
[18] Jackson, 'Mainstream . . .?', 23.
[19] Richard Last, 'BBC to Start Survey of Arts Viewers', *DT* (21 September 1978), 15.
[20] Peter Knight, 'BBC's Culture Drive to Empty the Pubs', *DT* (26 August 1976), 11.
[21] May, *Opera*, p. 6.

analyst, arrived in the United Kingdom as a young child in 1965, the son of Indian parents who, though enthusiastic about literature, had little interest in Western music, popular or classical. He discovered the latter of his own volition, attending performances by the Scottish National Orchestra and the BBC Scottish Symphony Orchestra whilst a student at Strathclyde University. In terms of opera, it was a television broadcast in 1977 of *Don Giovanni* from Glyndebourne (conducted by Bernard Haitink and with Benjamin Luxon) that lit the spark. Chatterjee recalls, 'I was a bit wary at first—operatic voices sounded a bit strange to my ears—but I had loved the symphonies and piano concertos of Mozart that I had already heard, and so I thought I'd give this a try. I really was entranced. And not just for the music: for the drama as well.'[22]

This experience led him to start buying opera records and borrowing them from the record library, near to his parents' home in Blackburn. Chatterjee never managed to persuade his parents to take an interest in opera, but he did introduce his brother to it, and recalls one Christmas morning when, under the Christmas tree, there was an LP box set of *Parsifal* for his brother and one of *Tristan und Isolde* for him. It was only a short leap from there to buying student tickets to see Scottish Opera in Glasgow and so a lifelong love of opera began.

Chatterjee's experience was not an unusual one for the time. The journalist Daniel Johnson, also raised in a non-musical household in the 1970s, has reminisced about discovering classical music through school concerts, rummaging around in record shops, travelling in from the London suburbs to Proms concerts as a treat, and listening to the radio. Opera soon followed: 'No phantom haunted the opera more assiduously: my first was *Don Giovanni* at the Coliseum and I can still sense the hairs on my neck standing up when I heard the voice of the Commendatore summon the Don to his final reckoning.'[23]

Happily, there was plenty of local live opera during the 1970s to satisfy new fans who had been converted by TV broadcasts or by the ongoing boom in opera recording. The problem of British operatic activity being overly centralised that had concerned commentators during the 1950s and 1960s was now being addressed. Scottish Opera was in particularly rude health in the 1970s, with the opening of the Theatre Royal Glasgow as a permanent

---

[22] Private correspondence with Himadri Chatterjee, 22 September 2021.
[23] Daniel Johnson, 'How I Discovered Classical Music', *The Critic* (7 July 2020), https://thecritic.co.uk/how-i-discovered-classical-music/ (accessed 14 October 2021).

Figure 7.1 Carol Neblett, Sherrill Milnes, Zubin Mehta in a London recording studio for *La fanciulla del West*, June 1977. Reproduced with permission from © Clive Barda/ArenaPAL.

opera house in 1975 and extensive tours of the Scottish regions and beyond with a wide repertoire.[24] Its spin-off troupe, Opera Go Round, used five singers, a conductor, a pianist, a producer, and a three-strong stage crew 'to preach the operatic gospel in areas that Scotland's premier company would not normally reach'.[25]

Welsh National Opera had established a second base in Birmingham and was touring far beyond Wales. Sarah Playfair, Controller of Planning for the company, later recalled a performance of *The Magic Flute* the company took to Peterborough in 1970—the first opera staged in the town in two decades—which the audience treated 'exactly as if it was a panto'.[26] The Glyndebourne Touring Company was performing with first-rate casts to large audiences around the country. All of these groups were putting on more opera in more places, and standards were rising. As the critic Rodney Milnes wrote in 1980, looking back over the previous decade, 'it is hard to say whether [more opera] was demanded, or whether availability has created the demand. Either way

---

[24] Robin May, *A Companion to the Opera* (Guildford: Lutterworth Press, 1977), p. 293.
[25] David Gillard, 'Clocking on to Opera', *DM* (31 January 1978), 6.
[26] Gerard van Werson, 'The Key of the Tour', *The Stage* (19 October 1989), 12.

it is healthy . . . the steady expansion of the regional companies has perhaps been the most heartening single trend of the last ten years.'[27]

In 1975, the Arts Council threw its weight behind Lord Harewood's scheme to set up a Leeds base for ENO, initially known as English National Opera North (ENON, renamed Opera North in 1981). Part of the rationale was to give a boost to touring: sets constructed for the Coliseum were often too large to be taken on tour; now sets could be tailor-made for Leeds and tour from there.[28] When the company launched in November 1978, *The Sunday Times* presented it as some sort of exotic endeavour, even the stuff of humour, headlining an article 'A Night at T'Opera' and writing, 'The truth is that Leeds and opera do not trip simultaneously off the tongue.'[29] Memories were evidently short: Leeds had been a particularly important operatic centre since the 1920s and demanding repertoire by touring companies sold out in Leeds in a way it would not in other cities.

Companies were also doing more to encourage new audiences to give opera a try, but having to work ever harder at it. Working-class opera-going, a fact of British life from the 1920s to the 1940s, was now declining. Robin May wrote in the 1970s that 'it is an accepted fact that the British working class as a whole do not go to the theatre, many feeling apparently that "it is not for the likes of us" . . . how much more, therefore, must they feel that opera is not for them—opera, which fills many middle-class folk with deep suspicion.'[30] This might seem depressing evidence of the elitism stereotype beginning to set in. However, opera companies were busy trying to buck the trend, even if it meant converting people by stealth. Scottish Opera's off-shoot for children, 'Opera for Youth', for example, hoped to target both open-minded youngsters and parents who might initially think 'Oh God, all this toffee-nosed stuff is not for me.'[31]

In 1977 Jimmy Milne, general secretary of the Scottish Trades Union Congress, and an opera lover, provided funding for over a thousand members of trade unions across Scotland to attend a performance of opera highlights. Factories laid on coaches to bus their workers to the performance. *The Daily Mail* interviewed Matty McKay, a wages clerk from Hamilton, near Glasgow, reporting, 'She has always loved opera and makes up wage packets

[27] Rodney Milnes, 'An Eventful Decade', *The Spectator* (5 January 1980), 24.

[28] *English National Opera at the London Coliseum. Review: 1976/78*, 4. BUTC, MM/REF/TH/LO/COL/56 (January–June 1976).

[29] Stephen Fay, 'A Night at T'Opera', *ST* (12 November 1978), 70–78.

[30] May, *Opera*, p. 6.

[31] Gillard, 'Clocking on to Opera', 6.

150   SOMEONE ELSE'S MUSIC

while singing snatches of arias "that I've heard on Sunday radio".[32] Matty had never heard an opera live before, but the scheme gave her the opportunity to go with five other clerks to see Scottish Opera perform excerpts from *The Magic Flute* and *La bohème*, paying between 75p and £2 for seats that would normally cost £8. Milne hoped that the initiative would lead to invitations for Opera for All to tour to canteens and working men's clubs across the country and made it clear that the Scottish TUC would subsidise the costs. Meanwhile, in 1979, opera singers gave lunchtime recitals in the canteens of four Yorkshire coal mines, an initiative billed by *The Daily Mirror* under the headline 'Cosi fan butty'.[33]

Even Covent Garden diversified its audience for certain performances by launching the Midland Bank Proms: subsidised performances at which audience members could buy extremely cheap tickets.[34] The initiative attracted many enthusiastic youngsters, now not consigned to the top of the theatre but able to occupy the stalls, albeit standing or sitting on the floor. People began queuing from the early afternoon, and the spirit of the interwar galleryites was back. Alastair Macaulay, who attended performances regularly from 1974, later recalled: 'I soon realised that I was in love with the Covent Garden Proms—not just for the performances they enabled me to attend, but also for their own sake . . . I learnt much about ballet and opera from more experienced neighbours in the queue. I made lasting friends in the queue and I introduced most of my best friends in the queue.'[35] By 1977—with tickets still priced at 50p versus the regular £12.50 seat price—the scheme had welcomed its twenty thousandth Prommer, with the Royal Opera House reporting that demand was such that many had had to be turned away.[36]

Meanwhile, the popular press still took evident delight in ordinary people 'making it' as opera singers. *The Daily Mail* hailed a succession of people from humble backgrounds who had gone on to achieve operatic success. One was Rita Hunter—dubbed 'the Wallasey boilermaker's daughter with the mighty voice'—who had been invited to choose her own role at the New York Met.[37] Another was David Rendall, the new star of ENO, who had worked

---

[32] Jane Gaskell, 'The Night the Workers Went to the Opera', *DM* (13 June 1977), 7.

[33] Anon., 'Cosi Fan Butty', *DMir* (31 July 1979), 5.

[34] *Royal Opera House Annual Report, 1972/1973*, p. 9. ROH archives file: Royal Opera House Annual Reports—1972/73–1991/92

[35] Alastair Macaulay, 'Bravo to the Midland', *FT* (19 October 1996), 53.

[36] William Mann, '*Faust*. Covent Garden', *The Times* (21 April 1977), 12; *Royal Opera House Annual Report, 1976/1977*, p. 8.

[37] David Gillard, 'Rita, Queen of New York', *DM* (23 September 1975), 20.

as a bricklayer before taking up a job in the BBC gramophone library, where a producer 'discovered' him after overhearing him singing along to a recording.[38] The 1970s witnessed a marked growth of amateur music-making, with the number of people joining operatic and dramatic societies, brass bands, choirs, and chamber music groups on the rise.[39] Opera remained something everyone could enjoy if they were so inclined, whether as an audience member or a participant. But were the British ready to embrace a 'national opera'?

The new ENO

In 1974 Sadler's Wells, now thriving at the Coliseum, changed its name to English National Opera, giving its first performance under the new name on 3 August. In part, it was a question of clarification—following the move of Sadler's Wells to the Coliseum, many opera-goers had been turning up at the wrong theatre.[40] But it was also a symbolic change, achieving a decades-long ambition—to establish a permanent 'national' opera in Britain.

The name change was not, however, without controversy, and objections came from groups with a wide variety of agendas. Some people, including company soprano Valerie Masterson, lamented the disappearance of a name that signified a certain sense of romance and had history attached to it.[41] Covent Garden initially tried to oppose any title involving the words 'National', 'British', or 'English'.[42] Some regional journalists complained that the new ENO no longer did enough touring to justify such an all-encompassing title, and tabloid newspapers didn't seem to understand how a company could be 'English' when it put on foreign operas.[43]

What should have been a celebratory moment was also overshadowed by its coinciding with a period of industrial action on the part of stage crew—the beginning of problems that would rumble on throughout the decade, with performances regularly being cancelled or staged in ordinary clothes.[44]

---

[38] Anon., 'Desert Island Discovery', *DM* (25 September 1978), 24.

[39] Ian Brown, 'A Nation of Telly-Addicts?', *DM* (25 October 1974), 7.

[40] Anon., 'Curtain Rises on New Name', *Reading Evening Post* (2 August 1974), 9.

[41] Ibid., 9.

[42] Gilbert, *Opera for Everybody*, pp. 263–265.

[43] Anon., 'London Calls the Tune', *The Liverpool Echo* (25 January 1974), 6; Anon., 'Why the Provinces See So Little of Opera', *The Birmingham Daily Post* (26 January 1974), 13; Anon., 'False Note', *DMir* (5 February 1974), 15.

[44] Gilbert, *Opera for Everybody*, pp. 266–269.

152   SOMEONE ELSE'S MUSIC

Nevertheless, as time went on, ENO would become a spectacular success in the 1970s, achieving the seemingly impossible: putting on a wide range of diverse and sometimes difficult repertory yet still attracting large audiences. Using a repertory company continued to be a winning strategy: audiences enjoyed the fact that they could 'get to know' singers by watching them over and over again.

Going to ENO remained cheap and accessible. Though the company occasionally had to increase ticket prices because of rising costs, it was at pains to stress its desire to keep them as low as feasibly possible.[45] There were various discount schemes: 30 per cent off in the balcony for regular attendees; group reductions for parties of children; and deals where a good seat could be combined at reasonable price with dinner at a restaurant or rail travel.[46] As *Opera* reported in 1975, 'Let it never be forgotten that you can get into the gallery at the Coliseum for less than it costs at any cinema, within a mile radius, a luxury that Londoners should beware of taking for granted.'[47]

And as at the Old Vic half a century earlier, ENO supplemented its performances with a range of activities to make audiences feel more involved. From the early 1970s, audience members could attend 'lunchtime at the Coliseum' events, featuring a talk by a notable figure from the opera world and a light lunch; by the end of the decade, a more formalised 'Opera in Depth' programme was offered by the University of London Extra-Mural Studies department.[48] Members of an affiliated group called 'The Opera Club' had the opportunity to attend rehearsals and parties, while children were invited to design the sort of poster that would encourage them to come and see *La Cenerentola*, in a competition that offered tickets, art materials, and dinner at the Café Royal as a prize.[49]

Even more direct participation was sometimes encouraged. Around one hundred children per year performed in ENO productions by the mid-1970s. 'ENO Workshop Opera' was a scheme where people around the

[45] 'English National Opera booking form'. BUTC, MM/REF/TH/LO/COL/51 (June–August 1974).

[46] 'Balcony Ticket Voucher Scheme' flyer, 1974. BUTC, MM/REF/TH/LO/COL/48 (January–March 1974); 'Sadler's Wells Opera at the London Coliseum, October 11–December 8', flyer, 1973. BUTC, MM/REF/TH/LO/COL/47 (October–December 1973).

[47] Cited in *The Opera Club* magazine, 15 (January 1975). BUTC, MM/REF/TH/LO/COL/48 (January–March 1974).

[48] 'Lunchtime at the Coliseum' flyer, 1973. BUTC, MM/REF/TH/LO/COL/46 (April–September 1973); 'Opera in Depth' flyer, 1979. BUTC, MM/REF/TH/LO/COL/68 (October–December 1979).

[49] *The Opera Club* magazine, 15 (January 1975). BUTC, MM/REF/TH/LO/COL/48 (January–March 1974); 'Design a poster' flyer, 1979. BUTC, MM/REF/TH/LO/COL/67 (August–September 1979).

A NATIONAL OPERA? 153

country could take part in specially devised new works, minimally costumed and accompanied by tape-recorder and synthesiser.[50] On the main stage at the Coliseum, contemporary works on a larger scale were also aired—with Harewood keen to promote new works, alongside a wide range of unusual older repertory. A particularly striking commission was David Blake and Anthony Ward's *Toussaint* (1977), about Toussaint Louverture, the leader of the Haitian Revolution.

ENO was keen to emphasise the same sort of populist credentials that had been underpinning the enterprise since the Old Vic days. Although advertisements in company programmes often played on the stereotypical trappings of opera-going, with images of champagne bottles and glasses, the company's own publicity looked rather different. An ENO calendar published in 1979 featured an advert (accompanied by a photograph of Groucho Marx) boasting, 'A night at the opera isn't all it's cracked up to be.' It informed readers that 'you don't have to speak Italian, own a dinner jacket or drink champagne', and that 90p bought you a seat at the Coli, 'where all the best operas come in English.'[51]

Meanwhile, a booklet published in 1980 reflecting on the first few years of ENO wrote of an audience made up both of 'a regular corps, intimately familiar with the Company's work and eager to applaud its favourite singers' and a more casual crowd, 'attracted to the theatre by its accessibility and to the Company by its consistent standards of good entertainment', boasting, 'With opera now filling London's largest theatre five nights a week English National Opera was indeed proving a "People's Opera" in the best sense of the word.'[52]

Opera at high cost

For all this, opera-going at its most glamorous was getting a bad press yet again, seeming out of step with the mood of the times in a decade plagued by economic travails and characterised by an egalitarian social mood. Even in opera-mad Italy, audiences in furs and jewels had been pelted with mud

[50] *English National Opera at the London Coliseum. Review: 1976/78*, 140. BUTC, MM/REF/TH/LO/COL/56 (January–June 1976).
[51] ENO calendar, 1979. BUTC, MM/REF/TH/LO/COL/66 (January–July 1979).
[52] Anon., *A History of Sadler's Wells and English National Opera* (London: ENO, 1980), p. 63. BUTC, MM/REF/TH/LO/COL/71 (October 1980–1982).

154　SOMEONE ELSE'S MUSIC

on their way to La Scala.[53] The Glyndebourne Festival remained as inaccessible to the majority as ever, with prices said to be 'now approaching the prohibitive'.[54] At Covent Garden there were also complaints that ordinary opera lovers, even members of the professional middle classes who formed the backbone of the audience, were being priced out, as a stalls seat rose, across the decade, from £4.50 to £21 (the relative rise at the Coliseum was from £2 to £7.90).[55]

Railing at Covent Garden for charging 'wildly inflated prices . . . which ordinary people can no longer afford to pay', the critic Harold Rosenthal asked in *Opera* magazine who the theatre was now supposed to be for. Was it for foreign tourists, expense-account young executives, or 'the "smart set" who think it fashionable to be seen in the Royal Opera's expensive surroundings and who help perpetuate the belief that opera is an elitist kind of entertainment?'[56] In any of these cases, Rosenthal wondered whether this was really the model of opera-going that should be funded by state subsidy.[57] To have the leading specialist opera magazine railing against Covent Garden was a troubling development indeed.

But the Royal Opera House was still struggling financially, particularly in the face of the imposition of VAT and a sharp rise in inflation, and felt the need to respond to criticism of ticket-price rises by commissioning the economist Mark Blaug to write a pamphlet entitled 'Why are Covent Garden Seat Prices So High?'[58] Responding to two typical criticisms made of the theatre, Blaug concluded that it was neither the staging of unusual operas (crucial for maintaining artistic vitality and company morale) nor the alleged extravagance of costly productions that was keeping prices high. Rather, the reason why Covent Garden was more expensive than the Coliseum boiled down to one thing: foreign guest stars, deemed necessary to the theatre's policy of performing opera at international standards.

Blaug noted that getting rid of expensive foreign stars could result in a saving of £379,000 per annum, but this would mean that the top tier of pricing could no longer be justified. Ticket prices could theoretically be brought down to the price of those at the Coliseum, but with so little to

---

[53] Haltrecht, *The Quiet Showman*, p. 17.
[54] May, *A Companion to the Opera*, p. 320.
[55] Milnes, 'An Eventful Decade', 24.
[56] The Editor, 'Opera For Whom?', *Opera*, 29/5 (May 1978), 444.
[57] The Editor, 'Covent Garden—1976-77 and Beyond', *Opera*, 27/8 (August 1976), 698–702, 702.
[58] Mark Blaug, 'Why are Covent Garden Seat Prices So High?' (London: The Royal Opera House, 1976).

A NATIONAL OPERA? 155

choose between the two enterprises in terms of personnel, the chances of the Royal Opera receiving its higher Arts Council grant would be reduced. Since ENO also received a grant from the GLC, Blaug concluded that

> any tendency to equalise the Arts Council grant to both houses ... would require higher prices at Covent Garden than at the London Coliseum, and would therefore drive Covent Garden out of business in the field of opera. In short, the idea of doing without guest artists at the Royal Opera House would imply the demise of opera at Covent Garden. If that is what is wanted, here is a formula for bringing it about.[59]

Other options open to Covent Garden were to lean more heavily on old favourites (running the risk of alienating more adventurous listeners), to skimp on new productions (with the same effect), or to put on more ballet, since ballets attracted consistently larger audiences and were cheaper to mount. But simply making drastic cuts to ticket prices was not a viable option.[60]

The theatre's fundraising strategies, meanwhile, often seemed to lead to controversy. In 1979 there was a public outcry when Princess Margaret, President of the Royal Ballet, was sent on a tour of the United States to raise funds from millionaires for a refit of the poor backstage facilities of the Royal Opera House.[61] A reader wrote to *The Daily Mirror* to express her disgust, suggesting the Princess make another tour to raise money for the starving in Cambodia, since 'it's only the rich who go to Covent Garden.'[62] Once again, arts funding was being set invidiously against worthier causes. This did not, however, reflect everyone's view, another reader writing to the same paper to protest, 'Covent Garden isn't just for the rich. As an ordinary housewife, I go there four or five times a year, and pay out no more than people spend on away football matches and the like.'[63]

Though arts funding remained controversial among the general public, there was now at least a growing cross-party consensus that the arts deserved subsidy. Arts funding rose in the first year of Edward Heath's Conservative government (1970–1971) to £2.6 million, more than the combined increases

---

[59] Ibid., p. 8.
[60] Ibid., p. 11.
[61] Anon, 'The Un-Royal Opera House', *DM* (5 July 1979), 11.
[62] James Morgan, letter to *DMir* (23 November 1979), 15.
[63] Margaret Watson, letter to *DMir* (5 December 1979), 13.

156   SOMEONE ELSE'S MUSIC

of the previous four years.[64] In 1972–1973, £1.75 million was granted to the
Royal Opera and £935,000 to Sadler's Wells. (For comparison, £398,000 went
to the National Theatre and £382,000 to the RSC.[65]) Opera now accounted
for only a quarter of the Council's budget, as opposed to half in 1956, yet the
Covent Garden grant remained the largest grant given and continued to be
'controversial year in, year out' over the course of a decade of rising unemployment, high inflation, and financial woes.[66]

Like Philip Snowden's embryonic subsidy of the 1930s before it, Heath's
generosity towards arts funding was, of course, the result of a personal interest in classical music. It also belied the truism that the left is always more
supportive of the arts than the right. In 1972 Heath appointed Lord Eccles,
another arts devotee, as Minister for the Arts. Eccles sounded positively evan-
gelistic when he argued that there were more important things in life than economic efficiency, writing that 'a nation is to be judged by the quality of life
it maintains and that life-quality involves something more than a swelling
torrent of cars, television sets and dishwashing machines'.[67] He recognised
that not everyone could access the high arts, just as not everyone could access the top jobs or live in the nicest houses, since such things could not be
produced in high enough numbers to go around, but he argued that good
things were worth preserving nonetheless, dismissing 'the familiar socialist
doctrine—what all cannot have, none must have'.[68] This could be construed
as an elitist argument, but it was one that militated in favour of funding the
arts, and both Eccles and Heath were keen to disseminate more arts funding
beyond London.

The Conservative Party would continue to be pro-opera in opposition.
Later in the 1970s, a group of its members, led by Paul Channon, formed
the Opera and Ballet Policy Group, which took advice from artists, including Sir Geraint Evans and Dame Alicia Markova.[69] In 1976 the group
published a policy report, endorsing Arts Council funding to support two
opera houses with permanent companies in London, calling for more tours
and the foundation of companies in Birmingham, Manchester, and Leeds.

---

[64] Russell Lewis, 'The State as Patron of the Arts', *DT* (16 February 1971), 12.

[65] Rene Elvin, 'German Subsidies', *The Stage* (21 November 1974), 21.

[66] Anon., 'Opera: Ideas for the Future', *The Economist* (26 August 1972), 28–29; Anon., 'Rich
Preserve?', *The Economist* (1 December 1979), 31–32, 32.

[67] Anon., 'Arts in the Provinces', *The Economist* (18 March 1972), 30.

[68] Roy Shaw, *The Arts and the People* (London: J. Cape, 1987), pp. 128–129.

[69] The Opera and Ballet Policy Group comprised Paul Channon, Toby Jessel, John Hannan, Sir
Geraint Evans, Michael Wood, Dame Alicia Markova, Nicholas Fairbairn QC, John Chesworth, and
Ernle Money.

The authors posited the Conservative Party as more friendly to opera, and indeed more in favour of democratic opera-going, than Labour—stressing the Conservatives' belief in the art form as a means of enrichment for all and not the preserve of a social elite.[70] In the years running up to the 1979 general election, Conservative Arts Spokesman Norman St John-Stevas made a number of speeches in favour of increasing funding to high-profile organisations such as the Royal Opera House, as well as advocating for presenting the arts outside their traditional settings and arguing vigorously for more arts teaching in schools.[71]

However, the Conservative position at this time was not entirely one of art for art's sake. Rather, supporting the arts was presented as a way of backing 'winners', who would benefit the nation economically by generating high levels of revenue and attracting tourists.[72] It was also couched as a patriotic act, with much positioning of the arts as one of the nation's great post-war achievements.[73] Nevertheless, there was little suggestion that the arts were a flippant, elitist luxury, as had been the message in earlier decades and would become so again later.

Sceptical about what the arrival of the Thatcher regime might really mean for the Royal Opera House subsidy, Claus Moser, the theatre's chairman, made an impassioned defence of its continued funding, calling indeed for that funding to be increased, warning that achievements that had taken twenty or thirty years to build up could disappear overnight and take decades to restore. At the centre of his manifesto was the idea that the Royal Opera House was the cornerstone of a civilised society, emblematic of the great strides that had been made in the arts since the war, and exactly the sort of 'centre of excellence' upon which the nation's reputation in the eyes of other nations depended.[74] Such patriotic words were calculated to appeal to traditional Conservative sensibilities, and to sound competitive and punchy in an age when European nations were trying to outdo each other in terms of bold artistic plans and cultural largesse, with France leading the way with the

---

[70] Opera and Ballet Policy Group. Report. Conservative Party Archive (CPA), Bodleian Library Special Collections, CRD 4/3/19.

[71] Norman St John-Stevas. The Richmond Lecture 1977, 'The Arts the Brightest Jewel in our Crown', CPA, CRD 4/3/23, 16. Norman St John-Stevas, 'Arts the Way Forward', 19 July 1978. CPA, CRD 4/3/23.

[72] Norman St John-Stevas, 'Making It happen', London University Institute of Education, 29 June 1978. CPA, CRD 4/3/23.

[73] Norman St John-Stevas, 'Arts the Way Forward'.

[74] *Royal Opera House Annual Report, 1978/1979*, pp. 6–7. ROH archive file: Royal Opera House Annual Reports—1972/73–1991/92.

158 SOMEONE ELSE'S MUSIC

construction of the Pompidou Centre. Idealistic talk about the connection between the arts, 'civilisation', and national pride, however, was on the point of becoming very unfashionable indeed.

Changing terms

The word 'elitist' was starting to enter the lexicon by the late 1970s. Sometimes it was simply a synonym for 'high art', or possibly even just 'art', but on other occasions it already had pejorative overtones. Certainly, it was a term that began to undermine hitherto confident talk of 'civilisation'. Paul Johnson, former editor of *The New Statesman* and a historian who had shifted allegiance during the 1970s from the political left to the right, lamented the turn against elites being regarded as 'the engine of civilisation'. This he attributed to a generational shift: the post-war generation, he argued, disparaged and even feared leadership, had less respect for authority figures, and was suspicious of anything that might be construed as 'elite'. Elitism had now become, Johnson argued, 'the all-purpose term of abuse, endlessly repeated in schools and universities, on the BBC and in newspapers and not least in politics'.[75]

The word 'elitism' was not yet heard regularly in an operatic context at this stage, but it did start to be used with noticeable regularity in one rather surprising place. On the face of it, it seems bizarre that *Opera* magazine, the opera industry's natural ally, should have started to rail against its purported 'elitism'. But here a generational shift explains the apparent paradox. Critics who had grown up in the immediate post-war years—a positive, hopeful time for democratic opera in the United Kingdom—evidently felt by the 1970s that Covent Garden, most particularly, was retreating from the ideals of that era.

It is worth looking in detail at an article from 1971 by the critic Rodney Milnes, a regular *Opera* contributor and member of the aforementioned demographic. Milnes expressed fear that opera as Britain currently knew it was under threat and might disappear within the next ten to twenty years. Aware of a wider change in the zeitgeist, he wrote that 'an increasingly influential body of opinion holds that opera is a waste of time, talent and money'.[76] Although obviously an advocate for the art form himself, Milnes argued that

---

[75] Paul Johnson, 'At Last Someone Who's Not Afraid to Lead', *DM* (31 August 1979), 6.
[76] Milnes, 'Ever Decreasing Circles', 945.

A NATIONAL OPERA? 159

the conditions under which opera was being currently performed went some way towards justifying such a negative view. There was, today, he wrote, 'an air of exclusiveness' about contemporary operatic life: 'an aura of colour supplement glamour, that is comparatively recent and quite undeserved'. Worse, opera was becoming 'an ingrown, inward looking minority cult almost entirely associated with one social class, and as such it cannot hope to survive'.

Milnes believed that opera was becoming 'remote' from audiences and from daily life and that the fault lay with the opera industry itself. It was remote, first, on account of ongoing debates about language, as original-language performances steadily began to become more common. (For example, ENON had recently performed *Samson et Dalila* in French.[77]) To Milnes, born in 1936 and raised at a time when opera was sung in English even at Covent Garden, this was anathema, 'castrating' the operatic experience by placing a barrier of incomprehensibility between audience and text.[78] Foreign-language productions catered, Milnes argued, to a 'shrinking corps of opera elitists', whom he dismissed as superficial people who liked their opera incomprehensible so as not to have to engage intellectually with the ways in which operas might be challenging, and questioned whether British singers singing in 'dubious Italian' deserved subsidy.[79]

Opera was also 'remote', Milnes believed, because of the illusion of luxury that persisted in surrounding it, at least at Covent Garden. High seat prices were helping to 'prolong the social function of opera', he wrote, 'the false glamour that I thought was dead in the 1950s and which does much to alienate potential audiences'.[80] Certainly this image of opera as a social event persisted in the wider public imagination. Bel Mooney, in an article about the exclusivity of Wimbledon, argued that 'Wimbledon is a ritual. For the few lucky (and wealthy) ones who can get tickets, it has as much to do with tennis as going to the opera has to do with singing'.[81]

A third reason for opera's remoteness, Milnes argued, was star singers who treated their adoring audiences with contempt in making no effort to engage with the drama or by behaving in an aloof manner. Again, the contrast with the repertory company at Covent Garden immediately after the war, not to mention Sadler's Wells, was stark. Speaking of recent performances at

[77] Gilbert, *Opera for Everybody*, p. 305, p. 312.
[78] Milnes, 'Ever Decreasing Circles', 947.
[79] Ibid., 947–949.
[80] Ibid., 948.
[81] Bel Mooney, 'Tennis for Anyone? No, Just for the Warm Champagne Set', *DMir* (28 June 1979), 9.

160 SOMEONE ELSE'S MUSIC

the Royal Opera House, he argued that singers had sung exquisitely but that 'Miss Price betrayed no involvement at all in the plot of *Il Trovatore*—this was truly a concert performance—while Miss Nilsson . . . chose not to "do" the production she was asked to do'.[82] And as for the recent rise in opportunities for British singers to perform internationally, that was for Milnes merely a circus, with young singers jetting off at the first opportunity in pursuit of higher fees.

Milnes also complained about the rise of a big-budget, filmic manner of staging opera that had, he argued, rendered opera production sterile, going against all the imaginative work that had taken place in earlier decades. He wrote: 'While in the late 1950s and 1960s the theatre has been forging new ideas, new principles, new techniques, too much British opera has been gently, prettily and very expensively embalmed by those two expert undertakers, Zeffirelli and Visconti, and most of us have been crowding round the coffin to kiss the glacial result.'[83]

Milnes was a highly regarded critic and one of the leading advocates of opera for all during this period. But there is, arguably, something rather aloof and purist in the way he writes about and writes off singers, popular productions inspired by film, and the sort of audience who admired them, resurrecting old clichés about celebrity, popular taste, and 'improper' ways of listening. Milnes had a bold, revolutionary vision for reforming opera, but it was one that ended up sounding more than a little elitist itself. Any over-familiar popular classic that had been performed for three years in a subsidised opera house should be banned for seven years and replaced by a more worthy, modern opera, by Henze, Hindemith, Janáček, Weill, Dallapiccola, Prokofiev, Berg, or Goehr. The 'microgroove maniacs', mean-while, were advised to go off and 'listen to foreign language warblers if they must, but in private somewhere and without the benefit of government subsidy.'[84]

Milnes's plan to confront the image of opera as 'a minority pastime ex-travagantly obsessed with its own past' reflected a 1970s vogue for deriding opera houses as museums—yet the analogy seems misplaced.[85] A surprising amount of modern and unusual repertory was being staged during the 1970s. Henze, for example, was on the bill at various theatres in the 1970s.

[82] Milnes, 'Ever Decreasing Circles', 950.
[83] Ibid., 947.
[84] Ibid., 952.
[85] Gilbert, *Opera for Everybody*, p. 245.

A NATIONAL OPERA? 161

Scottish opera performed his *Elegy for Young Lovers* several times and ENO put on *The Bassarids*. Other adventurous fare put on at ENO during the later 1970s included Ginastera's *Bomarzo* (which did well at the box office) and Smetana's *Dalibor* (which did not).[86] Operas such as *Werther*, *Euryanthe*, *From the House of the Dead*, and *The Adventures of Mr Brouček*, which would be considered rarities nowadays, were also staple fare.[87]

But ENO had built up a distinctively loyal, enquiring, and adventurous audience. Milnes's idea that modern works would entice the masses to the opera more generally was surely a pipe dream. The BBC was proud of the fact that Radio 3 was broadcasting unusual operas, boasting in its 1970 year-book of the station having put on works by Dallapiccola, Birtwistle, and Joubert.[88] However, none of this meant that the public at large was ready to embrace modern opera. After all, readers wrote to *The Daily Mail* in the 1970s to complain about Radio 3 prioritising 'obsolete operas' and contemporary music that 'could have been recorded in tin factories' over works 'the average listener to good music' could enjoy.[89] But perhaps Milnes's idea was not to entice the masses, but merely to please the 'right' people.

Elsewhere in *Opera* magazine, the editor Harold Rosenthal was also occasionally prone to demonstrating what seems like self-loathing. He wrote in 1976 that he sometimes wondered, when he was at a festival at home or abroad, 'where we all dress up and . . . pay outrageously high prices for this very elitist and specialist form of entertainment we call opera', whether it was all about trying to seek an escape from 'horrid reality'.[90] Rosenthal noted that 'Fortnum and Mason's hampers, popping champagne corks, arrival by helicopter are not exactly contributing to making opera less of the exclusive entertainment that many people think it is'.[91] Musing on whether he should be enjoying 'so rarified a piece as *Capriccio*', he seemed to fall into a slough of navel-gazing despond, simply muttering 'I do not really know'.[92]

Within the broader arts community, the high cultural status of the so-called high arts was now starting to be questioned. Cultural politics were changing in 1970s Britain, and debates were growing about whether the nation's culture was best fostered by promoting traditional forms of art that

[86] Ibid., pp. 295–296.
[87] Ibid., pp. 300–303.
[88] Anon., *BBC Handbook 1970* (BBC: London, 1970), p. 91.
[89] Y. Tissier, 'Bang On!', letter to *DM* (17 April 1972), 19.
[90] Harold Rosenthal, 'Capriccio. July 2', *Opera*, Autumn 1976 (Festival Issue), 39–41, 39.
[91] Ibid., 39–40.
[92] Ibid., 40.

162 SOMEONE ELSE'S MUSIC

were performed by a small, particularly talented group of artists or by encouraging art forms in which everyone could participate. Or, as Roy Shaw, Secretary-General of the Arts Council, put it, there was now a tension between the previously unquestioned policy of 'diffusing an essentially elitist culture to the people' and 'cultivating the artistic impulses of ordinary people'.[93]

The community art movement that had begun in the late 1960s was in full flower by the early 1970s, with performance art and 'happenings' at their peak, and there was much discussion about how to bring art back into contact with day-to-day social contexts.[94] Fundamental questions were beginning to be asked about the very nature of art. Culture, many now believed, should be about self-expression, active rather than passive. Some of this credo would find its way into the opera world over the coming decades, with community projects in which ordinary people could participate. However, it was simply not realistic for 'ordinary people' to participate actively in opera in its conventional manner of presentation, in the same way as they might in some other forms of art.

Furthermore, we can see in these ideas the beginnings of a rejection of the old view, widely held on the left in the interwar and immediate post-war years, that everyone, irrespective of background, should be able to access the so-called high arts. Su Braden, an artist, critic, and activist, argued in 1978 that high culture was the preserve of a certain social class, and that that class had no right to impose it upon other people. She wrote:

The so-called "cultured" people belong mainly to the professional and middle classes which are separate and distinct groups from those who seek to express and improve their condition by cultural means. There are exceptions, of course, but broadly speaking we can say that "High Art" is associated with the middle class and its values and that Community Art is associated with the working class and its values.[95]

Everyone must, to use a modern expression, remain in their own lane. Braden characterised community arts using words such as 'active', 'social', 'relevant', 'working-class', and 'concerned with relevance to the community'. Conversely the high arts were 'inactive', 'asocial', 'aesthetic', 'middle-class', and

---

[93] Roy Shaw, 'Dramatic Flourish in Regions', *The Times* (5 January 1977), IV.
[94] Su Braden, *Arts and People* (London: Routledge and Kegan Paul, 1978), p. 3.
[95] Ibid., p. 179.

'concerned with missionary zeal for cultural heritage'. For the Arts Council to award 99 per cent of its funding to the latter and only 1 per cent to the former was, she argued, a form of 'oppression'.[96]

In fact, the Arts Council, increasingly concerned about its traditional remit of prioritising 'high art', had been quite active across the 1970s in diversifying the types of artistic activity it supported, a move that had ironically proved far more contentious than funding opera. The tabloid press dug up obscure and sensationalist projects that had apparently been granted funding, including a 'porn-pop art' show called 'Prostitution', an exhibition featuring twenty-two dirty nappies, and electronic music and light shows in which women painted their bodies and 'simply sat around', leading *The Daily Mail* to pronounce that 'the council is now established as a patron of the underground-anarchist-drugs world'.[97]

Interestingly, though the Arts Council evidently regarded its new funding strategy as a democratising one, the popular press saw it as elitist, *The Daily Mirror* remarking that 'the hair-brained schemes of a few trendy elitists must not be given public money to masquerade as art' and urging for the money to be diverted back to more traditional sorts of art.[98] Here, interestingly, the term 'elitism' was used *not* for opera—presumably one of the worthy mainstream recipients of Arts Council funding—but for the sensational, the pretentious, and the weird. Perhaps this change of policy did no favours to the cause of arts subsidy in general.

Su Braden implicitly condemned the post-war Keynesian idea of 'the best for the most', since it presumed a hierarchy that she wholeheartedly rejected. For her and others of similar views, this was an example of 'cultural imperialism', the term being used explicitly some four decades before it would enter common parlance. Braden wrote:

> To take a particular art and expose a community to it in the hope that it will become less mysterious and more relevant . . . was confused and wrong. Such thinking, reminiscent of the imperialist beliefs of fifty years ago, when our society imposed religion, laws and systems of democracy on other societies which were totally unsuited to them, asserts that if it is good and right for us it must be good and right for them.[99]

---

[96] Ibid.
[97] Anon., 'Knowing What We Like', *DMir* (19 October 1976), 2; Anon., 'They're Giving Away Your Money', *DM* (16 March 1970), 9.
[98] Anon., 'Knowing What We Like'.
[99] Braden, *Arts and People*, p. 180.

164 SOMEONE ELSE'S MUSIC

Keynes had got it wrong, then, and so had Baylis. Their well-intentioned desire to share the high arts with everyone was now being characterised as a form of oppression. In the 1970s, Braden's ideas about cultural imperialism would doubtless have been dismissed as the cranky ideas of a fringe group, but many decades later these ideas would make their way into the mainstream—even be endorsed by those very arts administrators who had previously advocated for the so-called 'high arts'. The path towards elitism, in its most destructive sense, was slowly but steadily being laid.

8

The E-Word

Opera, like so many other things, was big and booming in the 1980s. The decade saw the launch of large-scale arena productions, the brainchild of the rock promoter Harvey Goldsmith, who was more used to organising stadium tours for the Rolling Stones or Pink Floyd. Goldsmith, a canny businessman, believed there was an appetite for popular opera, presented like popular music, particularly among baby boomers who had grown up with rock and now wanted 'something sophisticated'.[1] From 1988, he began putting on works such as *Aida* and *Carmen* at the 15,000-seater Earls Court arena, with spectacular staging.[2] He spoke of his longstanding desire to present opera in such a venue 'so that ordinary people won't feel excluded. I hate the elitist attitude that great music has some kind of No Entry sign outside making it a members-only affair ... Opera snobs don't approve, but we have reached a much wider than usual audience'.[3]

Between 1986 and 1990, audiences for opera—even performed in more conventional contexts—increased more than for any other art form, with a particularly dramatic rise in interest being reported among the young. ENO's managing director Peter Jonas stated that 'opera has never known such demand'.[4] When Covent Garden put on *La bohème* with Plácido Domingo, 2,000 people huddled in the rain to watch the performance on a screen in Covent Garden Piazza, some climbing lamp posts or standing on bins to get a better view.[5] At every turn, the clichés about opera seemed to be being confounded. In 1988, following an Opera North *Tosca*, Rodney Milnes reported that 'Arts Council mandarins should have been bussed up to Leeds to see how totally un-elitist the potential audience for opera is: this, the sixth

---

[1] Robin Simon, 'Tempestuous Toscas', *DM* (8 June 1991), 13–15, 14.
[2] Bryan Appleyard, 'The Greatest Showman on Earth', *The Times* (25 May 1989), 14.
[3] Shaun Usher, 'Live Aida', *DM* (25 June 1988), 26.
[4] Norman Lebrecht, 'Choruses of Approval', *The Times* (15 July 1987), 14; David Cairns, 'Your Tiny Funds Music Be Unfrozen', *ST* (16 February 1992), Section 4, 12.
[5] Daily Mail Reporter, 'Piazza for Free Big Screen Show', *DM* (10 June 1987), 3.

166 SOMEONE ELSE'S MUSIC

performance in the run, was relished by a heterogeneous assembly of every possible age, class and colour.'[6]

Mass media exposure was helping to take opera to new audiences. The year 1980 saw the first opera relay on commercial radio, when *Otello* was broadcast on Capital Radio.[7] The sheer amount of opera on television was astounding: in 1988 alone, the recently launched Channel 4 broadcast seventeen operas, with a further eleven being shown on the BBC, attracting a total audience of eleven million viewers.[8] By the end of the decade *The Times* was able to report that 'arts programmes have lost their minority interest tag.'[9] But in any case, broadcasters were still not worrying too much about ratings. As Brian Wenham, the BBC's Director of Programmes, wrote in 1984, 'We have effectively insulated two of our four channels from any major anxiety about numbers, and targeted them instead upon the high ground of plain public service aspiration.'[10] Roy Shaw, Secretary-General to the Arts Council in the early 1980s, saw television as taking over from touring—now prohibitively expensive—as the best way of engaging audiences who lived outside the major metropolitan centres.[11] This ethos would become more problematic in the following decades, when televised opera itself was allowed to dwindle.

Listeners were also spending huge amounts on CDs (£288 million by 1988).[12] It was a format that had been marketed explicitly towards 'upmarket consumers' and classical recordings were twice as popular on CD as they had been on cassette and three times more popular than on LPs.[13] The 1980s were something of a golden era for studio opera recordings—big-budget box-sets featuring the major stars of the day, Plácido Domingo, Luciano Pavarotti, and Kiri Te Kanawa. Some of these singers were also branching out into lighter repertory, Te Kanawa recording *My Fair Lady* with Jeremy Irons, for example, and *West Side Story* with José Carreras. Opera sat happily alongside popular culture in other ways too. Opera films were booming: Francesco

---

[6] Rodney Milnes, '*Tosca*. Opera North at the Grand Theatre, Leeds, May 5', *Opera*, 39/7 (July 1988), 867–870, 869.

[7] *Royal Opera House Annual Report, 1979/1980*, p. 4, p. 8. ROH archive file: Royal Opera House Annual Reports—1972/73–1991/92.

[8] Andrew Feist and Robert Hutchison (eds), *Cultural Trends in the Eighties*, 4 (London: Policy Studies Institute, 1990), p. 40.

[9] Simon Tait, 'TV Brings New Audience to the Arts Despite General Drop in Viewing', *The Times* (11 September 1990), 2.

[10] Brian Wenham, 'Focus on Range and Quality, Not Ratings', *The Stage* (20 September 1984), 14.

[11] Shaw, *The Arts and the People*, pp. 140–141.

[12] Simon Tait, 'Spending on the Arts Doubles', *The Times* (19 July 1990), 6.

[13] Feist and Hutchison (eds), *Cultural Trends in the Eighties*, p. 65.

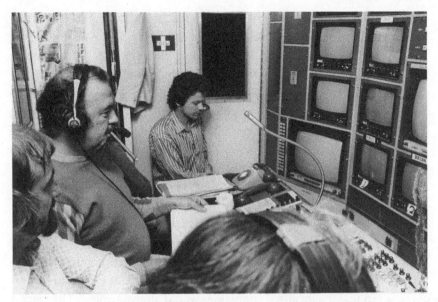

Figure 8.1 Peter Hall (director) in the control van with Robin Lough. *L'incoronazione di Poppea*, Glyndebourne Festival Opera, 1984. Reproduced with permission from © Glyndebourne Productions Ltd/ArenaPAL.

Rosi's *Carmen* (1984), filmed on location in Andalusia, was an international hit, receiving Golden Globe and BAFTA nominations.[14] Operatic excerpts also featured prominently in the soundtracks of films, including *Raging Bull* and *A Room With a View*.

A buzz was starting to build around opera, a renewed sense of optimism for the art form. A study of opera-going in the 1980s concluded that whereas opera had previously been perceived as 'an old-fashioned, elitist artform, patronised only by a wealthy minority', who were 'more interested in the occasion than the art', there was now a widespread belief that opera offered 'some of the most challenging performance work around—fresh, innovative and attracting young audiences'.[15] Opera had become fashionable and ENO's Peter Jonas went so far as to argue that 'the whole argument that it is elitist is now obsolete'.[16]

---

[14] Marianne Grey, 'Divine Divas!', *DM* (8 July 1985), 20.
[15] Devlin, 'Beggar's Opera', 11, 18.
[16] Simon Tait, 'TV Brings New Audience to the Arts Despite General Drop in Viewing', *The Times* (11 September 1990), 2; Norman Lebrecht, 'Choruses of Approval', *The Times* (15 July 1987), 14.

168 SOMEONE ELSE'S MUSIC

Unfortunately, not everybody agreed. In fact, it was during the 1980s that the terms 'elitist' (sometimes still accented as 'élitist') and 'elitism' became, almost overnight, *les mots du jour*—fashionable adjectives with which to pepper one's conversations about culture. By the end of the 1980s, it was not uncommon for journalists to refer routinely to opera as 'the most elitist of the arts'.[17] At the same time, opera was being presented in ways that brought it ever closer to the world of popular culture, attracting record audiences, and gaining countless new fans. Opera was, paradoxically, more popular than ever before and yet supposedly 'elitist'. How could this be?

Expense and exhibitionism

Ironically, opera was gaining in popularity just as it was becoming more expensive. Over the course of the 1980s, the average price of a ticket to see one of the seven major subsidised companies would almost triple.[18] The market seemed able to withstand the price hike, but such statistics made for good ammunition for a press determined to associate opera with extravagance. Peter Conrad wrote in *The Observer* in 1983, 'In the welfare state, opera might reasonably be expected to have withered away, ashamed of its exorbitant elitism. Not a bit of it, however: this most apparently excessive and superfluous of arts grows more popular each year.'[19]

There was a growing sense of discontent among opera's most devoted followers about opera's rising prices. *Opera* magazine received numerous complaints about the rising cost of tickets at Covent Garden from audience members who felt the institution had abandoned ordinary listeners by the late 1980s. Although there were still cheap tickets to be had in the gallery or at the Midland Bank Proms, it now cost £100 to watch Domingo from the best seats.[20] Noting that tickets were becoming 'virtually out of reach of people with an average income', a reader went so far as to argue for the withdrawal of the theatre's subsidy, on the grounds that 'I do not object to my taxes being used for the arts, but I object strongly to it being used to subsidize

---

[17] See, for example, Bryan Appleyard, 'The Greatest Showman on Earth', *The Times* (25 May 1989), 14. See also Patrick O'Neill, 'Anything Goes in the New Culture Club', *DM* (23 August 1984), 20; and Marianne Grey, 'Divine Divas!', *DM* (8 July 1985), 20.

[18] Feist and Hutchison (eds), *Cultural Trends in the Eighties*, p. 4.

[19] Peter Conrad, 'The Heights of Passion', *The Observer* (15 May 1983), 25.

[20] A. Middleton, 'The Axe Falls Again', letter to *Opera*, 38/7 (July 1987), 739.

THE E-WORD   169

the wealthy and the various companies and institutions who use Covent Garden as a means of flattering their business clients'.[21]

The subsidy question, as ever, was never far from the surface and calls were growing for it to be removed. In 1981, Covent Garden and ENO asked the government for increases of £2 million and £1 million to their annual subsidies, which already stood at £7 million and £4.5 million, respectively. When the figures were presented to the Commons Select Committee for Education, Science and the Arts, the Conservative MP Patrick Cormack asked: 'How can you justify asking for an increase in public funding for such an exclusive and expensive article?'[22] Moser's riposte was that 'opera and ballet bring unique experiences of joy and happiness and enrich the life of the community. They are not a luxury but a necessity, and a country which does not subscribe to this would be a poor place'.[23]

Unfortunately, Britain subscribed to this view rather less than other nations. Covent Garden repeatedly expressed despair at the fact that it had to recoup a far higher proportion of its costs from the box office than any continental house of similar size or stature: 40–45 per cent, whereas the norm in Europe was 25 per cent at most.[24] With costs rising exponentially, the House found itself in a desperate cycle of having to put up ticket prices—a partially self-defeating gesture, as attendance fell accordingly—and pare back its programming.[25] By the end of the decade, the theatre was facing its largest real terms decline in subsidy to date and was forced to put huge efforts into seeking new ways of generating private-sector funding.[26]

The very idea of subsidy was now coming under question, and not only from Conservative MPs. An investigation into cultural trends of the 1980s noted that 'those in higher socio-economic groups and on higher weekly incomes go to arts events much more than those in lower socio-economic groups and those on lower incomes. So the direct benefits of subsidy to the arts go mainly to those who are financially already relatively well off'.[27] Even more bluntly, the *TLS* in 1985 characterised arts subsidy as 'a net transfer

[21] K. J. Rhodes, letter to *Opera*, 40/5 (May 1989), 533–534, 533.
[22] Anon., 'Covent Garden and ENO ask for £3m Cash Aid', *The Times* (30 June 1981), 1.
[23] *Royal Opera House Annual Report, 1980/1981*, p. 6.
[24] Ibid., p. 5.
[25] *Royal Opera House Annual Report, 1981/1982*, p. 6, p. 5. ROH archives file: Royal Opera House Annual Reports—1972/73–1991/92.
[26] *Royal Opera House Annual Report, 1988/1989*, p. 2. ROH archives file: Royal Opera House Annual Reports—1972/73–1991/92.
[27] Feist and Hutchison (eds), *Cultural Trends in the Eighties*, p. 29.

170   SOMEONE ELSE'S MUSIC

of wealth from the poor and underprivileged to the rich and privileged.'[28] Unskilled workers were paying high taxes but never going to the opera; the university-educated middle classes were having their opera tickets subsidised by £19 per seat and should, the author argued, examine their consciences.

Opera's public image was further damaged in the 1980s by becoming associated with a particular type of conspicuous consumption, with Glyndebourne coming in for particular criticism. To its credit, the company was now engaged in outreach projects with the wider community and by the end of the decade was spending £100,000 annually on its educational work with local schoolchildren.[29] It was also hailed for Trevor Nunn's 1986 production of *Porgy and Bess*, conducted by Simon Rattle and starring Willard White and Cynthia Haymon, of which *The Economist* wrote, 'A success like this (a controversial, would-be populist work, receiving its first British production in the heartland of conservatism) may help dispel the charges of elitism sometimes levelled at Glyndebourne.'[30] But this was not what the wider world saw and the press talked endlessly about 'elitist alfresco frolickings' and about tickets that, by the end of the decade, had reached £65, or £480 for a box.[31]

The Festival was increasingly characterised as elitist for appealing to an old, establishment elite on the one hand and 'yuppies' on the other, as new wealth sought to emulate the habits of old money. On the first count, an opera-goer described attending Glyndebourne in 1982 and, within five minutes, spotting Edward Heath, John Julius Norwich, Rudolf Nureyev, Lord Hailsham, and Michael York. 'It was', he remarked, 'rather like Madame Tussaud's.'[32] This comment can be read on two levels, alluding both to the men's fame and to the fact that they may have seemed like stiff waxworks, establishment figures from an older era. We can see a shift in tone here: the presence of 'the established order' at the opera was no longer reported reverently as a matter of pride, something to be celebrated, but was becoming a matter of derision.

As for the yuppies, they were regarded with misgivings both by left-wingers who were becoming increasingly hostile to opera and (paradoxically) by opera's most ardent devotees. Both groups perceived that the

---

[28] Nicholas Shrimpton, 'Literature Without the State', *TLS* (15 March 1985), 286.

[29] Gerard van Werson, 'The Key of the Tour', *The Stage* (19 October 1989), 12.

[30] Anon., 'Porgy's Got Plenty o' Nuttin'', *The Economist* (26 July 1986), 91.

[31] David Gillard, 'Destined for Greatness ...?' *DM* (2 June 1981), 22; Jolliffe, *Glyndebourne*, p. 269.

[32] Revell D. Gaunt, 'Glyndebourne Contrasts', letter to *Opera*, 35/1 (January 1984), 37.

THE E-WORD   171

'wrong' type of audience member was driving the opera boom. Once again, *Opera* wrung its hands in anxiety at changes in Britain's operatic culture. The editor, Harold Rosenthal, expressed regret that Glyndebourne was increasingly characterised by an 'Ascot-like atmosphere', with Fortnum and Mason hampers being opened by hired butlers.[33] He wrote, 'I . . . find the sight of what I can only describe as superior-looking young bloods walking around the gardens clutching bottles of champagne and glasses particularly off-putting. Am I being particularly intolerant or am I right in suggesting that this kind of behaviour helps to contribute to the élitist image of opera in general and of Glyndebourne in particular?'[34]

On the other hand, there was a certain irony to Rosenthal's constant complaints about yuppies engrossed in interval conversations about stocks and shares or holidays on the Costa Brava.[35] A former schoolteacher, Rosenthal agonised repeatedly about his desire to make opera 'more accessible and more democratic'.[36] He was a vocal opponent of high ticket prices and wanted opera to appeal to a wide audience, but not, apparently, *this* audience. These were the wrong sort of people to be going to the opera, consuming opera in 'the wrong way'—an age-old complaint about those who attended opera primarily as an 'event'. Anti-elitists could, then, sometimes inadvertently end up sounding rather elitist themselves. All these paradoxes would come to the fore once more with the arrival of a ground-breaking new form of technology.

Communication and gatekeeping

The arrival of surtitles ought to have removed a structural plank in the very framework of the embryonic elitism stereotype. All those centuries-old refrains that it was impossible to understand an opera unless you were a highly educated polyglot disappeared in the blink of an eye. Reporting from the United States, *The Times* gushed that 'the elitist, highbrow atmosphere

---

[33] Harold Rosenthal, 'Contrasted Pleasures', *Opera*, Festival Edition (Autumn 1982), 18.

[34] Harold Rosenthal, 'Glyndebourne Welcomes Gershwin', *Opera*, Festival Issue (Autumn 1986), 12–13.

[35] Ibid. See also Rosenthal, 'Contrasted Pleasures' and Harold Rosenthal, 'A Less Than Vintage Glyndebourne', *Opera*, Festival edition (Autumn 1983), 47.

[36] Rosenthal, 'A Less Than Vintage Glyndebourne'.

172 SOMEONE ELSE'S MUSIC

of the opera is banished forever when the screen flashes up the translation "Back, dogs! Back". This is the stuff of Saturday matinées at the local cinema'.[37]

Surtitles were initially tried out on what were evidently deemed less 'specialist' audiences. Glyndebourne Touring Opera was an early adopter in 1984, but the Festival proper initially resisted them for operas except those by Janáček.[38] Covent Garden trialled surtitles for schools' matinées in the first instance, only gradually introducing them for regular productions in obscure languages, starting with *Jenůfa* in autumn 1986.[39] But surveys revealed that surtitles were popular: 80 per cent of opera-goers told the Royal Opera House in 1987 that surtitles had helped their understanding, and in March the following year the company announced that, 'in response to demand', it would henceforth use surtitles for all foreign-language productions.[40]

The fact that the presence or otherwise of surtitles was advertised in publicity materials and noted in reviews throughout the decade reflects the fact that they were not without controversy. While audiences adapted to them quickly, critics' acceptance was harder won. In 1986 Gerard Werson of *The Stage* wrote that the constant flitting of the eyes to the top of the stage felt distracting, though by 1989 had become a convert and complained when he attended a performance where they were not used.[41] *The Illustrated London News* declared surtitles to be an 'intrusion', though the review conceded that they were 'no doubt helpful to those who know nothing about the work'.[42]

Here a certain condescension may be detected. A hierarchy of viewers was implicitly established: surtitles were all right for the operatic newcomer but an unwelcome distraction for those who were really in the know. Many commentators asserted, as some still do today, that the use of a foreign language acts as a barrier between the artists and the audience even if a translation is provided and that only opera in the audience's native tongue is acceptable. Some of the most specialised opera critics declared themselves violently opposed to the new technology.

Rodney Milnes, whom we encountered in the last chapter, took over as editor of *Opera* in 1986 and from the editorial chair continued what had

---

[37] Mark Steyn, 'The Italian Lady Is Going Places...', *The Times* (18 July 1984), 10.

[38] Arthur Jacobs, 'All on a Paper Plate', *The Stage* (15 June 1989), 10.

[39] *Royal Opera House Annual Report, 1983/1984*, p. 7; ROH archives file: Royal Opera House Annual Reports—1972/73–1991/92; Margaret Davies, 'Opera', *ILN* (1 January 1985), 61.

[40] Fred Norris, 'Brom Set to Go Up in Lights for Opera', *Sandwell Evening Mail* (12 June 1987), 17; Anon., 'Opera "Explained"', *Aberdeen Press and Journal* (17 March 1988), 9.

[41] Gerard Werson, 'Red Letter Day for the Titled Revolutionaries', *The Stage* (27 November 1986), 21; Gerard Werson, 'Britten Theatre', *The Stage* (3 August 1989), 13.

[42] Margaret Davies, 'Novelties of *Jenůfa* at Covent Garden', *ILN* (1 January 1987), 48.

THE E-WORD   173

already become, via his reviews, a concerted campaign against surtitles. In 1988 he called Covent Garden's introduction of surtitles for all foreign-language performances 'high-handed and authoritarian' and proposed that conductors, singers, and producers might well object to having their work 'witnessed through a haze of celluloid'.[43] The fact that there was 'overwhelming demand' for surtitles was beside the point. Indeed, he argued, in a rather shocking analogy:

> The words "overwhelming demand" anyway strike a chill into liberal hearts. We have been reminded recently that there was undoubtedly an overwhelming demand for the *Anschluss* fifty years ago, and I have no doubt that there is an overwhelming majority in favour of capital punishment in this country. In the words of Henrik Ibsen . . . "the majority is always wrong".

The journal received an overflowing postbag from readers every time the subject of surtitles was raised. Some readers agreed with Rosenthal's stance but a great many wrote in to complain about intellectual snobbery and an unhelpful impression of gatekeeping. One reader said that Milnes's suggestion that opera-goers read up on opera plots beforehand reflected 'the often superior attitude of opera-goers in the metropolis', pointing out that libraries in small towns usually had only very small music sections.[44] Another remarked: 'We are not all in the privileged position of your reviewers and probably do not see as many performances as these sages.'[45] And a third, noting that surtitles made listeners more engaged, asked, 'Is it this sacrilegious involvement of the audience which Rodney Milnes finds so painful? Is it his wish to preserve opera as a pastime for the few, an obscure art open only to initiates, members of the "trade"? I do hope not.'[46]

An impression was forming, perhaps unfairly, of a coterie of critics who wanted to keep opera for themselves. This, on top of the growing perception that opera was becoming too expensive for anyone but merchant bankers, irritated ordinary people who enjoyed going, leading to an unfortunate situation whereby even opera lovers began to use the word 'elitist'. The idea of

---

[43] The Editor, 'Always Wrong', *Opera*, 39/4 (April 1988), 401.
[44] Mollie Warren, letter to *Opera*, 38/1 (January 1987), 16–17, 16.
[45] Steven J. McClue, 'High-Handed and Authoritarian', letter to *Opera*, 39/7 (July 1988), 786.
[46] Dr Colin Roth, letter to *Opera*, 37/12 (December 1986), 1348.

174   SOMEONE ELSE'S MUSIC

a snobbish metropolitan elite was already starting to emerge, and the debate over surtitles would run and run, well into the new century.

A new regime at ENO

There were, of course, no surtitles at ENO: with performances in English, there was ostensibly no need, though ironically the company would eventually capitulate and introduce them in 2005.[47] Nevertheless, surtitles—which presented a threat to ENO's USP of a direct line of communication between performers and audience—evidently made the company nervous. Rather than recognising them as a potentially democratising tool, ENO's managers spoke scornfully about the sort of people who appreciated them. Surtitles were, they declared at the beginning of the 1990s, something for the tourist, 'who looks but does not participate, and this is a betrayal of theatre's civic function as a place of communal experience'.[48] The management did not hold back from using a similarly emotive argument to Milnes's, stating, 'Let us admit at once that audiences like them. The same is apparently true of hanging. Neither would get our vote. There are, after all, limits to democracy.'[49]

These combative words—calculated to shock and unconcerned about alienating the 'wrong' type of opera-goer or sounding dismissive of popular taste—were uttered by the new broom that had taken hold at ENO during the 1980s. Mark Elder arrived as Music Director in 1979, David Pountney as Director of Productions in 1982, and Peter Jonas as General Director in 1985.[50] Collectively they oversaw what came to be known as the 'Power House' era. Challenging audiences, risk-taking, and revelling in controversy were the order of the day.[51] This had mixed results in terms of democratising opera.

Elder and Pountney's aim was to shake up the repertoire, staging little-known works in a 'radicalized . . . rumbustious, iconoclastic' production style.[52] The new regime was unapologetically political, on both sides of the

[47] https://wno.org.uk/news/surtitles-a-brief-history (accessed 16 March 2022).
[48] Peter Jonas, Mark Elder, and David Pountney, *Power House: The English National Opera Experience* (London: Lime Tree, 1992), p. 48.
[49] Ibid., p. 44.
[50] Robert Thicknesse, 'From Scaffolding to the Scaffold', *The Times* (12 July 2002), 3; Jonas, Elder, and Pountney, *Power House*, p. 78.
[51] Robert Henderson, 'Too Much Fun at the People's Opera?', *DT* (27 April 1993), 16.
[52] Jonas, Elder, and Pountney, *Power House*, p. 15.

curtain. Pountney, interviewed for the ENO Friends' magazine, urged audience members to write to their MPs about subsidy, arguing, 'The arts-going public has never grasped what a powerful lobby they are.'[53] Works that tackled political concerns and dealt with contemporary daily life were also commissioned, with Lord Harewood calling for operas to be 'made real in terms of contemporary anxieties, taboos and shibboleths.'[54]

Operatic updating, which had only really been common in the United Kingdom from the late 1970s onwards, was fully embraced at ENO, and the company hired daring continental producers to design provocative productions that would differentiate ENO from the more conventional model of opera being presented by the Royal Opera. Some within the musical world thoroughly approved of the Power House endeavour and saw it as a welcome shaking up of what had become an ossified art form. In 1985 Nicholas Kenyon reported in *The Sunday Times* that ENO was 'currently reinvigorating opera and pulling in a new audience for this supposedly most élitist of arts to an extent that few would have thought possible a decade ago.'[55] A contrast was drawn between ENO as a place of 'living theatre and potent drama' and other theatres (the swipe at Covent Garden was obvious), where star singers moved cautiously around the stage, unable to remember where the scenery was, because they had only just stepped off the plane from Milan. More broadly, the Power House experiment had, in some ways, given ENO a certain trendy allure, leading even *GQ*, the men's fashion magazine, to report that 'ENO has liberated opera from its highbrow constraints and sent it careering into the 21st century.'[56]

Others expressed concern that the showy antics at ENO were alienating, Rodney Milnes later reflecting that the Power House regime had gone too far in courting a new, non-operatic audience, at the expense of the company's traditional supporters.[57] Milnes had been concerned about the new broom at ENO from the outset, expressing concern about 'a new, young-Turkish regime at the Coliseum', whose productions could be summed up as 'the urban guerrilla *Elektra*, the anti-colonialist *Butterfly*', and asking, 'Must a philosophical art form be reduced to a merely political one?'[58] But three years

---

[53] 'ENO and Friends', 8 (Autumn 1985). BUTC, MM/REF/TH/LO/COL/82 (January–August 1985).

[54] Patrick Carnegy, 'Blood on the Carpet', *TLS* (1 January 2010), 3–4, 4.

[55] Nicholas Kenyon, 'All Things Bright and Musical', *ST* (14 April 1985), 65–68, 65.

[56] Cited in *Wozzeck* programme, ENO 1990/91 season, n.p. BUTC, MM/REF/TH/LO/COL/91.

[57] Rodney Milnes, 'Arias for Hard Times', *The Times* (11 February 1994), 31.

[58] Rodney Milnes, 'An Eventful Decade', *The Spectator* (5 January 1980), 24.

Figure 8.2 Jonathan Miller at the London Coliseum, *Rigoletto*, ENO, 8 January 1985. Reproduced with permission from © Conrad Blackmore/ArenaPAL.

later his colleague at *Opera* magazine, Harold Rosenthal, argued that such productions were doing good work in diversifying the audience for opera, writing, 'For too long opera has been regarded as elitist, and certainly I feel that the approach of producers like Pountney and Jonathan Miller has helped to bring in a different kind of audience to the opera house' (Figure 8.2).[59]

Some productions from this era succeeded in being both novel and accessible: Miller's mafia-inspired *Rigoletto* was hailed as a more democratic sort of opera, being hailed by the *Times Literary Supplement* as having won the director 'considerable popular acclaim in an art form long associated with exclusiveness and the rich'.[60] Edgier politicised productions that 'deconstructed' operas via a particular ideological lens were more divisive. 'Director's opera' could sometimes obfuscate rather than clarify. Lighting director Francis Reid argued in 1989 that 'wider access is unlikely to result from productions which develop minor aspects of an opera to such an extent

---

[59] Harold Rosenthal, 'People: 132. David Pountney', *Opera*, 34/10 (October 1983), 1072–1076, 1076.
[60] Stephen Pickles, 'Dating the Diva', *TLS* (13 February 1987), 162.

THE E-WORD   177

that the performance can only be understood by those in the audience who have already seen the work in several other stagings'.[61]

ENO was also keen to reiterate its commitment to using down-to-earth singers, Lord Harewood receiving praise for 'taking the stuffy elitist element out of opera' by building up an ensemble cast and nurturing home-grown talent, including Valerie Masterson, Josephine Barstow, and John Tomlinson.[62] The policy was a shrewd one: the company's predecessors at the Old Vic and Sadler's Wells had thrived because audiences developed a sense of loyalty to singers they would go back to hear repeatedly. This was the antithesis of Covent Garden where high fees were being paid to big-name foreign stars who did not even always show up. (There was a furore in 1983 when Pavarotti pulled out of a production of *Tosca*, claiming that a directorial stipulation to lie on the stage would aggravate a dust allergy.[63]) The fact that ENO would later abandon the repertory policy was surely a contributing factor in its relative loss of audience loyalty.

In Lesley Garrett, ENO had, from the mid-1980s, a particularly approachable leading lady, who in due course established herself as a household name via popular recordings and crossover projects. In dubbing Garrett, the daughter of a railway signalman, 'the diva from Doncaster', the press was keen to play on the usual supposed paradox between opera and northernness, but in fact, Garrett was following a well-trodden path of talented northerners making it in opera.[64] Another ENO principal, Janet Baker, wrote in a diary entry from 1982 on her retirement from the company: 'The years have taught me that the part of me which is a down-to-earth Yorkshire working woman and the part of me which is an artist, can live together peaceably and enjoy all the different facets of this extra-ordinary life of mine; the battle has ceased to rage.'[65]

Garrett's grandfather had been a self-taught cinema pianist; her parents had sung around the piano at home. A grammar-school education had given her many more musical experiences, but there was no record player at home and she saw only a single opera during her childhood. Thus, for the young Garrett, opera was not something particularly familiar—and yet this was part

[61] Francis Reid, 'Paying the Price for the Quality of Opera', *The Stage* (21 December 1989), 12.
[62] Shirley Lowe, 'Hedgehogs and High Notes', *The Times* (23 June 1983), 12.
[63] *Royal Opera House Annual Report, 1982/1983*, p. 5. ROH archives file: Royal Opera House Annual Reports—1972/73–1991/92.
[64] Michael Parkinson, introduction to Lesley Garrett, *Notes from a Small Soprano* (Bath: Chivers Large Print, 2000), p. ix.
[65] Janet Baker, *Full Circle: An Autobiographical Journal* (London: Julia MacRae, 1982), p. 122.

178   SOMEONE ELSE'S MUSIC

of its appeal. In her autobiography she wrote: 'Opera for me was a fairytale. I aimed for it because, to my adolescent mind, the more out of reach something was the more desirable it became. Opera was grand and exotic and fantastically glamorous and, most of all, it belonged to another world, away from Yorkshire and home and family.'[66] Again, it is worth reminding ourselves that, for some, opera's appeal lies precisely in its perceived glamour and its status as something 'special' or 'other-worldly', removed from everyday life—facets that many now attempt to construct as evidence of its elitism.

Towards the end of the 1980s and into the 1990s, however, some of the younger singers emerging from the ENO stable would score something of an own goal by starting to criticise their own art form. This may have been intended as a strategy to differentiate 'democratic' ENO from 'stuffy' Covent Garden, but the spectacle of opera singers calling opera elitist was a bizarre, ultimately self-harming PR exercise. Take, for example, the Californian tenor Tom Randle, who professed that 'opera for much too long has been an elitist thing, a star turn for someone big, fat and conceited. Thankfully, we're now seeing a new type of star—and I'm not interested in bouquets and curtain calls—and a new type of audience. For years lots of people felt too intimidated even to try opera.'[67] Randle clearly wanted to make opera seem more accessible, but his assumptions about audiences and his claim that opera had long been 'an elitist thing' betrayed a lack of awareness of the history of opera-going in twentieth-century Britain. American attitudes towards opera—drawn from a culture with different attitudes towards the arts, funding, class, and social status—would come to be increasingly influential as the century drew to its close.

Elitism and accessibility

In certain senses, then, the opera industry did not help itself during the 1980s. Rising prices and a growing aura of 'luxury' meant that the operatic establishment was often called upon to defend itself. But it often did so cack-handedly, either by giving an inadvertent impression of gatekeeping or by appearing to buy into the idea of opera's supposed elitism whilst simultaneously attempting to combat it. All these people loved opera, none of them

[66] Garrett, *Notes from a Small Soprano*, p. 57.
[67] Deborah Ross, 'Fan Time at the Opera', *DM* (26 August 1989), 7.

THE E-WORD 179

surely really thought it elitist, and yet many of them ended up stoking the stereotype.

Whence, then, this idea of elitism, which was—with seeming perversity—being trotted out with ever greater predictability as the 1980s progressed? 'Elitism' and 'elitist' had entered the lexicon abruptly at the end of the 1970s and were now being widely used, though dictionary definitions at the beginning of the decade were not yet pejorative. The 1982 edition of *The Concise Oxford Dictionary of Current English* defined 'elitism' as 'advocacy or reliance on leadership or dominance by a select group'.[68] There was no overt implication that this was a bad thing, because that 'select group'—the elite—was defined as something good: 'the choice part, the best'.

Some commentators within the arts also tried to insist that the term was merely a variation on the term 'elite', denoting high standards and aspiration. In 1984, for example, Sir Peter Hall wrote of the company he had long directed, 'Glyndebourne . . . was from the first unashamedly elitist, putting quality before quantity'.[69] And the journalist and broadcaster Bernard Levin exhorted colleagues to insist on using 'elite' in its original sense of meaning the best. But despite his attempts to reclaim the term 'elitist', Levin was well aware that he was fighting a losing battle, noting that 'there is at large in our society a dreadful hatred of anything rare and rich and strange, anything designed only to be beautiful, anything that cannot be reduced or diluted, anything that appeals, and of its nature can only appeal, to a few rather than the multitude, anything of which there isn't enough for everyone to have some, anything that many people cannot understand or appreciate'.[70]

Of course, there is plentiful evidence in the pages of this book that opera was capable of being understood by and appealing to 'the multitude'. However, it would certainly be a victim of the general shift in cultural attitudes that Levin identifies here, a particular mixture of a British anti-intellectualism (long present but now intensifying), post-1960s egalitarianism (suspicious of anything that smacked of the Establishment or elite institutions), with a dash of 1980s free-market utilitarianism thrown in. The politics of such attitudes are, on the face of it, inconsistent and illogical.

The voices that began to clamour against opera during the 1980s came from both sides of the political spectrum, with right-wing philistines and

---

[68] Sykes (ed.), *The Concise Oxford Dictionary of Current English*, p. 312.
[69] Sir Peter Hall, 'The Mozart Debt We Owe to Glyndebourne', *The Times* (12 May 1984), 6.
[70] Bernard Levin, 'Idealism amid the Idyllic', *The Times* (8 August 1988), 10.

180 SOMEONE ELSE'S MUSIC

left-wing class warriors each equally likely to jump on the opera and elitism bandwagon in a bid to serve their own interests and to impress the electorate. Let us consider, first, some examples from the right. A changing tone from government was apparent to arts organisations from the very beginning of the new Conservative regime, notwithstanding the pro-opera comments the party had made in the lead-up to the election.

Margaret Thatcher's government was famously ill-disposed towards the arts, dealing a blow to the prevailing post-war attitude that the arts were un-equivocally a good thing, like free health care or cheap housing, and indeed dismantling some aspects of the welfare state and refusing to increase government subsidy for the arts, which meant that the money available to the Arts Council fell in real terms.[71] Public subsidy was coming to be seen by some in government as 'yesterday's idea', with private sponsorship for the arts regarded as the way forward.[72] There was a growing perception on the right that the arts should be able to fight their way in the marketplace, rather than be reliant on something akin to benefits. Indeed, Sir William Rees-Mogg, as Chairman of the Arts Council, argued in 1987 that 'subsidy creates dependence'.[73] John Tooley, General Director of the Royal Opera House until 1988, later wrote: 'The theory of market forces so dominated [Thatcher's] thinking and that of her government that the true purpose and significance of public arts funding were lost on them. Financially, these were immensely difficult years for the arts, and ministers seemed reluctant to come to terms with the real issues.'[74]

Thatcher herself had no particular personal fondness for opera, though, as Sir Simon Rattle observed recently, she did at least watch *Porgy and Bess* at Glyndebourne and wasn't averse to being seen at the opera, unlike many present-day politicians.[75] Additionally, Thatcher was quick to defend herself against the charges of philistinism widely levelled by the left. In a speech at a banquet at the Royal Academy in May 1980, she dismissed suggestions that the arts were being left to stand on their own two feet, pointing to an increase in spending on the arts that year of £163 million, even in a time of straitened

---

[71] Amanda Eubanks-Winkler, 'Politics and the Reception of Andrew Lloyd-Webber's *The Phantom of the Opera*', *Cambridge Opera Journal*, 26/3 (November 2014), 271–287, 275.

[72] Shaw, *The Arts and the People*, p. 59; Bryan Appleyard, 'The Tories' New Culture Club', *The Times* (13 May 1992), 12.

[73] Roy Shaw, 'Sponsoring the Arts', in Roy Shaw (ed.), *The Spread of Sponsorship in the Arts, Sport, Education, the Health Service and Broadcasting* (Newcastle: Bloodaxe Books, 1993), pp. 13–32, p. 27.

[74] Tooley, *In House*, p. 232.

[75] Richard Morrison, 'Simon Rattle: "This Is a Desperate Moment: The Entire Art Form Is Threatened"', *The Times* (20 April 2023), n.p.

finances. While recoiling from the idea of state art, she argued that the arts were vital to Britain's vision, heritage, and national self-confidence.[76] Yet by 1983, Claus Moser was writing in the Royal Opera House's Annual Report of a widespread sense of concern in the arts world as to whether the great achievements of the post-war decades could be sustained in the current climate, noting that 'it does not seem to be sufficiently understood here—as it is throughout Europe—that the arts are one of the activities that make countries, indeed civilisations, great'.[77] Decline, Moser warned, could be fast and irreversible.

Similarly, there seemed to be a lack of interest in using culture to showcase British achievements on the world stage. In November 1980 Moser's colleague John Tooley noted that other countries, particularly in the Eastern bloc, attached great importance to the soft political power that could be gained by sending their artists on tour. The British government, however, seemed to be showing no interest in exporting the nation's cultural achievements, despite the fact that this might be a subtly productive way of encouraging trade.[78] If even the economic benefits of exporting British culture could not be seen, it went without saying that there had been an abrupt rejection of the warmer, *l'art pour l'art* attitude exhibited in the previous decade by the Heath administration, and seemingly little interest in competing with continental neighbours that were embarking upon large-scale cultural projects such as the Opéra de la Bastille, inaugurated in Paris in 1989 as part of President Mitterrand's programme of 'Grands Travaux'.

The argument that the arts ought to be able to be self-supporting through the box office encouraged a broader public hostility towards arts funding, reviving the tropes of the 1930s. In 1983 the National Audit Office began to scrutinise the finances of the arts as if they were merely a sector of the economy like any other, applying terms like 'economic efficiency' that were meaningless in a field whose achievements could not be quantified in purely financial terms.[79] Art was increasingly measured in terms of its 'impact' on some other aspect of life, and a new ethos of utilitarianism and managerialism began to set in that is still with us today.

---

[76] Prime Minister's Speech at Royal Academy Banquet, Tuesday, 27 May 1980, Conservative Party Archive, Bodleian Special Collections, CRD 4/3/22 (file 6.17), 1–2.
[77] *Royal Opera House Annual Report, 1982/1983*, n.p.
[78] *Royal Opera House Annual Report, 1979/1980*, p. 8.
[79] John Tusa, *Art Matters: Reflecting on Culture* (London: Methuen, 2000), p. 22.

182 SOMEONE ELSE'S MUSIC

The right-wing press exhibited a capricious attitude towards the arts during this decade. Throughout the 1980s, *The Times*—in a paradoxical position in having readers who included both wealthy opera devotees and hard-nosed free-marketeers opposed to arts funding—pursued a particularly surreal policy of alternating articles about opera's immense popularity with ones about its supposed 'elitism', such as one that concluded that 'we would be culturally better off not bothering to subsidize so vain, inferior and foreign an expression of art'.[80] It was unsurprising that the elitism stereotype should have been pushed by *The Times* because from 1981 it was part of the newspaper group owned by Rupert Murdoch. As Eliane Glaser notes, 'Murdoch's empire originated in Australia, where anti-elitism is particularly virulent, and by the 1980s he was already beginning to use the term elitism, both about culture and about society in general.'[81] Murdoch's focus here was not opera per se—he was equally likely to be found accusing 'up-market costume dramas' with 'strangulated English accents' of reflecting the values of a 'narrow élite' at the BBC as to be attacking opera. No surprise then that the term 'elitism' would seep into arts reportage so pervasively over the coming decades as it became the particular preoccupation of a figure who would come to play such a dominant role not only in international broadcasting but also in the British print media.

Meanwhile, at the other end of the political spectrum, elitism was also becoming a persistent refrain, and this was equally damaging in its own way. Many left-wing politicians favoured subsidy for the arts but had a particular blind spot for the 'high' arts. Since the 1970s, many on the left had begun to use the language of Marxist theory, as postmodern cultural theory began to make its way out of university common rooms and into the dining rooms of the chattering classes and pages of the left-wing press.

During this period the British left tended to favour community-focused arts projects, which allowed ordinary people to take a participatory role in artistic activities. The community arts movement, which had emerged in the late 1960s and was more usually focused upon deprived areas, had initially been associated with radical political activism and its aim remained to bring about social change by taking art into the streets and giving it back to the people.[82] Community artists often worked with working-class communities

---

[80] George Gale, 'Do We Really Need Opera?', *The Times* (23 May 1987), 20.
[81] Eliane Glaser, *Elitism: A Progressive Defence* (London: Biteback Publishing, 2020), p. 21.
[82] Owen Kelly, *Community, Art and the State: Storming the Citadels* (London: Comedia, 1984), p. 1, p. 2, p. 9.

THE E-WORD 183

whom the subsidised arts failed to reach. Though this was positive, less so was the movement's inherent hostility towards the sorts of art forms that had traditionally been funded. In his 1984 book *Community, Art and the State*, Owen Kelly, like Su Braden before him, called into question the hierarchical value system about what was worthy and what was not.[83] A process of 'persuasion' on the part of those controlling the dominant culture had been used, Kelly argued, to hold up opera as 'an alleged corner of civilisation', while downgrading other forms of musical activity.

Left-wing social activists and community artists of this period dismissed earlier endeavours that had been designed to take high culture to the masses. The community educator and social activist E. D. Berman, for example, referred to CEMA as 'an upper class, cultural imperialist trick'. He decried opera funding as insidious, its prioritisation over tiddlywinks or model aeroplane-making as a form of class warfare: a con by powerful people who had managed to persuade others that it had any relevance for twentieth-century British society.[84] This sort of talk perpetuated the idea that opera was not only something for a social elite but that it was 'foreign'. Thus, age-old clichés were given a new, fashionably activist spin.

Opera companies began to take note of the growing calls for art to be embedded in the community. Many explored ways of undertaking community projects, both during this decade and later, many of which were worthy, successful, and enjoyed by the people involved. But opera could never realistically qualify as community art, with its need for exceptionally talented, highly trained performers. For some on the left, opera therefore started to become anathema, the ultimate embodiment of the new 'elitism', although of course not everyone on the left subscribed to this view. (John Morton, general secretary of the Musicians' Union, for example, argued that 'elitism is a consequence of economic and social disadvantage—it's not a characteristic of the arts'.[85])

But the way in which the left was beginning to think about the arts had troubling implications for opera, its claims to funding and even its aspirations to reach wider audiences. A growing ethos of cultural relativism meant that some on the left believed there was no reason to share opera with people who might not have had an opportunity to encounter it. Kelly, for

[83] Ibid., p. 27, p. 54.
[84] Ibid., p. 55.
[85] Anon., 'Public Funding of the Arts Backed as Tory Ideas on Business Sponsorship are Rejected', *The Guardian* (12 September 1987), 5.

184 SOMEONE ELSE'S MUSIC

example, objected to 'the desire to instruct the "uncultured" working classes, and raise them to the state of the cultured'. He objected to the fact that what he called the 'court arts' had been allowed to prevail over the 'folk arts', which were passed orally between generations. And he objected to the 'cultural missionaries' to be found among aristocrats and 'the wives of politicians'— surely a not-so-veiled dig at Ethel Snowden.[86]

By this measure, the efforts of Victorian philanthropists to establish museums and galleries in provincial towns and cities became objectionable. So too did Baylis's efforts to bring opera to working-class Londoners and every subsequent well-meaning opera outreach scheme. So too did the Arts Council as envisaged by Keynes. Kelly was building upon the ideas of Su Braden, who had made the astonishing claim in 1979 that the notion that high art could be for the working classes as well as the bourgeoisie was 'the great artistic deception of the twentieth century'.[87] Such ideas fundamentally undermined the theory that the arts were for everyone.

The idea that 'people happily playing darts (or push-pin) need to be helped across the road into the opera house' was, in Kelly's reading, paternalistic, discriminatory, redundant, and offensive.[88] People should be left to enjoy their 'own' culture, and not have purportedly 'higher' art forms foisted upon them. People must, indeed, understand the way in which they were being 'oppressed' and understand 'the imperialist structures which nurture and propagate these oppressions'.[89] The ethos of 'Christian socialism' that had driven the Victorian upper classes (and later figures such as Baylis) to try to 'improve' the working classes was no better than colonialists imposing Western ways of living on the inhabitants of other countries.

All these ideas about cultural imperialism would re-emerge in the mainstream in the 2010s, and we shall return to them anon. In the 1980s, they would still have been considered marginal, strange, and extreme, but they were beginning, nevertheless, to underpin the developing elitism stereotype. Something had changed in the left-wing mindset. Access for all to the high arts in their highest manifestations was no longer the ambition; indeed, it was something from which the left began actively to recoil, despite the fact that, as Roy Shaw put it, 'one of the few things on which Marx, Lenin *and*

[86] Kelly, *Community, Art and the State*, p. 88.
[87] Cited in Shaw, *The Arts and the People*, p. 131.
[88] Kelly, *Community, Art and the State*, p. 88.
[89] Ibid., p. 92.

THE E-WORD   185

Trotsky were all agreed is that the best of bourgeois art must be available to the people.[90]

Why this shift in attitudes? A. C. Grayling, writing in 2002, attributed it to a change of mindset that began to develop after the war, gathered pace with the social changes that took place from the 1960s onwards and intensified exponentially as the twentieth century came to its end. A desire to 'valorise all cultural activities', privileging none above another, made it difficult for the left to 'be votaries of high culture without feeling the need to defend the preference'.[91] As time went on it would become particularly hard for some on the left to feel comfortable about supporting art forms such as opera, or to accept the idea that they were more deserving of subsidy than other, more comfortably proletarian, forms of culture.

The idea that one might have to put in a bit of effort in order to appreciate opera was also one that was becoming less acceptable by the 1980s. As Jonathan Rose puts it, 'The old classics-oriented autodidacts have disappeared with the factories that employed them.'[92] Grayling pointed to a slow decline in working-class autodidacticism and the culture of self-improvement after the war, partly as a result of distractions like television as well as changes in cultural attitudes that tended to make the traditional arts look conservative. The logical culmination of this was that some on the left would eventually feel instinctively that 'cultural aspiration is itself a form of betrayal, either of working-class roots or the battle for equal respect in one's own society'.[93] This was a baffling about-turn, given that so many Labour MPs had largely discovered the arts for themselves via access to public libraries.[94]

Of course, many working-class people still continued to seek out opera for themselves—often inspired by Radio 3 (which was broadcasting 125 operas a year in 1988) or the rich diet of operas that continued to be shown on TV.[95] However, autodidacticism would become a far less common point of entry, as the idea that the masses were not interested in 'high culture', repeated ever more frequently, started to become something of a self-fulfilling prophecy as the century neared its end. *The Stage* argued in 1984 that 'there is nothing to stop anybody who is turned on to the arts by television and radio from

---

[90] Shaw, *The Arts and the People*, p. 131; original emphasis.
[91] A. C. Grayling, 'A Question of Discrimination', *The Guardian* (13 July 2002), 58–60, 58.
[92] Rose, *The Intellectual Life*, p. 463.
[93] Grayling, 'A Question of Discrimination', 60.
[94] Ibid., 60.
[95] Mark Fisher, 'Opera Needs a Stronger Voice', *ST* (3 July 1988), 31.

186   SOMEONE ELSE'S MUSIC

walking into the nearest theatre and spending the money that would otherwise go on drink, football or taking the family for a day at the seaside'[96] But
the way in which the arts were spoken about in the media now made it far
less likely that certain sectors of society would think to do so.

Politics in practice

By the 1980s, then, opera had found itself in the unwelcome position of
being regarded with hostility from both right and left—for different ideological ends, but with the same negative outcomes. This shift in the elitism
debate would set the tone for decades to come, and it is a problem that
persists today: indeed, both positions have become entrenched. As the
decade progressed, an awareness developed in the opera world that this
multipronged perception of elitism posed a severe threat to the art form's
future prospects in the United Kingdom, casting opera adrift in terms of
institutional support to a greater extent than at any time since the war. As
Gavin Stamp wrote in *The Spectator* in 1987, 'What, unfortunately, is clear
is that help cannot any longer be expected from the government, whatever
its colour. The Conservative Party seems disinclined to subsidise any worth-
while enterprise while the Labour Party, despite its commitment to the "Arts",
now evidently regards opera as "élitist"'[97]

Even though Labour was in opposition throughout the decade, it could
determine cultural policy at the local level. In 1984 Edinburgh's newly
elected Labour council proposed removing subsidy from the Edinburgh
International Festival on the grounds that it was elitist and failing to cater
for ordinary people. Although the Festival put on a wide array of different
art forms, opera was singled out as a particular target, being dismissed as
something that 'benefits only a few'[98] The £560,000 spent on the Festival
should be diverted, it was suggested, towards community-oriented events,
public hygiene, or housing. Plans to replace the King's Theatre, at this time
a cramped and inadequate venue for opera, with a new opera house which
had been on the cards for almost two decades were abandoned as a deliberate vote-winning strategy. *The Guardian* reported: 'Now, here was a district council which had come to power declaring—insofar as it mentioned

---

[96] Anon., 'Silly Accusation of Elitist Arts', *The Stage* (17 May 1984), 14.
[97] Gavin Stamp, 'The Second Battle of Covent Garden', *The Spectator* (27 June 1987), 13–15, 13.
[98] Anon., 'Labour Council Threatens Edinburgh Festival', *The Times* (7 May 1984), 1.

THE E-WORD   187

the arts at all—the need to smash elitism and make community arts the priority; it was, in fact, widely believed to have been elected because of its doorstep promise *not* to build the city's long awaited opera house.[99]

Then there was Tony Banks, the chair of the Arts Committee of the Greater London Council. Banks came into office determined to reverse the arts policies of the previous Conservative incumbents, recommending in 1981 that the GLC should renege on the last two instalments of a £1 million development grant promised to Covent Garden to renovate backstage changing facilities. (His proposal to deny the Royal Opera House the remaining £250,000 was thwarted when some of his Labour colleagues voted in favour of the subsidy alongside Conservatives.[100]) And it was not only Covent Garden from whom Banks wanted to remove funding, recommending that a regular annual GLC payment of £850,000 to ENO be cut, with the burden to pass to the Arts Council instead. The money should be redistributed, Banks suggested, to street performers and entertainers attached to housing estates, which led to outraged responses from the Minister for the Arts, the General Secretary of the Arts Council, and even *The Guardian*.[101]

These moves were part of a broader aversion on Banks's part for anything that seemed to symbolise the 'luxurious' aspects of the contemporary arts scene. (In 1983 he closed the new champagne bar at the London Festival Hall.[102]) The GLC purported to be prioritising disadvantaged social groups, including the unemployed, women's groups, gay men's groups, the elderly, the disabled, and ethnic minorities, though Jonathan Rose notes that of the community groups generously funded by the GLC in the early 1980s, only 1 per cent were in working-class communities, and most catered to a university-educated audience.[103] Whether hypocritical or not, Banks sought to cultivate a 'man-of-the-people' image that did not sit logically with supporting Covent Garden.

The operatic establishment pointed out the illogicality of Banks's position. Harold Rosenthal took him to task in *Opera*, arguing that if opera were as middle-class as Banks suggested, it surely needed more rather than less

---

[99] Joyce McMillan, 'Share Out the Bread and Keep the Circuses Going', *The Guardian* (9 August 1985), 11; original emphasis.

[100] Our Reporters, 'The New Men in Charge at the GLC', *ILN* (1 September 1981), 35.

[101] Ibid.

[102] John Cunningham, 'Not Playing Our Tune', *The Guardian* (7 July 1981), 9; Shaun Usher, 'Man Who Put a Stopper on Bubbly', *DM* (14 April 1983), n.p.

[103] Kathryn Deane, 'Community Music in the United Kingdom: Politics or Policies?', in Brydie-Lee Bartleet and Lee Higgins (eds), *The Oxford Handbook of Community Music* (Oxford: Oxford University Press, 2018), pp. 323–342, p. 326; Rose, *The Intellectual Life*, p. 464.

188   SOMEONE ELSE'S MUSIC

subsidy to bring ticket prices within the reach of all. Rosenthal drew Banks's attention to what his 'comrades' in Eastern Europe had done to popularise the arts through generous subsidy and educational programmes, ruminating that 'I sometimes have the feeling that when the committed British socialist gets the bit between his teeth he often becomes very puritanical in his outlook'.[104] Banks's was a regrettable position, an about-turn on the one taken by earlier Labour figures such as Jennie Lee, under whom the arts had prospered.

Not all on the left, of course, talked in the same terms as Banks. Baron Kissin, a cross-bencher in the House of Lords but a Labour supporter and close confidante of Harold Wilson, wrote to *The Times* in 1986 to express concern that the Arts Council was increasingly funding small-scale arts projects outside London, at the expense of major national institutions. He asserted that:

> It is essential that the Government and the public should realise that the standards of excellence maintained by the national institutions are in no sense elitist, but are, on the contrary, fundamental for the preservation and progress of our national artistic life. They are a constant reminder of what can be achieved, and are a bastion against mediocrity and lack of discrimination.[105]

But Kissin, born in 1912, was of an older generation, and the way in which he spoke here represented a more old-fashioned left-wing attitude towards the arts, one more akin to that demonstrated by Ethel and Philip Snowden, whose desire to fund opera at the highest level was wildly removed from Banks's desire to defund the high arts. Kissin also thought in the same way as the composer Peter Maxwell Davies, who wore his traditional left-wing values on his sleeve when he stated that 'the working class deserves the best of whatever it is . . . It is elitism of the worst sort to pretend that the working class is not capable of understanding the best of the arts. It is inverted snobbery'.[106]

Central government was still supporting opera via Arts Council funding, but there was a nervousness about whether the funding status quo would remain in perpetuity. Nicholas Payne, General Administrator of Opera North,

---

[104] The Editor, 'Politics and Opera', *Opera*, 32/7 (July 1981), 672.
[105] Kissin of Camden, letter to *The Times* (11 December 1986), 17.
[106] Pearl Murray, 'Orkney . . . the Lure and the Inspiration', *Aberdeen Press and Journal* (21 June 1985), 12.

THE E-WORD · 189

expressed concern as early as 1983 that 'if the consensus swings against opera as an elitist art form—which it is quite possible it could do by, say, 1990— we could go out of existence', calling for greater consensus that minority interests were things worth supporting.[107] Opera had not gone out of existence by 1990, but with the term 'elitist' now being used not only by philistines but by opera fans disillusioned about everything from high ticket prices to gatekeeping critics, the battle surrounding opera and elitism was about to get very bloody indeed.

[107] Max Loppert, 'Northerly Direction', *Opera*, 34/10 (October 1983), 1079–1084, 1081.

9

A Perfect Storm

Excitement was at fever pitch. After a listless performance in the group stages, England had come back fighting through the round of sixteen and quarter-finals, and now faced West Germany for the nail-biting semi-final. Fans' nerves were shredded after an own goal in the second half, but Gary Lineker equalised with ten minutes to go, and the prospect of victory seemed tantalisingly close, the word 'Vincerò!' ringing in everyone's ears.

In the end, England did not triumph at Italia 90. West Germany won in a penalty shootout, and England went on to be beaten by the hosts Italy in the third-place play-off. The bubble had burst. But for a few weeks an entire nation—even people who normally had no interest in football—had been on a high. Perhaps the heat was a factor in why it felt so exciting, and the TV shots of beautiful Italian cities that put everyone in a holiday mood. But as with every cinematic or televisual fantasy, the soundtrack was also vital.

Opera, undoubtedly, played a large part in creating the particular thrill of that memorable World Cup, the BBC having chosen Luciano Pavarotti's 1972 recording of Puccini's 'Nessun Dorma' as the theme tune to its coverage of the tournament. The opera fever that had gripped the nation reached its apex on 7 July, the eve of the World Cup Final, when Pavarotti performed in a live concert from the Baths of Caracalla in Rome with Plácido Domingo and José Carreras, which was broadcast to a billion people worldwide.[1] The concert was a ratings hit for Channel 4, a spin-off album spent five weeks at number one in the UK album charts, and 'Nessun Dorma' reached number two in the singles charts.[2] A series of further concerts followed, with charity fundraisers and performances at sporting events, including three subsequent World Cups. In 1991, Pavarotti sang in Hyde Park and Domingo in Windsor Great Park.

---

[1] Anon., 'World Cup Encore', *Liverpool Echo* (23 August 1990), 40.
[2] Colin Symes, 'Beating Up the Classics: Aspects of a Compact Discourse', *Popular Music*, 16/1 (1997), 81–95, 85; https://www.officialcharts.com/search/albums/in%20concert/; https://www.officialcharts.com/search/singles/nessun-dorma/ (accessed 10 March 2021).

The razzmatazz surrounding the Three Tenors seemed like great news for the popularisation of opera, *The Sunday Times* rejoicing in the fact that 'Pavarotti in the Park has killed the elitist image dear to opera's opponents'.[3] But was it that straightforward? Although the singers sold plenty of records, astronomical ticket prices—£250 to hear Pavarotti at Covent Garden in 1992—made it difficult to see them live on stage.[4] In 1996 *The Financial Times* observed that 'the phenomenal success of the Three Tenors, which might have led to a new audience for opera, has been frittered away. The ageing trio set out again this year, hawking their money-making bandwagon around the world. Ticket prices started at £35 and went up to £1,000; programmes cost £10 ... Is this opera for the people? I think not'.[5]

Indeed, in some respects the Three Tenors phenomenon seemed to confirm some of the worst clichés about opera. With plenty of popular music on the bill, it wasn't opera so much as variety, yet the concerts played into all the popular signifiers of opera, the singers clad in tailcoats and white tie. Critics agonised about whether the 'Three Tenors', as a brand, was more about music or celebrity. For Victor Lewis-Smith in *The Mirror*, the whole phenomenon boiled down to nothing more than people showing off their knowledge of high culture based on 'a CD sampler of the Three Tenors' concert, given free with two gallons of super unleaded'.[6]

Unfortunately, however, the way in which some commentators scoffed at the Three Tenors merely reinforced a perceived divide between the opera world and 'the people', reminiscent of the way in which 1920s critics had fretted about 'celebrity concerts' attracting audiences who were interested more in personalities than music. Anthony Holden in *The Times* claimed that football fans had no more sought out complete performances of *Turandot* than film enthusiasts who had enjoyed *Brief Encounter* had joined the Rachmaninov Society, while Michael Kennedy in *The Spectator* rubbished all talk of opera being popularised, arguing that the vast majority of listeners only wanted the soundbite.[7]

---

[3] David Cairns, 'Your Tiny Funds Music Be Unfrozen', *The Sunday Times* (16 February 1992), 12.

[4] John Storey, '"Expecting Rain": Opera as Popular Culture?', in Jim Collins (ed.), *High-Pop: Making Culture into Popular Entertainment* (Malden, MA: Blackwell's, 2002), pp. 32–55, p. 42; Stephen Fay, 'Sticking Up for Jeremy Isaacs', *The Spectator* (12 September 1992), 27–28, 28.

[5] Richard Fairman, 'Elitist Image Loses Its Fizz: Opera in 1996', *FT* (23 December 1996), 15.

[6] Victor Lewis-Smith, 'Shame of the Free Tenners', *The Mirror* (4 December 1999), 6.

[7] Anthony Holden, 'A Bite, or Two, at the Opera', *The Times* (23 September 1995), 6; Michael Kennedy, 'Down with Accessibility!', *The Spectator* (22 February 1997), 36.

192 SOMEONE ELSE'S MUSIC

Patronising? The Three Tenors phenomenon might not have expanded the opera-going audience vastly—*The Economist* reported in 1992 that 1.7 million more people in Britain owned an opera record after the World Cup but that opera attendance was static—but *some* people's embryonic interest in opera must have been fuelled by hearing Pavarotti sing 'Nessun Dorma'.[8] Indeed, I speak as one of them. Looking back, supercilious comments about the impossibility of anyone coming to opera after hearing the Three Tenors do create a rather unfortunate impression of gatekeeping.

Opera goes pop

'Opera has entered the world of popular entertainment', *The Financial Times* declared in 1991.[9] The pan-global, high-profile encounters between opera and popular culture continued as the decade progressed. In 1992, the Freddie Mercury/Montserrat Caballé duet 'Barcelona'—operatic at least in spirit—was chosen as the theme-tune of the 1992 Olympic Games. Pavarotti, meanwhile, was moving further towards the world of pop, collaborating with Sting, Bob Geldof, and Elton John via his 'Pavarotti and Friends' benefit concerts in Modena.

Back home in Britain, opera was ubiquitous on TV, from the soundtrack of the defining detective series of the decade, *Inspector Morse*, to adverts for everything from ice-cream to electronics.[10] *Lesley Garrett—Tonight!*, a prime-time light-entertainment TV show, featured opera arias and duets with Michael Ball and Andrea Boccelli, alongside performances by the Grimethorpe Colliery Band and Gary Barlow.[11] And the popular TV comedian Harry Enfield released his 'Guide to the Opera' in 1993. Enfield discovered opera after borrowing CDs from the library in the mid-1980s, stating, 'I had a CD player and no CDs, so I went to the local library . . . All they had was classical music. The only thing I had was The Police's Greatest Hits. I listened to the whole of *La Traviata* and really liked it. After that I went out and bought a lot of opera.'[12]

---

[8] Anon., 'A Fight at the Opera', *The Economist* (17 October 1992), 36.
[9] Andrew Clark, 'Pop Goes the Opera', *FT* (30 November 1991), 23.
[10] Robin Simon, 'Tempestuous Toscas', *DM* (8 June 1991), 13–15, 14.
[11] Hugh Canning, 'Opera for the Masses', *ST* (8 November 1998), 33.
[12] Jill Parsons, 'Harry's Fright at the Opera', *DM* (29 December 1992), 33.

A PERFECT STORM   193

This was a decade when 'high culture' was being turned into popular culture, a phenomenon that Jim Collins would later label 'high pop'.[13] 'Higher' forms of culture were suddenly being marketed using techniques borrowed from popular culture: 'blockbuster' museum shows were given massive advertising campaigns; film adaptations of Jane Austen novels were runaway box office hits. Harvey Goldsmith was still putting on his stadium-style operas at Earl's Court, and other impresarios such as Victor Hochhauser and Raymond Gubbay jumped on the bandwagon with vast arena-style 'Opera Spectaculars' at the Royal Albert Hall. The audience even had a chance to sing along to popular arias and choruses at a vast 'Opera Singalong' organised by Gubbay and Goldsmith in 1994, hosted by popular TV stars Gloria Hunniford and Matthew Kelly.[14]

Classic FM (established in 1992), a new commercial radio station, played operatic arias alongside other popular classics in a format that was closer to pop-music radio and attracted sniffy comments from critics. Michael Kennedy, for instance, wrote, 'No doubt there will be some good points about Classic FM but I don't think it's too difficult to guess what its main diet will be. Those who want dawn-to-dusk Kanawa and Pavarotti will, I suspect, be well catered for.'[15]

Classic FM often promoted classical music in functional terms, as something for relaxing, gardening, or driving to, and record labels soon began to borrow the strategy. Serious music lovers scoffed, but all of this cut through some of classical music's 'sacral' associations and aligned it more closely with everyday life, as well as with consumer culture, blurring the divide between popular and classical music. However, there was still scepticism about whether any of this might encourage people to see an opera in a theatre. As one journalist wrote in 1999, 'Sales of opera CDs continue to soar, but for most people the idea of going to see an opera ranks on the social calendar alongside having dinner with Hannibal Lecter.'[16]

Again, this was overly simplistic and did not capture personal experience. Kate Hopkins, later Content Producer for Opera at the Royal Opera House, recalled listening to opera records with her grandparents Arthur and Kathleen during the 1990s. Both were of working-class origins but keen

---

[13] Jim Collins (ed.), *High-Pop: Making Culture into Popular Entertainment* (Malden, MA: Blackwell's, 2002).

[14] Royal Albert Hall archive file, RAHE/1/1994/46, programme for 'Opera Singalong', 26 June 1994.

[15] Michael Kennedy, 'On the Crest of a Wave', *The Sunday Telegraph* (14 June 1992), 74.

[16] Tim Marsh, 'Under a Tenor', *The Times* (7 August 1999), 15.

194   SOMEONE ELSE'S MUSIC

opera and operetta enthusiasts, Arthur having seen *The Merry Widow* in Cairo during the war. Though the couple didn't watch opera performances live, since there were none available locally, they enjoyed opera on CD and DVD with their granddaughter, and both were able to talk discerningly about singers. Hopkins recalls, 'Like a lot of people who are coming to an art form completely fresh they were also interestingly open-minded.' She was struck by the fact that her grandparents never described opera as 'inaccessible' and 'boring', in contrast with some colleagues she later met working in the opera industry itself.[17]

The success of the Three Tenors album, as well as that of Nigel Kennedy's *The Four Seasons* brought about structural change in the record industry. Record executives realised that the classical market could be promoted to multiple different groups of listeners and divided the sector into separate 'core classical' and 'strategic classical' areas. In the latter, marketing and promotional practices were borrowed from popular music, placing a large emphasis on performers and their image rather than on musical works themselves. *The Guardian* reported in 1991 that the classical departments of Virgin's twelve megastores had recently seen sales rise by 11 per cent as operatic highlights albums by star singers boomed.[18]

One interesting way in which opera and 'image' converged in the 1990s can be seen in the way in which the opera world began to associate itself with designer fashion. This was an international trend, but it was a bandwagon upon which the Royal Opera House was keen to jump. In 1991 it put on a production of Strauss's *Capriccio* using sumptuous costumes designed by Gianni Versace.[19] Four years later, for a Jonathan Miller production of *Così fan tutte*, it used clothes that were not so much 'costumes' as an advertisement for a fashion house, being lines from the 1995 Armani ready-to-wear-collection. Indeed, the clothes were supplied free of charge on the basis that they would gain high-profile publicity. Here was opera associating itself with extreme luxury—the sort of clothing almost nobody could afford to buy. This might well have worked against the Royal Opera House, compounding an image of exclusivity and expense. Instead, it proved highly popular, drawing people in who might not otherwise have attended an opera. As ever, the expense and exclusivity of high fashion was perceived as aspirational rather

---

[17] Private email correspondence with Kate Hopkins.
[18] Louise Gray, 'Divas Take a Dive', *The Guardian* (19 August 1991), 28.
[19] Helena Matheopoulos, *Fashion Designers at the Opera* (London: Thames and Hudson, 2011), pp. 156–163.

A PERFECT STORM   195

than elitist and an association with this sort of luxury seemed, oddly, to work in Covent Garden's favour.

More generally, the opera world seemed to feel the need to make the art form 'cool' and 'sexy'. English National Opera produced posters depicting leather-clad bikers attending a performance, semi-clad prima donnas, and bare-chested men from the backstage crew.[20] CD marketing campaigns eroticised young female musicians. In 1991 *The Guardian* applauded the release of Lesley Garrett's first album, 'A Soprano at the Movies', noting that 'the message . . . is that classical music is sexy, that the walls separating pop from classical are long overdue for a storming, and that musical elitism has had its day'.[21] But the way the reporter writes here is counterproductive, a classic example of ostensibly confronting stereotypes whilst actually reinforcing them in people's minds. What Garrett was doing was nothing new: opera singers had been crossing over into the world of film since the 1920s. And since Garrett was a principal soprano at ENO, which had been established as the home of opera for the people, where exactly was the musical elitism that had had its day?

As opera began to be presented in ever more diverse ways in the 1990s, arguments broke out between different parties within the opera world, each keen to defend their own patch. One such row was occasioned by Rodney Milnes, now chief opera critic of *The Times*, writing a scathing review of a Raymond Gubbay production of *La bohème* at the Royal Albert Hall. Gubbay responded with the accusation that Milnes was an out-of-touch purist—objecting now not only to surtitles but to the amplification required by arena-style opera—and the newspaper published an exchange of open letters between the two men.[22] Gubbay wrote, 'You perceived a threat to the operatic establishment and what better way to assert your authority than by a total put-down in print?', while Milnes insisted that his criticism was merely of a poorly directed production.

Gubbay's shows—some of which Milnes would later praise—followed in the footsteps of many historic ventures to put commercial opera on in popular settings for a broad audience.[23] There had always been different types of opera coexisting in the United Kingdom. What was different now, however,

[20] Anon., 'A Fight at the Opera', *The Economist* (17 October 1992), 36.
[21] Louise Gray, 'Divas Take a Dive', *The Guardian* (19 August 1991), 28.
[22] Raymond Gubbay and Rodney Milnes, 'Seconds Out For a Real Fight at the Opera', *The Times* (12 April 1996), 29.
[23] Rodney Milnes, 'Packing a Real Punch', *The Times* (10 February 1997), 18; Milnes, 'Electric, Sexy and Right on Song', *The Times* (22 February 1999), 19.

196 SOMEONE ELSE'S MUSIC

was the antagonism that was developing between different factions in the opera world: the promoters of popular opera—self-styled ambassadors against elitism—versus more traditional members of the operatic establishment, whom they characterised as elitists.

So heated did the row become that *The Times* devoted an editorial to it, asserting that 'anything which impedes the greatest possible access to opera is to be abhorred'. Although it was fairly even-handed towards both antagonists, the paper ultimately sided with its own critic. The leader writer argued that high standards did not have to mean elitism, writing, 'If the workers of Milan can appreciate opera, why shouldn't Basildon man go to *Bohème*? But arguing for access should not mean demanding dilution. Opera, like wine, should not be watered down and Mr Milnes is right to insist that standards be maintained.'[24] At a time when opera was so routinely and casually disparaged as elitist in the British press, it was heartening to see a national newspaper arguing that audiences—all audiences—deserved to be given a chance to experience opera straight, in its very best manifestations, without dumbing down and without apology.

Access and the media

Alas, such attitudes were rare. Ironically, this was a period when the newspapers were devoting more and more space to the arts—between 1989 and 1994 *The Times* expanded its daily arts coverage from one page to three—while simultaneously disparaging them as elitist.[25] Brian McMaster, former MD of WNO and now Director of the Edinburgh Festival, was deeply frustrated that stereotypes were hampering the work of opera companies and said in 1998, 'That elitist image has now been extended to the arts as a whole. It seems to be coming from the government, and it's certainly coming from the media.'[26] Yet this was paradoxical, given the 'high pop' vogue mentioned above. People wanted to consume culture and they wanted to read about it. But the type of coverage the arts were receiving was changing.

Specialist critics complained that they were being marginalised and pushed aside by general arts journalists, celebrities, and even political

[24] Editorial, 'Duets and Duels', *The Times* (12 April 1996), 17.
[25] Richard Morrison, 'Critics at the Blunt End', *The Times* (19 October 1994), 33.
[26] Andrew Clark, 'Brian McMaster', *Opera*, 1998 Festival Edition, 16–23, 23.

correspondents writing PR-driven features.[27] A prime example of the general journalist offering 'comment' on the arts was an article in *The Observer* by a young freelance journalist called Jay Rayner, who would later become a leading food critic. Rayner admitted to knowing little about opera; he had struggled through a few recordings and performances but still couldn't stand it. Yet he was categorically certain that it was elitist and he itemised the reasons why.[28]

First, Rayner argued, opera was expensive: top-price tickets at Covent Garden cost £112 and despite a subsidy of more than £7 million, the place still had a deficit of £4.5 million. Second, opera was for entitled, ignorant toffs 'with fur coats, animals slung dead-eyed across their backs'. Third, opera was conservative: its traditional fans booed ENO's adventurous reworkings and regarded the use of 'Nessun Dorma' as the World Cup theme as 'the equivalent of grand larceny'. Fourth, opera was weird: 'an overblown banquet of aesthetic excess' featuring singers who were 'like steroid-drenched body builders, fanatics who have over-exercised their larynxes'. Fifth, opera was un-British: 'we don't even have a tradition of opera in this country'. Sixth, opera was old-fashioned and out of touch: people should watch musicals, 'the people's entertainment'. 'So out with your kings and queens', Rayner concluded, 'junk your love-struck gods. Give them all their P45s and send them down to the dole office. It will shut them up at last.'

Rayner trotted out every cliché about opera in the book, subjecting not a single one of his acquired prejudices to critical scrutiny. Some of them contained a grain of truth; most were patently exaggerated. The article was entitled 'Spleen'. It was an exercise in provocation, an excuse to vent a personal antipathy. Humorous? Certainly, but unhelpful, too. For stereotypes become gospel truth when recycled frequently enough in respected news outlets.

Elitism was, by this time, more than just a buzzword. The idea that opera was elitist had been repeated so many times that it had become every journalist's opening gambit. Referring to Radio 4's *Today* programme, Simon Jenkins observed:

> You can see it coming. James Naughtie or Sue MacGregor has some hapless defender of culture in their sights. The subject may be Covent Garden

[27] Michael Kennedy, 'Down with Accessibility!', *The Spectator* (22 February 1997), 36.
[28] Jay Rayner, 'Spleen: Opera Buffoonery', *The Observer* (5 May 1991), 77.

198 SOMEONE ELSE'S MUSIC

or provincial rep or Shakespeare in schools. A question or two passes, and then the e-word swoops. Horny-handed populists watch from the *Today* programme's control room: "Use the word", they mouth through the glass. And out it comes, "Minister, isn't this all rather *elitist*?" A sigh of relief rises from a million working-class breakfast tables. The Corporation has done its proletarian duty.[29]

Even when the opera world did something laudable in the 1990s, the spectre of elitism was invariably hovering in the wings. In 1993, for example, the Royal Opera House ran a 'Saturday special' scheme, where tickets for six performances were available for between £1.50 and £20 (set against the then-current top price of £118) to the unemployed, those on income support, and students. But *The Guardian*'s headline 'Lofty Culture at Low Prices' was hardly likely to sell the scheme to those new to opera, suggesting, as it did, that opera was elitist in ways unconnected with price.[30]

Meanwhile, notwithstanding the ubiquity of opera in soundtracks and celebrity-fronted shows, the amount of *actual* opera on television was declining. Occasionally, opera could still be a television 'event', notably when BBC Two cleared the schedules for Covent Garden's new *La traviata* in 1994 (directed by Richard Eyre), propelling the then little-known Romanian soprano Angela Gheorghiu into international stardom. You could still expect to see the odd opera at Christmas: Channel 4 broadcast Thomas Adès's *Powder Her Face* on Christmas night in 1999, inconceivable today. But when the critic Richard Morrison scrutinised the TV listings for a week in 1996, he found that less than 2 per cent of the week's programming had anything to do with the arts.[31] Given the rich fare available on television throughout the previous two decades this was a step backwards, which can only have contributed to a growing sense that opera was detached from everyday life.

One of the problems facing those who sought to make the case for opera in the 1990s, whether critics, broadcasters, or opera companies themselves, was that the elitism stereotype was so ubiquitous that it forced everyone on to the defensive. No longer was it possible to give the public opera on its own terms. When Channel 4 broadcast *Operavox*—six operas presented as half-hour animations—in 1995, the series was billed apologetically. Only five years

---

[29] Simon Jenkins, 'The E-Word That Sends a Shudder Down the Spine', *The Spectator* (21 October 1995), 38; original emphasis.

[30] Anon., 'Lofty Culture at Low Prices', *The Guardian* (20 August 1993), 6.

[31] Richard Morrison, 'What's BBC TV Got Against Culture?', *The Times* (1 June 1996), 17.

after Channel 4's runaway ratings success with the Three Tenors concert, *The Times* reported, 'The plan is to demystify what is seen as elitist, impenetrable art, to present good music and coherent stories.'[32] Similarly, an evening in which soloists from Scottish Opera entertained diners at a Harry Ramsden's fish-and-chip restaurant—the sort of occasion that would previously have been presented as a quirky bit of fun—now became a bold attempt to 'shake off opera's elitist image'.[33] Nobody had spoken about opera like this in previous decades; now it seemed impossible to talk about it without mentioning the e-word.

Crisis at Covent Garden

Opera's 'elitist' image was compounded when Covent Garden was hit by a perfect storm of problems in the mid-1990s. The Royal Opera was still doing many good things: around 40,000 people annually were enjoying the company's performances for free or only a small sum.[34] Yet such achievements were eclipsed by a crisis that would do long-term damage both to the Royal Opera House itself—dubbed by *Opera* magazine as 'the national Soap Opera House'—and to the cause of opera in Britain more generally.[35] The triggers for the crisis were many: a lottery grant that was characterised by *Newsnight*'s Jeremy Paxman as 'a massive public subsidy for the entertainment of the nobs', widely reported institutional mismanagement, and a fly-on-the-wall documentary series that would turn out to be a colossal own goal.[36] All of this would compound an image of an aloof, arrogant institution, derided by *The Evening Standard* in 1996 as 'an elitist, indulgent, inefficient and preposterously expensive house of camp'.[37]

At the turn of the 1990s, the financial woes of the Royal Opera House persisted, a consequence of the particular way in which opera was funded in the United Kingdom. Jeremy Isaacs reported that at an international conference of opera-house directors, 'the British representatives were the only ones

---

[32] David Flusfeder, 'Drawn, Yes, But Hardly Drawn Out', *The Times* (4 February 1995), 3.

[33] Shirley English, 'Opera Sings for Its Supper in Return to Populist Roots', *The Times* (28 September 1998), 10.

[34] *Royal Opera House Annual Report, 1991/1992*, p. 6.

[35] John Allison, 'An American in London', *Opera*, 50/12 (December 1999), 1388–1395, 1388.

[36] *Newsnight*, 20 July 1995, shown on *Trouble at the House*.

[37] Rupert Christiansen, 'Trouble at the House—Again', *The Spectator* (27 January 1996), 36–37, 36.

200 SOMEONE ELSE'S MUSIC

for whom finance was a major and persistent difficulty'.[38] Over the coming years, there was little of good news to report in the theatre's annual reports, with a steady decline of subsidy as a proportion of income, with any attempts to increase box office income via ticket price rises leading both to lower attendance and charges of elitism.[39]

In July 1995, Covent Garden was awarded £55 million from the Arts Council's Lottery Fund towards a major redevelopment project of a building substantially unmodernised since World War One, with a further £23 million to follow.[40] Renovation works had to be carried out, for health-and-safety and accessibility reasons, backstage facilities needed modernising, a second auditorium was to be constructed, and new spaces created to accommodate the ballet company. The Floral Hall would become a new, elegant public forum. There is no doubt that the Royal Opera House genuinely needed the money; indeed, the grant would cover only a third of its costs, with more to be raised from a fundraising appeal and renting out commercial space in the Piazza.[41] However, the vast sums involved, a blaze of publicity, and the way in which the issue was handled by the theatre's management led to bad PR that seriously aggravated the perceived 'scandal'.

Nobody had taken much notice of arts funding in recent times when it was taken from general taxation, but the high-profile lottery grant attracted public attention and public ire.[42] It was like 1930 all over again, except that this time the money was perceived to be being taken directly from the less well-off (who were particularly inclined to buy lottery tickets) and given to the rich. It was not apparent to the public that this 'subsidy' was a mechanism for providing cheaper seats and expanding the audience, though both were stipulated in the terms of the award.

Sectors of the right-wing press, perhaps surprisingly, defended the grant. *The Spectator*, indeed, argued it should have been doubled in order to expand the capacity of the theatre, thus bringing ticket prices down to a level everyone could afford: 'End of elitism'.[43] *The Daily Telegraph* argued that

---

[38] *Royal Opera House Annual Report, 1989/1990*, p. 6. ROH archives: ROH Annual Reports—1972/73–1991/92.

[39] *Royal Opera House Annual Report, 1991/1992*, p. 2, ROH archives: ROH Annual Reports—1972/73–1991/92.

[40] Dalya Alberge, 'Arts Council Backs £55m Lottery Gift to Opera House', *The Times* (21 July 1995), 5; Simon Tait, 'A Garden in Bloom', *The Times* (12 January 1995), 34.

[41] *Royal Opera House Annual Report, 1995/1996*, p. 4. ROH archives: Royal Opera House Annual Reports 1992/93–2005/06.

[42] Fairman, 'Elitist Image Loses Its Fizz', 15.

[43] John Parry, 'A Study in Spending', *The Spectator* (26 October 1996), 67–68, 67.

A PERFECT STORM   201

whether one liked opera or not, 'the retention of and investment in a resource such as Covent Garden is essential if Britain is to make any pretence of maintaining a civilised culture.'[44] But civilisation, in abstract terms, was becoming an unfashionable concept few were willing to defend, and the response to the lottery grant was highly critical from a populist media determined to whip up a storm. As Rodney Milnes stated a few years later, 'I think nobody realised what an anti-arts ethos was abroad in the country.'[45]

The Sun railed against opera to such an extent that, in Bernard Levin's words, the very word 'opera' had been 'transmogrified into something so shocking that when they hear it, stern mothers feel obliged to tell their offspring to go and wash their mouths out.'[46] Covent Garden was by far 'the biggest and most gleaming target' for those with a class-war agenda, but as so often, Covent Garden and opera were indistinguishable to most people reading their daily papers. Furthermore, the perceived 'elitism' of the award had a knock-on effect for other arts institutions. An application for lottery funds to pay for a new opera house in the regenerated Cardiff Bay, to be designed by Zaha Hadid, was turned down, after opera found itself up against rugby in a battle for funding. The local press, in Richard Morrison's words, 'decided that an opera house, especially one designed by an architect with a funny foreign name, was a "toffy" idea, and campaigned relentlessly against it.'[47] The Millennium Stadium (projected cost: £100 million) was approved, while the Cardiff Bay Opera House (£87 million) was not.[48]

Reminiscent of the calls in the 1930s for the proposed subsidy to be used on orphans and allotments for the unemployed, charities argued they would have been more worthy recipients of such a large sum. A spokesperson for Cancer Research stated, 'Cancer isn't elitist. One in three of us will get cancer ... The British people would agree that the lottery was never intended to top up elitist ventures.'[49] The charity's sense of grievance was understandable, but the terms in which it expressed it called into question once more whether the arts should be funded at all. The shock on the face of Keith Cooper, PR director at the Royal Opera House, was palpable as he struggled

---

[44] Anon., 'Garden For All the Nation', *DT* (21 July 1995), 22.
[45] *Trouble at the House.*
[46] Bernard Levin, 'Come Into the Garden', *The Times* (23 February 1996), 16.
[47] Richard Morrison, 'An M-Word to Be Proud Of', *The Times* (15 December 2003), T2, 3.
[48] Anon., 'And Not a Dome in Sight', *The Guardian* (20 September 2003), C9.
[49] Dalya Alberge, 'Arts Council Backs £55m Lottery Gift to Opera House', *The Times* (21 July 1995), 5.

202 SOMEONE ELSE'S MUSIC

to defend the lottery award on the daytime TV chat show *Kilroy*, in front of an audience irate that the money hadn't gone to hospitals.[50]

There was now widespread discussion of the possibility of Covent Garden's subsidy being removed altogether, Chris Smith admitting in 1998 that this was 'one possibility'.[51] It was astonishing to find this call coming from the left, which had been behind the initiatives to subsidise opera both in 1930 and in 1945. *The Guardian* even argued that 'the time has surely come for Covent Garden to be financed by private money'.[52] Though the author of the article, Claire Armitstead, conceded that opera was 'special' and 'the greatest theatrical experience of them all', she also asked what the point was, in 'the "people's century"', of funding 'an elitist art form appealing to a privileged minority' that had been 'commandeered by the rich' and had an 'off-putting upper-class aura'. Even a cursory glance at the popularisation of opera in the 1980s and 1990s, never mind a backward glance at the rich democratic history of earlier twentieth-century opera-going, should have disproved such clichés.

That said, some loyal Covent Garden audience members did feel that the newly renovated house, when it reopened, was not the same place it had once been, and complaints about opera's 'real' enthusiasts being priced out continued. In an open letter to *The Guardian* in 1999, a reader lamented the disappearance of the old inhabitants of the gallery, who had represented the 'heart' of the place: 'retired ladies having a rare treat, young people devoting much of their disposable income to a special night out, music lovers indulging themselves in their one passion'. All talk about 'access' (which amounted to opening the foyers, the odd free concert, and uncomfortable cheap seats) was, he said, 'bullshit'. Access should mean one thing: 'enabling people of modest means who love opera to attend performances in the house their taxes pay for'.[53]

In addition to all the negative press attention it was receiving about the lottery grant, the Royal Opera House came under scrutiny in the 1996 BBC documentary *The House*.[54] The theatre hoped that allowing the cameras in would show the public why subsidy was needed, as well as demonstrating the commitment of artists and staff.[55] The venture backfired, exposing a state of

---

[50] *Trouble at the House.*
[51] Wyatt, 'Blowing in the Wind', 20.
[52] Claire Armitstead, 'No Go Aria', *The Guardian* (11 July 1997), A2.
[53] Gareth James, '... And the Most Expensive', letter to *The Guardian* (22 December 1999), 15.
[54] Jeremy Isaacs, 'The Royal Opera House: My Part in the Drama', *The Times* (25 October 1999), 37.
[55] Royal Opera House Annual Report, 1995/1996, p. 6. ROH archives: Royal Opera House Annual Reports 1992/93–2005/06.

managerial turmoil, which appalled figures from the arts world and alienated fans, such as Mike Martineau, whose working-class parents had saved up to take him to Covent Garden countless times as a child. He wrote, 'It would be no bad thing if this monument to waste, greed and vanity, totally divorced from reality, went out of business for ever. I say this as an opera lover, who was taken to see more than twenty Covent Garden productions before I was 16.'[56] Despite the programme's hatchet job—or perhaps because of it—an audience of four million viewers tuned in.[57]

The furore about the lottery grant and *The House* was accompanied by a sharp decline in sponsorship, disappointing box office, and a resulting cut in budgets that meant cancelling productions and laying off staff, all of which caused pain and dented morale.[58] A period of disorientating managerial change, with three director generals between January 1997 and March 1998, meant that the governance of the organisation came perilously close to falling apart. With catastrophic budget losses there was a prospect of the company going into administration, a scenario that was eventually averted thanks to a bail-out from donors.[59] Suitable venues to perform in during the renovation period were not found, staff redundancies were mishandled, and in December 1997, the entire board resigned. Opera's supporters looked on aghast, with Simon Jenkins arguing that the company had 'tested the elitist fallacy to destruction.'[60]

Even the gala in July 1997 to mark the theatre's closure was mishandled, reinforcing rather than combating negative perceptions. Westminster Council decreed that, for health and safety reasons, the audience at the free outdoor screening in the Piazza would have to stand rather than being provided with seats.[61] In contrast, the scene within the theatre was described as one of untrammelled luxury and stuffiness, resembling, according to one eye-witness, 'a filmset of the Austro-Hungarian empire', with guests 'tied up in dinner jackets like lobsters in a cauldron, an occasional claw breaking free to wave for air or a glass of champagne.'[62] This whole period was a PR disaster, and talk of making the theatre more accessible after the renovation was

---

[56] Mike Martineau, 'Opera Obscenity', letter to *DM* (28 February 1996), 51.

[57] Isaacs, 'The Royal Opera House', 37.

[58] Royal Opera House Annual Report, 1995/1996, p. 6.

[59] Mary Allen, *A House Divided: The Diary of a Chief Executive of the Royal Opera House* (London: Simon & Schuster, 1998), p. 80, p. 131, p. 181.

[60] Simon Jenkins, 'What News from the Piazza', *The Times* (16 July 1997), 18.

[61] Dalya Alberge, 'Standing Room Only for Opera House's Swansong', *The Times* (14 July 1997), 5.

[62] Jenkins, 'What News from the Piazza', 18.

Figure 9.1 Audience entering for a performance of Richard Strauss, *Salome*, Royal Opera House, Covent Garden, April 1997. Reproduced with permission from © Clive Barda/ArenaPAL.

undermined when Sir Colin Southgate, who took over as Chairman in 1998, said, 'We mustn't downgrade the opera house. I don't want to see a pair of shorts and smelly trainers.'[63] Perceptions of elitism at Covent Garden were now so ingrained that, as Simon Jenkins observed, 'You could cut the price of the Royal Box to zero and advertise it in *The Big Issue*, and still nobody would notice.'[64]

Although many commentators blamed Covent Garden's incompetence for the mess into which it had got itself, the director Peter Hall thought that the state of affairs had, in some measure, been caused by politicians. Successive government cuts, and an insistence that seat prices be raised in place of an increase in subsidy, had created a situation where the theatre had had to turn to corporate entertainment in order to cover its costs. It was political decisions, Hall argued, that had made Covent Garden 'elitist' and 'an indefensible "toffs" venue'—and these had been made by both right and left.[65]

[63] Dalya Alberge, 'Opera to Get a New Leader, Love and a Cuddle', *The Times* (16 January 1998), 10.
[64] Simon Jenkins, 'Smith Wins the House', *The Times* (1 July 1998), 20.
[65] Peter Hall, 'The New Cromwellians', *The Spectator* (27 June 1998), 16–17, 16.

The politics of anti-elitism

As the son of a music-hall artist, John Major was more naturally inclined to favour the arts than Thatcher had been, though he struggled to overcome the misgivings of his colleagues. Stressing the importance of enjoyable activities in a rounded life, he wrote in his autobiography: 'My interest in promoting a renaissance in sport and the arts . . . was thought to be rather quirky by some of my colleagues. I disagreed with them then, and do now.'[66] Major was an opera enthusiast and—unlike most later prime ministers—happy to be seen at operatic performances, posing for the cameras with artists taking part in a Royal Opera performance of *Turandot* at Wembley Arena in 1992.[67] Thanks in part to the keenness of the then Secretary of State for National Heritage David Mellor, it became acceptable once again to talk about the arts in idealistic terms, as an essential human need, though commentators on the right criticised Major for his unexpected Reithian paternalism.[68] Mellor managed to achieve a huge increase in the Arts Council's grant and exerted pressure for the Coliseum to be bought for the nation, arguing, 'For me, the chance to guarantee great opera at affordable prices in the heart of London was irresistible. It was not so easy to persuade my colleagues.'[69]

But the arts world was largely unconvinced by any purported new Conservative friendliness to the arts after the Thatcher years, and many feared that the introduction of lottery funding might lead to the removal of Arts Council subsidies altogether. Furthermore, the Major government's rebranding of the arts as 'heritage', lumping them with sport and broadcasting into a new 'Ministry for National Heritage', was largely reviled. This move signalled that the arts were part of the leisure industry, something that potentially undermined their claim to subsidy, and favoured what some saw as artistic conservatism and blandness, what Robert McCrum called 'the Marks & Spencer approach to the nation's cultural satisfaction.'[70]

When New Labour came to power in 1997, hopes within the arts world were high. Speaking at the South Bank Show awards, Tony Blair said that the arts were central to Labour's vision of a decent and just society, not just

---

[66] John Major, *John Major: The Autobiography* (London: HarperCollins, 1999), p. 412.

[67] Royal Opera House Annual Report, 1991/1992, p. 6.

[68] Bryan Appleyard, 'The Tories' New Culture Club', *The Times* (13 May 1992), 12.

[69] Tooley, *In House*, p. 207; David Mellor, 'Why It Is Time to Speak Out', *The Sunday Telegraph* (19 November 1995), 49.

[70] Robert McCrum, 'The Flight of the Culture Vultures', *The Guardian* (23 July 1992), 26.

206 SOMEONE ELSE'S MUSIC

something to be tucked away on page twenty-four of a manifesto.[71] Peter Hall wrote that the Conservatives had 'quietly decimated the arts over the past eighteen years in the cause of free enterprise' and generated hostility against artists by disparaging them as 'luvvies'.[72] Nevertheless, he expressed anxiety about New Labour, whose arts manifesto seemed 'tentative and muddled', wedded to funding local community centres but mistrustful of landmark institutions such as the National Theatre and Covent Garden. Once the party had been elected, disillusionment soon set in, as its arts policy turned out to be, in Richard Morrison's words, not so much the end of an eighteen-year dark age as 'a flimsy tissue of vague buzzwords'.[73]

Blair had promised creativity would be 'cherished and honoured', yet cut the Arts Council grant by £3 million.[74] Hall argued that an arts world of international repute that had taken fifty years to build and that had been sustained by subsidy, which had promoted new talent, kept ticket prices low, and built new generations of audiences, was being dismantled.[75] Pointing to a 'narrow-minded and joyless' ethos that was 'indifferent to what really matters in life', Hall wrote, 'Oliver Cromwell destroyed English art because he wanted to level everything in the name of Christianity. New Labour looks set to do the same in the name of egalitarianism.'[76] For Thatcher, the arts were 'left-wing'; for Blair, they were 'elitist'.

Access was one of the vague buzzwords of the new administration. Chris Smith wrote of the aims of the newly renamed Department of Culture, Media and Sport, 'This is a profoundly democratic agenda, seeing cultural access as one of the egalitarian building blocks of society.'[77] Such aims were undoubtedly laudable, but the flip side to access was 'elitism', another buzzword that was repeated over and over again. In attempting to define what 'culture'—a word now widely preferred to 'art'—actually was, Smith wrote, 'Culture can embrace a broad sweep of fine and high-quality activity, of all kinds. It does not need to be highbrow to qualify as "culture". It does not need to be élitist.'[78] In talking in these terms, Smith seemed to confirm that culture, as traditionally conceived, was indeed 'highbrow' and 'elitist'. Certainly, some of

---

[71] Richard Morrison, 'Labour's Empty Canvas Put on Show', *The Times* (12 January 2001), 24.
[72] Peter Hall, 'I Shan't Vote for These Philistines', *The Times* (8 March 1997), 20.
[73] Richard Morrison, 'Luvvies Fall Out of Love with Labour', *The Times* (21 November 1997), n.p.
[74] Peter Hall, 'The New Cromwellians', *The Spectator* (27 June 1998), 16–17, 16.
[75] Ibid., 16.
[76] Ibid.
[77] The Rt Hon Chris Smith, MP, *Creative Britain* (London: Faber and Faber, 1998), p. 3.
[78] Ibid., p. 4.

A PERFECT STORM 207

Britain's opera companies felt a chill wind was blowing. John Tooley wrote in 1999: 'The age of populism is with us, and high culture—for want of a better term—ranks low in the present government's rating of the arts scene.'[79]

In a speech at the Royal Academy in May 1997, Smith stated that the arts were 'not optional extras for government' but 'at the very centre of our mission', arguing that any civilised government was duty-bound to support the arts.[80] All of this sounded positive, but Smith was quietly shooting himself in the foot under the table. In a speech to the Fabian Society conference that September, he stated, 'There is a perpetual danger that "culture" will be seen as something alien to the vast majority of people, something just for an élite and for special people in privileged places. We must fight as sturdily as we can against such notions.'[81] Yet the way in which the government talked about opera reinforced such notions at every turn.

This had practical ramifications, as patrons became increasingly fearful of being seen to be supporting 'elitist' art forms. The Midland Bank announced in 1997 that it would end its twenty-six-year sponsorship of the Royal Opera House Proms. The bank's head of advertising and promotions was quoted as saying, 'The opera house has always been elitist. The ballet is less so but it's still a bit niche. We want to interact more with customers.'[82] There was talk of launching a rock festival instead.

The Blair government presented itself as very interested in culture, so long as it was culture that was unambiguously 'of the people' and the here and now. Whereas the Conservatives had been keen to talk about the arts primarily in terms of a historic national legacy, Smith stated, 'We must not define ourselves solely in terms of the past, or tradition, or what we have inherited.'[83] New Labour had inherited the Conservative term 'heritage', but spun it in a negative manner, lumping the arts in with museums, stately homes, and other things that were cosy, conservative, and supposedly backward-looking.

Time and again, New Labour pitted new against old. Blair held up *The Full Monty* as representing the 'inventive, creative, dynamic' spirit of modern Britain; Smith urged the BBC to stop producing 'formulaic' historical drama based on novels like *Pride and Prejudice* (notwithstanding the immense popularity of Andrew Davies' 1995 adaptation). British pop and rock

[79] Tooley, *In House*, p. 214.
[80] Smith, *Creative Britain*, pp. 42–43.
[81] Ibid., p. 37.
[82] Nigel Reynolds, 'Midland Drops Opera Funding', *DT* (19 November 1997), 1.
[83] Smith, *Creative Britain*, pp. 37–38.

208 SOMEONE ELSE'S MUSIC

were held up by the new government as world-leading; the D'Oyly Carte Company lost its Arts Council funding.[84] The New Labour project was all about rebranding, and soon the nation itself was being reinvented as 'Cool Britannia'.

Was personal taste guiding public policy? John Tusa, head of the Barbican Centre, argued that the arts were being harmed by the Prime Minister's personal apathy towards them, as a child of the sixties whose instinctive penchant was for pop and rock.[85] Almost as soon as he had been given the keys to 10 Downing Street, Blair started to invite the stars of popular culture—Noel and Liam Gallagher, DJs, and soap-opera casts—to visit. If corresponding invitations were offered to the nation's leading actors, classical musicians, and novelists, they were not well-publicised: Chris Smith protested that the press simply didn't take pictures.[86]

Blair's particular championing of film, video, TV, design, rock, and pop corresponded with his conversion to the idea of the 'creative industries', support for which had become central to New Labour Ideology. Applied art was much in favour—fashion and interior design, radio and TV production, film and animation.[87] The pure arts—opera, ballet, drama—were not so favoured. The term 'creative industries'—still pervasive today—had the benefit of making certain art forms (or applied extensions of them) sound more dynamic, more like the sciences, more hard-working, and more capable of earning their keep. But it was an interesting turn of priorities for a Labour government, in favouring utilitarianism over art for art's sake. Tusa argued that 'in backing "the arts that pay", and overlooking and undervaluing "the arts that cost"', Blair had shown himself to be 'the true son of Margaret Thatcher'.[88]

New Labour would redefine culture in two ways in the late 1990s: as a commodified economic phenomenon ('the creative industries'), and as a mechanism for combatting social exclusion (the 'access agenda'). Art was now to be co-opted in order to combat unemployment, crime, health, and educational challenges and targets were set to increase attendance at the arts by various minority groups.[89] As Robert Hewison notes, 'This placed

---

[84] Hal Colebatch, *Blair's Britain* (London: The Claridge Press, 1999), p. 40, p. 80.

[85] John Tusa, 'Why I'm Worried About Tony', *The Times* (11 March 1998), 31.

[86] Wyatt, 'Blowing in the Wind', 20.

[87] Smith, *Creative Britain*, p. 8.

[88] Tusa, 'Why I'm Worried About Tony'?

[89] Robert Hewison, *Cultural Capital: The Rise and Fall of Creative Britain* (London: Verso, 2014), p. 87.

A PERFECT STORM   209

previously unheard-of expectations on the arts and heritage' as culture was placed 'at the service of the economy and the government's social agenda'.[90]

In its commitment to combating 'elitism', and wary after the Royal Opera House scandal, the government decided that something would have to be 'done' about opera. Chris Smith posited himself as the champion of a 'people's opera' and commissioned a report into Covent Garden's affairs by the National Heritage Select Committee, chaired by Gerald Kaufman, which would turn out to be damning. A year later he commissioned the Eyre Report, which delved deep into the workings of the Royal Opera, the Royal Ballet, and ENO.[91] Eyre specifically attacked the elitism of Covent Garden, noting that everything about the place exuded grandeur, expense, and exclusivity, and arguing that potential audience members were 'put off, much as people are put off hunting, not by the activity itself, as by the perceived behaviour—or the social class—of some of its enthusiasts'.[92]

Eyre was asked to investigate whether Covent Garden could become fully privatised, and the idea of housing the Royal Opera, Royal Ballet, and ENO under one roof was also explored. ENO was going through a difficult period, with ticket sales falling despite an array of promotions and marketing strategies.[93] The sensationalist, confrontational Power House productions had alienated some core audience members, leading both to falling ticket sales and—ironically—perceptions of elitism.[94] Sir Charles Mackerras, who had directed ENO in the 1970s, urged the company to put on 'accessible, comprehensible' productions and to ditch the 'drab backcloths or politically correct social comment on sleaze in the Balkans'.[95] 'Concept productions', the conductor argued, were often so obscure that they only made sense to an audience that knew the original: updating that was justified in the name of accessibility could, in other words, leave 'uninitiated' audiences baffled, fuelling the notion that opera was remote and recherché.[96]

But despite these woes, opera-lovers were appalled by the government's suggestion that ENO might be subsumed by Covent Garden, and influential figures spoke out against the proposal. The novelist Doris Lessing wrote

[90] Ibid., p. 29.

[91] Dalya Alberge and Stephen Farrell, 'Opera House Accused of Elitism and Arrogance', *The Times* (1 July 1998), 1.

[92] Sally Pook, 'Opera Debacle Has Tarnished Britain's Arts', *DT* (1 July 1998), 9.

[93] Antony Thorncroft, 'Hitting the Right Note To Fill The Seats', *FT* (27 November 1993), 48.

[94] Rodney Milnes, 'Arias for Hard Times', *The Times* (11 February 1994), 31.

[95] Anon., 'Grasping the Nettle: Response to a Crisis', *Opera*, 49/1 (January 1998), 24–32, pp. 31–32.

[96] Alan Blyth, 'Mackerras at 70—Straight from the Shoulder', *Opera*, 46/12 (December 1995), 1408–1414, 1413.

210   SOMEONE ELSE'S MUSIC

of being 'charmed out of my wits' when she first attended an opera, after arriving in Britain from Southern Rhodesia in 1949.[97] In response to the government's plans for ENO, she wrote to *The Times*:

> The arts are what we are good at. Other countries know this, if we don't. I have been struck by the spiteful pleasure in some of the comments on the opera crisis made by people who should be rejoicing that our opera and theatre are so good that visitors come here from all over the world. If the ENO is destroyed—and there are those who want that—it will be the end of one of the liveliest, bravest and genuinely popular artistic efforts in London. This can be such a nasty little country; so philistine, so mean, and often so stupid.[98]

Thankfully for ENO, the project to merge it with Covent Garden ultimately came to nothing. National opera, for the time being, lived on, but Lessing's words about philistinism, meanness, and stupidity would have enduring resonance.

Doubling down on elitism

For all the populist razzle-dazzle, for all the best-selling CDs, for all the worthy educational initiatives, opera had been comprehensively rebranded as elitist by the 1990s, and it felt as if some in the opera world had given up the fight. Those involved in promoting and writing about opera increasingly seemed to be atoning for the art form, such as when leading critics and representatives from major opera companies attended a public debate organised by *The Times* which was billed 'As the millennium approaches, has opera lost its way and adopted a blinkered, elitist approach, ignoring a wider public as it appeals to an increasingly marginalised audience?'[99] Rodney Milnes, furthermore, reminisced about the 'epic moment' when director David Pountney had admitted, 'Sorry, opera *is* elitist, it's a challenge that you have to make an effort to go out and meet.'[100]

---

[97] 'The ENO Experience', *Coliseum*, 7 (Autumn 1998), 6–7, 6. BUTC, MM/REF/TH/LO/COL/105.
[98] Doris Lessing, letter to *The Times* (15 November 1997), 23.
[99] 'At the Heart of Opera', *The Times* (28 June 1995), 36.
[100] Rodney Milnes, 'New Brooms at Broomhill', *Opera*, 49/7 (July 1998), 777–781, 780; original emphasis.

A PERFECT STORM 211

Yes, there were pockets of operatic activity in the United Kingdom where privilege was certainly apparent. The Glyndebourne experience was in danger of becoming a parody of itself. A 1996 article in *The Illustrated London News*, showing picnickers in black tie, seen through a soft-focus haze of cow parsley, listed all the accessories the fashionable Glyndebourne picknicker might need: binoculars 'for monitoring who's arriving by helicopter'; a £650 cocktail shaker for making fresh Pimm's; a £4,100 hamper complete with cashmere rug, silver-plated cutlery, and fine porcelain; a £4,790 Hermès chaise-longue.[101]

The critic Hugh Canning called Glyndebourne 'a byword for opera at its most epicurean'.[102] Country house opera was, in a strange sort of way, tied to preserving this image, irrespective of its negative connotations, because it was fundamental to its brand image and its economic model. As Canning observed: 'Glyndebourne sees itself as a luxury product and it is important for the festivals that its wealthy benefactors do too.' Though elitism was, by now, an insult, exclusivity remained a marketing tool. On the other hand, the construction of a new theatre at Glyndebourne did mean more people could now buy tickets.

Glyndebourne was what Glyndebourne was—the company had always been a thing apart. However, there was a whole other face to the enterprise that rarely made headlines: the company's extremely active work in education and outreach, which at this time involved the composer Jonathan Dove working with people in Hastings, Ashford, and Peterborough to devise new works that were meaningful to local communities.[103] This was something that the company took extremely seriously, and the projects changed perceptions, albeit on a modest scale. One woman from Peterborough reported being 'hooked', despite her initial perception that opera 'has always seemed a bombastic artificial privilege for the overpaid—totally superficial, and completely unbelievable'.[104]

There was plentiful evidence that British opera—taken in the round—had not lost its way and become the preserve of the rich. Top-priced tickets at Covent Garden and Glyndebourne might be becoming increasingly expensive, but most people going to watch an opera in the United Kingdom were paying less than they would for a West End musical, rock concert, or Premier

[101] Anon., 'Pack a Power Picnic', *ILN* (3 June 1996), 36.
[102] Hugh Canning, 'How Does Glyndebourne Do It?', *ILN* (3 June 1996), 30–36, 32.
[103] Anon., *The Opera Education Workbook* (London: Opera and Music Theatre Forum, n.d.), 6–9.
[104] Ibid., 8.

212 SOMEONE ELSE'S MUSIC

League match. Half the seats at ENO cost less than £25 in 1999, whereas a ticket to watch West Ham cost £27.[105]

There were estimated to be forty to fifty small opera or music-theatre companies working in the United Kingdom by the early 1990s.[106] This was the decade that saw the foundation of Opera Holland Park by Michael Volpe, the son of working-class Italian immigrants, and James Clutton, a former West End producer. City of Birmingham Touring Opera was taking performances to sports halls, its repertoire including an opera by Ravi Shankar and a scaled-down version of *The Ring* rescored for eighteen players.[107] And after watching a performance of *Carmen* by the Moldovan National Opera in Southend-on-Sea in 1998, John Allison wrote, 'Anyone who still thinks opera "elitist" should have been here, on a damp mid-week evening when the auditorium was packed by people of all ages looking for a good night out.'[108]

Many groups were now reaching out to parts of the community highly unlikely to have encountered opera before. The southeast London-based Opera Factory ran projects for the homeless. Opera Spezzata ran a workshop with inmates in Brixton Prison, devising an improvised work based upon *The Escape from the Seraglio*.[109] English Touring Opera ran a rich programme of projects with disabled people, finding imaginative ways to perform opera using sign language.[110] And all the major opera companies now ran activities for schoolchildren, as did a number of specialist music education bodies.

For all this good news, the opera world was going through a crisis of confidence, and it was one that was specifically British. As Peter Jonas, former manager of ENO and by the late 1990s Staatsintendant of the Bavarian State Opera, explained, opera was not perceived as 'a toff's plaything' in Vienna, Munich, or Berlin: only in London.[111] And stereotypes that set in during this period laid the ground for the terms in which opera would be discussed into the twenty-first century; attitudes towards opera began to harden and many of the negative ideas about it established at this time have proved impossible to shake off.

---

[105] Tusa, *Art Matters*, p. 15.
[106] Devlin, 'Beggar's Opera', 21.
[107] Ibid., 15, 81.
[108] John Allison, 'Opera on the Fringe', *Opera*, 49/4 (April 1998), 480.
[109] Anon., *The Opera Education Pack* (London: Opera and Music Theatre Forum, n.d.), n.p.
[110] Anon., *The Opera Education Workbook*, 10.
[111] Cited in Anon., 'Grasping the Nettle', 29.

A PERFECT STORM 213

Formerly accepted ideas of 'excellence', 'quality', or 'good taste' had become unfashionable not just in tabloid culture but also among the intelligentsia. Ever more in thrall to postmodern theory—itself surely 'elitist' in using arcane language only the initiated could understand—academia and the radical left became obsessed with the notion of cultural relativism. While the cultural levelling of the postmodern project had benefits—opening up rich fields of enquiry about art forms that had hitherto been disdained—it also had troubling consequences. As Robert McCrum argued in *The Guardian*, people had become 'jumpy' about culture, because there was no longer a common agreement as to what it was any more, now that society had 'become fragmented along the San Andreas faults of Class, Race, Gender and Generation', with even the Arts Council going so far as to declare that 'there is no hierarchy of art forms'.[112] On the face of it, this lack of hierarchy seemed like a positive thing. But the problem was that, in time, commentators would not simply be content for all the arts to be put on an equal plane. Rather, those art forms that had historically been given special status had to be comprehensively demoted. The consequences for opera—and for access to opera for all—in the twenty-first century would be grave.

---

[112] McCrum, 'The Flight of the Culture Vultures', 26.

10

Twenty-First-Century Blues

Denise Leigh was a blind housewife and mother of three, Jane Gilchrist, a Tesco checkout assistant. In 2003 these two women found themselves thrust into the limelight as the winners of Channel 4's reality TV show *Operatunity*, a cross between a talent contest and a fly-on-the-wall docusoap, which sought to discover an amateur singer with no formal training who could sing a leading role at ENO. Adverts were sent to amateur choirs, brass bands, and working-men's clubs, and auditionees could sing any genre of music. The series followed the progress of a small group of participants (whittled down from 2,500 applicants) over fifteen months and Leigh and Gilchrist were ultimately selected as joint winners and given the opportunity to perform in *Rigoletto*, sharing the role of Gilda.[1]

Operatunity was promoted in similar vein to the talent contests with a pop music focus that were dominating the television schedules, without the public phone-in or humiliation that typically characterised the format. The stereotypical 'clash' between banal everyday life and the perceived 'high' status of opera was predictably played up as a hook with which to draw in viewers: publicity homed in on such participants as a builder, a supermarket assistant, a chef, a club singer and a pig farmer.[2] Nevertheless, all this was done with affection, and *Operatunity* avoided the extremely negative stereotypes that were, by now, swirling around opera, instead documenting the workings of ENO in a respectful format. And no wonder, because it was an exercise in public broadcasting, funded by the Arts Council as a way of making opera more accessible to a wider public, challenging public perceptions of opera, and identifying and coaching singers who might otherwise never be discovered.[3]

---

[1] Arts Council England, 'The New Audiences Programme 1998–2003'. https://www.artscoun cil.org.uk/sites/default/files/download-file/New-Audiences-Final-Report.pdf (accessed 6 June 2022), 35.

[2] Ibid., 36.

[3] Arts Council England, 'The New Audiences Programme 1998–2003', 35.

The series was successful in challenging the elitism stereotype at a number of levels. It built a taste for opera among the participants, not all of whom were previously familiar with it. It showed opera houses to be unstuffy places where friendly people from varied backgrounds could be found, encouraging people to attend an opera for the first time. And it defied fears that a series about opera might be thought too highbrow, attracting between 1.5 and 1.8 million viewers per episode. Hits on the ENO website doubled during the series and numerous first-time opera-goers booked to see a show.[4]

The programme also seemed, on the face of it, to challenge the opera-elitism stereotype by suggesting that anyone could have a go. Yet although the winners would go on to record an album and pursue careers in singing, neither achieved the high-profile success of the winners of a spin-off series, *Musicality*, who secured roles in West End musicals. Interestingly, *Operatunity*'s producer, Michael Waldman, said that the series aimed to show precisely how hard it is to become an opera singer, claiming, 'However well it goes for the winner on the final night, it is inconceivable that the Met or La Scala will be phoning the next morning to say "please play the lead in our next production".'[5] And yet, in this book we have encountered miners, telephonists, secretaries, and farmhands who *did* manage to 'make it' as opera singers, some even becoming international stars. So why was this no longer so easily achievable?

The beginning of the twenty-first century was a testing time for the opera industry. ENO was experiencing particular difficulties, making it highly unlikely that the *Operatunity* winners would have been invited to join the company, in the way that Sadler's Wells or the Old Vic might have recruited them. Just after *Operatunity* broadcast, the company was reported to be 'at its lowest ebb', as a result of mismanagement, high debts, and the threat of industrial action from its chorus.[6] (Jane Gilchrist reported a frosty reception from them during filming.[7]) As Richard Morrison noted, 'Sending these starry-eyed hopefuls to the near-bankrupt ENO for tuition, just as the company is axing dozens of its own singers and players, does seem like screening *Titanic* to illustrate safety procedures at sea.'[8]

---

[4] Ibid., 36; James Rampton, 'And For Our Encore', *The Independent on Sunday* (2 November 2003), 27.

[5] James Rampton, 'Pigaro, Pigaro!', *Radio Times* (8–14 February 2003), 26–27, 26.

[6] The Editor, 'Chorus Line', *The Times* (26 February 2003), 21.

[7] Richard Morrison, 'The Cash Lady Sings', *The Times* (26 February 2003), 7.

[8] Richard Morrison, '*Operatunity* Is Pitched Somewhere Between *Popstars* and the Karaoke Night from Hell', *The Times* (7 February 2003), 3.

216 SOMEONE ELSE'S MUSIC

But there were other factors at play—broader changes at the institutional, rather than the local, level, which made it more difficult for a novice opera singer to be 'discovered' out of nowhere. By the later decades of the twentieth century, operatic training had become more formalised and more expensive. Becoming an opera singer was now bound up with having money, though it was not the only musical sphere to which affluence granted access: by 2010 it was estimated that at least 60 per cent of chart pop and rock acts were former private-school pupils, compared with just 1 per cent twenty years previously.[9]

The opera industry in the United Kingdom had become far more professionalised, and indeed more internationalised. ENO, whose USP had previously been its use of talented British singers, was now casting from an international pool. The rather hazy line between professional and amateur opera that had existed in the touring companies of the early twentieth century, or even at Covent Garden after the war, had now entirely disappeared. Audience expectations of what they might hear on the professional operatic stage had changed. That standards should be higher was in many respects a good thing, but if 'accessibility' was perceived to be bound up with participation, the fact that few ordinary people could become opera singers did in some senses fuel the elitism stereotype.

Talented amateurs were perhaps more likely to become 'crossover' artists, a distinct, marketable category that had emerged by the 2000s. Crossover repertoire spanned a range of musical genres, from popular operatic arias delivered 'straight' to pop songs sung in a quasi-operatic manner, and was disseminated via recordings, TV shows, and major sporting events. On the face of it, the crossover movement seemed as if it might break down barriers between different types of musical theatre and provide opportunities for more people to enter opera from a background in musicals or pop. But for the most part this was not to be. Indeed, this apparent convergence of opera and popular culture fuelled an increase, rather than a decrease, in tension between the two spheres. Depressingly, it also served to reinforce some of the most damaging stereotypes about opera.

The crossover movement was a broad church. Some artists were established opera singers with broad appeal who also sang light music: notable in this category were Lesley Garrett and Bryn Terfel. Others were conservatoire graduates trying to establish a career outside of opera, such as the classical

---

[9] David Thomas, 'Why Are Today's Pop Stars So Posh', *DM* (6 December 2010), 15.

boyband G4, whose members met at the Guildhall School of Music and Drama before deciding to enter *The X Factor*. Some, such as the members of the classical girl-group All Angels, were brought together via an audition format, in similar vein to fabricated pop bands such as The Spice Girls. And among the most successful crossover performers were singers with no advanced classical training (or no training at all) who were simply 'spotted' and cultivated by impresarios. One was the former girl chorister Charlotte Church, discovered in the late 1990s after entering a TV breakfast show phone-in; another was Russell Watson, who was discovered performing in a working men's club and swiftly dubbed 'the people's tenor'.

With the exception of Garrett, Terfel, and a very few others who moved one way or the other between the two groups (notably Alfie Boe and Nicky Spence), these performers had not sung complete performances of live opera on stage. Most crossover artists made no actual claim to be 'opera singers'. Garrett, distancing herself from the rest of the crossover movement, emphasised this fact, describing bands such as Il Divo as 'little hors d'oeuvres' for listeners and writing, 'I think they're absolutely fine, but don't confuse them with real opera singers, who take seven years to train.'[10] Yet the papers certainly had trouble differentiating between different types of singers. In *The Daily Express* Mark Pappenheim remarked that 'the great British public may not love opera . . . but they certainly love their opera singers, so long as they restrict themselves to only a sprinkling of arias and the blizzard of crossover pop pap and merry Christmas jingles'.[11]

So what if listeners could not tell their José Carreras from their Russell Watson? Middlebrow listening had always included a bit of this and a bit of that. Wasn't it a good thing that barriers should be coming down between opera per se and operatic numbers performed in a popular music context? Eclectic tastes were, in themselves, no problem. Unfortunately, however, as Richard Morrison observed, a 'vicious little turf war' was being waged, with mutual loathing on both sides, 'as the various factions tug and heave at the proprietorial rights to those troublesome words "classical music"'.[12] Only occasionally could the breach be successfully navigated, and for the most part, the crossover phenomenon only served to exacerbate the pop versus posh cliché.

---

[10] David Stephenson, 'Opera Isn't Elitist, It's Like a Soap', *SE* (3 February 2008), 67.
[11] Mark Pappenheim, 'Opera', *DE* (24 November 2000), 71.
[12] Richard Morrison, 'Raw Talent or Hot Air on a G-String', *The Times* (1 May 2001), 16.

218 SOMEONE ELSE'S MUSIC

Everyone in the crossover/'core classical' debate was annoyed. Jobbing opera singers who had trained for years to enter the profession and were poorly remunerated for their work were resentful of the hype surrounding crossover singers, the high fees they commanded, and the public platform they were being given. Where once opera singers might have been invited on to chat shows, the invitations now went to crossover singers, and the same went for high-profile civic events such as the annual Festival of Remembrance. But the crossover stars weren't happy either, regarding the opera world as snobbish gatekeepers who looked down on them and did not regard them as serious artists. Dame Kiri Te Kanawa poured oil on the flames in 2008 by telling a New Zealand newspaper that crossover singers were 'the new fakes'.[13]

Crossover was really something quite separate from opera, yet it was, at the same time, a sort of parody of opera, thanks to artists' appropriation of all the most stereotypical glamorous 'signifiers' of opera—black tie and elaborate evening dresses—and marketing labels like 'the people's tenor'. The schism between the two ostensibly similar-looking groups—one perceived as popular and accessible, the other as aloof and uptight—merely added to public perceptions that opera was elitist. Where *Operatunity* was a boon to the opera world's image, in-fighting between the opera and classical crossover worlds most certainly was not.

Access all arias?

The Arts Council remained wedded, in the 2000s, to the idea that opera was best made accessible by practical immersion. Where, in decades long past, those attempting to broaden the audience for opera had relied heavily on recordings or broadcasts, the emphasis had now passed from listening to participating, with the 'music appreciation' movement increasingly being belittled as old-fashioned. Every opera company in the land now had a busy outreach and education department, offering schools' workshops, activities with marginalised social groups, and community programmes. Of course, it was rarely possible for untrained singers to participate in standard repertory

[13] Reported in Robert Sandall, 'Meeting Katherine Jenkins', The Arts Desk (4 September 2009), https://theartsdesk.com/classical-music/meeting-katherine-jenkins (accessed 27 January 2022).

TWENTY-FIRST-CENTURY BLUES 219

works; thus, activities often revolved around works specially written for or devised by the community group itself.

There were ambitious exceptions, however. Director Graham Vick achieved astonishing things with the Birmingham Opera Company, finding innovative ways to involve community groups in deprived inner-city areas in productions of full-length operas. Performances in venues such as The Warehouse, a former council depot amid high-rise housing blocks in the deprived Ladywood area, a branch of Tesco's, and in a big top next to Villa Park football ground introduced people to opera who had almost certainly never encountered it before, whether as performers or as audience members.[14] Among the works performed was Berg's *Votzek* (so-spelled), sung in English and in modern dress, using nine professional singers, twenty-one orchestral musicians, and almost two hundred amateur actors and dancers, among them unemployed youngsters doing apprenticeships in the creative arts, many from ethnic minority backgrounds.

Such initiatives were widely praised for the benefits to the participants involved. Whether participants made the leap from taking part to going to watch operas was, however, another matter. The Arts Council–affiliated group Opera and Music Theatre Forum collected feedback after a number of education projects in Sutton Coldfield, Norwich, and Epping Forest. The activities were certainly successful in countering clichés about opera. Participants typically reported expecting it to be characterised by 'big hair, big chests, warbling voices, language you can't understand, love stories . . . chandeliers, rich people' and had those expectations confounded.[15] However, some made comments like 'Doing it yourself is one thing, but having to sit and watch someone else do it is different, isn't it?'[16] Thus, the activities perhaps succeeded in some of their social aims, but arguably failed to do much in terms of building an audience for the future.

Perhaps, however, that was enough? By the early 2000s, the access movement had become a political initiative, part of a functional ethos that was coming to colour all aspects of public life. It had been on the rise since the 1980s, when the Conservatives began to demand that the arts demonstrate their economic value to society. However, the subsequent Labour

---

[14] Belina-Johnson and Scott, *The Business of Opera*, p. 4; Fiachra Gibbons, 'Opera Woos Radical Hero to Escape £3m Mire', *The Guardian* (19 November 2002), 7.

[15] Opera and Music Theatre Forum, 'Opera for Now: A Profile of Opera and Music Theatre Companies in Britain' (The Arts Council of England, January 2001), 20.

[16] Ibid., 21.

administration had done nothing to redress this way of thinking; indeed, it was pursuing the access agenda with ever greater enthusiasm. Its mission was wrapped up in terms of social worthiness—improving lives, redressing social inequality, and so on—but it remained a sort of utilitarianism nonetheless.

Though an expansion in outreach programmes might seem, on the face of it, only a good thing, there was something slightly dispiriting about the box-ticking aspect to it. Endless policy documents were published and the arts world, like education and public health, began to become relentlessly bureaucratised. The onus appeared to be shifting away from merely introducing children, or indeed adults, to something new that they might enjoy for its own sake. The director Richard Eyre noted that the Arts Council was now bogged down in finding ways to measure the social usefulness of the arts rather than promoting it in terms of 'its ability to enchant and entertain'.[17]

Initially compelled to subscribe to the government's agenda for fear of losing subsidy, arts organisations began to buy into it, seeing its social inclusion agenda as an unalloyed good. What arts organisations failed to notice, however, was the way in which the access agenda worked against their own interests, in making it harder to advocate for the arts on their own terms. Increasingly, culture was being valued only in terms of its social worthiness, rather than for its inherent artistic qualities. Arts managers seemed to be embarrassed about talking about any intellectual or spiritual satisfaction one might derive from an opera, play, or visit to a gallery. To do so suddenly seemed old-fashioned, out of touch, even vaguely elitist, so much did it go against the prevailing narrative that art had to change lives in demonstrable material or social ways.

Eliane Glaser, a rare voice from the left willing to question the wisdom of the access agenda, wrote in 2020:

> Forcing arts and culture organisations to be socially useful and "engage new audiences" is an unquestioned good to many right-thinking people, but I believe it undermines their core purpose and imposes burdens on them that they are hard pressed to fulfil. The point of these bodies should be to make great art and great culture, and to create and disseminate the highest forms of knowledge. It should not be to solve social problems that

[17] Richard Eyre, 'Why British Culture Needs a Healthy Dose of Elitism', *The Guardian* (25 March 2000), B3.

are the rightful preserve of governments and the state. By making culture, education and journalism into public relations arenas for tackling inequality, politics has given up on trying to improve society in any kind of organised way.[18]

The access agenda has undoubtedly, ironically, fuelled the elitism narrative. When the Arts Council talks relentlessly about access, diversity, and relevance—to a far greater extent than it does about artistic excellence—it reinforces negative perceptions of the arts as inaccessible, limited in appeal and irrelevant, rather than simply presenting them as interesting or capable of sparking the imagination.[19] The consequence of this has been that, as Glaser notes, 'arts organisations no longer seem convinced by their own right to exist' and as such they find it hard to defend their core purpose.[20] Advocating for art for art's sake now seems impossible, playing straight into the hands of culture's populist detractors.

By the 2000s, changing lives was the new agenda—but certainly not in the 'civilising' or 'transcendent' senses that had been fashionable in the past. For the opera world this meant something quite different from the many earlier twentieth-century initiatives to engage audiences. 'Inclusion' no longer meant taking high culture to everyone; it meant tailoring the culture to the perceived interests and 'identity' of the particular communities arts organisations were attempting to target. Seemingly worthy, the access agenda was far from entirely benign. Indeed, it did much to fuel the elitism stereotypes that were becoming ever more entrenched in the early twenty-first century—and this would intensify in the following decade.

Reinventing opera

By the 2000s, opera companies were acutely aware of the negative stereotypes surrounding the art form and constantly searching for ways of countering it. By the turn of the twenty-first century, 'elitism'—now an idea that seemed to go hand-in-glove with opera in the public imagination—had become something about which every right-thinking person was worried. George Walden

[18] Glaser, *Elitism*, pp. 47–48.
[19] Ibid., pp. 50–52.
[20] Ibid., p. 57, p. 58.

222 SOMEONE ELSE'S MUSIC

wrote satirically (but with more than a grain of truth), 'The Government condemns it, the BBC are fervently against it, writers go to great lengths to disclaim it, the schools inoculate children against it as they once did smallpox or diptheria.'[21]

The Arts Council published reports stating that the young were deterred from attending arts events not only by cost but by peer pressure, negative perceptions about venues and audiences, and a perceived lack of 'relevance'.[22] Opera companies devised a vast array of initiatives to demonstrate their appeal to new audiences. Some were imaginative and could be said to have been genuinely successful; others were gimmicky, embarrassing, or downright counterproductive, further fuelling negative public perceptions.

On the positive side there were companies such as Opera Holland Park. Based in a leafy, affluent area of West London, this summer festival nevertheless sought to eschew the social trappings of Glyndebourne or Garsington. The emphasis, the company asserted, was on the works themselves: the theatre was a temporary structure, partly exposed to the elements, and on inclement evenings the audience was as likely to be dressed in jumpers and cagoules as suits and cocktail dresses. In fact, the festival sought to attract all comers: those who might be willing to pay high prices elsewhere but also those entirely new to opera, some of whom the company would attract by offering free seats. The company's modus operandi was not to promote opera using gimmicks, but to give away free tickets to a normal production on a normal night, just like 'giving a free sample of washing powder or shampoo'.[23]

Over in East London, meanwhile, there was Grimeborn. Based at the Arcola Theatre, a converted textiles factory in Hackney, worlds apart from the lush gardens of Glyndebourne (upon whose name it punned), this festival was founded in 2007 by Mehmet Ergen with the explicit aim of challenging perceptions of opera as elitist, by putting on new and rare works in combination with radical adaptations of traditional operas, all in surroundings that were far from stuffy or grand. The company also placed an emphasis upon fostering the careers of new artists and directors from diverse backgrounds, and engaging the local community.

In the commercial West End, meanwhile, Raymond Gubbay was back in 2004 with a season of opera at the Savoy Theatre, featuring popular

---

[21] George Walden, *The New Elites: Making a Career in the Masses* (London: Allen Lane, 2000), 7.

[22] Arts Council England, 'The New Audiences Programme 1998–2003', 10, 12.

[23] Warwick Thompson, 'An Opera You Can't Refuse', *The Times* (2 June 2006), 20; Anna Picard, 'No Black Tie', *The Independent on Sunday* (22 May 2011), 56–57, 57.

crowd-pleasers in safe, traditional stagings.[24] His premise was that opera, if competitively priced, well-marketed, and run on a tight budget, could be sold like a West End musical, and flourish on ticket revenue alone.[25] Unfortunately this failed to happen, despite the fact that the enterprise attracted much press comment and publicity. Performances attracted a nightly audience of barely 200, when 500 was required to break even, and the enterprise was abandoned prematurely.

In a sense, the Savoy experiment followed the model used by the old early twentieth-century touring companies. Opera *had* been successfully sold to audiences as a form of entertainment little different from any other night out in decades long past, but the business model had been different. Touring companies of old had typically presented a different opera each night during a week's residency in any given town. Gubbay's model of alternating *The Marriage of Figaro* and *The Barber of Seville* nightly for weeks on end—in the West End, where alternative entertainment options were abundant—proved unsustainable, particularly when reviews were mediocre.[26] The enterprise had positioned itself badly in the marketplace, by going head-to-head with ENO, without offering any significant reduction in price.[27] Critic Rupert Christiansen argued that Gubbay had, ironically, made a mistake in spinning the notion of 'people's opera', deliberately stripping the enterprise of all glamour, big names, spectacular sets, and beautiful costumes so as to avoid the charge of elitism. Christiansen argued that 'a lot of people with only a casual interest prefer their *Bohème* and *Traviata* to come surrounded by a bubble of glamour and "exclusivity", something that lifts you out of the humdrum to take you to places that you've never been before'.[28] This is a refrain we have heard several times before: removing opera's glamour, its sense of occasion, is not necessarily the way to win new fans.

An even more rough-and-ready, unpretentious sort of opera emerged in the 2000s in the form of East European touring opera companies that began to appear and embark on tours around the United Kingdom. Superficially, this seemed positive, since the companies toured to out-of-the-way towns that never normally saw an opera, but unfortunately the enterprise had a darker side. The Polish or Moldovan singers were, in many cases, being exploited

---

[24] Janet Street-Porter, 'These Opera Snobs Are So Short-Sighted', *The Independent* (8 April 2004), 33.

[25] Andrew Clark, 'Finale for Opera Beggared By Poor Sales', *FT* (8–9 May 2004), 3.

[26] Hugh Canning, 'Savoy Opera Can Only Get Better', *ST* (25 April 2004), S9, 32–33, 32.

[27] Anon., 'Spoilt for Choice', *ST* (9 November 2003), S11, 29.

[28] Rupert Christiansen, 'Opera Is So Much Better When It's Expensive', *DT* (12 May 2004), 19.

224 SOMEONE ELSE'S MUSIC

by unscrupulous agents, made to stay in low-grade accommodation—sometimes even tents—or to sleep on buses as they moved between venues. As Shirley Apthorp observed in *Opera*, 'This isn't an operatic world of first-class flights and international glamour. It's one of gruelling schedules, penny-pinching managers, and no-star conditions.'[29] The price being paid, in this case, for 'no-frills opera' was surely too high.

Meanwhile, even the most high profile of the United Kingdom's opera companies were going to great lengths in the 2000s to counter the poor image acquired by the art form during the 1990s, with initiatives to take performances to new audiences. As a 'taster' of the art form, Opera North put on a season of what it called 'eight little greats'—short operas ranging from well-known crowd-pleasers (*Pagliacci*) to works that were considerably less well-known (Zemlinsky's *The Dwarf*). The operas were paired in double bills, with the proviso that people paid by the opera and were welcome to leave (or arrive) at the interval if they didn't fancy both.

In 2008, the Royal Opera House offered cut-price tickets via a scheme in *The Sun*, an unlikely venture, since the newspaper had spent years proclaiming opera was for toffs. The newspaper put a predictable tabloid spin on the offer, reporting, 'Most operas are dirtier than Amy Winehouse's beehive, riper than a full-on effing rant by Gordon Ramsay and more violent than a Tarantino bloodfest . . . It's full of sex, violence and great singing.'[30] ENO, meanwhile, put on the third act of *The Valkyrie* at Glastonbury, which was reportedly greeted with cheers and generally appreciated in this un-expected context. Nevertheless, the critic Philip Hensher argued that such ventures could only ever act as 'a sort of trailer, encouraging customers to take the plunge and come in. Despite all appearances, it isn't, and can't be, the real thing.'[31]

Companies were quick to exploit social media as a way of reinventing opera's image, with the Royal Opera even commissioning *The Twitter Opera* (2009), a project in which a libretto composed entirely of tweets would be set to a mixture of original music and familiar operatic tunes. Though the company claimed that 'it's the people's opera. The perfect way for everyone to become involved with the inventiveness of opera as the ultimate form of storytelling', public interest was limited and the project roundly mocked.[32]

---

[29] Shirley Apthorp, 'What Price Opera?', *Opera*, 51/12 (December 2000), 1416–1422, 1416.

[30] All cited in Roland White, 'Tabloid Week', *ST* (3 August 2008), 11.

[31] Philip Hensher, 'Is Opera Really Meant to Be Populist?', *The Independent* (9 July 2004), 33.

[32] Rachel Shields, 'Overtures, Arias and Tweets', *The Independent on Sunday* (9 August 2009), 7.

TWENTY-FIRST-CENTURY BLUES 225

More broadly, the extent to which YouTube videos, Facebook, podcasts, and websites spoke to anyone beyond those already interested in opera or altered popular perceptions of the art form was moot.

In a bid to attract the youth audience, the Royal Opera distributed advertising flyers at the Ministry of Sound in 2003, using a Royal Opera House logo mimicking the nightclub's own, with the slogans 'dance music' (for ballet), 'soul music' (opera), and 'house music' (the opera house itself) leading to much press ribaldry about the sort of scantily clad clientèle who might turn up. The director Jonathan Miller called the initiative grotesque, imagining a scenario where the National Gallery advertised an exhibition of Giovanni Bellini paintings as if they were Soho pornography. Miller argued that it was imperative to have confidence in the art form on its own terms, lamenting that 'this awful word elitism has come along and in order to convince people that these things aren't elitist, people feel they have to show that it's something that's indistinguishable from something else that's popular, like *Pop Idol*'.[33]

Miller put his finger on the perversity of a typical 2000s publicity conceit. Opera was repeatedly being sold to audiences by being compared to popular culture or by 'sexing up' the content, a strategy that was often highly misleading. Perhaps the problem was that arts organisations were increasingly being forced to chase an audience that might take a fleeting interest in an individual event but were less likely to become long-term enthusiasts. Had the opera fanatics of the past, willing to camp out overnight for cheap gallery tickets and listening repeatedly to recordings, had their day? Brian Hunt argued in 2001 that the nature of audiences had quite simply changed. The old, 'Victorian' ethos that art was good for you now seemed distinctly old-fashioned, and had been replaced by a new doctrine: 'the principle that art isn't worth expending time, energy or money on if it doesn't have immediate mass appeal'.[34]

Opera was also being 'rebranded' in terms of how it was staged. Like most major opera houses worldwide, the Royal Opera House was exploring ways of making opera more visually appealing in the HD age, as performances began to be screened in cinemas. This led to adjustments in casting strategy, with a move towards hiring singers who looked attractive and age-appropriate on screen. The company's Elaine Padmore stated, 'It is expected

---

[33] James Morrison, 'Introducing the Kickin' New Royal Opera House', *The Independent on Sunday* (4 May 2003), 3.

[34] Brian Hunt, 'Why the Public Is Putting Art in Peril', *DT* (20 January 2001), A8.

226   SOMEONE ELSE'S MUSIC

these days, when people are used to seeing beautiful people in films and on the television.'[35] But the drive towards hiring 'slimmer, fitter and more glamorous singers' sometimes created PR disasters, such as when the press picked up on the fact that the Royal Opera had fired Deborah Voigt from a production of *Ariadne auf Naxos* in 2004 because she could not fit into the dress designed for the role.

By the turn of the twenty-first century, updated productions were becoming standard in the United Kingdom: some were relatively 'straight' performances, which happened to be transplanted to recent times; others were what might be called 'concept' productions, where a director's vision and message, however incongruous, were imposed upon a work. Some such productions were bewilderingly obscure—so recherché that one might almost see the underlying mentality as rather elitist—and would certainly have been unappealing as a draw for prospective audiences seeking the sort of lavish visual spectacle they could see in film. Others pitched themselves squarely at current, popular preoccupations in order to demonstrate their relevance to the current moment, and often this was used in marketing materials as a hook to attract new audiences.

Updated productions sometimes used shock tactics as a way of generating interest, controversy, and newspaper headlines and of shaking up opera's fusty old image. A Glyndebourne production of *La bohème* in 2000 that featured cocaine use (a conceit that soon became a cliché) epitomised the trend. But did opera need drug references in order to sell? Vanessa Thorpe of *The Observer* argued that 'the tragic *La bohème*, first performed in Turin in 1896, is one of the most romantic works in the classical canon but until now had few points of reference for younger people.'[36] The claim was patently absurd: *La bohème* is an opera preoccupied almost like no other with the idea of youth, evoking as it does that sweet spot between gaining maturity and taking on the responsibilities of adult life. Its themes range across first love, jealousy, possessiveness, struggling to pay the rent, and believing your friends are your family. But no, Thorpe claimed, there had been nothing in *La bohème* to appeal to the young until a drugs theme was introduced.

Thorpe's faux pas—and Miller's comments about *Pop Idol*—spoke to a wider truism that was taking hold within the arts world: that opera had to be presented to audiences by reference to contemporary fashions or

---

[35] Ian Griggs, 'Too Big for La Bohème', *The Independent on Sunday* (14 September 2008), 22–23.
[36] Vanessa Thorpe, 'Now It's Sex, Drugs and Opera', *The Observer* (15 October 2000), 9.

preoccupations that, in some cases, had nothing to do with the original work. Access projects were increasingly geared around gritty themes deemed particularly 'relevant' to particular socio-economic groups or 'communities', as in the case of the Birmingham *Votzek* project. Berg's opera was chosen because, Graham Vick explained, its themes of single parenthood, prostitution, teenage pregnancy, and the dispossessed had much to say to the local community. All of this was a very different sort of 'access' strategy from that taken by companies such as the Old Vic, which had engaged audiences suffering social deprivation, but presented a wide range of repertory operas 'straight', with no feeling that they must be tailored to, or chosen to resonate in any direct way with, the audience's lives.

Access no longer meant simply giving people the opportunity to attend opera cheaply, or broadcasting it for free on television, but making it seem 'relatable' (a neologism drawn from reality TV) to certain target groups by reflecting their own lives back at them. But who decided what was relevant to these groups? Very often these were middle-aged, middle-class perceptions of what the lives of young or socially deprived people must be like, which presumed all those within a certain age bracket or socio-economic group or age bracket to have the same experiences, to feel the same emotions, and to perceive the world in the same way. In other words, stereotypes. As George Walden noted in 2000, 'The most striking aspect of anti-elitism as a social and cultural doctrine in Britain is that it is propagated not from below, but largely from above.'[37]

Was this really any less patronising than the 'paternalist' approach of the old music-appreciation evangelists, whose approach was looked on with such scorn by the twenty-first century? One might argue that it was, in fact, a good deal more so, since it denied potential audiences access to anything that would stretch them beyond their existing cultural parameters. For all the marketing gimmicks and access strategies, opera's elitist image remained firmly, stubbornly, in place in the 2000s. The project to make it so, long waged in the media, was complete. Had the damage done to opera's public image during the 1990s simply been so grievous that its reputation could never be repaired? Or were some of the new strategies being used to promote opera actually counterproductive?

When *The Independent* interviewed a cross-section of regulars at the Royal Opera House in 2004, it found plenty who went after work, bought

---

[37] Walden, *The New Elites*, p. 11.

228 SOMEONE ELSE'S MUSIC

standing tickets, and wore jeans.[38] But in a vox pop conducted outside the Southbank Centre four years later, it found members of the public with no particular interest in opera who were happy to proclaim that there was 'a sense of exclusivity' at the opera house or that 'theatres and opera houses are still full of toffs'.[39] The fact that the young people questioned were asked a leading question—whether they thought art, broadly defined, was the exclusive preserve of a white, middle-class elite—almost certainly coloured the answers received.

But it was small wonder that people now had such negative perceptions of opera, as unremitting negative messaging from the media combined with a reduction in opportunities to encounter opera, or indeed classical music, in their daily lives, and as the amount of classical music on television or in the school curriculum was progressively eroded. Richard Eyre argued that young people were, for the most part, not being offered the opportunity to go the theatre by parents or schools and, consequently, 'feel that theatre-going is not for them. If they feel anything at all about the theatre, they feel disenfranchised. The consequence of this disaffection is that politicians have been able to dismiss the theatre as an irredeemably elitist activity'.[40]

Politicians and the press

And so they did. The message that opera specifically and the high arts in general were elitist continued to be disseminated by New Labour. There were undoubtedly many positive achievements for the arts under this administration, such as the abolition of museum entry charges, increased funding for British film-making, the refurbishment of ENO, and the launch of the Wales Millennium Centre, the long hoped-for new home for WNO, even if many in the press noted the carefully avoidance of the word 'opera'.[41] But this was an administration that was widely perceived to be comparatively uninterested in the art works themselves.[42] As Richard Morrison wrote in 2001, 'If those

---

[38] Louise Jury, 'West End Story: Will Cheaper Seats Lower the Tone of Opera?', *The Independent* (17 April 2004), 14–15, 15.

[39] Anon., 'Vox Pop', *The Independent on Sunday* (9 March 2008), 44.

[40] Eyre, 'Why British Culture Needs a Healthy Dose of Elitism', B3.

[41] Giles Worsley, 'Wales Can Be Proud of Its Slate Armadillo', *DT* (10 February 2004), 17; Anon., 'And Not a Dome in Sight', *The Guardian* (20 September 2003), C9.

[42] Nigel Reynolds, 'Blair Hails Golden Age for Culture and the Arts', *DT* (7 March 2007), 12.

in the highest government circles can't see the point of the arts, the illness spreads insidiously downwards.'[43]

New Labour politicians were almost never spotted at theatres, galleries, or cinemas, unless on official business, though they were often seen at sporting events and contemporary political rhetoric was littered with references to sport. Indeed, arts budgets were usually the first to be raided when sport needed additional funding.[44] The government's attitude seemed to be shaped by a combination of ideological cultural relativism and pragmatic political expediency. On the latter, Stephen Johnson wrote in *The Guardian*, 'Classical music isn't People's Music. Most important of all, it isn't Young People's Music. Supporting it won't win votes. Attacking it just might.'[45]

Let us consider a few examples of this mentality. In 2003, extracts from a speech to be given by the Arts Minister Estelle Morris at the Cheltenham Literature Festival were leaked, in which it was reported that she planned to 'pour scorn on Britain's top galleries and museums, saying they are too middle-class, elitist and off-putting for the working classes and ethnic minorities'. Morris denied it and the speech was not, in the event, given.[46] Later, in 2008, Margaret Hodge gave a speech in which she attacked the Proms for attracting a narrow, unrepresentative cross-section of the public and failing to bring people together or create a sense of shared British identity. The Proms was not, she argued, a festival where people from different backgrounds could 'feel at ease'.[47] Questioning whether Hodge had ever stood in the Proms queue, the cellist Steven Isserlis observed witheringly that she would never have attacked a rap artist, for fear it might lose her votes, arguing that classical musicians resented having the art they loved assigned, mindlessly, to one particular sector of society.[48]

Almost as troubling as overt suggestions that the arts were elitist were flat refusals to contradict the idea. Richard Eyre wrote, 'Refusing to take a stand to say that the arts are not elitist is to condone the sheer shoddiness of much popular culture and implicitly to consign us all to the worst aspects of consumer capitalism.'[49] Eyre was writing in 2000: since then, cultural relativism has taken root to such an extent that it would be improbable to see a figure

---

[43] Richard Morrison, 'Labour's Empty Canvas Put on Show', *The Times* (12 January 2001), 24.
[44] Ben Macintyre, 'How Labour's Philistines Grabbed Gold', *The Times* (13 April 2007), 17.
[45] Stephen Johnson, 'Larger Than Live', *The Guardian* (19 January 2001), B10–B11, B10.
[46] Nigel Reynolds, 'Art Elitist? I Never Meant to Say That', *DT* (16 October 2003), 15.
[47] Patrick Wintour, 'Hodge Attacks Proms', *The Guardian* (4 March 2008), n.p.
[48] Steven Isserlis, 'Acts of Cultural Supremacy', letter to *The Guardian* (6 March 2008), n.p.
[49] Eyre, 'Why British Culture Needs a Healthy Dose of Elitism', B3.

230　SOMEONE ELSE'S MUSIC

from the arts world daring to attack popular culture in these terms. But at this stage, high-profile figures in the literary world were willing to attack the government for its opposition to the high arts and particularly for its constant use of the elitism slur.

For example, the novelist Doris Lessing, a staunch defender of ENO, told Radio 4's Today Programme how concerned she was about the 'very philistine' government's tendency to rubbish high culture and even likened Blair to Robert Mugabe, claiming that New Labour 'played the "class card" by bashing so-called cultural elites every time it got in trouble in the same way the Zimbabwean prime minister played the race card'.[50] Even more irate was V. S. Naipaul, who called Blair 'a cultural vandal destroying the idea of civilisation in this country' and stated, 'Every day you hear on the radio some minister from this appalling government saying something about things no longer being for the privileged few . . . It is terrible, this plebeian culture that celebrates itself for being plebeian.'[51] He declared that he had only been to the opera twice in his life, but that he was 'thrilled' by the thought that London contained one of the greatest opera houses in the world, and felt 'demeaned' by the fact that Britain was now seen in the wider world as the home of 'the Dome, the Spice Girls and Manchester United'.[52]

All these comments were made at the start of the 2000s. It would be hard for figures in the arts world to make similar remarks today without being accused of being elitists. The idea of cultural relativism, a debate that had been rumbling since the 1960s, was becoming entrenched in the United Kingdom at this time. However, it was not, at this stage, a sacred totem that made it difficult to have nuanced debates about the merits of different forms of culture, as would become the case by the late 2010s. The philosopher A. C. Grayling wrote in 2002 that the term 'high culture' was used 'to differentiate what is most valued and esteemed by those supposed to be in a position to judge; and the term is therefore expressly discriminatory. The question therefore becomes: does an enjoyment of high culture involve a justifiable form of discrimination? I think most would still think that the answer is "Yes" '.[53]

Later this would change. Quarrels about the aforementioned issues would grow to hitherto unimaginable proportions over the course of the 2000s and

---

[50] Fiachra Gibbons, 'Novelist Lessing Likens "Philistine" Blair to Mugabe', *The Guardian* (13 July 2000), 8.

[51] Phillip Oppenheim, 'Deathly Arts of the Cultural Commissars', *ST* (16 July 2000), 18; Gibbons, 'Novelist Lessing Likens "Philistine" Blair to Mugabe'.

[52] Tom Utley, 'Why We All Owe So Much to the Privileged Few', *DT* (12 July 2000), 24.

[53] A. C. Grayling, 'A Question of Discrimination', *The Guardian* (13 July 2002), 4.

TWENTY-FIRST-CENTURY BLUES 231

into the 2010s. And the high arts—and opera in particular—would continue to find themselves under attack from both ends of the political spectrum: from sectors of, as Grayling put it, the lowbrow right, opposed to what it perceived to be 'Islington trendiness', and the anti-highbrow left, so concerned about cultural relativism and perceived injustice that it found itself unable to defend the arts.[54] From now on it would become extremely difficult indeed for opera to be presented in the public arena as a simple source of entertainment—even as opera continued to interact with popular culture—or to be discussed in terms that were not political.

By the 2000s, a nervousness had set in around opera, meaning that figures from within the opera world itself often spoke about it in ways that were apologetic. Some went so far as to insult those who bought tickets. Director Graham Vick railed against the 'existing [opera] audience' for supposedly putting others off attending, while Mark-Anthony Turnage—who had composed operas for ENO—declared himself uninterested in the opera world, where he did not feel at home because of its 'stifling and snotty atmosphere'.[55] None of this seemed sensitive to opera devotees or indeed good PR for the art form as a whole.

In the press, every initiative to take opera 'to the people' was mentioned in the same breath as stereotypes about the elitism of opera in its more conventional modes of presentation. But what did journalists really seek to achieve? Why did *The Guardian* contrast Vick's *Votzek* with a highly clichéd vision of opera as 'a privileged and exclusive club', which appealed to 'an overwhelmingly pink-skinned, dinner-jacketed and bejewelled elite'?[56] Did an article in *The Independent* about ticket-price cuts at WNO and ENO hold readers' attention beyond the opening claim that 'a night at the opera was once the province of the upper classes, a black-tie occasion for the champagne-swilling rich'?[57] Why report on Gubbay's Savoy season by telling readers that 'this was no tight-lipped upper-class audience expanding their minds with a high-brow art form'?[58] And how useful was it for an *Observer* article about young, casually dressed opera-goers at Covent Garden to open with the bold claim that 'for generations, the popular image of the average Covent Garden

---

[54] Ibid., 4, 6.

[55] Chris Arnot, 'Voices of the People', *The Guardian* (14 February 2001), B6; David Lister, 'It's Not Opera That Is Behind the Times', *The Independent* (9 October 2004), 49.

[56] Arnot, 'Voices of the People', B6.

[57] Louise Jury, 'A Cheap Night at the Opera: Prices Cut in Drive to Boost Attendances', *The Independent* (11 March 2004), 5.

[58] Jury, 'West End Story', 14.

232 SOMEONE ELSE'S MUSIC

operagoer has remained the same: grey-haired and doddery, the men wearing formal evening dress, the women draped in the family jewels'?[59]

And on it went ad nauseam. *The Times* seemed to sum up the trend by reporting a price cut at Covent Garden and simultaneously asking readers to email in their responses to the question, 'Is opera too elitist—despite cheap seats?'[60] The opera world and the media seemed to believe, by the 2000s, that there was only one way of promoting opera: by playing up all the worst clichés and then knocking them down. As a means of countering the stereotypes surrounding opera, this approach patently was not working.

By the 2000s the media had its knives out for opera, having learnt from the Royal Opera House furore of the 1990s that opera—if presented in scandalous or sensationalist enough terms—sold copy. Predictably, then, it was having a particular field day with Glyndebourne, that epitome of opera at its most glamorous, which by the early 2000s had 7,000 people on the waiting list to become members, with those on the upper tier of membership willing to pay up to £5,796 for the privilege.[61] But did it really matter if these small pockets of 'luxurious' opera existed? If people wanted to save up to go as a special treat—at a similar cost to attending a major sporting event or going to a fancy restaurant—that was surely their own business. Yet critic Rupert Christiansen observed that Glyndebourne inspired 'an astonishing amount of puritanical vitriol' and that 'nothing seems to bring the simmering class-hatred that infects our cultural attitudes to the boil faster than the thought of people paying a lot of money to get out their gladrags, listen to unamplified music and eat a picnic'.[62]

Christiansen was even willing to defend the country-house opera audience. He noted that this audience was not comprised, as many evidently still believed, of decadent aristocrats but largely of middle-class professionals, who had saved up for a treat.[63] Yet here was the rub, for increasingly these people were characterised as embodying 'privilege'. In 2007, two sociologists at the University of Oxford, Tak Wing Chan and John Goldthorpe, concluded that 'social status' in Britain was now no longer based upon noble birth or wealth but upon a person's professional status. There were, then, both economic elites and occupational elites, and the two were not necessarily the

---

[59] Vanessa Thorpe, 'Why Trainers, Not Tiaras, Are the Order of The Day for a Night at the Opera', *The Observer* (17 February 2002), 7.

[60] Dalya Alberge, 'Take Your Tenner to the Opera', *The Times* (7 April 2004), 9.

[61] Rupert Christiansen, 'Glyndebourne and the Grim Gawpers', *DT* (15 May 2002), 19.

[62] Rupert Christiansen, 'Opera Is So Much Better When It's Expensive', *DT* (12 May 2004), 19.

[63] Ibid.

same thing. Social class no longer had much bearing upon someone's cultural tastes but education and professional status did. The authors wrote: 'The newspaper a person chooses, and the forms of entertainment that person enjoys are all tied up with ideas about social status. That does not mean that professionals in elite jobs restrict themselves to "elite" arts, but it does mean that the opera houses and specialist art galleries are likely to be filled with people who have "status".'[64]

By this measure, even someone who came from a relatively poor background but worked hard to 'better themselves' through education and professional advancement would technically be regarded as a 'privileged' member of the opera audience by those determined to demonstrate that opera was 'elitist'. Jeanette Winterson was exactly such a person, brought up in Manchester as the adopted child of working-class, evangelical Christian parents, who had dramatically changed her circumstances via education, winning herself a place at Oxford and ultimately becoming a well-respected novelist. Hers was exactly the sort of autodidact success story that would have been celebrated in previous decades, yet by the twenty-first century she might be labelled as possessing 'privilege'.

In 2006, Winterson wrote a lengthy tribute to Glyndebourne in *The Independent*. It was a striking article not only for the poetic language in which it was written but for the way in which it went against the grain, defending opera in ways that were no longer often seen. Winterson characterised Glyndebourne as a place of eccentricity and inclusivity, its opera-goers—including 'kids with more piercings than a medieval martyr' and 'guys so gay that they could no more climb in the closet than get back to Narnia'—defying stereotype. It was somewhere where she, a working-class lesbian, had been able to feel at home. Pointing to the gender-bending nature of many of the works performed, the propensity of trouser roles and countertenors, Winterson wrote that 'opera is a kind of torment for the conventional mind . . . subversive, definitely not submissive. Opera is a present-tense art form, not some mothballed number from the days of snobbery and stupidity'.[65]

With its beautiful gardens, Glyndebourne was, as Winterson characterised it, 'the Elysian fields', 'just about the happiest place in England . . . like a

---

[64] Andy McSmith, 'Cultural Elite Does Not Exist, Academics Claim', *The Independent* (20 December 2007), 20.

[65] Jeanette Winterson, 'Operas Are Not the Only Joy', *The Independent* (19 May 2006), 2–4, 4.

234 SOMEONE ELSE'S MUSIC

dream of some ideal childhood, the one that we never had'. Travelling there on the train, among people in evening dress who seemed like 'visions from another life', Winterson felt that she might have stepped into the pages of Virginia Woolf's diary.[66] This sort of nostalgia for a long-lost or imagined Englishness might seem appealing to some readers, albeit nauseating to others. Winterson herself acknowledged that she was teetering perilously close to stereotype but countered it by emphasising that Glyndebourne was a world of pure, knowing fantasy. She wrote: 'Here are people who have decided to DRESS UP, and they are playing it as hard as anything out of Noël Coward, which is why it is a game, not a class nightmare.' In this comment, perhaps, lies a nugget of hope for an alternative way of thinking about opera. Would it not be better to reframe opera in affectionately humorous terms, even to rejoice in its absurdities, than to keep calling it elitist?

Yes, it might be expensive to go to Glyndebourne, Winterson acknowledged, but other activities were expensive too: people in Manchester had recently paid more than £500 to hear Barbra Streisand. Yes, there was a certain amount of social etiquette, but nobody would care if you did your own thing: 'If you want to bring a bowl of cornflakes and a cheese triangle, you can picnic on the lawn with the best of them, and you can see the show for less than a ticket to *The Da Vinci Code*.'[67] Glyndebourne might be hedonistic, but it was a soul-enriching type of hedonism, an antidote to busy, fragmented modern life. In short, Winterson concluded, it was rather like wild smoked salmon: special and seasonal; a bit more expensive than the farmed variety, but the real thing. 'If life is about heightened moments, and living well when we can', Winterson concluded, 'then Glyndebourne is an essential part of life.' It had become unfashionable to talk about opera in these terms, but how refreshing when someone actually did. There was still something special about opera, Winterson proposed. Over the next decade, it would become ever more difficult to say so.

---

[66] Ibid., 2.
[67] Chris Arnot, 'Voices of the People', *The Guardian* (14 February 2001), 3.

11

This Sceptic Isle

Alfie Boe had a lot to get off his chest. In 2011 the popular tenor appeared on an episode of the long-running BBC Radio 4 series *Desert Island Discs*. The programme, which often coaxes intimate confessions from its famous interviewees, prompted from Boe a large dose of apathy and ennui. Disdaining to include among his chosen tracks any 'high opera', as host Kirsty Young put it, he told listeners he never went to the opera, stating, 'I go there and feel very uncomfy . . . When I'm up there doing it, that's my world, that's what I really enjoy. But sitting in the audience and watching it, I'm bored stiff.'[1] It was a broadcast that provoked anger in the opera world, not so much because of Boe's antipathy towards opera but because of the damage the episode did in stoking the elitism cliché.

Boe grew up in a working-class Lancashire family where opera records were shelved alongside albums by Frank Sinatra, Glenn Miller, and Elvis. After leaving school he worked as a car mechanic, but singing in an amateur operatic society led to his joining the D'Oyly Carte chorus, studying at the Royal College of Music, touring Scotland with Opera Go Round, and ultimately playing leading roles on the Glyndebourne tour and at ENO. Boe was awarded a place on the prestigious Vilar Young Artists' Programme at the Royal Opera House and finally catapulted into international fame when he starred in Baz Luhrmann's *La bohème* on Broadway.

It should have been a heart-warming story, like those of the many twentieth-century working-class singers whose success had been celebrated in the press. But by the time he appeared on *Desert Island Discs*, Boe had developed an apparent loathing of what he regarded as the operatic 'establishment', and proceeded to outline further grievances in his autobiography.[2] It was not that barriers had been put in Boe's way, for he had received coveted opportunities, but he felt ill-at-ease on the Vilar programme, baulking at

---

[1] *Desert Island Discs*, 'Alfie Boe' (5 June 2011) https://www.bbc.co.uk/sounds/play/b011p13c (accessed 25 March 2022).

[2] Alfie Boe, *Alfie: My Story* (London: Simon and Schuster, 2012).

Figure 11.1 Alfie Boe, Melody Moore, David Stout, Pauls Putnins, *La bohème*, ENO, The London Coliseum, 29 January 2009. Reproduced with permission from © Elliott Franks/ArenaPAL.

being asked to wear a shirt and tie and ultimately walking out.[3] Boe had come to see the operatic world as profoundly class-ridden, repeatedly stating that it did not feel like 'his world', and telling the press it was 'snooty and elitist'.[4]

It is perfectly possible that Boe had a negative experience on the training programme and encountered difficult or snobbish people. Some of the reactions to Boe's interview did add grist to his mill. *The Spectator* accused Boe of playing 'the Wat Tyler card', and Jonathan Miller, in whose *La bohème* Boe had performed at ENO in 2009, retorted, 'He sings rather well but I know he comes from something other than opera. He was a car mechanic, I believe.'[5] However, Boe's version of events made him sound arrogant ('I'd done all that') and deliberately provocative (drinking heavily before a special performance 'just to make a point'), as he styled himself as the bad boy

---

[3] Ibid., pp. 138–142.
[4] Richard Kay, 'Pin-Up Tenor Slams "Snooty" Royal Opera', *DM* (6 January 2011), 39.
[5] Michael Henderson, 'Let's Hear It for Elitism', *The Spectator* (26 October 2011); Boe, *Alfie*, p. 252.

of opera.[6] If the Royal Opera House came out of his account badly, Boe did himself few favours, with comments like 'I'm flying back... to shit. I'm flying back to my life at the Royal Opera House' and 'It's a bloody wooden platform. No better than the Marine Hall in Fleetwood.'[7]

Opera singers were frustrated that one of their own had bitten the hand that had fed him, and in the process, made life more difficult for his former colleagues by fuelling unfair stereotypes. Boe's claim, for instance, that the operatic world didn't recognise opera as 'legitimate' unless it was put on somewhere like the Royal Opera House, ENO, or La Scala was highly questionable.[8] 'We should rename him Alfie Boellocks', retorted Opera Holland Park's Michael Volpe; Boe replied scathingly that 'it entertains me when their feathers get ruffled.'[9] But Volpe—the tattooed, football-loving son of Italian immigrants, brought up by a single mother in a council flat, who wrote that 'I see no reason why opera cannot become the preserve of the reformed hooligan, the bin-person, the builder'—was as far removed as you could get from the operatic establishment of crude caricature.[10] Opera Holland Park offered countless discounted or free tickets to young people, the elderly, and NHS staff, undertook work with people with learning difficulties and asylum seekers, and made films showing opera could speak to football fans, inner-city teenagers, and traumatised services personnel. The two men should have been singing from the same hymn sheet. As it was, they found themselves at loggerheads: the all-pervading elitism stereotype had fractured the classical music world, its members increasingly divided over how to make opera accessible.

Elsewhere, even well-meaning efforts to popularise opera by people deeply committed to it had become confused, drawing attention to the elitism stereotype in ways that compounded rather than confronted it. The BBC's promotion, for example, of soprano Danielle De Niese's radio show 'How to Watch an Opera' was downright cack-handed. Radio 4 publicised the programme with a tweet asking, 'Which way do I face?', 'Should I get up there and join in?', and 'Are monocles obligatory?'[11] Though doubtless

---

[6] Boe, *Alfie*, p. 139, p. 141.
[7] Ibid., p. 148, p. 143.
[8] Ibid., p. 150.
[9] Emily Dugan, 'Opera Singer Boe Bites the (Tiny) Hand That Feeds Him', *The Independent* (5 June 2011); Boe, *Alfie*, p. 253.
[10] Michael Volpe, 'The Marriage of Figaro and Footie', *The Independent* (1 July 2011), 19.
[11] https://www.bbc.co.uk/programmes/p07glyf2 (accessed 13 July 2019). Tweets posted by @BBCRadio4 on 12, 14, 15 July, and 25 September 2019.

238 SOMEONE ELSE'S MUSIC

intended to be witty, the tweet prompted a mixture of irritation, derision, and parody from the large community of opera fans on Twitter. Laudable projects aimed at encouraging people to give classical music a go were therefore still focusing on imagined malign gatekeepers: 'classical purists [who] ensure maximum discomfort for anyone unfamiliar with the rules of the game', to quote broadcaster Clemency Burton-Hill, promoting her podcast 'The Open Ears Project'.[12] But did such people really exist or hold any cultural sway? The truth of the matter seemed to be that by the end of the 2010s, a type of populism had emerged that was based entirely upon defining the 'good' anti-elitist against the 'bad' snob, even if the latter was merely the stuff of caricature. This mindset had, unfortunately, laid down deep roots.

Populism and politics

By the 2010s, broadcasters appeared to have lost confidence in how to promote classical music to a general audience. Looking back over the century discussed in this book, which corresponds with the BBC's existence, we see that the Corporation has done invaluable work historically to disseminate and popularise opera, not only through specialist radio channels but also through more mainstream programming. It was therefore depressing to see that, by the 2010s, opera was not only largely marginalised—with the notable exception of Radio 3 and a large-scale season across multiple channels in 2017 called 'Opera: Passion, Power and Politics'—on the BBC, but sometimes maligned.

Possibly the most egregious example was a 2013 radio interview on the World Service's *HARDtalk* programme. The episode in question, an interview with the American baritone Thomas Hampson, called upon him to defend his art form against a series of attacks, beginning with the charge from presenter Sarah Montague that 'opera is one of the least-watched art forms in the world'. The interview proceeded to wheel out every cliché in the book, with Montague countering Hampson's informed, well-reasoned responses with assertions like 'the only people really watching opera are the richest, most educated in the world'.[13] When Montague cited studies that quoted

---

[12] Clemency Burton-Hill, 'We Need to Get Emotional About Classical Music', *The Guardian* (8 October 2019), n.p.

[13] HARDtalk, 'Opera Singer Thomas Hampson', World Service (29 July 2013). https://www.bbc.co.uk/programmes/p01cg1zv (accessed 2 September 2019).

people saying opera is 'not for people like me' as further evidence of the art form's elitism, she failed to spot that her own repetition of stereotypes was part of the problem.

As John Allison, editor of *Opera*, pointed out, this broadcast came from the same BBC that had broadcast *Götterdämmerung* only the previous night.[14] What on earth did the Corporation think it was doing? But by the end of the decade, Allison had become wearily resigned, stating in 2019 that 'the sorry state of arts representation by our national broadcaster is, alas, something we've become quite used to' and 'if you take classical music and opera off national television and out of the wider consciousness, people will believe that these art forms are dead after all'.[15] High hopes that the appointment as Director General of Tony Hall—former Chief Executive of the Royal Opera House—would herald a return to the Corporation's core values had been dashed.[16]

If the BBC seemed to be taking a turn to the populist, it was under severe pressure to do so from successive hostile Conservative administrations, who were sceptical of, if not downright hostile towards the Corporation for perceived political bias, and who saw attacking any remaining 'rarefied' aspects of programming as a good way of courting populist favour. In 2020 the Culture Secretary Oliver Dowden stated in *The Telegraph* that 'someone switching on their TV from their semi in Bradford should feel just as represented by the Beeb as a person watching in their Islington townhouse'.[17] The BBC had, from its earliest days, sought to speak to the entire population. But it had done so by giving high art to all, and this was plainly not what Dowden had in mind.

Everybody reading the article knew what the geographical shorthand stood for: the much-reviled Islington (supposed home of wealthy Labour-supporting luvvies and intellectuals) for the 'metropolitan elite', Bradford for working-class people who could not possibly be interested in the arts. It was a comment seemingly calculated to stoke class antagonism, which perpetuated stereotypes about the north-south divide, made sweeping generalisations about the sort of person who might live in the north or in a semi-detached house, and showed a blithe disregard for, or ignorance of, the ways in which

[14] The Editor, 'Auntie Knows Best?', *Opera*, 64/9 (September 2013), 1093.

[15] The Editor, 'Strictly Come Singing', *Opera*, 70/8 (August 2019), 941.

[16] Peter Aspden, 'High Culture and Safe Hands Have Returned to the BBC', *FT* (24–25 November 2012), 13.

[17] Oliver Dowden, 'It's Time to Ask Big Questions About the Future of the BBC', *The Telegraph* (10 November 2020), n.p.

240   SOMEONE ELSE'S MUSIC

people of all classes had consumed the arts in the past. At the same time, it invoked the dreary mantra of 'relevance', the assumption that broadcasting should reflect people's (presumed) worlds back at them, confirming their biases and prejudices, rather than introducing them to new experiences and viewpoints. Dowden appeared, on the face of it, to be speaking up for the underprivileged; in fact he was doing no such thing, but, rather, advocating for dumbing down.

Of the BBC's three founding principles, to 'inform, educate and entertain', it was the last that loomed largest on British TV by the 2010s, as the schedules were devoted to an ever-greater extent by reality TV formats and talent contests, often featuring celebrity participants. British society was ever more in thrall to the all-pervasive cult of populist celebrity and occasionally the opera world engaged with it. The year 2011 saw the Covent Garden *première* of Mark-Anthony Turnage's *Anna Nicole*, about the Texan former *Playboy* model Anna Nicole Smith, who married an 89-year-old billionaire and died of an overdose. Operas based upon real-life people you could read about in the tabloids corresponded with the need to appear 'relevant' and ironically employed the age-old ploy of counterpoising so-called ordinariness with the perceived grandeur of the art form. The Royal Opera House declared works like *Anna Nicole* to be essential in attracting younger audiences, and replaced the usual glitzy, expensive opening night of the season with a cheaply priced performance entirely reserved for students.[18]

Aptly, the opera itself was somewhat overshadowed by the media circus surrounding the celebrities who came to watch, including Graham Norton, Boy George, and Dame Vivienne Westwood. But did this do anything to cultivate new audiences? Perhaps the prospect of seeing a famous face was sufficient to attract some people to attend. Evidently this was what ENO thought in 2019 when it decided to emulate the old model of high society at the opera. The company courted the popular celebrities of daytime and reality TV (Holly Willoughby, Davina McCall), comedians (Alan Carr), and sportsmen (various Chelsea footballers) and treated them as 'influencers', giving them free tickets and encouraging them to post about their night out on Twitter or Instagram.[19] This was part of a resolutely populist approach taken by the

---

[18] Adrian Hamilton, 'When Soap Meets Opera', *The Independent* (27 January 2011), 12–13, 12; Richard Morrison, 'Why £1 Tickets to Covent Garden Are Something to Sing Loudly About', *The Times* (31 March 2014), 8–9, 8.

[19] Anita Singh, 'ENO's Stuart Murphy on Free Tickets', *The Telegraph* (3 April 2019), n.p.

new CEO Stuart Murphy, formerly of SkyTV, who elsewhere likened opera to the final of *Love Island*.[20]

Murphy claimed that the initiative had had an 'amazing' effect on ticket sales.[21] But was laying out the red carpet, cordoning off sections of the foyer, and offering free-flowing champagne to a portion of the audience designated as a special 'elite' the right look for the national opera company, one that had always tried to distance itself from showiness? The image of opera houses as somewhere the rich, powerful, and influential go to hob-nob and show off—while taking relatively little interest in the music or drama—has been a strong facet of the elitism charge. Was it different when the glamorous elite was made up of TV personalities, rather than the aristocrats who had attended Covent Garden galas in the interwar and post-war years?

If fame-hungry celebrity influencers were prepared to take the free tickets and the publicity in return for tabloid exposure, politicians continued to be extremely reluctant to be seen at the opera. Although Angela Merkel was happy to be photographed at the opera, even seeing attendance as a civic duty, British politicians known to have operatic leanings—Michael Gove and George Osborne, for instance, who were spotted watching Wagner at Covent Garden and Bayreuth—seemed loath to court the cameras.[22] A sociological study that examined the cultural preferences of the socially significant 0.5 per cent (MPs, judges, ambassadors, FTSE CEOs and the like) via the pages of *Who's Who* noted that since the turn of the millennium, members of the establishment had tended to emphasise everyday activities in order to 'establish their authenticity, normality, and ordinariness ... and ward off moral suspicions that their highbrow or aristocratic tastes may position them as snobbish, status-seeking, and aloof'.[23] It was better, from the point of view of winning votes, to 'perform "ordinariness"', by listing one's hobbies as football and 'spending time with family' than by admitting to an enjoyment of opera or theatre.[24]

The same phenomenon was observable on *Desert Island Discs*. Guest choices had historically been dominated by classical music: between 1956

---

[20] Stuart Murphy, 'Love Island Withdrawal Syndrome?', *ES* (7 August 2019), n.p.

[21] Singh, 'ENO's Stuart Murphy'.

[22] Hannah Furness, 'Politicians Scared by Elitist Label Says Opera Chief', *DT* (12 May 2014), 11; Hannah Summers, 'Epic Night Out', *The Guardian* (10 August 2017), n.p.

[23] Sam Friedman and Aaron Reeves, 'From Aristocratic to Ordinary: Shifting Modes of Elite Distinction', *American Sociological Review*, 85/2 (2020), 323–350, 342.

[24] Libby Purves, 'Elites Who Show Off Their Lowbrow Taste Cannot Be Trusted', *The Times* (17 April 2020), n.p.

242 SOMEONE ELSE'S MUSIC

and 2016, 592 tracks by Mozart were chosen, 498 by Beethoven, 223 by Verdi, and 200 by Puccini. This compared with 235 requests for Beatles records and 161 for Frank Sinatra; all other rock or pop artists were requested fewer than 100 times apiece.[25] Margaret Thatcher, in 1978, took Beethoven, Dvořák, Verdi, Mendelssohn, Saint-Preux, and Mascagni to her desert island.[26] More recent prime ministers, however, have been keen to demonstrate their man-of-the-people credentials. David Cameron chose tracks by Bob Dylan, Pink Floyd, Radiohead, The Smiths, R.E.M., The Killers, and even a sketch by Benny Hill, with a single nod to popular classical music in 'On Wings of Song' (which had been played at his wedding).[27] Gordon Brown's top choice was Bach's Suite no. 3 in G Major, but 'Jerusalem' was the only other 'classical' music in his list.[28] The marked move away from public figures using culture as a badge of status and towards displaying omnivorous tastes may have made these figures more 'approachable' in an era when nobody wanted to be seen as 'posh', but it had the unfortunate result of side-lining classical music in the national cultural conversation. *Guardian* journalist Martin Kettle went so far as to observe that 'in British politics today, a cultural life remains almost as much a taboo as a secret sexuality once was.'[29]

By the end of the 2010s, politicians were falling over themselves to present themselves as having 'the common touch'. This was a tendency that had begun in the Blair years and gained ground over the subsequent two decades. Bar the occasional maverick such as Jacob Rees-Mogg, politicians worked hard to appear as 'ordinary' as possible. Gravitas was strangely absent from political life; indeed, gravitas was no longer a quality to which politicians seemed to aspire. Yet, ironically, many of those in politics claiming to be 'men of the people' and driving the international populist agenda, such as Donald Trump and Nigel Farage, were in fact multi-millionaires. Everybody knew this, and yet it didn't seem to matter.

The high arts, so-called, sat ill at ease within this new ethos of political populism, in which people had 'had enough of experts', in the infamous

---

[25] Simon Frith, 'What Does It Mean to be Cultured? *Desert Island Discs* as an Ideological Archive', in Julie Brown, Nicholas Cook, and Stephen Cottrell (eds), *Defining the Discographic Self: Desert Island Discs in Context* (Oxford: The British Academy, 2017), pp. 125–144, pp. 130–133.

[26] Tia DeNora, 'Public and Narrative Selves in *Desert Island Discs*', in Brown, Cook, and Cottrell (eds), *Defining the Discographic Self*, pp. 215–237, p. 232.

[27] https://www.bbc.co.uk/programmes/p0093vjz (accessed 2 October 2022).

[28] https://www.bbc.co.uk/programmes/p0093nrg (accessed 2 October 2022).

[29] Martin Kettle, 'Why You Won't Catch a British Politician at the Opera', *The Guardian* (30 July 2015), n.p.

words of Michael Gove.[30] Expertise and intellectualism had fallen out of fashion, together with anything that demanded a sustained concentration span. Society was in thrall to the stars of popular culture, whose ostentatious wealth (again) was, perversely, never characterised as 'elitist'. Rationally, in this context, the idea that opera's 'luxuriousness' made it elitist ought to have made no sense. Was the problem with opera in fact now something else—its perceived refinement and intellectualism, which seemed out of keeping with the populist spirit of the times? Whereas a century ago intellectualism was an aspiration, including for people with little material wealth, it has latterly come to be seen as eccentric. In many respects, of course, most operas are not in any meaningful sense intellectual, but the art form is still widely perceived as such. Here we find a perverse state of affairs, for while 'elitist' high culture is potentially available to all for free (via libraries and the internet), access to the world of populist celebrity—with its supercars, private jets, and mansions with swimming pools—most definitely is not.

Seismic shocks

Populism had a significant hand in the first all-consuming 'culture war' of our time. The Brexit debate tore families and friendship groups apart, demanded people nail their political colours to the mast and permitted no fence-sitting. Leaving the EU had very real consequences for those involved in the opera industry, particularly for singers who, by the 2010s, were operating in a global economy and depended upon freedom of movement. Many of those starting out in the profession served 'apprenticeships' at German repertory theatres, while those at the peak of their careers were as likely to be singing in Paris or Vienna as in London. The practical ramifications of Brexit in terms of red tape are likely to pose problems for singers for the foreseeable future. Singers who became extremely vocal on the subject included mezzo-soprano Dame Sarah Connolly—often seen at anti-Brexit rallies—and soprano Anna Patalong, who wore a yellow ballgown with a blue star-spangled sash for a concert at the Royal Albert Hall and was instructed by Raymond Gubbay's management to choose a different outfit next time.[31]

---

[30] Henry Mance, 'Britain Has Had Enough of Experts, Says Gove', *FT* (3 June 2016), n.p.
[31] Anon., 'Royal Albert Hall Singer Asked to Change Pro-EU Dress', BBC News (26 March 2019).

244   SOMEONE ELSE'S MUSIC

But the connection between opera and Brexit went deeper than this. Opera had been dragged repeatedly into discussions about the British sense of identity, and there could be no bigger conversation on that topic in the early twenty-first century than the Brexit debate, concerned as it was with so many fundamental questions of 'who we are'. To be a 'hard Remainer' or 'hard Leaver', as characterised by the media, was to take a position on a far wider range of issues than EU membership, including culture. Back in 1973, upon the entry of the United Kingdom into the European Community, opera was used as a symbol of international cooperation and unity. The 'Fanfare for Europe' celebrations were launched at Covent Garden in January of that year with a gala performance of music and spoken word, in the presence of the Queen and numerous European ambassadors and diplomats.[32] In the late 2010s opera also came to be associated with the issue of European unity, this time more negatively.

The Brexit debate became bundled up with a wider contempt for metropolitan elites and their supposed advocation of rootless cosmopolitanism. In a parliamentary debate in March 2019, Brexit-supporting Conservative MP Sir John Hayes fantasised about the perfect day out for a Remainer encompassing 'Glyndebourne, the Henley regatta, and the People's Vote march'.[33] This was a shorthand way of disparaging Remainers as champagne socialists, with the implication that their cultural tastes were dubiously 'foreign'. Yet, opera's place in this debate was a complicated one, as it was also loved by some ardent leavers such as Gove. Cultural tastes never map simplistically on to political allegiances, but that was not the story the media chose to tell.

The view from abroad, as captured by a 2019 review for *The New Yorker* of *La forza del destino* with Anna Netrebko and Jonas Kaufmann, was that 'the fierce anti-Europeanism of economically uncertain Britons, who were swayed by populist demagogues to support the Brexit referendum, might even be partly directed against precisely the sort of prosperous, cosmopolitan European operagoers who converged on Covent Garden this week in a spirit of artistic communion'. The performance became symbolic, this critic argued, as the audience cowered inside the Royal Opera House, seeking an escape from the 'political insanity' raging outside, which he characterised as being driven by 'a hatred of immigrants, a hatred of Europe, and, perhaps, a

---

[32] Royal Opera House Annual Report, 1972/1973, p. 8. ROH archives: Royal Opera House Annual Reports—1972/73–1991/92.
[33] HoC debate, 14 March 2019: 'UK's Withdrawal from the European Union', Hansard, Vol. 656.

THIS SCEPTIC ISLE   245

hatred of élite European culture itself as summed up, in its very essence, by the opera'.[34]

If Brexit had seemed bad enough for opera, another cataclysmic event was to follow swiftly in its wake. The Covid-19 crisis overwhelmed the world, affecting all aspects of life. During the Spanish flu epidemic, the disruption to the arts seems to have been minimal: the show quite literally went on, as witnessed by a 1920 report on activities at the People's Palace that made no mention of the epidemic and stated that since World War One 'the activities at the Palace appear to have taken a new lease of life'.[35] But the reaction to Covid-19 was entirely different, with almost all aspects of normal activity simply grinding to a halt. For opera, the lights went out, seasons were cancelled, and singers dropped without payment of fees. Companies were resourceful in finding opportunities to perform and earn revenue by producing streamed performances. Nevertheless, the opera community found itself in a state of existential angst.

Initially, Boris Johnson's government vacillated about how, or indeed whether, to support the performing arts. *The Telegraph* warned in May 2020 that without a government rescue package, 70 per cent of performing arts companies were expected to be out of business by the end of the year, and more than 1,000 theatres insolvent.[36] Leading arts venues such as the Globe Theatre, the Albert Hall, and the Old Vic warned that they were all facing a very real prospect of closure.[37] In time, a rescue package for major institutions was announced, and such crises were averted, but it helped only some. While some freelance musicians were able to access state support, others—confounded by loopholes that meant they did not meet the criteria—were cast adrift. As theatres reopened, extreme social distancing was initially required to protect audiences, leading to colossal losses in ticket revenue; even with full reopening, some companies reported that audiences were not back at full strength. Gloomy predictions circulated about the bleak future for opera in the longer term.

As things began tentatively to open up, there was felt to be a particular need to get football going again, to boost morale, and in recognition of its revenue-raising power. Discussions on social media became heated. Some

---

[34] Larry Wolff, 'Opera and Brexit in London', *The New Yorker* (2 April 2019), n.p.

[35] 'Report of the Work of the People's Palace for Period Ending 31st July 1920', QMUL archives.

[36] Sonia Friedman, 'Theatre Stands on the Brink of Ruin', *The Telegraph* (21 May 2020), n.p.

[37] Charlotte Higgins, 'After the War the Arts Came Back Stronger', *The Guardian* (18 May 2020), n.p.

246   SOMEONE ELSE'S MUSIC

sectors of the arts-loving community expressed concern that a populist government was prioritising bread and circuses. On the other hand, countless social media users did believe that football ought to be put first and were scornful of any suggestion that the arts should be prioritised. In a fevered atmosphere, with people on all sides of the debate feeling frustrated by the drastic limitations placed on their lives, angry voices argued hammer-and-tongs about whose interests were more important.

All these tensions were encapsulated in a speech given in Parliament in November 2020 by Conservative MP Jake Berry, the day after Oliver Dowden had published his article about the Bradford semi-dweller. In a debate about economic support for the north of England and calling for government support for regional football, Berry stated:

> Opera and ballet will be at the heart of the culture of many people who live in London and the south of England, but for many of us in the north it is our local football club—our Glyndebourne, Royal Ballet, Royal Opera House or Royal Shakespeare Company will be Blackburn Rovers, Accrington Stanley, Barrow, Carlisle or Sunderland.[38]

Apparently ignorant of the thriving cultural history of the north and even of the existence of Opera North, the Hallé Orchestra, Northern Ballet, or the Liverpool Philharmonic, Berry fell back upon the crudest stereotypes about audiences for the arts. He did not explicitly use the word 'elitism', but the suggestion of it could not have been clearer.

Thus, even the Covid crisis—and the deep soul-searching it prompted about what sort of a society people wanted to see once normality returned—fuelled the elitism stereotype, leading to an intensification of the age-old narrative that opera was frivolous, posh, and not even truly British. This was a line pushed by a philistine right that was prepared to trample art underfoot as it opportunistically played to the gallery in pursuit of votes. Yet at the same time, opera found itself ever more reviled by the radical left, as the Covid crisis became embroiled with a wider explosion of global social unrest and calls for social justice. And so, opera found itself in a vexed position: disparaged as much by the intellectual left as by the populist right.

---

[38] HoC debate, 11 November 2020: 'North of England: Economic Support', Hansard, Vol. 683.

Culture wars

As the 2010s gave way to the 2020s, politics was no longer simply about domestic and foreign policy, education, defence, transport, or health, nor was it, any more, a private matter between the voter and the ballot box. The United Kingdom, strongly influenced by the United States, witnessed an explosion of 'culture wars', as all aspects of life took on a politicised hue, thanks to the inexorable power of social media. There was no chance that opera would escape from highly contentious debates about identity politics, 'relevance', and 'privilege'. Its status already weakened in Britain by the crises of Brexit and Covid and the relentless prods from a lazy, cliché-loving press, opera now found itself being fundamentally reappraised as an art form even by people who might seem like natural advocates for it.

As we have seen, the debate about opera and elitism has largely been one about the *trappings* of opera—money, dress, grand buildings—and about perceived snobbery on the part of opera-goers. Until recently, very few people would have attempted to sustain an argument that opera *itself* is elitist. This now seems to be changing, as opera, like other art forms, has become caught up in a broader debate about identity politics, social justice, and 'problematic canons', with many long-beloved operas now being chastised for their connections with historic power structures.

Opera hits the headlines regularly in one political controversy after another. Of course, it has always been inherently political: composers have, since its very beginnings, used it to challenge or to endorse the prevailing power structures of the day. The very existence of operatic censorship, widely used in the nineteenth century and still employed in certain cultures today, is testament to the fact that regimes of various types have perceived operas as potentially dangerous vehicles of political dissent. At the same time, it has been possible to disconnect an opera from its political message and simply treat it as an evening's entertainment, at least in the case of the familiar Mozarts, Verdis, and Puccinis (less so, of course, in the case of a work like *The Death of Klinghoffer*, about the hijacking of a passenger liner by the PLO).

Operas can, in other words, be 'read' at a variety of different levels—some deep, some less so—an unsurprising situation given that they constitute at once art and entertainment. Increasingly, however, simple enjoyment of opera at the level of entertainment is becoming more difficult. Operas that long seemed uncontroversial are suddenly being held up for scrutiny and

248   SOMEONE ELSE'S MUSIC

found wanting. This is a new and troubling twist in the development of the elitism trope, emerging as it has at a time when the place of classical music in society and in education is already under severe threat.

A view espoused by many who teach humanities disciplines in the United States—and increasingly in the United Kingdom—is that the university curriculum must be 'decolonised'. The proponents of this viewpoint, hyper-alert to unfair power dynamics, argue that the canonical art works that have long dominated the curriculum are in many cases so deeply intertwined with cultural and social privilege that they should be demoted from their elevated position. For some, the canon has become inherently objectionable and a bit of tinkering around the edges will not suffice; rather, it must be actively 'dismantled'. These recent discussions about the operatic canon and about representations of race and gender are too complex to discuss here in detail but are useful for our purposes insofar as they intersect with the elitism trope, pouring hot oil as they have upon a debate that was already ablaze. Opera's naysayers now have even more ammunition with which to depict the art form as elitist and exclusionary.

It is unfortunate that British discourses around opera are increasingly being shaped by ideas emanating from a country with a very different operatic history from our own. Opera has interacted with class and privilege very differently in the United States, and some of the discussions currently taking place there around the arts reflect anxieties specific to that nation's own cultural past. Transplanting American ways of thinking to the UK context does a great disservice to the long British history of accessible, popular opera. We might also reflect on the fact that there is a decidedly nationalist, anti-European tone to some of the American attacks on 'imperialist art forms', and, arguably, a quasi-colonial desire to promote American popular culture above all.

Postmodern race and gender theory has, nevertheless, made its way out of American academe and come to be applied to almost every aspect of humanistic endeavour in the United Kingdom. Academic work and activism have converged, as righting social wrongs is seen to be as much a part of the business of an academic as engaging in research. This trend was accelerated by the Covid crisis, the #MeToo movement, the rise of the BLM movement, and the environmental protest movement. The loudest voices in this discussion contend that culture cannot be examined *except* through a social-justice perspective. Such discussions have swiftly moved beyond academia and into the arts world and the general consciousness. The right-wing press gleefully reports the most excessive case studies and delights in stoking the so-called 'culture wars'.

These intellectual trends have had a knock-on effect in terms of arts practice, prompting arts organisations to make visible change in the works they programme and the artists they hire. This diversification of the canon and the employment of artists from previously marginalised groups is to be welcomed, and much good will surely come of it both for those employed in the arts and for audiences. However, the tendency to condemn or outlaw artistic works has been far less helpful. As a case in point, the bandying about of the label 'dead white men' as an expression of contempt when referring to hitherto celebrated writers, painters, and composers, or the rubbishing of certain art works as 'pale and stale', is surely fatuous and unproductive.

Academics have been talking about the representation of race and gender in opera since the 1990s, taking their cue from Edward Said's *Culture and Imperialism*. Similarly, they have been analysing the social and political mechanisms that shaped the canon for over thirty years. But while such 'deconstruction' of the canon was for many years merely abstract, by the turn of the 2020s it had become not only harder-edged but a practical aspiration. In an age in which statues of offending figures from the past are being pulled down and stately homes reproached for historic associations with slavery, many voices are clamouring for art works that offend contemporary sensibilities to be removed from view or, in the case of opera, the stage.

Art works have always addressed challenging and disturbing topics: tragedies are, by their very nature, tragic. It would be simple-minded to assume that in representing unpleasant situations or behaviours, an artist is necessarily endorsing them, yet this is often the level of commentary offered today. It has become far harder in the 2020s to argue that an opera might be a cautionary tale, to advocate for its artistic value even as it affronts modern sensibilities, or to accept it as a product of a time when things were done differently. Meanwhile, popular culture—in which gratuitous violence against women is routine on both the large and small screen and in song lyrics—draws comparatively little censure.

The contemporary opera world has realised that these debates are something it cannot ignore. As companies began to resume operations after the first wave of the Covid pandemic, many showed signs of taking active steps to diversify their repertoires—a good thing, since we can all surely benefit from the opportunity to hear a wider range of works. Nevertheless, companies were aware that they had to please constituencies with sharply differing views on matters of tradition and innovation—and put on works that would be guaranteed 'sellers' in order to recoup losses. They find themselves in a vexed position today, knowing that they are likely to face a stern backlash if they alienate more 'traditional' audiences with a wholesale 'decolonisation' of the operatic repertoire, as demanded by (social) media commentators who might or might not actually buy tickets. 'Problematic' operas are, however, now increasingly framed in apologetic or condemnatory fashion. Commentators from outside the musical world are often called upon to set the agenda, such as when WNO accompanied its new staging of *Madama Butterfly* in 2021 with an online event entitled 'The Long Arm of Imperialism', chaired by Priyamvada Gopal, Professor of Postcolonial Studies at the University of Cambridge, or when ENO held a private 'race consultation' in February 2020 dominated by members of the British East-Asian activist group BEATS.[39]

The idea of actually suppressing well-known art works from the past has recently gained traction in conversations about accessibility. After decades of educational initiatives by opera companies under the banner of opera for all, the conversation has suddenly become more complicated, as some argue that marginalised groups ought not to be offered 'high art' after all. Contemporary society has become increasingly preoccupied with so-called 'relevance'. This is the idea that people should study, watch, engage with, and perform culture that is their 'own': culture with which they can *identify*, which was created by people of similar backgrounds and experiences. The idea of 'lived experience' has become totemic. In 2019 *The Guardian* quoted an English teacher as saying that 'disaffected teens with terrible lives do not want to be studying Dickens and Shakespeare ... We should be encouraging these pupils, not boring them half to death—why not study literature that is relevant to their lives?'[40]

There is an impulse, today, to baulk at the paternalism of people who are 'in the know' sharing their love of art, of whatever form, with others who know less about it. But there is no getting away from the fact that gatekeepers will *always* attempt to guide the cultural tastes of others. Indeed, the new guardians of culture turn out to be more authoritarian than the old. Where earlier generations of privileged tastemakers gave 'ordinary people' access

[39] https://www.youtube.com/watch?v=-clyCR6kpQU(accessed 25 March 2025). The author was in attendance at the ENO event.

[40] Sally Weale and Naomi Larsson, '"Students Don't See the Value": Why A-Level English Is in Decline', *The Guardian* (16 August 2019), n.p.

to so-called high art, the new anti-elitist gatekeepers would, in many cases, deny them it.[41] In a thoughtful study that argues well-meaning progressives have bought far too willingly into a perversely self-harming anti-elitism narrative, Eliane Glaser writes: 'Now high culture is proscribed in the name of inclusivity. Yet this has the opposite impact to what was intended: it effectively denies that the masses are able to grasp anything challenging or avant-garde.'[42]

In the musical sphere, it has become commonplace to suggest that young people can only be engaged via popular music. In 2019, the chief executive of the charity 'Youth Music', which was undertaking a study of pupil exclusion, proposed that Stormzy should be taught in schools instead of Mozart, because his music was 'more relevant'.[43] Although the organisation later suggested young people should be taught about both, it tweeted, 'Engaging young people with music that speaks to them opens doors to broader, more diverse musical learning that can have benefits for attendance, attainment and wellbeing.'[44]

Laudable though the charity's aims were, its strategy seems more than a little problematic, albeit being perfectly in step with contemporary ideas about arts education and access. The purpose of education has historically been seen as introducing people to information and perspectives that are new to them, even if these initially challenge them and do not correspond with their personal tastes. But in the twenty-first century, this idea has been flipped on its head. There is a prevailing view that the art and culture to which schoolchildren and university students are introduced must mirror those with which they are already familiar, or presumed to be.

Presumed, of course, is the operative word here, for crude assumptions are often made about the relationship between taste and age, race or class. Young people are not one homogeneous group; it is as reductive to presume they all like Stormzy, or that Mozart does not 'speak to them', as it would be to assume that everyone over 65 is stuck in a time-warp of listening only to Cliff Richard. To give people more of the same is not 'access', nor is it education. The fashion for 'relevance'—allied to the contemporary obsession with identity politics—narrows horizons, effectively boxing people into a world they

---

[41] Rose, *The Intellectual Life*, p. 438.
[42] Glaser, *Elitism*, p. 79.
[43] Gabriella Swerling, 'Stormzy Should Be Taught in Schools', *The Telegraph* (22 May 2019), n.p.
[44] Tweeted by @youthmusic, 3.56 p.m., 22 May 2019.

252 SOMEONE ELSE'S MUSIC

already know, together with other people who are patronisingly presumed to be 'like them'.

Indeed, in contemporary discourse, when people talk about certain cultural products being more 'relevant', they often mean that they are simply more familiar. Assigning value to art works on the basis of familiarity sounds a death knell for opera, because the chance of opera being familiar to young people today is slim indeed. Classroom music lessons and instrumental tuition have been pared back progressively since the late twentieth century, with the Conservative governments of recent times particularly keen to diminish the arts with their relentless utilitarian obsession with STEM subjects. The arts and humanities have been progressively defunded at university level and at the time of writing are under severe threat at some institutions. Even those small numbers studying music will find little opera on the curriculum.

Opera stars are no longer household names: a Classic FM poll of 2017 found that half of its respondents could not name a single opera singer.[45] There has been a decline in arts broadcasting, and if opera features in the media at all, it is routinely dismissed as elitist. What chance is there today of a teenager who likes a good story and a good tune but who has had little prior introduction to classical music stumbling across opera, as I did when taken on a school trip to see Opera North in Bradford in the late 1980s? If young people are to be engaged with the arts only by what they already know, and familiarity with classical music is limited to those who attend private schools or whose parents are enthusiasts, doesn't that serve only to make it all the more 'elitist'?

In our age, where anything that smacks of paternalism is disdained, a Reithian ethos of educated people telling others what is good for them is widely scorned. But the suggestion that people should be given access only to culture that is 'relevant' to them raises the same old unpalatable questions. Who decides what is relevant, and for whom? The uncomfortable truth is that it is typically highly educated, middle-class, middle-aged people waving the banner for 'inclusion' who sit in arbitration, often making decisions that guarantee younger generations have less access to the arts than they did.

Attitudes towards music education have changed radically over the course of the period under investigation in this book. Let us think back to the teacher from the Isle of Dogs, putting on *The Magic Flute* with working-class schoolboys in the 1920s. He was certainly not giving them music that

---

[45] Adrian Lee, 'World of the Opera Elite', *DE* (6 December 2017), 19.

reflected their lives. Mozart was no more familiar to them than it would be to those with whom 'Youth Music' works today, and it was equally novel to their parents in the audience. And yet the novelty was, in a way, the point. Smith reported that the experiment brought pleasure to everyone who participated or watched. The boys, he reported, 'enter into their parts so intensely simply because they are *happy*'.[46] Laughter and smiles had emerged from beneath what were sometimes 'cheerless, saddened exteriors'; one boy even turned away from a life of petty crime as a result of his encounter with opera.

The fact that such enterprises would now be far less likely to take place because the idea of cultural 'enlightenment' has become almost laughably unfashionable, even politically unacceptable, is surely only something to lament. As the composer Sir James Macmillan wrote in 2019, 'Youngsters from less well-off homes are being discouraged away from the world of music, sometimes by budget cuts, but also poisonously abetted by media pressure.'[47] Who really gains from having their cultural opportunities restricted? How unimaginative, how small-minded, we have become.

In our current era of 'relevance', opera is presumed to be irrelevant because it is not in the musical mainstream, even though most people are subconsciously familiar with some operatic music. But there are many ways in which operas are 'relevant' to people of all ages and social backgrounds in their subject matter, as are the works of Dickens and Shakespeare. Sexual violence, gang rivalry, political corruption, revenge, and westerners meddling in eastern cultures are all to be found here; so too are issues of disability, race, and gender politics. If it is imperative to find a connection to the present in everything we study, this is an art form that offers rich pickings.

The extent to which music administrators have become complicit with the opera-elitism stereotype is depressing. Susanna Eastburn, Chief Executive of the organisation Sound and Music and former Director of Music at Arts Council England, wrote in 2018 that the term 'classical music' conveys 'connotations of clear hierarchies, of value judgements that are somehow objective and fixed across time, and of a principally Eurocentric view of culture.'[48] As such, she argued, the classical-music world ran the risk of

---

[46] Smith, *The School of Life*, p. 87; original emphasis.

[47] James Macmillan, 'What Has the Guardian Got Against Classical Music?', Unherd (https://unherd.com/2019/07/what-has-the-guardian-got-against-classical-music/), 12 July 2019.

[48] Susanna Eastburn, 'Is Classical Music a Living or Heritage Art Form?', in Chris Dromey and Julia Haferkorn (eds), *The Classical Music Industry* (New York: Routledge, 2018), pp. 141–147, p. 141.

254 SOMEONE ELSE'S MUSIC

becoming 'hopelessly outdated and irrelevant, increasingly distant from the diverse realities of British society today' unless it transformed itself entirely.[49]

Such ideas appear to be deeply ingrained at Arts Council England (ACE). Throughout this book we have seen the vital role played by the Arts Council in funding and promoting opera, a benevolent initiative that widened the audience for opera and as a result gave pleasure, enjoyment, and, dare one even say, enlightenment to countless people. In recent times, however, the institution has become so squeamish about its own remit that it has even shied away from using the word 'art'. In 2020 ACE announced in its latest strategy document, 'Let's Create', that it would stop using the terms 'art' and 'artists', substituting instead 'culture', 'cultural content', and 'creative practitioners', on the grounds that 'many people are uncomfortable with the label "the arts" and associate it only with either the visual arts or "high art" such as ballet or opera'.[50]

Add all this self-flagellation in the arts to the practical problems faced by the opera industry as a result of Brexit and Covid, and the opera world, at the turn of the 2020s, found itself in a very dark place indeed. And then, in 2022, ACE decided to redistribute its funding, no doubt offering a lifeline to some worthy new organisations but inflicting major cuts on the British opera scene. It was under the cosh from a government whose motivations were guided both by saving money and holding on to 'red wall' voters: disaffected working-class residents of northern towns and cities who felt abandoned by a Labour Party they perceived as catering to middle-class professionals.[51] Being seen to move arts investment out of the South East was part and parcel of the Conservative administration's 'levelling up' agenda. But not all the blame could be placed on the government: ACE itself made the fine-grained decisions about which organisations to fund and defund, and it chose to hit classical music, and opera in particular, hard.

The reduction by a third of WNO's funding led to a swift announcement that it would be scaling down its touring schedule. Similarly, Glyndebourne announced that it would not be able to tour as planned in 2023, having lost funding previously granted for its tour and its learning and engagement work. ENO's entire grant was removed, with a one-off sum over three

---

[49] Ibid., p. 145.
[50] Charlotte Wace, 'Artists Get Rebranded as Creative Practitioners', *The Times* (28 January 2020), n.p.
[51] David Skelton, *The New Snobbery: Taking on Modern Elitism and Empowering the Working Class* (Croydon: Biteback Publishing, 2021), p. 30.

years being offered on the condition of relocating outside of London. In due course, after a public outcry and angry statements in the House of Commons from MPs of all political colours—all of which proved that the British were not as hostile to opera as many in the media would have it—the company was given a tentative year's reprieve and the opportunity to apply for more funds. But relocation to Manchester—an unfeasible proposition for most chorus members and orchestral musicians, as a questionnaire of company staff revealed—was still on the cards, and artists were made redundant in 2024.[52] There remains at the time of writing much uncertainty about the company's long-term future, and the suspicion lingers that it might have to change its core business, prioritising performances in car parks rather than theatres. As Sir Simon Rattle observed, 'For me, the notion that you can say to an opera company, as the Arts Council has said to ENO, "Move somewhere else in the country and reinvent your art form," is like some sort of bad joke in a novel.'[53]

The 'levelling up' rationale for the cuts made no sense. What was being chipped away at was opera at its most accessible: opera in English, opera in the regions—Liverpool lost all its annual opera visits in one fell swoop—and the company (ENO) that had been 'the people's opera', in one guise or another, for over a century. This was unconscionable cultural vandalism by an organisation that had originally prized opera so highly. Sir Antonio Pappano, music director of the Royal Opera, called the proposal to force ENO out of the West End ('a hugely successful portion of real estate that the British should be proud of') reckless and pointed out that it didn't even square with the Brexit mantra of showing the world what Britain could achieve by itself.[54]

Since the ACE decisions defied all logic, it was tempting to conclude that its managers were motivated first and foremost by jitters about opera's supposed 'elitism'. But they also betrayed a deeper antipathy towards the very idea of national opera, towards taking pride in the nation and its accomplishments, and towards using London as the shop window for them. The days when John Maynard Keynes had said that 'it is . . . our business to make London a great artistic metropolis, a place to visit and to wonder at' seemed but a distant memory. ACE, then, was not only removing musicians' livelihoods and depriving audiences of the opportunity to hear wonderful

---

[52] Matthew Hemley, 'ENO Agrees to Move Out of London in £24m Deal with Arts Council', *The Stage* (20 April 2023), 2.

[53] Richard Morrison, 'Simon Rattle: "This Is a Desperate Moment: The Entire Art Form is Threatened"', *The Times* (20 April 2023), n.p.

[54] Richard Morrison, 'Antonio Pappano, "It's Scary How Opera Is Still Viewed as Elitist", *ST* (23 April 2023), n.p.

256 SOMEONE ELSE'S MUSIC

performances, but it was also betraying its own founding principles. It had originally provided what we would now call 'access' to large numbers of people of all backgrounds, over a large geographical area, though of course it would not have used the term. In the 2020s, we hear the word all the time, but it becomes empty and insincere when opportunities for listeners to encounter the arts are simultaneously being removed by the very organisations set up to champion them.

ACE executives seemingly oblivious or indifferent to the worth and vulnerability of the cultural treasures in their own hands were, by the early 2020s, doing the Conservative government's bidding but also demonstrating an ideological hostility towards classical music that seemed to go beyond it. (The Chair of the All-Party Parliamentary Group for Opera Sir Bob Neill told Parliament that 'the ineptitude of Arts Council England has undermined and discredited the Government's policy intention' in terms of levelling up.[55]) The terrain had been laid for such cuts by the relentless recycling of the elitism stereotype, over four decades, by people and organisations many and varied, including some who in the past would have been opera's natural allies. Describing opera as elitist was not only terrible PR—how many people would be tempted to explore an art form that had been thus characterised?— but played straight into the hands of anyone looking to make cuts.

At this point it seems difficult at times to imagine opera as we know it surviving the many charges thrown at it for much longer. Against a backdrop of profound government hostility, opera needs every endorsement it can get from people who know how it can transform lives. Thus, the ever-more aggressive claims, sometimes perpetuated by its own practitioners, that it is complicit in great social ills seem particularly painful. If culture is viewed entirely through the lens of grievance politics, then opera's case is irrevocably doomed. If one is determined to judge an art form by the power structures that shaped its creation as entertainment for the aristocracy over four hundred years ago, opera falls at the first hurdle. If art must be participatory, one gets nowhere with an art form that demands high-level skills possessed only by a minority. If one views opera purely in dogmatic, resentful terms, there is no scope to celebrate it, nor to inspire new audiences who might enjoy it. As Glaser notes, the populist right has done its best to associate the arts with elite privilege, but the left-leaning arts world and education sectors have

---

[55] HoC debate, 18 January 2023: 'Arts Council England: Funding', Hansard, Vol. 726.

THIS SCEPTIC ISLE 257

often shown themselves to be 'timid and tongue-tied, stricken to silence in the face of anti-elitist attacks'.[56]

These latest twists in the elitism debate have been nothing other than catastrophic for opera. The circular arguments that swirl incessantly around the art form's supposed elitism and irrelevance to the modern world ultimately go nowhere: their logical conclusion can only be that opera must die. As we enter the second quarter of the twenty-first century, Britain shows every sign of confirming its reputation as the land without music. But it does not have to be this way. It is time to change the conversation about opera.

---

[56] Glaser, *Elitism*, p. 45, p. 122.

Conclusion

Stereotypes are damaging. Contemporary society likes to see itself as egalitarian and open-minded, purporting to despise old-fashioned, reductive thinking on all manner of issues. Paradoxically, ours is also an era that seeks to label to an ever-greater extent. Social media has fostered a type of public discourse in which nuanced debate has left the room. In an age of polarised viewpoints, in which one fraught public debate after another rages, people are exhorted to 'pick a side' or be 'on the right side of history'. We are constantly urged to nail our political colours to the mast, and question the morality of those who hold different views. All these imperatives to pigeon-hole people, ideas, and tastes lead to the reinforcement of divisive stereotypes.

Stereotypes are also immensely difficult to shift. Once an idea has circulated endlessly in the public sphere, it becomes normalised, beyond challenge. Dave Russell wrote pessimistically in 2017: 'In the final analysis, it is tempting to suggest that the concept of opera as elitist has simply proved too powerful to be discarded, a convenient populist discourse that everyone outside of the wealthiest in the country could unite in using as a convenient shorthand with which to confer and condemn patrician and/or supposedly pretentious lifestyles.'[1] A *Daily Mail* poll found people were assumed by readers to be 'posh' if they attended an opera, though the same went for people who ate hummus.[2] In a society that has—according to several recent prime ministers—supposedly become classless (though of course it has not really), crude class signifiers are reinforced ever more relentlessly.

Opera is the only art form that is written off wholesale as elitist, followed closely by classical music in general, around which unhelpful stereotypes also swirl. Other art forms are sometimes called elitist for their intellectualism, including poetry (perceived by the public as 'out-of-touch, gloomy, irrelevant, effeminate, high-brow and elitist', according to an Arts Council report) and even jazz.[3] But poetry makes no demands on the public purse,

[1] Russell, 'Reaching the Operatic Stage', 338.
[2] Sean Poulter, 'Supper, Waitrose and £10 Bottles of Wine? You're Posh', *DM* (4 June 2010), 11.
[3] Cited in David Lister, 'Poets' Image: Gloomy, Elitist and Irrelevant', *The Independent* (28 June 1996), n.p.; Andrew Ross, *No Respect: Intellectuals and Popular Culture* (New York: Routledge, 1989), 67, 81.

CONCLUSION 259

jazz is 'cool', and neither is associated with social extravagance. It is unimaginable that the word 'elitism' would be applied systematically to *all* drama, literature, or fine art, let alone cinema—notwithstanding the existence of numerous challenging plays and novels, bizarre art installations, and pretentious art-house films. Yet opera is dismissed systematically as elitist, irrespective of the fact that many operas are immensely well-liked and their music familiar.

The opera-elitism stereotype is not an inherent truth, however, but an ideological construct. The idea that opera is elitist, fuelled so determinedly in recent decades, comes from a combination of ignorance (a hazy idea of picnickers in black tie and overweight divas in horned helmets), personal distaste, and partisan agendas. As we have seen, it is an idea that has been promoted from both ends of the political spectrum—often by people who do not like opera but identify ways of exploiting it, via its denigration, as a way of furthering a particular ideological agenda. Though different parties in the debate may be at cross-purposes as to what elitism really means, the stereotype has been endlessly disseminated by a lazy media, which has learned that the magic words 'opera' + 'elitism' = clicks. In short, as the journalist Adrian Hamilton wrote in 2011, 'More nonsense is talked about opera than any other single art form.'[4]

If we want to share a love of opera with others, it is essential that we find ways to mount a defensive action, for lazy words have real-life ramifications. The elitism stereotype has become a problem that inhibits accessibility and even threatens to strike an existential blow to some of our greatest artistic institutions. The relentless boosting of the elitism stereotype since 2000 has enabled a situation where opera has become highly vulnerable. ACE acts as a stooge for a government trying to appease the populist, philistine right while simultaneously exhibiting an ideological loathing for the so-called high arts that emanates from parts of the left under a false guise of egalitarianism.

Opera is often proclaimed to be elitist by people who claim to want to make the arts more accessible. Since some of these people work within the arts themselves, or allied areas such as music education, this is confusing for the opera world, leaving it uneasy about whether it can still legitimately advocate for its own business. In reality, talking obsessively about how elitist (or racist or sexist) opera is does nothing to make it appeal to new audiences. Far from creating opportunities for all, the current elitism rhetoric does nothing

[4] Adrian Hamilton, 'When Soap Meets Opera', *The Independent* (27 January 2011), 12–13, 12.

260 SOMEONE ELSE'S MUSIC

more than stoke social division and tell people that opera is 'not for the likes of them'.

Anyone who knows the therapeutic benefits, as well as the sheer pleasure, that opera can offer will find this troubling. The benefits of the arts for mental health, for rehabilitation after trauma, and for building stronger communities are increasingly recognised, and there are numerous examples in this book of opera bringing comfort to people who had the privilege—in the Streatfeild sense—of stumbling across it. But labelling it as elitist slams the door shut from the off. The elitism stereotype hampers the efforts of opera companies to reach new audiences through their educational and outreach work.

In the face of this pernicious stereotype, arts organisations do their best. However, a major stumbling block is that people with no prior exposure to the arts are now far less likely to discover them for themselves than would have been the case in the past. For at least the first two-thirds of the twentieth century, the autodidacticism movement introduced countless people to literature and various forms of 'high art'. In his history of working-class culture, Jonathan Rose cites the example of one Jim Turnbull, a barely educated blacksmith from unemployment-stricken Jarrow, brought up by drunks. Despite his many disadvantages, Turnbull read Dickens and Darwin, built up a record collection, went to the opera, and dreamed of a future where 'the symphonies of Beethoven and the operas of Mozart will be played in public halls everywhere'.[5] During the war and in the post-war decades, many people continued to discover the arts and were encouraged to do so by radio and television programmes, the founding of the Open University, evening classes, and more. There was a spirit of enquiry abroad in the land.

Autodidacticism encouraged intellectual independence in those who aspired to it and gave them opportunities beyond their social environment: knowledge was power. Jonathan Rose, the leading documenter of this movement, laments the fact that 'the withering away of the autodidact tradition has been a great loss'.[6] But not everyone sees things this way. In a detailed study of the music-appreciation movement, musicologist Kate Guthrie worries about its underpinning Victorian ideals of cultivation and 'uplift', its perpetuation of the musical canon, and its so-called 'presumptive paternalism' in guiding people's listening habits. She objects to the system of 'cultured values, of cultured discourse, of high cultural products' upon which

---

[5] Rose, *The Intellectual Life*, pp. 456–457.
[6] Ibid., p. 464.

CONCLUSION 261

the movement was based and argues that the music appreciationists' shared understanding of what constituted 'the best', in cultural terms, seems 'insolent' from today's perspective.[7]

But at a time when the arts are off most people's radar, marginalised in the school curriculum, and defunded, is this our biggest worry? Surely we can find much to admire in the well-intentioned, well-received endeavours of earlier times, when, as Guthrie herself concedes, the arts became, for many, 'a sought-after leisure pastime variously pursued for enjoyment, self-improvement, or intellectual stimulation'?[8] Today many baulk at the idea of people aspiring to become more 'cultivated', but what is wrong with treating ideas and art as part of a healthy culture of aspiration? Isn't it more positive to promote such things over the mansions, fast cars, and expensive fashion that are celebrated by popular culture?

It goes without saying that earlier efforts to use music to create 'good citizens' are now derided. Yet it was this ethos that persuaded post-war governments to invest in music education and public libraries, things whose current demise many would surely lament. Lilian Baylis put on opera for all because she was fervently committed to the idea of giving everyone good art so that it might improve their lives in meaningful ways, not because she had boxes to tick. Her initiatives might have been 'Victorian' in spirit but at least they were motivated by a genuine love of art. The same cannot be said for the attitude that currently abounds in British society.

Perhaps most troublingly, there has been a fundamental shift in attitudes regarding who the arts are 'for'. The notion, emanating from the 1970s community-arts movement, that the middle classes have no right to impose 'their' [sic] art on everyone else has gone mainstream. The Guardian—a predominantly middle-class newspaper—appears to have become a particular agent provocateur on this issue. In one example of many of opera-bashing in the paper, the crime novelist Dreda Say Mitchell wrote gleefully in 2015 of attending a debate about elitism at the Royal Opera House and provoking Puccini fans by suggesting they were 'braying snobs who only mix with other braying snobs'.[9] Poking fun at the idea of an elite wanting everyone else to be like them by attending the opera, Say Mitchell wrote, 'In the past, the conservatively cultured said, "You'll never be like us". Now the progressively

[7] Guthrie, The Art of Appreciation, p. 3, p. 24, p. 167, p. 208.
[8] Ibid., p. 3.
[9] Dreda Say Mitchell, 'We Can't Leave It to the Elite to Decide Who's Cultured', The Guardian (21 September 2015), n.p.

262 SOMEONE ELSE'S MUSIC

cultured say, "You can be like us but you've got to put some effort in". Neither have an answer to the question: "But what if we don't want to be like you?"'

Opera is not everyone's cup of tea, nor need it be, but what is concerning here is the total rejection of the idea of sharing the arts (or what *The Guardian*'s sub-editor called the tastes of 'the posh few') with everyone. This was the noble buttress of the Vic-Wells venture, the early BBC, and the Arts Council, and it continues to inform arts outreach today. But if it is no longer agreed to be a good thing, the whole idea of 'access', in its most positive sense, crumbles. All the good work by the dynamic opera advocates of the early twentieth century broke the upper-class monopoly of the so-called 'high arts'. That work is now rapidly being undone by evangelists of 'inclusion', who label such art works as irrelevant to people's lives.

Nowadays, it is widely stated as a matter of categorical fact that only those who are 'privileged' will encounter the arts. Opera and classical music in general are maligned as interests of the white middle classes (often by commentators who are white, middle-class, and classically trained themselves). This point is asserted particularly dogmatically in a recent book by sociologist Anna Bull, who received an intensive music education when growing up in New Zealand and became a professional musician, though eventually gave up playing because of what she perceived to be classical music's upholding of 'hegemonic' structures.[10] Bull's study of music-making among contemporary young people in the United Kingdom is underpinned by the credo that classical music is associated with 'classed, gendered, and racialized identities', and that the middle classes use it to 'safeguard their privilege', reproduce inequality, and 'clos[e] off their protected and exclusive spaces to the other groups in society'.[11]

Sociologists like to talk about the ways in which social elites use 'highbrow' culture to demarcate themselves from other social groups, drawing heavily upon Pierre Bourdieu's hypothesis of taste as a form of 'cultural capital'. Such assumptions contribute towards fuelling the elitism stereotype yet very often rely upon broad-brush hypotheses, which are not necessarily grounded in historical evidence.[12] Bull draws upon countless theoretical studies but overlooks the history of classical music consumption in this country. Anyone reading her book would come away believing that classical music constitutes

---

[10] Anna Bull, *Class, Control, and Classical Music* (New York: Oxford University Press, 2019), p. 174.

[11] Ibid., xii–xiv, xvi.

[12] Friedman and Reeves, 'From Aristocratic to Ordinary', 323.

CONCLUSION 263

a 'closed world': class-based musical tastes are seen as somehow monolithic. The numerous examples of working-class engagement with opera presented here vigorously disprove such an argument.

Perhaps it is because I am, unlike Bull, a musical autodidact, and thus lacking any sense of self-loathing at my youthful 'privilege', that I find myself baulking not at the classical music world itself but at the sweeping statements uttered by many writing about classical music today, some of whom seem to want to pull up the ladder behind them. Confounding the contemporary truism that people who enjoy opera must have parents who introduced them to it, I did not come from a 'musical family', and my teenage interest in classical music was entirely self-driven. The records in our home were pop and rock; my parents did not play musical instruments, read music, or go to classical concerts. Yet I badgered them to buy me a second-hand piano they could ill afford, having taught myself to play at a friend's house. My pathways into opera were school trips, organised by enthusiastic music teachers at my York comprehensive school, and hearing snippets of opera in *A Room with a View* and *Inspector Morse*. As a student in the early 1990s, I bought cheap tickets to see Scottish Opera in Newcastle, borrowed CDs of opera's greatest hits from the public library, and sang Gilbert and Sullivan. Opera, to me, was a colourful, exuberant, life-affirming way of telling stories through music and drama, and throughout this journey of discovery, nobody, bar nobody, told me opera was elitist, or said it wasn't for people like me. But they would today.

What can be done to counter the misleading or downright factually inaccurate stereotypes that surround opera and present it to potential new listeners in more positive ways? Perhaps it is helpful to return to first principles. Though operas often debate the key issues of the era in which they were composed, opera's purpose is, at root, to entertain. An overwhelming sense of people having fun at the opera emerges from the earlier periods considered here, and that was my own formative experience in the 1990s. The alliance of opera to negative stereotypes and politics means that that spirit of enjoyment seems to have been lost in recent decades.

Historically, the most successful way of getting people interested in opera in the past was simply to present it straight, in imaginative places and at affordable prices, and to say, 'Try this. You might like it. And if you don't, that's fine.' (We must, incidentally, abandon the received wisdom that things only have worth if they are approved by a majority, and acknowledge that just because something is a minority taste does not make it elitist.) Less successful

264 SOMEONE ELSE'S MUSIC

ways of presenting opera to the public have included using desperate gimmicks to present opera as something it is not, either via strained attempts to sell opera like pop music or edgy productions with a high shock factor. There is little evidence that such strategies have had any significant success in attracting new audiences; indeed, they may well be counterproductive. As Rupert Christiansen writes, 'It doesn't work; none of it works. The harder you try to sell opera as groovy, the greater the suspicion and resistance, the stronger the shrieking fat lady stereotypes, the louder the catcalls of elitism and anachronism.'[13]

A good recent example of presenting opera accessibly was Stephen Medcalf's low-budget production of *Gianni Schicchi* for Grange Park Opera, filmed on location in a Chelsea house in 2021 and broadcast for free on YouTube. This was an immensely appealing production, which poked fun at archetypal British class tensions, in similar vein to comedies such as *Keeping up Appearances*. It was a production packed full of human touches: Schicchi was a car mechanic and Lauretta his apprentice; one of the social-climbing relatives pilfered items and stuffed them in a Sainsbury's bag; the small boy ran off to buy a Beano from a shabby-looking corner shop. There was nothing stuffy about opera presented in such a natural and contemporary way. It was hard to see how anyone, however sceptical about opera, could fail to be charmed.

But the challenge is getting people to watch in the first place. It is far harder for new listeners to come to opera nowadays without prejudice. Today's opera companies have to fight against a great deal more ingrained suspicion and inverted snobbery than did the Old Vic, wartime Sadler's Wells, or Opera North in the 1970s. The politics of opera undoubtedly became muddier in the later decades of our century. It is far less likely today that people will stumble across opera in their daily lives, and if they do, it is far less likely that they will approach it with an open mind.

This is where the dots need to be joined. We need more music in schools and more school trips. We need more opera on radio—Radio 2 and Radio 4 as well as Radio 3—and on television. We need more repertory companies that can build up a loyal local following. All these things used to be normal in this country: there is no fundamental reason why they could not be again. We also need political parties that address the arts seriously in their

---

[13] Rupert Christiansen, 'Opera Must Bring Down the Curtain on Gimmickry And Gore', *DT* (9 April 2016), 22.

CONCLUSION   265

election manifestos and on entering government. Sir Bob Neill, Chair of the All-Party Parliamentary Group for Opera, said in a Parliamentary debate about the ACE cuts, 'We need a proper strategy for opera. Opera is a major part of the British music scene. Some people think it is a bit of a foreign thing . . . It is not. It is fundamental.'[14]

Above all, we need to break the unhelpful cycle of circular arguments within which current operatic discourse would appear to have become stuck. The so-called high arts are often discussed in terms that tend towards the nihilistic, and we desperately need to find new, more positive and productive ways to talk about them. At a time when funding for the arts is being cut and arts education is the lowest priority for successive governments, the British cultural scene is facing possibly the greatest crisis in its history. Disparage the arts long and hard enough for their supposed ideological baggage and we shall lose them forever. And though it may sound unfashionable to say so, we shall all be diminished in the process.

If opera is to survive in the United Kingdom, everyone who cares about it—whether it be musicians, educationalists, critics, opera-loving MPs, or audience members—must find the courage to speak up for it, without being deterred by fear of being called 'elitist'. John Tusa lamented the fact that 'classical music walks on the fragile eggshells of British class sensitivity— mightily powered by social guilt—not because of what it is but what it is presumed to signify'.[15] To put it bluntly, we need to get over this. So long as opera is available to all, via cheap tickets, television and radio broadcasts, recordings, and streaming, the fact that somebody somewhere has bought an expensive ticket, dressed up, and packed a fancy picnic should be neither here nor there.

Rather than apologising for opera, the opera world needs to advocate for it—for the art form itself as well as its social benefits. It must take control of the narrative, wresting the story of what opera is out of the hands of loud, sometimes ill-informed people with malign agendas. It must be prepared to challenge (or at least ignore) not only philistinism from the populist right but unhelpful, destructive ideas from the radical left. Countering such narratives will require courage, not least because it involves overcoming qualms about cultural relativism, which have rendered redundant the idea of providing the best for the most, since nobody is allowed to claim that their art form is better

---

[14] HoC debate, 18 January 2023: 'Arts Council England: Funding', Hansard, Vol. 726.
[15] John Tusa, *Pain in the Arts* (London: I. B. Tauris, 2014), p. 117.

or special. The opera world will have to find ways of arguing that opera is at once ordinary (in the social sense) and yet extraordinary in the aesthetic sense, in the way in which it brings together so many different forms of art in one. If it cannot do this, it will have no means of fighting its corner, no argument with which to justify its high subsidies. Valuing opera need not mean devaluing other forms of culture. It must be possible to talk about opera as inspiring and magnificent without casting implied aspersions on any other form of music. Will anyone dare, in an age of information overload and reduced attention spans, to make the case that 'long-form' art works, whether operas, symphonies, or epic novels, offer something that makes them particularly meaningful and satisfying?

Above all, we must counter crude ideas about who opera is 'for'. In the pages of this book, we have heard about expensive tickets, snooty gatekeepers, and opera-goers in tiaras or black tie. It would be disingenuous to try to conceal these aspects of British operatic culture. However, if you had told the audience at the Old Vic that the art form about which they were so passionate was elitist, they would have laughed. You would have received blank expressions from the people who wrote to Lilian Baylis to say that going to Sadler's Wells was 'my weekly pick-me-up' or 'my tonic'.[16] The idea would have seemed equally illogical to the people who went to see a touring opera production during the war, to the many ex-miners who forged careers as opera singers, to the children having fun devising their own operas. To all these people and more, opera offered something of value and they took it as they found it.

It is horrifying to think of the way opera might now elude people who could, potentially, gain so much from it. Let us think back to the Yorkshire housewife who found consolation in her dead son's opera records after the war. In an analogous situation today, such a bereaved mother, having been told that opera was not for 'ordinary folks', would probably approach her son's music collection with suspicion. Indeed, the son probably wouldn't have had opera in his collection in the first place. The thought that people of today should have the potential comfort that this woman experienced denied to them reveals the true ugliness of the elitism mantra. We need the arts, and we need them even when times are tough. Indeed, perhaps that is when we need them the most.

Opera has, quite simply, meant too much to too many people for us not to fight for its future. In this book we have met countless British people who

---

[16] Lilian Baylis, 'Wanted: 2,000 People!', *OVSWM*, 1/5 (September and October 1931), 2–3, 3.

CONCLUSION   267

have derived enjoyment, solace, and inspiration from opera. There is no reason why it should not be equally meaningful to future generations, no justification for treating it as a vaguely suspect relic. Opera could become a source of lifelong enjoyment for so many people who have not yet discovered it; it is a crying shame that most will never have the opportunity to do so, or will be put off by negative clichés. Perhaps we can find hope for Britain's cultural future by looking to the lessons of the past. This book reveals that opera used to be for everyone—and shows us how it could be again.

Music brings people together. The rhetoric of elitism seeks to divide them. The elitism stereotype is destructive rather than constructive: it closes doors and it closes minds. We have spent decades trying to give people of all backgrounds equal access to education and the arts, yet people are now being told that works from the operatic or literary canon are not relevant to them. It is when we do this, when we try to confine people to what they already know and tell them that certain forms of culture are 'not for them', that we become the real elitists. To talk endlessly about opera being elitist is, it turns out, just about the most elitist thing one can do.

Selected Bibliography

Anon., *The Arts in War Time: A Report on the Work of C.E.M.A 1942 and 1943* (London: Council for the Encouragement of Music and the Arts, 1944)

Anon., 'The Opera in Britain', *Planning*, 15/290 (8 November 1948), 147–162

Anon., 'List of Operas and Operettas for Schools and Youth Clubs' (London: National Operatic & Dramatic Association, 1957)

Anon., 'London Opera Centre: Report of the Committee Appointed by the Governing Body to Investigate Recent Criticisms of the Centre' (London: St Clement's Press, 1964)

Anon., *A History of Sadler's Wells and English National Opera* (London: ENO, 1980)

Anon., *The Opera Education Pack* (London: Opera and Music Theatre Forum, n.d.)

Anon., *The Opera Education Workbook* (London: Opera and Music Theatre Forum, n.d.)

Allen, Eleanor, *Heddle Nash: Singing against the Tide* (London: Jubilee House Press, 2010)

Allen, Mary, *A House Divided: The Diary of a Chief Executive of the Royal Opera House* (London: Simon & Schuster, 1998)

Arrandale, Karen, 'The Scholar as Critic: Edward J. Dent', in Jeremy Dibble and Julian Horton (eds), *British Musical Criticism and Intellectual Thought, 1850–1950* (Woodbridge: Boydell, 2018), pp. 154–173

The Arts Council of Great Britain, *A Report on Opera and Ballet in the United Kingdom, 1966–69* (Colchester: Benham and Company, 1969)

Baker, Janet, *Full Circle: An Autobiographical Journal* (London: Julia MacRae, 1982)

Bakewell, Joan, and Garnham, Nicholas, *The New Priesthood: British Television Today* (London: Allen Lane, The Penguin Press, 1970)

Bartley, Alan, *Far from the Fashionable Crowd: The People's Concert Society and Music in London's Suburbs* (n.p.: Whimbrel Publishing, 2009)

Beaven, Brad, *Leisure, Citizenship and Working-Class Men in Britain, 1850–1945* (Manchester: Manchester University Press, 2005)

Binney, Marcus, and Runciman, Rosy, *Glyndebourne: Building a Vision* (London: Thames and Hudson, 1994)

Blaug, Mark, *Why Are Covent Garden Seat Prices So High?* (London: The Royal Opera House, 1976)

Blunt, Wilfrid, *John Christie of Glyndebourne* (London: Geoffrey Bles, 1968)

Boarder, Sylvia, *They Made an Opera* (London: University of London Press, Ltd, 1966)

Boe, Alfie, *Alfie: My Story* (London: Simon and Schuster, 2012)

Boughton, Rutland, *The Glastonbury Festival Movement* (Bloomsbury: Somerset Folk Press, 1921)

Braden, Su, *Arts and People* (London: Routledge and Kegan Paul, 1978)

Brecknock, John L., and Melling, John Kennedy, *Scaling the High Cs: The Musical Life of Tenor John L. Brecknock* (Lanham, MD: The Scarecrow Press, 1996)

Bridges, Lord, *The State and the Arts: The Romanes Lecture* (Oxford: The Clarendon Press, 1958)

Bridges, Lord, Albemarle, Diana, Annan, Noel, Barnes, George, *Help for the Arts* (London: The Calouste Gulbenkian Foundation, 1959)

Bull, Anna, *Class, Control, and Classical Music* (New York: Oxford University Press, 2019)

Carpenter, Humphrey, *The Envy of the World: Fifty Years of the BBC Third Programme and Radio 3, 1946–1996* (London: Phoenix, 1996)

270 SELECTED BIBLIOGRAPHY

Chamier, J. Daniel, *Percy Pitt of Covent Garden and the B.B.C.* (London: Edward Arnold and Co., 1938)

Christie, George, *A Slim Volume. Glyndebourne: An Anecdotal Account* (Lewes: Glyndebourne Productions, 2016)

Cohen-Portheim, Paul, *England the Unknown Isle*, trans. Alan Harris (London: Duckworth, 1930)

Cohen-Portheim, Paul, *The Spirit of London* (London: Batsford, 1935)

Colebatch, Hal, *Blair's Britain* (London: The Claridge Press, 1999)

Collins, Jim (ed.), *High-Pop: Making Culture into Popular Entertainment* (Malden, MA: Blackwell's, 2002)

Collins, Sarah, 'Anti-intellectualism and the Rhetoric of "National Character"', in Jeremy Dibble and Julian Horton (eds), *British Musical Criticism and Intellectual Thought, 1850–1950* (Woodbridge: The Boydell Press, 2018), pp. 199–234

Cook, Ida, *We Followed Our Stars* (London: Hamish Hamilton, 1950)

Dawson, Sandra Trudgen, *Holiday Camps in Twentieth-Century Britain* (Manchester: Manchester University Press, 2011)

Deane, Kathryn, 'Community Music in the United Kingdom: Politics or Policies?', in Brydie-Lee Bartleet and Lee Higgins (eds), *The Oxford Handbook of Community Music* (Oxford: Oxford University Press, 2018), pp. 323–342

Deathridge, John, *Wagner Beyond Good and Evil* (Berkeley: University of California Press, 2008)

DeNora, Tia, 'Public and Narrative Selves in *Desert Island Discs*', in Julie Brown, Nicholas Cook, and Stephen Cottrell (eds), *Defining the Discographic Self: Desert Island Discs in Context* (Oxford: The British Academy, 2017), pp. 215–237

Drogheda, Lord, *Double Harness: Memoirs by Lord Drogheda* (London: Weidenfeld and Nicolson, 1978)

Dwyer, Terence, *Opera in Your School* (London: Oxford University Press, 1964)

The Earl of Harewood, *The Tongs and The Bones: The Memoirs of Lord Harewood* (London: Weidenfeld and Nicolson, 1981)

Eastburn, Susanna, 'Is Classical Music a Living or Heritage Art Form?', in Chris Dromey and Julia Haferkorn (eds), *The Classical Music Industry* (New York: Routledge, 2018), pp. 141–147

Eubanks-Winkler, Amanda, 'Politics and the Reception of Andrew Lloyd-Webber's *The Phantom of the Opera*', *Cambridge Opera Journal*, 26/3 (November 2014), 271–287

Evans, Geraint, with Goodwin, Noël, *Sir Geraint Evans: A Knight at the Opera* (London: Michael Joseph, 1984)

Fawkes, Richard, *Welsh National Opera* (London: Julia MacRae, 1986)

Feist, Andrew, and Hutchison, Robert (eds), *Cultural Trends in the Eighties*, 4 (London: Policy Studies Institute, 1990)

Fielding, Helen, *Bridget Jones's Diary* (London: Picador, 1996)

Findlater, Richard, *Lilian Baylis: The Lady of the Old Vic* (London: Allen Lane, 1975)

Forsyth, Cecil, *Music and Nationalism: A Study of English Opera* (London: n.p., 1911)

Friedman, Sam, and Reeves, Aaron, 'From Aristocratic to Ordinary: Shifting Modes of Elite Distinction', *American Sociological Review*, 85/2 (2020), 323–350

Frith, Simon, 'What Does It Mean to Be Cultured? *Desert Island Discs* as an Ideological Archive', in Julie Brown, Nicholas Cook, and Stephen Cottrell (eds), *Defining the Discographic Self: Desert Island Discs in Context* (Oxford: The British Academy, 2017), pp. 125–144

Gardiner, Juliet, *The Thirties: An Intimate History* (London: HarperPress, 2011)

Garrett, Lesley, *Notes from a Small Soprano* (Bath: Chivers Large Print, 2000)

Gass, Irene, *Through an Opera Glass* (London: George Harrap and Co., 1957)

Gibson, Lorna, *Beyond Jerusalem: Music in the Women's Institute, 1919–1969* (Aldershot: Ashgate, 2008)

SELECTED BIBLIOGRAPHY 271

Gilbert, Susie, *Opera for Everybody: The Story of English National Opera* (London: Faber and Faber, 2009)

Glaser, Eliane, *Elitism: A Progressive Defence* (London: Biteback Publishing, 2020)

Glendinning, Victoria, *Family Business: An Intimate History of John Lewis and the Partnership* (London: William Collins, 2021)

Goff, Martyn, *A Short Guide to Long Play* (London: Museum Press, Ltd, 1957)

Gray, Linda Esther, *Dame Eva Turner: 'A Life on the High Cs'* (New Malden: Green Oak Publishing, 2011)

Guthrie, Kate, *The Art of Appreciation: Music and Middlebrow Culture in Modern Britain* (Oakland: University of California Press, 2021)

Guthrie, Tyrone, *A Life in the Theatre* (London: Columbus Books, 1987)

Guthrie, Tyrone, Evans, Edwin, Cross, Joan, Dent, Edward J., and de Valois, Ninette, *Opera in English* (London: John Lane the Bodley Head, 1945)

Hall, Duncan, *'A Pleasant Change from Politics': Music and the British Labour Movement Between the Wars* (Cheltenham: New Clarion Press, 2001)

Haltrecht, Montague, *The Quiet Showman: Sir David Webster and the Royal Opera House* (London: Collins, 1975)

Hamilton, Cicely, and Baylis, Lilian, *The Old Vic* (London: Jonathan Cape, 1926)

Hammond, Joan, *A Voice, A Life* (London: Victor Gollancz Ltd, 1970)

Harding, Thomas, *Legacy: One Family, a Cup of Tea, and the Company That Took On the World* (London: Windmill Books, 2019)

Heath, Edward, *Music: A Joy for Life* (London: Sidgwick and Jackson, 1976)

Hecht, Katharina, McArthur, Daniel, Savage, Mike, and Friedman, Sam, 'Elites in the UK: Pulling Away?' (The Sutton Trust, 2019)

Hendy, David, *The BBC: A People's History* (London: Profile Books, 2022)

Hewison, Robert, *Cultural Capital: The Rise and Fall of Creative Britain* (London: Verso, 2014)

Holden, Raymond (ed.), *Glorious John: A Collection of Sir John Barbirolli's Lectures, Articles, Speeches and Interviews* (London: The Barbirolli Society, 2007)

Hollis, Patricia, *Jennie Lee: A Life* (Oxford: Oxford University Press, 1997)

Hope-Wallace, Philip, 'Opera at Glyndebourne', in Anna Instone and Julian Herbiage (eds), *Selections from the BBC Programme Music Magazine* (London: Rockliff, 1953), pp. 110–113

Howes, Frank, and Hope-Wallace, Philip, *A Key to Opera* (London: Blackie and Son Ltd, 1939)

Hunter, Rita Nellie, *Wait Till the Sun Shines, Nellie* (London: Hamish Hamilton, 1986)

Hurd, Michael, *Young Person's Guide to Opera* (London: Routledge and Kegan Paul, 1963)

Jacob, Naomi, and Robertson, James C., *Opera in Italy* (London: Hutchinson, 1948)

Jolliffe, John, *Glyndebourne: An Operatic Miracle* (London: John Murray, 1999)

Jonas, Peter, Elder, Mark, and Pountney, David, *Power House: The English National Opera Experience* (London: Lime Tree, 1992)

Kelly, Owen, *Community, Art and the State: Storming the Citadels* (London: Comedia, 1984)

Kynaston, David, *Modernity Britain: 1957–62* (New York: Bloomsbury, 2014)

Laslett, Peter, *The Future of Sound Broadcasting: A Plea for the Third Programme* (Oxford: Basil Blackwell, 1957)

Levin, Bernard, *The Pendulum Years: Britain and the Sixties* (London: Jonathan Cape, 1970)

Linklater, Eric, *The Music of the North* (Aberdeen: The Haddo House Choral Society, 1970)

Little, Robert, *Edgar Evans—Extempore* (St Albans: Bob Little Press and PR, 2005)

Lowerson, John, *Amateur Operatics: A Social and Cultural History* (Manchester: Manchester University Press, 2005)

Major, John, *John Major: The Autobiography* (London: HarperCollins, 1999)

Mandler, Peter, *The English National Character: The History of an Idea from Edmund Burke to Tony Blair* (New Haven: Yale University Press, 2006)

Martin, Steven Edward, 'The British "Operatic Machine": Investigations into Institutional History of English Opera, c. 1875–1939', unpublished PhD dissertation, University of Bristol (2010)

272 SELECTED BIBLIOGRAPHY

Marwick, Arthur, *The Sixties: Cultural Revolution in Britain, France, Italy, and the United States, c. 1958-1974* (Oxford: Oxford University Press, 1998)

Matheopoulos, Helena, *Fashion Designers at the Opera* (London: Thames and Hudson, 2011)

May, Robin, *Operamania* (Wimbledon: Vernon and Yates, 1966)

May, Robin, *Opera* (Sevenoaks: Hodder and Stoughton, 1977)

May, Robin, *A Companion to the Opera* (Guildford: Lutterworth Press, 1977)

McKibbin, Ross, *Classes and Cultures: England 1918-1951* (Oxford: Oxford University Press, 1998, repr. 2013)

McLeod, Ken, 'Bohemian Rhapsodies: Operatic Influences on Rock Music', *Popular Music*, 20/2 (May 2001), 189-203

McWilliam, Rohan, *London's West End: Creating the Pleasure District, 1800-1914* (Oxford: Oxford University Press, 2020)

Merriman, Andy, *Greasepaint and Cordite: The Story of ENSA and Concert Party Entertainment During the Second World War* (London: Aurum, 2013)

Mirsky, Dmitri, *The Intelligentsia of Great Britain*, trans. Alec Brown (London: Victor Gollancz, 1935)

Mitford, Nancy, *The Pursuit of Love* (London: Penguin, 1949)

Oliver, Cordelia, *It's a Curious Story: The Tale of Scottish Opera 1962-1987* (Edinburgh: Mainstream Publishing, 1987)

Opera and Music Theatre Forum, 'Opera for Now: A Profile of Opera and Music Theatre Companies in Britain' (The Arts Council of England, January 2001)

Parry, Elisabeth, *Thirty Men and a Girl: A Singer's Memories of War, Mountains, Travel, and Always Music* (Guildford: Allegra, 2010)

Payne, Nicholas, 'Trends and Innovations in Opera', in Anastasia Belina-Johnson and Derek B. Scott (eds), *The Business of Opera* (Farnham: Ashgate, 2015), pp. 17-29

Pick, John (ed.), *The State and the Arts* (London: City University, Centre for the Arts, 1980)

Potter, Simon J., *This Is the BBC: Entertaining the Nation, Speaking for Britain? 1922-2022* (Oxford: Oxford University Press, 2022)

Priestley, J. B., *English Journey* (London: William Heinemann, 1934)

Priestley, J. B., *The Arts under Socialism* (London: Turnstile Press, 1947)

Reynolds, Ernest, *The Plain Man's Guide to the Opera* (London: Michael Joseph, 1964)

Richards, Marjorie, *Opera House* (London: Hutchinson and Co., 1935)

Rose, Jonathan, *The Intellectual Life of the British Working Classes* (New Haven, CT: Yale University Press, second edition 2010)

Ross, Andrew, *No Respect: Intellectuals and Popular Culture* (New York: Routledge, 1989)

Russell, Dave, 'Reaching the Operatic Stage: The Geographical and Social Origins of British and Irish Opera Singers, c.1850-c.1960', *Cambridge Opera Journal*, 29/3 (November 2017), 312-352

Sackville-West, Edward, and Shawe-Taylor, Desmond, *The Record Guide* (London: Collins, 1951)

Salter, Lionel, *Going to the Opera* (London: Penguin Books, 1958)

Scholes, Percy, *Everybody's Guide to Broadcast Music* (London: Oxford University Press, 1925)

Shaw, Roy, *The Arts and the People* (London: J. Cape, 1987)

Shaw, Roy, 'Sponsoring the Arts', in Roy Shaw (ed.), *The Spread of Sponsorship in the Arts, Sport, Education, the Health Service and Broadcasting* (Newcastle: Bloodaxe Books, 1993), pp. 13-32

Shawe-Taylor, Desmond, *Covent Garden* (London: Max Parrish, 1948)

Silex, Karl, *John Bull at Home*, trans. Huntley Paterson (London: George G. Harrap & Co., 1931)

Sinclair, Andrew, *The Need to Give: The Patrons and the Arts* (London: Sinclair-Stevenson, 1990)

Skelton, David, *The New Snobbery: Taking on Modern Elitism and Empowering the Working Class* (Croydon: Biteback Publishing, 2021)

SELECTED BIBLIOGRAPHY 273

Sladen, Chris, 'Holidays at Home in the Second World War', *Journal of Contemporary History*, 37/1 (January 2002), 67–89

Smith, Charles T., *The School of Life: A Theatre of Education* (London: Grant Richards, Ltd, 1921)

Smith, Chris, *Creative Britain* (London: Faber and Faber, 1998)

Snowman, Daniel, *Just Passing Through: Interactions with the World* (Bristol: Brown Dog Books, 2021)

Stapleton, Michael, *The Sadler's Wells Opera* (London: Adam and Charles Black, 1954)

Storey, John, '"Expecting Rain": Opera as Popular Culture?' in Jim Collins (ed.), *High-Pop: Making Culture into Popular Entertainment* (Malden, MA: Blackwell's, 2002), 32–55

Streatfeild, Noel, *Enjoying Opera* (London: Dennis Dobson, 1966)

Strong, Roy, *The Spirit of Britain: A Narrative History of the Arts* (London: Hutchinson, 1999)

Swanston, Hamish F. G., *In Defence of Opera* (London: Penguin, 1978)

Symes, Colin, 'Beating Up the Classics: Aspects of a Compact Discourse', *Popular Music*, 16/1 (1997), 81–95

Tooley, John, *In House: Covent Garden. 50 Years of Opera and Ballet* (London: Faber and Faber, 1999)

Tusa, John, *Art Matters: Reflecting on Culture* (London: Methuen, 2000)

Tusa, John, *Pain in the Arts* (London: I. B. Tauris, 2014)

Walden, George, *The New Elites: Making a Career in the Masses* (London: Allen Lane, 2000)

Walpole, Michael (ed.), *Midland Music Makers Opera: The First Fifty Years, 1946–1996* (Birmingham: Midland Music Makers, n.d.)

Weingärtner, Jörg, *The Arts as a Weapon of War: Britain and the Shaping of National Morale in the Second World War* (London: Tauris, 2006)

White, Jerry, *The Battle of London, 1939–45: Endurance, Heroism and Frailty under Fire* (London: The Bodley Head, 2021)

Whitehead, Kate, *The Third Programme: A Literary History* (Oxford: Clarendon Press, 1989)

Willatt, Hugh, *The Arts Council of Great Britain: The First Twenty-Five Years* (London: Arts Council of Great Britain, 1973)

Williams, Stephen, *Come to the Opera!* (London: Hutchinson and Co., 1948)

Williams, Stephen, *In the Opera House* (London: Stratford Place, 1952)

Williams, Stephen, *You and the Opera: A Pocket Guide* (London: MacDonald and Evans, Ltd., 1952)

Wilson, Alexandra, *Opera in the Jazz Age: Cultural Politics in 1920s Britain* (New York: Oxford University Press, 2019)

Woodhouse, Frederick, *Opera for Amateurs* (London: Dennis Dobson, Ltd, 1951)

Index

For the benefit of digital users, indexed terms that span two pages (e.g., 52–53) may, on occasion, appear on only one of those pages.

Figures are indicated by an italic *f* following the page number.

Allen, Thomas, 114
Allison, John, 212, 239
amateur opera, 3, 26–27, 29, 34, 43–44, 84,
    113–15, 116–17, 119, 129–30, 134, 150–51,
    214–16, 219, 235
Arlen, Stephen, 126–27, 142
Arts Council, 74, 81–82, 89, 99–101, 107, 108–
    9, 117, 127, 128–29, 133, 134, 135, 137–38,
    149, 154–55, 156–57, 161–63, 165–66, 180,
    184, 187, 188–89, 200, 205, 206, 207–8,
    213, 214, 218–19, 220, 221, 222, 253–55,
    256, 258–59, 262
Attenborough, David, 145
Auden, W. H., 113
Austria, 8, 64–65, 87, 88–89, 212, 243
autodidacticism, 27–28, 41–42, 91–92, 111–12,
    113–14, 124, 185–86, 233, 260–61, 263

Baker, Janet, 130, 177
Banks, Tony, 187–88
Barbirolli, John, 44, 59, 69
Baylis, Lilian, 17, 28, 29, 30–31, 59–62, 66–67,
    142, 164, 184, 261, 266
Beecham, Thomas, 35–36, 47, 50, 53, 54, 85–86
Bennett, Richard Rodney, 124
Berry, Jake, 246
Bing, Rudolf, 102
Birmingham Opera Company, 8–9, 219, 226–27
Bizet, Georges, 1, 26, 50, 55, 56*f*, 61–62, 68, 122,
    130, 145, 165, 166, 212
Black, Peter, 144
Blair, Tony, 205–6, 207–8, 230, 242
Blaug, Mark, 154–55
Boarder, Sylvia, 129
Boe, Alfie, 217, 235–37, 236*f*
Boughton, Rutland, 26
Bourdieu, Pierre, 262–63
Braden, Su, 162, 163–64, 182–83, 184
Brexit, 21–22, 243–45, 247, 254, 255
Bridges, Lord, 99–100, 130–31

British National Opera Company, 25, 40, 44, 46
Britten, Benjamin, 54–55, 85–86, 96, 97, 110,
    114, 117–19, 129, 140–41
Bull, Anna, 262–63
Burton, Humphrey, 145–46
Burton-Hill, Clemency, 237–38
Butlin's, 3, 94–95
Butt, Alfred, 48

Callas, Maria, 10, 98, 105–6, 122–23, 135–
    36, 139
canon, 3–4, 20–21, 226, 247, 248, 249, 260–
    61, 267
Carl Rosa Opera Company, 17, 25–26, 51, 55–
    56, 58, 76, 84, 90, 95, 107
Carreras, José, 166, 190–92, 217
Caruso, Enrico, 24, 40, 118
CEMA, 74, 77–78, 81, 82, 95, 183
Channon, Paul, 156–57
Chatterjee, Himadri, 146–47
Cheverton, Una, 55
Christiansen, Rupert, 223, 232–33, 263–64
Christie, John, 7, 59–60, 63, 64–67, 85–
    86, 103–5
class, 2–3, 5, 6–15, 16–17, 18, 20–22, 23, 25,
    26–28, 30–31, 32–39, 40, 41–44, 45–46,
    51–64, 65–67, 70, 72, 76–77, 78, 80, 89, 93,
    94–95, 96–99, 100–2, 103–8, 109–10, 116,
    124, 125, 127–28, 130–32, 133–34, 135–36,
    137–38, 139–40, 141–42, 149–51, 153–54,
    155, 156, 158–59, 160–62, 163–64, 165–66,
    167, 168–71, 177–78, 179–80, 182–86,
    187–88, 193–95, 196, 197, 199, 200, 201,
    202–4, 209, 211–13, 214–15, 217, 219, 224,
    227–28, 229, 230, 231–34, 235–37, 239–40,
    241–43, 246, 247, 248, 251–53, 254, 256–
    57, 258, 260–63, 264, 265, 266, 267
Clutton, James, 212
Cohen-Portheim, Paul, 49
Cole, Hugo, 119

276 INDEX

Connolly, Sarah, 243
Conservative Party, 12, 15, 21–22, 48, 82, 98–99,
133, 155–58, 169–70, 179–81, 186, 187,
205–6, 207, 219–20, 239, 241–42, 244, 246,
252, 254, 256
Cook, Ida, 23–25, 27
Cook, Louise, 23–24, 27
Cool Britannia, 15, 21–22, 207–8
Coronation, 21–22, 96, 98, 110, 116–17
Corri, Charles, 32, 33
Covid-19 pandemic, 10–11, 245–46, 247, 248–
50, 254
Cross, Joan, 74, 97, 138–39
Crozier, Eric, 85

Davies, Peter Maxwell, 93, 188
Davies, Tudor, 84, 107–8
Davies, Walford, 23
De Niese, Danielle, 237–38
Deathridge, Leslie, 113
Dent, Edward J., 29, 83, 87, 91–92
Dickie, William and Murray, 86
Domingo, Plácido, 165–66, 168–69, 190–92
Dove, Jonathan, 211
Dowden, Oliver, 239–40
Dwyer, Terence, 129–30

East End, 3, 33–35, 37–38, 53, 55–56,
131, 138–39
Eastburn, Susanna, 253–54
Ebert, Carl, 64–65, 105
Eccles, Lord, 156
Elder, Mark, 174–75
elitism debate, 2–17, 18–19, 25, 27, 35, 38, 39,
42–43, 53, 63–64, 70–71, 78, 81–82, 90, 94,
101, 109–10, 114–15, 116, 127–28, 129,
133–34, 143–44, 145, 146, 149, 154, 156,
157, 158–59, 160, 161–62, 163, 164, 165–
66, 167–72, 173–74, 175–80, 182, 183, 184–
85, 186–87, 188–89, 191, 194–204, 206–7,
209, 210–13, 215, 216, 218, 220, 221–22,
223, 224, 225, 226, 227–30, 231–34, 235–
40, 241, 242–43, 246, 247–48, 250–51, 252,
253–54, 255–57, 258–60, 261–64, 265–67
Enfield, Harry, 192
English National Opera, 5–6, 7, 8, 32, 149,
150–53, 154–55, 160–61, 165–66, 167,
169, 174–77, 178, 187, 195, 197, 209–10,
211–12, 214–15, 216, 223, 224, 228–29,
230, 231–32, 235, 236–37, 236f, 240–41,
249–50, 254–55
ENSA, 78, 79, 82
Evans, Edgar, 24, 54

Evans, Geraint, 27, 40, 132, 156–57
Eyre, Richard, 198, 209, 220, 228, 229–30

Ferrier, Kathleen, 85–86, 117–18
Festival of Britain, 21–22, 102, 117
film, 2, 3–4, 5–9, 14, 15, 17, 18, 20–21, 25–26,
35–36, 37–38, 42, 43, 45–46, 48, 55–56, 57,
58, 60, 67, 68–69, 74, 76, 79–80, 83–84, 89,
105, 111, 118, 121, 123, 125, 130–31, 132,
141, 143, 145–46, 152, 160, 166, 171–72,
177–78, 190, 191, 193, 195, 207–8, 225–26,
228–29, 234, 258–59
Forsyth, Cecil, 21
France, 8, 19–20, 68, 97–98, 118–19, 141–42,
157–58, 181, 243

Galli-Curci, Amelita, 23–24
Garrett, Lesley, 177–78, 192, 195, 216–17
Garsington Opera, 222
Gass, Irene, 106, 112–13
Germany, 19, 21, 24, 32, 49, 64–65, 88–89, 106–
7, 141–42, 190, 212, 243
Gheorghiu, Angela, 198
Gibson, Alexander, 134
Gilbert and Sullivan, 26, 113, 130, 263
Gilchrist, Jane, 214, 215
Glaser, Eliane, 182, 220–21, 250–51, 256–57
Glyndebourne, 4–5, 7, 39, 59–60, 62–67, 73, 85–
86, 102–5, 110, 117, 121, 124, 132–33, 134–
35, 143–44, 146–47, 148–49, 153–54, 167f,
170–71, 172, 179, 180–81, 211–12, 222,
226, 232, 233–34, 235, 244, 246, 254–55
Goff, Martyn, 79
Goldsmith, Harvey, 165, 193
Gordon, June, 130
Gove, Michael, 241, 242–43
Grace, Harvey, 50, 53
Grange Park Opera, 264
Grayling, A. C., 185, 230–31
Grimeborn, 222
Gubbay, Raymond, 193, 195–96, 222–23, 231–
32, 243
Guthrie, Tyrone, 13, 28, 62, 85, 98

Hall, Peter, 93, 167f, 179, 204, 205–6
Hall, Tony, 111, 239
Hammond, Joan, 72–73, 76, 78
Hampson, Thomas, 238–39
Harding, Denys W., 70
Harewood, Earl of, 45, 79, 97, 149, 152–53,
174–75, 177
Heath, Edward, 26, 79, 127–28, 155–56,
170, 181

INDEX 277

Hely-Hutchinson, Victor, 83
Hensher, Philip, 224
Heyworth, Peter, 122
Hodge, Margaret, 229
Holden, Anthony, 191
Hope-Wallace, Philip, 122–23
Hopkins, Kate, 193–94
Hughes, Spike, 79–80
Hunter, Rita, 107–8, 150–51
Hurd, Michael, 4, 126–27
Huxley, Aldous, 38, 67

Isaacs, Jeremy, 199–200
Italy, 19–20, 44, 79–81, 83, 86, 87, 94, 106–7,
    133–34, 153–54, 175, 190, 196

Jacob, Naomi, 80–81
Janáček, Leoš, 1, 160–61, 172
Jenkins, Simon, 197, 203–4
John Lewis Partnership, 64, 102, 113, 119
Jonas, Peter, 165–66, 167, 174, 212

Kaufman, Gerald, 209
Kaufmann, Jonas, 10–11, 244–45
Kelly, Owen, 182–84
Kennedy, Michael, 191, 193
Kenyon, Nicholas, 175
Kissin, Baron, 188
Kramer, Daniel, 7

Labour Party, 15, 21–22, 25, 47, 48, 57, 82, 133,
    156–57, 185, 186–88, 205–9, 219–20, 228–
    29, 230, 239–40, 241–42, 254
Lee, Jennie, 133–34, 142, 187–88
Legge, Walter, 78
Leigh, Denise, 214
Leoncavallo, Ruggero, 45, 60–61, 94, 110, 224
Lessing, Doris, 209–10, 230
Levin, Bernard, 124–25, 179, 201
Lewis, John Spedan, 64, 102

Mackerras, Charles, 140–41, 209
Macmillan, James, 253
Major, John, 205
Manners, Charles, 50
Mascagni, Pietro, 34, 45, 94, 241–42
Masterson, Valerie, 151, 177
May, Robin, 6–7, 9–10, 123, 146, 149
Maynard Keynes, John, 77, 81–82, 163–64,
    184, 255–56
McCrum, Robert, 205, 213
Melba, Nellie, 34–35, 107–8
Mellor, David, 205

Mercury, Freddie, 144, 192
Midland Bank Proms, 150, 168–69, 207
Mildmay, Audrey, 59–60
Miller, Jonathan, 175–77, 176f, 194–95, 225,
    226–27, 236–37
Milne, Jimmy, 149–50
Milnes, Rodney, 1, 148–49, 158–61, 165–66,
    172–73, 174, 175–76, 195–96, 200–1, 210
Mirsky, Dmitri, 42–43
Mitford, Nancy, 24
Moffat Ford, Robert, 49–50
Montague, Sarah, 238–39
Moore, Grace, 58
Morris, Estelle, 229
Morrison, Richard, 198, 201, 205–6, 215,
    217, 228–29
Moser, Claus, 157–58, 169, 180–81
Mozart, Wolfgang Amadeus, 27, 29, 40, 44, 64–
    65, 129–30, 141, 145, 146–47, 148–50, 223,
    241–42, 247, 251–53, 260
Murdoch, Rupert, 182
Murphy, Stuart, 240–41
Musgrave, Thea, 132
music hall/variety, 8, 9, 10–11, 14–15, 17, 25–
    26, 28, 33–34, 35–36, 40, 43, 45–46, 60, 93–
    95, 111, 132, 137–38, 141, 143, 191, 205
musical theatre, 5–6, 10–11, 48, 69, 106, 109,
    193–94, 197, 211–12, 215, 216, 222–23

Naipaul, V. S., 230
Nash, Heddle, 29, 30–31
Neill, Bob, 256, 264–65
Netrebko, Anna, 10–11, 244–45
Newman, Ernest, 33, 50
northern England, 3, 11, 25, 33, 36, 54, 57, 61,
    72, 94, 95, 117–18, 134, 135, 149–50, 156–
    57, 165–66, 177–78, 224, 233, 234, 235,
    239–40, 246, 252, 254–55, 263, 264, 266

Old Vic, 17, 28–33, 37–38, 43–44, 55, 60–62, 81,
    94–95, 127, 139, 152, 153, 177, 215, 226–
    27, 245, 262, 264, 266
Oliver, Vic, 111
O'Mara company, 33–34
Opera Go Round, 147–48, 235
Opera Holland Park, 212, 222, 237
Opera North, 149, 165–66, 188–89, 224, 246,
    252, 264
Operatunity, 214–15, 218
Ormsby-Gore, William, 48
Orwell, George, 68
Osborne, George, 241
Owen, Idloes, 84

278 INDEX

Pappano, Antonio, 255
Parry, Elisabeth, 76, 79, 107
Patalong, Anna, 243
Pavarotti, Luciano, 145–46, 166, 177, 190–92, 193
Paxman, Jeremy, 199
Payne, Nicholas, 5–6, 9, 188–89
Pears, Peter, 97
People's Palace, 34–35, 37–38, 55–56, 245
Pinter, Harold, 93
Piper, John, 85
Pomeroy, Jay, 86–87
Ponselle, Rosa, 51
popular music/jazz, 2, 6, 10, 18, 19–21, 24, 34–35, 51–52, 55, 57–58, 78, 111, 125, 127, 131, 132–33, 144, 146–47, 165, 191, 192, 193, 194, 195, 207–8, 211–12, 214, 216–17, 225, 230, 234, 235, 241–43, 251, 258–59, 263–64
Pountney, David, 174–76, 210
Priestley, J. B., 57, 61, 82, 90–91
Princess Margaret, 155
Proms concerts, 21, 54–55, 147, 229
Puccini, Giacomo, 9–10, 35–36, 44, 45, 50, 58, 60–61, 68–69, 72, 76, 79–80, 94, 105, 107, 110, 122–23, 132, 134, 137f, 139, 143, 145–46, 149–50, 165–66, 175–76, 177, 190, 191, 192, 195, 196, 197, 205, 223, 226, 235, 236–37, 236f, 241–42, 247, 249–50, 261–62, 264
Purcell, Henry, 87, 114, 129–30

Queen, 144
Queen Elizabeth II, 96, 97, 244
Queen Elizabeth, the Queen Mother, 130, 137–38

radio, 3, 14, 17, 18, 23, 24, 25, 40–42, 47–48, 57–58, 69, 79–80, 92–94, 97–98, 108–10, 111, 116–17, 118, 127, 131, 132–33, 147, 149–50, 161, 166, 185–86, 193, 197, 198–99, 205, 208, 218–19, 230, 235–39, 252, 260, 264–65
Randle, Tom, 178
Rankl, Karl, 87, 90
Rattle, Simon, 170, 180–81, 254–55
Rayner, Jay, 196–97
recording, 3, 17, 23–24, 25, 27, 40, 45, 62, 72, 79, 92, 98, 102, 108, 111–12, 131, 147–48, 148f, 150–51, 166, 177, 190–91, 192, 193–94, 195, 196–97, 210, 215, 216, 218–19, 225, 235, 241–42, 263, 265, 266
Rees-Mogg, William, 180
Reith, John, 21–22, 41, 127, 146, 205, 252

Richards, Marjorie, 55
Rosenthal, Harold, 154, 161, 170–71, 173, 175–76, 187–88
Rossini, Gioachino, 33–34, 44, 50, 86, 94, 116–17, 223
Royal Opera House, Covent Garden, 4–5, 6–7, 8, 9–10, 13–14, 17, 18, 24–25, 28, 29, 34–39, 40, 42, 44, 47–48, 50, 51–55, 64–65, 73, 74, 76–77, 81–82, 83, 86–90, 93–94, 96–102, 103, 105–8, 111, 114–15, 117–20, 121, 122–23, 124, 126–27, 128–29, 130–31, 133, 134–40, 141–42, 150, 151, 153–58, 159–60, 165–66, 168–69, 172–73, 175, 177, 178, 180–81, 187, 191, 193–95, 197, 198, 199–204, 205–6, 207, 209–10, 211–12, 216, 224, 225–26, 227–28, 231–32, 235, 236–37, 239, 240, 241, 244–45, 246, 261–62

Sadler's Wells, 53–54, 59–63, 74, 75f, 76–77, 81, 83, 84–85, 86–87, 90, 105–6, 107, 117, 122, 124, 126–27, 128–29, 132, 135, 137–39, 140–42, 151, 155–56, 159–60, 177, 215, 262, 264, 266
Said, Edward, 249
Salter, Lionel, 13–14, 110–11
Say Mitchell, Dreda, 261–62
Schmitz, Oscar, 21
Scholes, Percy, 40
school opera, 26, 27, 53, 91, 107, 114–15, 129–30, 140, 170, 172, 212, 218–19, 251, 252–53, 261, 263, 264–65
Scotland, 44, 85–86, 113, 130, 132–34, 146–48, 149–50, 160–61, 186–87, 196, 198–99, 235, 263
Scottish Opera, 132–33, 134, 147–48, 149–50, 160–61, 198–99, 263
Secombe, Harry, 132
Sekers, Nicolas 'Miki', 103
Shakespeare, William, 4–5, 20–21, 28, 48, 60, 61–62, 115, 143–44, 197, 246, 250, 253
Shaw, George Bernard, 26, 74
Shaw, Roy, 161–62, 166, 184–85
Shawe-Taylor, Desmond, 74, 95
Short, George A., 49
Sladen, Victoria, 78, 108–9
Smith, Charles T., 27, 252–53
Smith, Chris, 3, 202, 206–8, 209
Snowden, Ethel, 47, 50, 51, 183–84, 188
Snowden, Philip, 47, 49–50, 51, 156, 188
Snowman, Daniel, 62, 105–6, 108
Solti, Georg, 135–37, 145–46
Southgate, Colin, 203–4
Spence, Nicky, 217

INDEX 279

sport, 4, 5, 6, 10, 12, 13–14, 15, 16, 20–21, 32, 34, 35–36, 41–42, 43, 45–46, 48, 54, 62–63, 69–70, 95, 112–13, 115–16, 155, 159, 185–86, 190, 197, 201, 205, 206–7, 211–12, 216, 219, 229, 230, 232, 237, 240–41, 245–46

St John-Stevas, Norman, 156–57

Stoll, Oswald, 74, 83, 106–7, 141

Strauss, Richard, 50, 161, 175–76, 194–95, 204f

Streatfeild, Noel, 1, 2, 111–12, 260

Strong, Roy, 125

Stuart, Robert, 59

subsidy, 5, 15, 18, 19, 25, 38, 47–51, 61–62, 70–71, 74, 81–82, 89, 98–102, 107, 108–9, 117, 126–27, 128–29, 133, 134, 135, 136–38, 149, 154–58, 159, 160, 161–63, 165–66, 168–70, 174–75, 180, 182, 184, 185, 186–89, 197, 199–203, 204, 205, 206, 207–8, 213, 214, 218–19, 220, 221, 222, 253–56, 258–59, 262

surtitles, 4–5, 171–74, 195

Sutherland, Joan, 135–36

Te Kanawa, Kiri, 131, 166, 193, 218

Teatro San Carlo, Naples, 79–80, 87, 94–95

television, 3, 6–7, 13–14, 18, 20–21, 110–11, 118, 125, 126, 127, 132–33, 139–40, 143–44, 145–48, 156, 166, 185–86, 190, 192, 193, 198–99, 201–2, 207–8, 214–15, 216–17, 225–26, 227, 228, 239–41, 260, 264–65

Terfel, Bryn, 216–17

Thatcher, Margaret, 21–22, 157–58, 180–81, 205, 206, 208, 241–42

Tippett, Michael, 118–19

Tomlinson, John, 177

Tooley, John, 180, 181, 206–7

touring opera, 6, 17, 25–26, 28, 34, 35–36, 37–38, 43–45, 50, 51, 55–56, 58, 74–76, 80, 81, 84, 90, 95, 107, 133, 134, 135, 147–49, 151, 156–57, 166, 172, 212, 216, 223–24, 235, 254–55, 266

Toye, Francis, 5, 53–54, 67

Toye, Geoffrey, 60

Turnage, Mark-Anthony, 231, 240

Turner, Eva, 36, 44

Tusa, John, 208, 265

USA, 23–24, 39, 52–53, 98, 102, 127, 150–51, 178, 248–49

Vaughan Williams, Ralph, 21, 50, 117

Verdi, Giuseppe, 26, 29, 44, 45, 50, 53, 54, 55, 68–69, 79, 83, 92, 95, 111, 113, 130, 134, 139–40, 143–44, 159–60, 165, 166, 176–77, 192, 198, 214, 223, 241–42, 247

Vick, Graham, 219, 226–27, 231–32

Volpe, Michael, 212, 237

Wagner, Richard, 1, 4–5, 29, 35–37, 40, 43, 44, 45, 50, 58, 67–68, 77, 92, 105, 111, 113, 114, 122, 131, 134–35, 147, 212, 241

Walden, George, 221–22, 227

Wales, 11, 24, 27, 40, 54–55, 84, 90, 107, 133–34, 148–49, 196, 201, 228–29, 231–32, 249–50, 254–55

Wallace, Ian, 132–33

Walpole, Hugh, 67–68

Walton, William, 118–19

war, 21–22, 42, 60, 72–81, 83, 86, 87, 90–91, 94–95, 102, 107, 193–94, 260, 264, 266

Watson, Russell, 216–17

Webster, David, 88, 98–99, 134–35, 140

Welsh National Opera, 84, 107, 148–49, 196, 228–29, 231–32, 249–50

West End, 6, 8, 9, 26, 33, 34–35, 52–53, 54–55, 58, 61, 86, 89, 141, 142, 211–12, 215, 222–23, 255

Whitehorn, Katharine, 121

Widdop, Walter, 79

Wilde, Oscar, 13

Williams, Stephen, 14, 85, 92, 111–12, 115

Wilson, Harold, 127–28, 188

Wilson, Steuart, 119–20

Winterson, Jeanette, 233–34

Wood, Anne, 138–39

Woodhouse, Frederick 114–15

Zeffirelli, Franco, 122–23, 160